Civil Rights Issues Facing Asian Americans in the 1990s

A Report of the United States
Commission on Civil Rights
February 1992

Letter of Transmittal

THE PRESIDENT
THE PRESIDENT OF THE SENATE
THE SPEAKER OF THE HOUSE OF REPRESENTATIVES

Sirs:

The United States Commission on Civil Rights transmits this report, *Civil Rights Issues Facing Asian Americans in the 1990s*, to you pursuant to Public Law 98-183, as amended.

This report was prompted by a series of three roundtable conferences held by the Commission in 1989. At these conferences local representatives of the Asian American communities were asked to inform the Commission about civil rights concerns within their communities. The clear and unambiguous message we received was that Asian Americans face serious civil rights problems that touch both U.S.- and foreign-born Asian Americans, and exist at all social and economic levels and in virtually all walks of life. The record of these roundtable conferences was published as *Voices Across America: Roundtable Discussions of Asian Civil Rights Issues.*

The research and field investigations conducted for this report establish these concerns as national problems. Asian Americans suffer widely the pain and humiliation of bigotry and acts of violence. They also confront institutional discrimination in numerous domains, such as places of work and schools, in accessing public services, and in the administration of justice. Although Asian Americans face prejudice and discrimination as a racial minority in this country, their experiences are also shaped by the unique history of persons of Asian descent in America and by the fact that many Asian Americans are immigrants and language minorities.

The more than 40 recommendations contained in this report, although not a total solution to the civil rights problems facing Asian Americans, prescribe actions that must be taken if progress is to be made. Central to the Commission's recommendations are specific legislative, programmatic and administrative efforts that the Federal, State and local governments, must undertake. The Commission looks to Congress and the President, in their crucial leadership roles in advancing civil rights, to move aggressively to adopt the Commission's recommendations and to encourage action by State and local governments and the private sector.

Respectfully,

For the Commissioners,
Arthur A. Fletcher
Chairperson

Preface

In the summer of 1989 the U.S. Commission on Civil Rights held a series of three Roundtable Conferences across the country to hear about the civil rights concerns of the Asian American community. Roundtable conferences were held in Houston, Texas, on May 27; in New York, New York, on June 23; and in San Francisco, California, on July 29. Participants at the Roundtable Conferences addressed a wide variety of civil rights issues facing today's Asian American community. An accompanying volume[1] contains transcripts of the Asian Roundtable Conferences. Using the information gathered at these conferences as a point of departure, Commission staff undertook a study of the wide-ranging civil rights issues facing Asian Americans in the 1990s. This report presents the results of that investigation.[2]

The purpose of this report is to investigate and heighten public awareness of the broad range of serious civil rights issues facing Asian Americans today and to make recommendations for enhancing civil rights protections for Asian Americans. It should be recognized at the outset that many of the civil rights problems confronting Asian Americans also confront other minority groups, and many of the recommendations made in this report for enhancing Asian Americans' civil rights protections could equally well be made for other minority groups.

The report reflects the continuing concern of the Commission for the civil rights advancement of Asian and Pacific Americans. It adds to the list of Commission reports on Asian and Pacific Americans, that includes:

U.S. Commission on Civil Rights, *The Economic Status of Americans of Asian Descent: An Exploratory Investigation*, Clearinghouse Publication 95, October 1988;

U.S. Commission on Civil Rights, *Recent Activities Against Citizens and Residents of Asian Descent*, Clearinghouse Publication 88, 1986;

U.S. Commission on Civil Rights, *Success of Asian Americans: Fact or Fiction?*, 1980;

U.S. Commission on Civil Rights, *The Tarnished Golden Door: Civil Rights Issues in Immigration*, September 1980;

U.S. Commission on Civil Rights, *Civil Rights Issues of Asian and Pacific Americans: Myths and Realities*, A Consultation, May 8-9, 1979, Washington, DC;

U.S. Commission on Civil Rights, *Civil Rights Digest*, [issue on Asian Americans] vol.9, no. 1 (Fall 1976);

---

1   U.S. Commission on Civil Rights, *Voices Across America: Roundtable Discussions of Asian Civil Rights Issues* (1991).

2   Asian American groups considered in this report are persons having origins in the Far East, Southeast Asia, and the Indian subcontinent. At times, the report also includes information about Pacific Islanders, but limited resources precluded a systematic investigation of the civil rights issues facing Pacific Islanders.

New York State Advisory Committee to the U.S. Commission on Civil Rights, *Asian Americans: An Agenda for Action*, February 1980;

Hawaii State Advisory Committee to the U.S. Commission on Civil Rights, *Breach of Trust? Native Hawaiian Homelands*, 1980;

New York State Advisory Committee to the U.S. Commission on Civil Rights, *The Forgotten Minority: Asian Americans in New York City*, 1978;

California State Advisory Committee to the U.S. Commission on Civil Rights, *Asian American and Pacific Peoples: A Case of Mistaken Identity*, February 1975;

California State Advisory Committee to the U.S. Commission on Civil Rights, *A Dream Unfulfilled: Korean and Pilipino Health Professionals in California*, 1975.

Acknowledgments

This report was researched and written by Ki-Taek Chun and Nadja Zalokar. Additional contributions were made by Brenna Mahoney, Victoria Ni, Mark Regets, and Eileen Rudert. Jennifer Cutler provided competent research assistance as the report neared completion. Audrey Wright and Clarence Gray provided secretarial support for this project. Carol Booker, Barbara Brooks, and Tino Calabia provided comments on the draft report. Editorial assistance and preparation of the report for publication were provided by Gloria Hong Izumi. The report was prepared under the general supervision of James S. Cunningham, Assistant Staff Director for Programs, Policy, and Research.

Several outside experts made valuable comments on a draft version of this report. They were: Sonya Chung, Japanese American Citizens League; Won-Moo Hurh, Western Illinois University; Kenji Ima, California State University at San Diego; Kathryn Imahara, Asian Pacific American Legal Center; K. Connie Kang, *San Francisco Examiner*; Peter Kiang, University of Massachusetts at Boston; Stewart Kwoh, Asian Pacific American Legal Center; Daphne Kwok, Organization of Chinese Americans, Inc.; K.W. Lee, *Korea Times—Los Angeles*; Bill Wong, *Oakland Tribune*; and Melinda Yee, formerly of Organization of Chinese Americans, Inc.

In addition, the following individuals provided valuable assistance in gathering information for this report: Peter Hong, *Business Week*; Eugene C. Kin, California State University of Sacramento; Kapson Lee, *Korea Times—Los Angeles*; Kay Lee, *New York Asian News*; Lee Maglaya, Asian Human Services; Dung Nguyen, California Legislative staff; Nguyen T. Ngyuen, California Senate Joint Committee on Refugee Resettlement; Chong W. Pyen, *Ann Arbor News*, S.K. "Chhem" Sip, Socioeconomic Development Center for Southeast Asians; Mayley L. Tom, California State Legislature, Office of Asian and Pacific Islander Affairs; Paul Bock, University of Connecticut; and Robin Wu, Chinese for Affirmative Action.

The Commission wishes to thank the participants at the Commission's Asian American Roundtable Conferences held in Houston, New York, and San Francisco in the summer of 1989 for the information they provided on the civil rights concerns of Asian Americans. The participants at the Houston Roundtable Conference were: Harry Gee, Theresa Chang, Steven Hoang, Michael Yuan, Glenda Kay Joe, Michael Chou, Ning Chiu, James T. Loh, Dr. Martha Wong, Manuel Pacheco, Wei-Chang Wayne Liauh, Robert Lay-Su, William W. Chang, Gordon Quan, Albert T. Wang, Rong-Tai Ho, Harb S. Hayre, George R. Willy, and Mark Chang. The participants at the New York Roundtable Conference were: Walter Oi, Setsuko Nishi, May Ying Chen, Mini Liu, Shirley Lung, Stanley Mark, Tsiwen M. Law, Charles Wang, Rockwell J. Chin, Pat Eng, Carlton Sagara, Margaret May Chin, Amy Chu, Theresa Ying Hsu, Romesh Diwan, Betty Sung, and Jackson Chin. The participants at the San Francisco Roundtable conference were: Patrick Andersen, Henry Der, Raj Prasad, Karl Matsushita, Leland Yee, Tom Kim, Stewart Kwoh, Bok Lim Kim, Francis C. Assisi, Tom Surh, Andy Anh, Tou Doua Kue, Prasert Duangmala, Vu-Duc Vuong, Kevin Acebo, Paul Wong, C. Vinod Patwardhan, David Chen, Virginia Barrientos, George Kita, Roger Chin, and Harold Yee.

Contents

Chapter 1

Introduction

In the spring of 1991 the *Wall Street Journal* and NBC News conducted a national poll of voters' opinions about a variety of social and economic issues. The poll revealed that the majority of American voters believe that Asian Americans[1] are not discriminated against in the United States. Some even believe that Asian Americans receive "too many special advantages."[2] The poll shows plainly that the general public is largely unaware of the problems Asian Americans confront. Considering the widely held image of Asian Americans as the "model minority," this is hardly surprising. Yet participants at the Civil Rights Commission's Roundtable Conferences in Houston, San Francisco, and New York[3] recounted numerous incidents of anti-Asian prejudice and discrimination. Their statements made evident that, contrary to the widespread belief captured in the *Wall Street Journal*/NBC News poll, Asian Americans encounter many discriminatory barriers to equal opportunity and full participation in our society.

This report seeks to focus attention on the civil rights issues that confront Asian Americans in the 1990s.[4] The report compiles evidence confirming that Asian Americans do face widespread prejudice, discrimination, and barriers to equal opportunity. Asian Americans are frequently victims of racially motivated bigotry and violence; they face significant barriers to equal opportunity in education and employment; and they do not have equal access to a number of public services, including police protection, health care, and the court system.

This chapter is intended as a general introduction to facilitate understanding of the civil rights issues Asian Americans face in the 1990s. It begins with a review of the history of Asian Americans in the United States that both demonstrates the long-standing anti-Asian bias in this country and shows how that history shaped today's Asian American population. It then paints a demographic and socioeconomic portrait of today's Asian Americans that shows the heterogeneity of the Asian American population. The diversity among Asian Americans means that Asian Americans as a group will confront an entire spectrum of civil rights issues, ranging from those that affect new immigrants with low skills to those that affect highly educated professionals and their offspring. Finally, the chapter discusses several factors that underlie discrimination against Asian Americans.

---

1   The term Asian Americans is used in this report to refer to persons of Asian descent who are either citizens or intending citizens of the United States, or who plan to spend the rest of their lives in the United States.

2   Michel McQueen, "Voters' Responses to Poll Disclose Huge Chasm Between Social Attitudes of Blacks and Whites," *Wall Street Journal,* May 17, 1991, p. A16.

3   The Commission's Roundtable Conferences on Asian American Civil Rights Issues for the 1990s were held in Houston, TX, on May 27, 1989; in New York, NY, on June 23, 1989; and in San Francisco, CA, on July 29, 1989.

4   Asian American groups considered in this report are persons having origins in the Far East, Southeast Asia, and the Indian subcontinent. At times, the report also includes information about Pacific Islanders, but limited resources precluded a systematic investigation of the civil rights issues facing Pacific Islanders.

Asians in the United States: A Brief History

The first Asians to arrive in the United States in large numbers were the Chinese, who came to work on Hawaiian plantations by the 1840s and to the West Coast of the mainland starting in the early 1850s to work in gold mines and later to help build the cross-country railroads. The Chinese were followed in the late 19th and early 20th centuries by Japanese and Filipinos and, in smaller numbers, by Koreans and Asian Indians. Restrictive immigration laws produced a 40-year hiatus in Asian immigration starting in the 1920s, but in 1965, when anti-Asian immigration restrictions were liberalized, a new wave of immigration began bringing people from Southeast Asia, China, Korea, the Philippines, and other Asian countries to the United States.

The history of Asian Americans in this country is replete with incidents of discrimination against them. Asian Americans experienced, at one time or another, discriminatory immigration and naturalization policies; discriminatory Federal, State, and local laws; discriminatory governmental treatment; considerable prejudice on the part of the general public; and outright violence. Not only was today's Asian American community shaped by historical forces, but today's civil rights issues need to be viewed in the context of past discrimination against Asian Americans.

Naturalization and Immigration Laws

Throughout most of their history in this country Asians have been victimized by discriminatory naturalization and immigration laws. These laws have had the legacy of making Asian American newcomers feel unwelcome in their adopted country and have also been important in shaping the Asian American community as it exists today.

As this country became a nation, its founders sought to restrict eligibility for citizenship. In 1790 Congress passed a law limiting naturalization to "free white persons."[5] The law was modified in 1870, after the adoption of the 14th amendment, to include "aliens of African nativity and persons of African descent." At that time Congress considered and rejected extending naturalization rights to Asians,[6] thus making Asian immigrants the only racial group barred from naturalization.[7] Because the 14th amendment granted citizenship to all persons born in the United States, however, the American-born children of Asian immigrants were citizens. Filipinos and Asian Indians were granted eligibility for naturalization in 1946,[8] but it was not until 1952, with the McCarran-Walter Act,[9] that naturalization eligibility was extended to all races.[10] Thus, through most of this country's history, immigrant Asians were ineligible to become citizens.

Despite these anti-Asian naturalization laws, immigrants came to the United States from sev-

---

5   U.S. Commission on Civil Rights, *The Tarnished Golden Door: Civil Rights Issues in Immigration* (September 1980), p. 10 (hereafter cited as *The Tarnished Golden Door*).

6   Roger Daniels, *Asian America: Chinese and Japanese in the United States Since 1850* (Seattle, WA: University of Washington Press, 1988), p. 43 (hereafter cited as *Asian America*).

7   These laws were widely held to bar the naturalization of the Chinese. In 1922 the Supreme Court held that the naturalization bar applied to Japanese (Ozawa v. United States, 260 U.S. 178 (1922)). The following year, the Supreme Court held that East Indians were also barred from naturalization, because the term "white" did not include all Caucasians (United States v. Thind, 261 U.S. 204 (1923)).

8   *The Tarnished Golden Door*, p. 10.

9   Pub. L. No. 82-414, 66 Stat. 163 (1952).

10   Don Teruo Hata, Jr., and Nadine Ishitani Hata, "Run Out and Ripped Off: A Legacy of Discrimination," *Civil Rights Digest*, vol. 9, no. 1 (Fall 1976), p. 10 (hereafter cited as "Run Out and Ripped Off").

eral Asian countries starting in the mid-19th century. As each successive Asian group arrived in this country, increasingly harsh immigration laws restricting the group's immigration were imposed. The first immigration ban was against the Chinese. In the 1850s Chinese immigrants began coming to the United States mainland to work in California's gold mines and quickly spread to mining in other Western States as well. Later, they played an essential role in building this country's transcontinental railroads. After the railroads were completed in 1869, jobs became scarcer on the West Coast, and worker resentment of the low wage rates accepted by Chinese workers intensified. Pressure built to limit the immigration of Chinese, culminating with the passage of the Chinese Exclusion Act in 1882,[11] which suspended the immigration of Chinese laborers for 10 years.[12] In 1892 the Geary Act[13] extended the immigration ban for another 10 years and required Chinese living in the United States to obtain "certificates of residence" to prove that they were legal residents.[14] In 1904 the Chinese immigration ban was extended indefinitely.[15] Since the Chinese living in this country were predominately male, the result of these immigration restrictions was that the Chinese population in the United States declined from 105,465 in 1880 to 61,639 by 1920.[16]

Shortly after Chinese immigration was halted by the Chinese Exclusion Act, a new wave of Asian immigration began, this time from Japan. Although a few Japanese had immigrated to Hawaii in the 1870s and 1880s, Japanese did not come to the mainland in noticeable numbers until the 1890s.[17] At first largely urban, the Japanese soon became engaged predominantly in agricultural pursuits and related trade.[18]

Although the number of Japanese in this country was not large (fewer than 25,000 in the 1900 census),[19] pressure soon developed on the West Coast to restrict Japanese immigration. In response to this pressure, the Japanese Government, fearing a loss of international prestige if U.S. immigration laws banned Japanese immigration, negotiated the Gentleman's Agreement[20] with President Theodore Roosevelt in 1907.[21] According to this agreement, the Japanese Government would voluntarily restrict the emigration of unskilled Japanese to the United States. In return, the parents, wives, and children of Japanese already in the United States would be allowed entrance. Unlike the Chinese Exclusion Act, the Gentleman's Agreement permitted the entrance of large numbers of Japanese "picture brides."[22] As a result, the Japanese population in the United States, initially much smaller than the Chinese population, grew from

---

11   Ch. 126, 22 Stat. 58 (1882).

12   *The Tarnished Golden Door,* p. 8. In 1888 the Scott Act widened the immigration ban to all Chinese except for officials, merchants, teachers, students, and tourists. The Scott Act also denied reentry to any Chinese who had left the United States, even though the Chinese Exclusion Act had allowed reentry of all Chinese who had been in this country in 1880. Ibid. and *Asian America,* p. 57.

13   Ch. 60, 27 Stat. 25 (1892).

14   *Asian America,* p. 58.

15   Ch. 1630, 33 Stat. 428 (1904); *The Tarnished Golden Door,* p. 8. As noted below, the ban was eventually lifted in 1943.

16   Ronald Takaki, *Strangers from a Different Shore: A History of Asian Americans* (Boston: Little Brown, 1989), pp. 111-12 (hereafter cited as *Strangers from a Different Shore*).

17   *Asian America,* pp. 101-02.

18   Ibid., p. 107.

19   Ibid., p. 115.

20   Exec. Order No. 589.

21   *Asian America,* p. 125.

22   Ibid., pp. 125-27.

roughly 25,000 in 1900 to almost 127,000 in 1940, far exceeding the 1940 Chinese population of roughly 78,000.[23]

Asian immigration was further limited by the Immigration Act of 1917,[24] which banned immigration from all countries in the Asia-Pacific Triangle except for the Philippines, a U.S. territory, and Japan.[25] Japanese immigration was subsequently limited by the Immigration Act of 1924.[26] This act restricted annual immigration from all countries to 2 percent of the countries' national origin populations living in the United States in 1890, with an overall cap of 150,000, and also specifically banned immigration of persons who were ineligible for citizenship, i.e., Asians.[27] Since immigration from all other Asian countries had already been halted, this provision appeared to be targeted at the Japanese.

The immigration to the U.S. mainland by Filipinos, largely laborers, which had begun just after 1900, increased substantially in the 1920s as demand for their labor increased, at least in part as a result of the exclusion of the Japanese.[28] Filipinos spread across the country quickly, most of them working in agriculture and in domestic service.[29] Immigration from the Philippines, a U.S. territory, continued apace until a few years before the Tydings-McDuffie Act of 1934,[30] which gave the Philippines Commonwealth status and defined Filipinos not born in the United States as aliens. The Tydings-McDuffie Act placed a quota of 50 immigrants per year on immigration from the Philippines[31] and did not allow the families of resident Filipinos to immigrate.[32] One year later, the Repatriation Act[33] authorized funds to pay for one-way tickets back to the Philippines for resident Filipinos, provided that they agreed not to return to the United States. Only 2,000 Filipinos took advantage of this offer, however.[34]

The discriminatory immigration laws were relaxed slowly starting in 1943, when the Chinese Exclusion Act was repealed[35] and an annual quota of 105 Chinese immigrants was set.[36] The Filipino and Indian quotas were increased by presidential proclamation in 1946.[37] The 1945 War Brides Act[38] permitted the immigration of Asian (and other national origin) spouses and children of American servicemen.[39] It was only in 1952 that the McCarran-Walter Act ended the ban on Asian immigration and for the first time in American history granted Asian im-

---

23   Ibid., p. 90 and p. 115.

24   Pub. L. No. 301, 39 Stat. 874 (1917).

25   *Asian America,* p. 150.

26   Pub. L. No. 139, 43 Stat. 153 (1924).

27   Except for Filipinos, who, as residents of a U.S. territory, were United States nationals.

28   *Strangers From a Different Shore,* pp. 57-58.

29   Ibid., pp. 316-19.

30   Ch. 84, 48 Stat. 459 (1934).

31   State of California, Attorney General's Asian/Pacific Advisory Committee, *Final Report* (December 1988), p. 38 (hereafter cited as Attorney General's Report).

32   *Strangers From a Different Shore,* p. 337.

33   Pub. L. No. 202, 49 Stat. 478 (1935). The time in which Filipinos could "benefit" from the statute was extended in Congress' next session. Pub. L. No. 645, 49 Stat. 1462 (1936).

34   *Strangers From a Different Shore,* pp. 332-33.

35   Pub. L. No. 199, 57 Stat. 600 (1943).

36   *The Tarnished Golden Door,* p. 10.

37   Proc. 2696, 3 C.F.R. 86 (1946).

38   Pub. L. No. 271, 59 Stat. 659 (1945).

39   *The Tarnished Golden Door,* p. 10.

migrants naturalization rights. The act, however, retained the national origins system established in the Immigration Act of 1924.[40] Since very few Asians (apart from Chinese) resided in the United States in 1890, this provision effectively continued discrimination against Asian immigration.[41] It was not until 1965 that amendments to the McCarran-Walter Act[42] replaced the national origins system with a fixed annual quota of 20,000 per country, permitting a sizable Asian immigration.[43] The 1965 amendments retained a preference for highly skilled workers first introduced in the 1952 act.[44]

Beginning in the late 1960s, the opening of the doors to Asian immigrants produced a second major wave of Asian immigration. Many of these new immigrants were highly educated professionals as a result of the preference system for skilled workers. In the 1970s and early 1980s immigration from Asia intensified, as Southeast Asian refugees came to this country as a result of upheavals in Southeast Asia brought on by the Vietnam War. Over 400,000 Asians came to the United States during the 1960s, and Asians constituted roughly 13 percent of all immigrants during the decade. During the 1970s Asian immigration increased to roughly 1.6 million, constituting 36 percent of all immigration.[45] Asian immigration continued apace into the 1980s. The second wave of Asian immigration was heavily Filipino, Korean, and Southeast Asian, and to a lesser extent Chinese and Indian. Japanese immigrants continued to come, but in much smaller numbers than the other groups.

The net effect of the changing immigration and naturalization policies towards Asians is that some Asian Americans, predominantly Japanese Americans and to a lesser extent, Chinese Americans,[46] have been here for generations, while a great number of Asian Americans are immigrants (many of whom entered the United States after 1965) or their children.

Anti-Asian Bigotry and Violence

Bigotry and violence against Asians began almost as soon as Asians arrived in this country, making Asian Americans feel that they were unwelcome outsiders in the United States. As early as the late 1840s, the Know-Nothing Party, which was largely anti-Catholic in the Eastern United States, promoted anti-Asian sentiments in the Western United States.[47] In the 1860s and 1870s, before the Chinese Exclusion Act, many unions and political parties in the West adopted anti-Chinese platforms. In 1862 anti-Coolie clubs formed in San Francisco and spread to other cities in California.[48] In 1870 a large-scale "anti-Oriental" mass meeting took place in San Francisco,[49] and several California unions, including the Knights of St. Crispin, "organized on

40   Ibid., p. 11.

41   Ibid., p. 11. Another provision of the McCarran-Walter Act counted persons of half-Asian descent against the quotas for their Asian country of origin.

42   Pub. L. No. 89-236, 79 Stat. 911 (1965).

43   E. P. Hutchinson, *Legislative History of American Immigration Policy: 1798-1965* (Philadelphia: University of Pennsylvania Press, 1981), pp. 369-78.

44   Ibid., pp. 308-09, 377-78.

45   U.S. Commission on Civil Rights, *The Economic Status of Americans of Asian Descent: An Exploratory Investigation* (Clearinghouse Publication 95, October 1988), p. 19 (hereafter cited as *The Economic Status of Americans of Asian Descent*).

46   As noted above, because the 19th century Chinese immigrants were heavily male, the Chinese American population fell precipitously after the Chinese Exclusion Act of 1882, and only a small proportion of today's Chinese Americans are descendants of the early Chinese immigrants.

47   *The Tarnished Golden Door*, p. 7.

48   *Asian America*, p. 36.

an anti-Chinese basis."[50] By 1871 both the Democratic and Republican parties in California had adopted platforms opposing Chinese immigration,[51] and both national parties had anti-Chinese resolutions in their platforms in the years 1876, 1880, 1888, and 1904.[52]

Anti-Chinese sentiments were propagated by the Western media, joined occasionally by the eastern press. For example, the *New York Times* warned:

We have four millions of degraded negroes in the South. We have political passion and religious prejudice everywhere. The strain upon the constitution is about as great as it can bear. And if, in addition, to all the adverse elements we now have, there were to be a flood-tide of Chinese population—a population befouled with all the social vices, with no knowledge or appreciation of free institutions or constitutional liberty, with heathenish souls and heathenish propensities, whose character, and habits, and modes of thought are firmly fixed by the consolidating influence of ages upon ages—we should be prepared to bid farewell to republicanism and democracy.[53]

The anti-Chinese sentiments of western workers erupted into violence in the 1870s. In October 1871 roughly 20 Chinese were massacred in Los Angeles by a white mob who also burned and looted their homes and stores.[54] In 1877 a similar incident occurred in San Francisco's Chinatown, and in Chico, California, five Chinese farmers were murdered.[55] The violence spread to other Western States in the 1880s. There were anti-Chinese riots in Denver and Rock Springs, Wyoming, and the cities of Seattle and Tacoma chased their Chinese residents out of town. In 1887, 31 Chinese miners were "robbed, murdered, and mutilated" in the Snake River (Oregon) Massacre.[56]

After the Chinese Exclusion Act of 1882, anti-Asian sentiments were directed against the Japanese, and later, at the Filipinos. In the early 1900s, many white workers began to resent competition from Japanese workers, and in 1905 delegates from more than 67 labor organizations formed the Asiatic Exclusion League in San Francisco.[57] The Asiatic Exclusion League spoke of the "yellow peril" and the "Asiatic horde" threatening to invade the United States.[58] Like the Chinese before them, the Japanese and the Filipinos were shunned. Anti-Filipino race riots broke out in 1928 and 1930 in Washington and California. In California, the rioting that took place in Watsonville was prompted by press coverage of the arrest of a Filipino man for walking with a white girl to whom he was engaged.[59]

State and Local Anti-Asian Laws

Although United States immigrants of many ethnic groups (for instance, Irish, Jews, and Italians) have experienced bigotry and violence akin to that experienced by Asian Americans, Asian Americans share with American blacks the distinction of having been the targets of widespread legal discrimination that hindered their

---

49   "Run Out and Ripped Off," p. 5.

50   *Asian America*, p. 38.

51   Ibid., p. 37.

52   Ibid., p. 45.

53   "Growth of the United States Through Emigration—The Chinese," *New York Times*, Sept. 3, 1865, p. 4.

54   "Run Out and Ripped Off," p. 5.

55   Attorney General's Report, p. 34.

56   *Asian America*, pp. 60-64.

57   "Run Out and Ripped Off," p. 7.

58   Attorney General's Report, pp. 34-35.

59   *Strangers From a Different Shore*, pp. 326-30.

ability to participate fully in the American dream.

The strong anti-Asian sentiments in the Western States led to the adoption of many discriminatory laws at the State and local levels, similar to those aimed at blacks in the South. Many of these laws took advantage of the discriminatory aspect of naturalization laws by restricting the rights of persons "ineligible to become citizens," i.e., Asians.[60] In addition, segregation in public facilities, including schools, was quite common until after the Second World War.

As early as the 1850s laws discriminatory against the Chinese were enacted by the State of California. In 1852 California imposed a "foreign miner's tax" of $3 for any miner who was not an intending citizen.[61] In 1855 California imposed a tax on ships landing at California ports amounting to $50 per disembarking passenger ineligible to become a citizen, and in 1858 California temporarily prohibited Chinese from landing in California altogether.[62] In 1862 California passed a head tax of $2.50 per month on most Chinese living in the State.[63]

In 1880 California enacted a miscegenation law prohibiting whites from marrying "negro, mulatto, or Mongolian."[64] After a Filipino successfully argued his right to marry a white woman in court on the basis that Filipinos are Malay and not Mongolian, the legislature extended the marriage prohibitions to Filipinos in 1933.[65] Laws prohibiting intermarriage between Asians and whites were widespread in other States as well.[66]

Whereas the earlier California anti-Asian laws were targeted at the Chinese, the 1913 Alien Land Law was targeted at Japanese farmers. This law prohibited persons ineligible to become citizens from purchasing land in the State of California and limited lease terms to 3 years or less. Many Japanese got around this law by leasing or purchasing land in the name of their American-born children.[67] To close the loopholes in the 1913 law, a stricter law was passed in 1920 preventing Japanese immigrants from acting as guardians for minors in matters pertaining to land ownership and also prohibiting them from leasing land.[68] Other States also had similar laws preventing Asian immigrants from owning land.[69]

Local laws were also discriminatory. For example, the city and county of San Francisco passed ordinances that were apparently race neutral but that had adverse impacts on Chinese residents. As a case in point, in 1873 the city of San Francisco passed the Laundry Ordinance, which imposed a tax on laundries of $1.25 on a laundry employing one horse-drawn vehicle, $4 on a laundry employing two horse-drawn vehicles, and $15 on laundries employing more than two horse-drawn vehicles. The ordinance also imposed a $15 tax on a laundry that had no horse-drawn vehicles at all.[70] This law was clearly targeted at the Chinese, since virtually no Chinese laundries operated horse-drawn vehi-

---

60   See above discussion of naturalization laws that made Asians ineligible to become citizens.

61   "Run Out and Ripped Off," p. 4. Price levels have increased by a factor of 10 since the mid-19th century, so a tax of $3 in 1850 would be equivalent to a tax today of $30.

62   Ibid. pp. 4-5.

63   *Strangers from a Different Shore*, p. 82.

64   Ibid., pp. 101-02.

65   Ibid., p. 330.

66   Ibid.

67   *Asian America*, pp. 139-44.

68   Ibid., pp. 145-47.

69   For example, the State of Washington also had such a law. Ibid., pp. 146-47.

70   A $15 tax is the equivalent of roughly $150 in today's dollars.

cles.[71] In a similar vein, San Francisco passed the Cubic Air Ordinance, requiring that living spaces have at least 500 cubic feet of space per person, and this law was only enforced in Chinatown.[72]

Asians often fought both State and local laws in the courts. Sometimes they were successful, but the courts were also discriminatory. For example, in 1854 the California Supreme Court decided in the case of *People v. Hall*[73] that Chinese could not testify against whites in court. Hall, a white man, had been convicted of murdering a Chinese man on the basis of testimony by one white and three Chinese witnesses. The supreme court overthrew his conviction, ruling that the Chinese witnesses should not have testified based on a State law that did not allow blacks, mulattos, or Indians to testify in favor of or against whites in court.[74] The wording of the decision illustrates the degree of racial bigotry against Asians even among those in the judiciary:

Indian as commonly used refers only to the North American Indian, yet in the days of Columbus all shores washed by Chinese waters were called the Indies. In the second place the word "white" necessarily excludes all other races than Caucasian; and in the third place, even if this were not so, I would decide against the testimony of Chinese on grounds of public policy.[75]

Despite the discriminatory tendencies of the courts, Chinese residents of San Francisco successfully fought the discriminatory enforcement of San Francisco's Laundry Ordinance, passed in 1880, which governed the sites and manner of laundry operations. Their fight led to the United States Supreme Court landmark decision, *Yick Wo v. Hopkins.*[76] In the early 1880s there were about 320 laundries in San Francisco. Of these, about 240 were owned and operated by Chinese residents, and about 310 were constructed of wood, as were about nine-tenths of the houses in the city of San Francisco at that time. The Laundry Ordinance prohibited wood construction for laundries, since wood construction purportedly constituted a fire and public safety hazard. In 1885, upon expiration of his business license, Mr. Yick Wo, who had operated a laundry at the same site for 20 years, applied for a renewal of his business license but was turned down because his building was of wood construction. Subsequently, he was found guilty of violating the Laundry Ordinance and imprisoned. Two hundred other Chinese laundries were also denied license renewals, although all had operated at the same sites for over 20 years. In contrast, all license renewal applications by non-Chinese laundries (even those with wooden buildings) were approved. In 1886 the United States Supreme Court ruled in favor of plaintiff Yick Wo in *Yick Wo v. Hopkins,* reasoning that:

The effect of [such selective enforcement]. . .would seem to be necessarily to close up the many Chinese laundries now existing, or compel their owners to pull down their present buildings and reconstruct of brick or stone. . . . [It] would be little short of absolute confiscation of the large amount of property. . . .If this

---

71   "Run Out and Ripped Off," p. 5.

72   *Asian America,* p. 39.

73   4 Cal. 309 (1854).

74   "Run Out and Ripped Off," p. 4.

75   *Asian America,* p. 54.

76   118 U.S. 356 (1886). The case was a landmark decision for several reasons: 1) it brought heightened scrutiny to cases involving improperly motivated classifications; 2) it is a clear example of how discriminatory impact alone can be used to unmask invidious classifications; and 3) it extended Federal equal protection guarantees under the 14th amendment beyond United States citizens to temporary or permanent residents. (Philip T. Nash, "Asian Americans and the Supreme Court: Employment and Education Issues," 1991, pp. 6-7.)

would not be depriving such parties of their property without due process of law, it would be difficult to say what would effect that prohibited result. The necessary tendency, if not the specific purpose, of [such selective enforcement] is to drive out of business all the numerous small laundries, especially those owned by Chinese, and give monopoly of the business to the large institutions.[77]

The Court concluded that:

No reason. . .exists except hostility to the race and nationality to which the petitioners belong, and which in the eye of the law is not justified. The discrimination is, therefore, illegal, and the public administration which enforces it is a denial of the equal protection of the laws and violation of the Fourteenth Amendment of the Constitution. The imprisonment of the petitioners is, therefore, illegal, and they must be discharged.[78]

The public school systems of California and other Western States were generally segregated. In 1860 California barred Asians, blacks, and Native Americans from attending its public schools. In 1884 the California Supreme Court held that the 1860 law was unconstitutional. As a result of this decision, the State set up a system of "oriental" (usually, Chinese) schools starting in 1885. In a 1902 decision, the U.S. Supreme Court upheld the constitutionality of separate but equal schools for Asian students.[79]

In 1906 the city of San Francisco decided that Japanese and Korean students could not attend white schools and instead had to attend Chinese schools, setting off an international incident. The Japanese Government protested the decision vigorously, and as a result, President Theodore Roosevelt persuaded San Francisco to back down with respect to Japanese students. It was this incident that heightened Japanese awareness of anti-Japanese sentiments in the U.S. and prompted the negotiations that ultimately led to the Gentleman's Agreement of 1907.[80]

Internment of Japanese Americans During World War II

Perhaps the most disgraceful incident in this country's history of discrimination against Asian Americans is the wartime evacuation and internment of Japanese Americans during the 1940s. On February 19, 1942, 2½ months after Japan attacked Pearl Harbor, President Roosevelt signed Executive Order 9066 authorizing the Army to evacuate any persons from sensitive areas for reasons of national defense,[81] and on March 2, 1942, General DeWitt announced the evacuation of persons of Japanese descent from an area bordering the Pacific Ocean.[82] Initially, evacuated persons were merely relocated to other areas of the country, but the decision was made quickly to intern them in relocation camps.[83] In evacuating the Japanese, the Army generally gave less than 7 days notice, thus forcing families to sell their properties and possessions at a fraction of their true value.[84] Persons were allowed to bring to the camps only what they could carry. Eventually over 100,000 Japanese Americans were moved to internment camps in the Midwest, and many remained there for the duration of the war. They were officially released on January 2, 1945.[85]

---

77   118 U.S. at 362.

78   *Id.*, at 374.

79   Connie Young Yu, "The Others: Asian Americans and Education," *Civil Rights Digest*, vol. 9, no. 1 (Fall 1976), p. 45.

80   *Strangers From a Distant Shore*, pp. 201-03.

81   "Run Out and Ripped Off," p. 8.

82   *Asian America*, p. 214.

83   Commission on Wartime Relocation and Internment of Civilians, *Personal Justice Denied* (Washington, DC: Government Printing Office, 1982), pp. 101-07 (hereafter cited as *Personal Justice Denied*).

84   Ibid., p. 217, and Attorney General's Report, p. 38.

Executive Order 9066 and General DeWitt's evacuation order were made despite the fact that government intelligence reports did not support the notion that resident Japanese posed a threat to national security.[86] No similar evacuation was ordered for persons of German or Italian descent. The Commission on Wartime Relocation and Internment of Civilians (CWRIC), established by Congress in 1980 to investigate the wartime internment, concluded that:

The promulgation of Executive Order 9066 was not justified by military necessity, and the decisions which followed from it—detention, ending detention and ending exclusion—were not driven by analysis of military conditions. The broad historical causes which shaped these decisions were race prejudice, war hysteria and a failure of political leadership. Widespread ignorance of Japanese Americans contributed to a policy conceived in haste and executed in an atmosphere of fear and anger at Japan. A grave injustice was done to American citizens and resident aliens of Japanese ancestry who, without individual review or any probative evidence against them, were excluded, removed and detained by the United States during World War II.[87]

Contemporaneous newspaper coverage of the internment process reflected its racist character. For example, consider the following quotes:

It is this inscrutability not general to other groups, that makes the application of the order immediate upon the Japanese.[88]

"Once a Jap always a Jap!" he [Congressman Rankin] shouted. "You can't any more regenerate a Jap than you can reverse the laws of nature. I'm for taking every Japanese and putting him in a concentration camp."[89]

Executive Order 9066 was upheld by the Supreme Court in two famous wartime cases, *Korematsu v. United States*[90] and *Hirabayashi v. United States*,[91] which upheld the criminal convictions of Korematsu and Hirabayashi for challenging the evacuation and internment orders. It was not until the mid-1980s that their convictions were overturned when it was discovered that the U.S. Government had "'deliberately omitted relevant information and provided misleading information' to the Supreme Court on the crucial 'military necessity' issue."[92]

Redress for the Japanese Americans interned during the war was slow in coming. In 1948 Congress passed the Japanese American Evacuation Claims Act, which appropriated $38 million to reimburse Japanese Americans who had been interned for their losses. This amounted to only 10 cents on the dollar of actual losses.[93] In 1976 President Ford issued Presidential Proclamation 4417, which rescinded Executive Order 9066 and apologized to those who had been interned.[94]

---

85   "Run Out and Ripped Off," p. 8.

86   *Personal Justice Denied*, pp. 51-60.

87   Ibid., p. 18.

88   *San Francisco Chronicle*, editorial, Feb. 23, 1942, as quoted in Gina Petonito, "Racial Discourse, Claims Making and Japanese Internment During World War II" (paper presented at the 86th Annual Meeting of the American Sociological Association, Cincinnati, OH, Aug. 23-27, 1991), p. 11.

89   *San Francisco Chronicle*, Feb. 19, 1942, p. 9, as cited in Petonito, "Racial Discourse," p. 11.

90   323 U.S. 214 (1944).

91   320 U.S. 81 (1943).

92   Peter Irons, "Justice Long Overdue," *New Perspectives*, vol. 18, no. 1 (Winter/Spring 1986), p. 6, quoting Judge Patel's decision vacating Korematsu's conviction.

93   "Run Out and Ripped Off," p. 8.

94   *Asian America*, p. 331.

Finally, in 1988, prompted by the conclusions of the CWRIC report, Congress passed the Civil Liberties Act of 1988,[95] authorizing compensation of $20,000 for living survivors of the internment camps. This money has only just begun to be paid, however.[96]

Nearly 50 years later, the issues surrounding Japanese internment remain emotional. In 1989 the State of California legislature passed a resolution "requiring schools to teach that the internment stemmed from racism, hysteria over the war and poor decisions by the country's political leaders."[97] In response to the passage, Assemblyman Gil Ferguson introduced a new resolution in 1990 that would have required schools to teach that there was some justification for the internment.[98] Although the measure was overwhelmingly defeated, its introduction demonstrates that the issue is not yet resolved in the minds of all Americans.

Anti-Asian Sentiments and America's Nativist Tradition

The brief summary of America's history of anti-Asian policies and incidents offered in the foregoing pages needs to be understood in the larger context of America's nativist tradition. Throughout U.S. history, Americans have frequently exhibited a general hostility towards groups whose cultures or traditions were different from those of the mainstream. According to historians, those from foreign lands and those subscribing to nonmainstream religions have been targets of suspicion, distrust, repulsion, and sometimes even hatred throughout American history.[99] This nativism predated the arrival of Asians in America and was directed towards Catholics and immigrants from European countries as well. One historian noted that "during the colonial times, suspicion of those who were 'foreigners' either through religion or national background, or both, was not uncommon."[100]

During the early years of our nation, nativistic sentiments were prevalent among the public, and national leaders often shared these views. Such historical figures as George Washington,[101] Benjamin Franklin, Thomas Jefferson, and John Quincy Adams[102] all had reservations about and were at best ambivalent toward immigrants and

---

95 28 C.F.R. 74.

96 In October 1990 the first Japanese internment camp survivors—those who were the oldest—received their reparation checks. (Michael Isikoff, "Delayed Reparations and an Apology: Japanese Americans Held During War Get First Checks," *Washington Post,* Oct. 10, 1990.) The second round of checks began in October, 1991. (Japanese American National Library, *Bulletin,* vol. 2, no. 4 (Summer 1991), p. 1.)

97 Steven A. Capps, "Assembly Kills 'Justification' for Internment," *San Francisco Examiner,* Aug. 29, 1990.

98 Ibid.

99 For panoramic coverage, see Ray Allen Billington, *The Protestant Crusade, 1800-1860: A Study of the Origins of American Nativism* (New York: Macmillan, 1938); and John Higham, *Strangers in the Land: Patterns of American Nativism, 1860-1925* (New Brunswick, NJ: Rutgers University Press, 1955).

100 Milton M. Gordon, *Assimilation in American Life: The Role of Race, Religion, and National Origins* (New York: Oxford University Press, 1964), p. 89.

101 In 1794 George Washington wrote:
"My opinion, with respect to immigration, is that except for useful mechanics and some particular descriptions of men or professions, there is no need of encouragement, while the policy or advantage of its taking place in a body (I mean the settling of them in a body) may be much questioned; for, by so doing, they retain the language, habits and principles (good or bad) which they bring with them." Cited in Gordon, *Assimilation in American Life,* p. 90; see n. 7, p. 90, for the original source of the quotation.

102 John Quincy Adams, then Secretary of State, wrote in 1818:
"If they [immigrants to America] cannot accommodate themselves to the character. . . of this country. . . , the Atlantic is

the effects of a free immigration policy. For example, in 1753 Benjamin Franklin wrote:

[He] had misgivings about the Germans because of their clannishness, their little knowledge of English, the German press, and the increasing need of interpreters. . . .I suppose in a few years they will also be necessary in the Assembly, to tell one-half of our legislators what the other half say.[103]

In the 1780s Thomas Jefferson commented that:

They [the immigrants] will bring with them the principles of the governments they leave, imbibed in their early youth; or, if able to throw them off, it will be in exchange for an unbounded licentiousness, passing, as is usual, from one extreme to another. It would be a miracle were they to stop precisely at the point of temperate liberty. These principles, with their language, they will transmit to their children. In proportion to their numbers, they will share with us the legislation. They will infuse into it their spirit, warp and bias its directions, and render it a heterogeneous, incoherent, distracted mass.[104]

In reviewing the early- and mid-19th century sentiments about immigrants, one historian observed:

Many Americans believed that the influx of aliens threatened their established social structure, endangered the nation's economic welfare, and spelled doom of the existing governmental system.[105]

Hatred of Catholics and foreigners had been steadily growing in the United States for more than two centuries before it took political form with the Native American outburst of the 1840's and the Know-Nothingism of the 1850's.[106]

Incidents of an anti-Catholic, anti-European-radical, anti-Semitic, and anti-foreigner nature continued into the current century and are well documented.[107]

Viewed from this perspective, it should be apparent that Asians were not the only victims of American nativism.[108] America's history has been one of unceasing struggles and eventual victories in ridding itself of various exclusionary, nativistic barriers. The Asian American civil rights struggle is only one part of a larger struggle over the past 50 years to overcome all forms of prejudice (e.g., anti-Catholic, anti-Semitic, anti-Euroethnic, anti-black, and anti-Hispanic, as well as anti-Asian) and barriers to equal opportunity.

This section has offered a sketch of what immigrants from Asia and their descendants had to endure in becoming part of contemporary America. The restrictive immigration policy and discriminatory laws and regulations of the past effectively barred most Asian Americans from enjoying the full benefits of American citizenship, isolated them from mainstream American society, and prevented many from receiving the love and support that comes from family life. Their complete isolation from their families and from American society and their realization that

---

always open to them to return to the land of their nativity and their fathers. . . .They must cast off the European skin. . .They must be sure that whatever their own feelings may be, those of their children will cling to the prejudices of this country." Cited in ibid., p. 94.

103   Cited in ibid., p. 89; see n. 6, p. 89, for the original source of this quotation.

104   Cited in ibid., pp. 90-91; see footnote 8, p. 91, for the original source of this quotation.

105   Billington, *Protestant Crusade*, p. 322.

106   Ibid., p. 1.

107   See John Higham, *Strangers in the Land*, and also his more recent work, *Send These To Me: Jews and Other Immigrants in Urban America* (New York: Atheneum, 1975).

108   One historian argues, however, that "no variety of anti-European sentiment has ever approached the violent extremes to which anti-Chinese agitation went in the 1870s and 1880s." Higham, *Strangers in the Land,* p. 25.

they had only limited opportunities in America may have led many early Asian immigrants to turn to socially impermissible forms of behavior, such as drug use and frequenting prostitutes, and persons with anti-Asian sentiments may have in turn seized upon such behavior as a weapon against Asian Americans in their attempts to gain the right to full participation in American society. It is a testament to Asian Americans and their culture that, in face of the extreme hostility and restrictions on opportunity confronting them, Asian Americans persisted in this country, eventually gaining the right of citizenship, and that they made incalculably important contributions to the American society, culture, economy, and democratic tradition.

Although the United States has made much progress in demolishing many of the barriers confronting Asian Americans in the past, Asian Americans continue to confront discriminatory treatment and barriers to equal opportunity today. The remainder of the report highlights the need for continued vigilance and commitment to tearing down the remaining barriers to equal opportunity for Asian Americans and to rooting out all anti-Asian discrimination.

Asian Americans in the 1990s: A Demographic and Socioeconomic Portrait

The demographic and socioeconomic portrait of Asian Americans contained in this section reveals that today's Asian American community is extremely heterogeneous—comprised of many ethnicities, new immigrants and persons whose families have been here for generations, and persons of all socioeconomic statuses. This diversity means that the civil rights issues facing Asian Americans are themselves diverse, ranging from issues facing those who are not proficient in English, such as inadequate bilingual and English as a Second Language programs in our public schools, to issues affecting highly educated professionals, such as the existence of an invisible "glass ceiling" that limits opportunities for Asian Americans at the top of their professions.

Demography of Asian Americans

With a population of roughly 7.3 million, Asian Americans today make up slightly less than 3 percent of the United States population. Table 1.1 shows that over the past decade, their population share has risen dramatically, from 1.5 percent to 2.9 percent of the total population. The Asian American population more than doubled, growing by 108 percent, twice as fast as the Hispanic population, which grew by 53 percent, 8 times as fast as the black population, which grew by 13 percent, and 15 times as fast as the white population, which grew by 6 percent. The Asian American population is expected to continue to grow rapidly.

The principal reason for the growth in the Asian American population is the post-1965 influx of immigrants and refugees from Asia and the Pacific Islands.[109] After 40 years of being virtually banned from the United States by immigration laws, people from Asia began to come here in greater numbers starting in 1965, when the United States abandoned the "national origins" system of immigration. The Vietnam War and its aftermath caused Asian immigration to accelerate starting in the mid-1970s. In every year since 1974 (except for 1977), immigrants from Asia made up over 40 percent of all immigrants to this country.[110] Not only do Asian immigrants make up a large percentage of all new immigrants, but new Asian immigrants

---

109   During the decade of the 1980s immigration has been responsible for roughly two-thirds of the population growth of Asian Americans. See U.S. Bureau of the Census, *United States Population Estimates, by Age, Sex, Race, and Hispanic Origin: 1980 to 1988,* Current Population Reports, Series P-25, No. 1045 (January 1990), p. 82, table 7.

110   Ibid., p. 27, table X.

make up a large percentage of the total Asian American population. Asian immigrants arriving in 1980, for instance, constituted 6.4 percent of the total Asian American population that year. The percentage of the Asian American population who were new immigrants declined gradually over the 1980s, but was still as high as 2.8 percent in 1988.[111]

Because of these high recent rates of immigration, a large proportion of Asian Americans are foreign born. Table 1.2 shows that as of 1980, 62.1 percent of Asian Americans were foreign born, compared with 6.2 percent of the general U.S. population. Because of the high rates of immigration since 1980, the current proportion of Asian Americans who are foreign born is likely to be substantially higher.[112] On the other hand, because of the restrictive immigration laws of the past, Asian American adults who are native born are likely to belong to families that have been here for several generations.

Although the overall proportion of foreign born among Asian Americans is high, this proportion differs substantially across subgroups. Table 1.2 shows that in 1980 over 90 percent of Southeast Asians (Vietnamese, Laotians, Cambodians, and Hmong) but only 28 percent of Japanese Americans were born abroad. Recent Japanese immigration has been slight and largely temporary, and most Japanese Americans are descendants of Japanese immigrants who came here before 1924. The two other groups that came to this country in large numbers before Asian immigration was restricted, Chinese and Filipinos, both had percentages of foreign born of around 64 percent in 1980.[113]

The large number of recent immigrants among Asian Americans translates into a large percentage of Asian Americans with limited English proficiency. As of 1980, 15 percent of Asian Americans did not speak English well, or did not speak it at all. Consistent with the immigration patterns discussed above, the extent of limited English proficiency was least prevalent among Japanese Americans (9 percent) and among Asians whose countries of origin use English (Indians and Filipinos) and most common among Southeast Asian groups (60 percent or more).[114]

Asian Americans are heavily concentrated in certain geographic areas. Coming to the United States across the Pacific Ocean, most Asian groups initially settled in the Western United States. Although only 19 percent of the general U.S. population lived in the West in 1980, 56 percent of the Asian American population did. Three non-Western States also have sizable Asian American populations: New York, Illinois, and Texas.[115] The percentage living in the West varies considerably across Asian groups, however. Japanese Americans, 80 percent of whom lived in the West in 1980, are the most concentrated in the Western United States. Around half of Chinese Americans and less than half of Americans from Southeast Asia lived in Western States in 1980. Asian Indians and Pakistanis were the least concentrated in the West, with 19 and 24 percent, respectively, living in the West in 1980.[116]

---

111 Ibid., p. 83, table 7.

112 As of November 1991, the 1990 census detail had not been released.

113 The percentage foreign born is higher for both of these groups than for the Japanese for two reasons. First, there has been a substantial post-1965 immigration from both the Philippines and China. Second, when Asian immigration was cut off by restrictive immigration laws in the 1920s, the majority of Chinese and Filipinos in this country were men, and thus early Chinese and Filipino immigrants had fewer children than the Japanese, among whom women numbered almost as many as men.

114 See table 1.2.

115 U.S. Bureau of the Census, *We, the Asian and Pacific Islander Americans*, p. 3, table 1.

TABLE 1.1
U.S. Population by Race and Ethnicity: 1990 and 1980

| | 1990 | | 1980 | | |
	Population (thousands)	Percentage of total	Population (thousands)	Percentage of total	Population growth rate: 1980-1990
White	199,686	80.3	188,372	83.1	6.0
Black	29,986	12.1	26,495	11.7	13.2
Hispanic	22,354	9.0	14,609	6.4	53.0
Asian & Pacific Islander	*7,274*	*2.9*	*3,500*	*1.5*	*107.8*
Native American	1,959	0.8	1,420	0.6	37.9

Source: U.S. Bureau of the Census, Racial Statistics Division.

TABLE 1.2
Characteristics of Asian Americans by Country of Origin

	Percentage of Asian American population [a]	Percentage foreign born [b]	Percentage who do not speak English well [b]	Percentage who live in the West [b]
Chinese	22.6	63.3	23	52.7
Filipino	19.3	64.7	6	68.8
Japanese	11.6	28.4	9	80.3
Asian Indian	11.2	70.4	5	19.2
Korean	11.0	81.9	24	42.9
Vietnamese	8.4	90.5	38	46.2
Laotian	2.0	93.7	69	45.7
Thai	1.3	82.1	12	43.0
Cambodian	2.0	93.9	59	55.6
Hmong	1.2	90.5	63	37.4
Pakistani	–	85.1	10	23.5
Indonesian	–	83.4	6	56.2
All Asian Americans	*100.0*	*62.1*	*15*	*56.4*

[a] Source: Barbara Vobejda, "Asians, Hispanics Giving Nation More Diversity," *Washington Post*, June 12, 1991.
[b] Source: U.S. Bureau of the Census, *We, the Asian and Pacific Islander Americans*, p. 11, table 7, and U.S. General Accounting Office, *Asian Americans: A Status Report*, p. 44, table 6.1.

Socioeconomic Status of Asian Americans

Summary statistics show that Asian Americans as a group are more educated, more likely to be in high-paying occupations, less likely to be unemployed, and have higher family incomes than the general population. It may be tempting to conclude from these statistics that Asian Americans do not face discrimination or encounter barriers to equal opportunity, that they have fully overcome them, or that they have not suffered the adverse consequences of racial prejudice. However, such a conclusion would be totally unwarranted and misleading. For one thing, focusing on the average experience of Asian Americans masks large socioeconomic differences among Asian American subgroups, as well as differences within groups. Many Asian Americans have not achieved the high socioeconomic status enjoyed by the fictional "average" Asian American. More important, socioeconomic status is at best a poor indicator of the discrimination experienced by Asian Americans or any other group. Even those Asians who appear to be doing well by "outcome" measures of socioeconomic status may experience barriers to equal opportunity that keep them from achieving the full measure of their potential. Furthermore, they may have to bear significant costs along the road to socioeconomic success, and their experiences with discrimination may leave scars that are not discernible in statistics that measure socioeconomic status.

The Asian American population is extremely heterogeneous in terms of socioeconomic status. Many Asian Americans do not share in the relatively favorable socioeconomic outcomes attributed to the "average" Asian American. In particular, the newer immigrant groups from Southeast Asia have sharply lower socioeconomic status than other Asian Americans. Table 1.3 shows that, whereas 34 percent of all Asian Americans were college graduates in 1980, the proportion of college graduates among Southeast Asians ranged from 13 percent for the Vietnamese, to 3 percent for the Hmong. Similarly, whereas Asian Americans as a group had a median family income almost 20 percent higher than that of the general population,[116] Southeast Asian family incomes ranged from 35 percent lower than the national average for the Vietnamese to 74 percent lower for the Hmong. Southeast Asian unemployment rates and poverty rates were also substantially higher than those of Asian Americans as a group.

There is also considerable variation in socioeconomic status even among the more established Asian American groups. Even though Chinese, Asian Indians, and Koreans all had higher median family incomes than the general population, these groups also had poverty rates as high or higher than that of the general population, indicating that not all members of these groups are doing as well.[117]

Asian Americans' high average levels of family income, educational attainment, and occupational prestige do not necessarily mean that Asian Americans do not face significant barriers to equal economic opportunity or other forms of discrimination and prejudice. Barriers to equal opportunity may force Asian Americans to expend extra efforts as they strive to reach socioeconomic success, and they may retard or ultimately prevent Asian Americans from reaching the full measure of their potential. Discrimination and prejudice may also exact a toll of pain

---

116   It should be noted that the census does not distinguish between Asian Americans—i.e., Asians who are either citizens or intending citizens or who plan to remain in the United States for their entire lives—and Asian nationals temporarily living in the United States. To the extent that the income of Asian nationals (often highly paid Japanese executives) are reflected in the summary statistics of Asian Americans' incomes, the average income of Asian Americans may be overstated.

117   See table 1.3.

TABLE 1.3
Characteristics of Asian Americans by Country of Origin: 1980

	Percent college graduates [a]	Percent managers or professionals [b]	Unemploy-ment rate [c]	Relative median family income [d]	Poverty rate [e]
Chinese	36.6	32.6	3.6	1.13	10.5
Filipino	37.0	25.1	4.8	1.19	6.2
Japanese	26.4	28.5	3.0	1.37	4.2
Asian Indian	51.9	48.5	5.8	1.25	10.6
Korean	33.7	24.9	5.7	1.03	12.5
Vietnamese	12.9	13.4	8.2	.65	33.5
Laotian	5.6	7.6	15.3	.26	67.2
Thai	32.3	23.4	5.5	.97	13.4
Cambodian	7.7	10.8	10.6	.45	46.9
Hmong	2.9	9.4	20.0	.26	65.5
Pakistani	58.4	45.2	5.7	1.08	10.5
Indonesian	33.3	24.2	6.1	1.06	15.2
All Asian Americans	34.3	29.7	4.6	1.19	10.3
Hawaiian	9.6	15.9	7.0	.96	14.3
All Pacific Islander Americans	9.3	15.6	7.3	.90	16.1
All Americans	16.2	22.7	6.5	1.00	9.6

Source: U.S. Bureau of the Census, *We, the Asian and Pacific Islander Americans*, pp. 12-13, Table 7.

[a] Percentage of all persons age 25 and over who have completed 4 or more years of college.
[b] Percentage of employed persons age 16 and over whose occupation is in a managerial or professional specialty.
[c] Unemployment rate for persons age 16 and over.
[d] Median family income as a fraction of the median family income for the entire U.S. population.
[e] Percentage of families with income below the poverty level.

and suffering that cannot be compensated for by mere socioeconomic success.

There are indications that high levels of family income may be an artifact created by Asian Americans' concentration in high cost of living areas, the larger average number of workers in many Asian American families, or the high education levels of many Asian Americans. Furthermore, if Asian Americans have larger than average families, high levels of total family income may not necessarily translate into high levels of per capita income. The Commission's recent study on the economic status of Asian Americans showed that it is important to look beyond total family income when examining the socioeconomic status of population groups. For example, the study found that:

1) Taking the different regional distributions of Asian Americans and non-Hispanic whites into account lowers the average family incomes of most Asian American groups relative to the average family income of non-Hispanic whites; this effect is greater for foreign-born Asian Americans than for those born in the United States.[118]

2) The percentage of family income coming from the earnings of family members other than the husband is larger for Asian American families than for non-Hispanic white families.[119]

3) Although most foreign-born Asian American groups have total family incomes that are as high or higher than those of U.S.-born non-Hispanic whites, the reverse is true for per capita income: for most foreign-born Asian American groups, per capita income is less than that of U.S.-born non-Hispanic whites.[120]

4) When differences in education and other skills are taken into account along with region of residence, Asian American men earn about the same as or less than white men.[121]

Furthermore, as will be discussed in greater detail in subsequent chapters, even Asian Americans with comparatively high levels of family income and occupational prestige may still suffer from discrimination that impedes their success.[122] For instance, the Commission study found that highly educated Asian Americans earned less relative to their white counterparts than Asian Americans with less education, suggesting that Asian Americans may have difficulty translating their greater educational attainment into increased income.[123] Moreover, Asian Americans were much less likely to be in managerial jobs than comparable non-Hispanic whites, suggesting the existence of a "glass ceiling" that blocks Asian Americans from achieving managerial positions.[124] Finally, racial prejudice and resulting bigotry and violence know no socioeconomic barriers: Asian Americans with high socioeconomic status are just as likely as those with low socioeconomic status to be targets of hatred.

Discrimination and Barriers to Equal Opportunity for Asian Americans: Some Contributory Factors

Knowledge of the history of Asian Americans in the United States and of the nature and diver-

---

118 *The Economic Status of Americans of Asian Descent*, p. 31.

119 Ibid., pp. 35-36.

120 Ibid., p. 42.

121 Ibid., pp. 68-69 and 78-79.

122 For instance, chap. 5 looks at the possibility that admissions quotas in highly selective colleges and universities might limit Asian Americans' educational opportunities, and chap. 6 discusses the "glass ceiling" that appears to place limits on the career advancement of Asian Americans.

123 *The Economic Status of Americans of Asian Descent*, pp. 70-71.

124 Ibid., pp. 72-76.

sity of today's Asian American population are essential to a full understanding of the civil rights problems confronting Asian Americans in the 1990s. It is equally important to have an appreciation of some basic underlying factors that contribute to discrimination against Asian Americans and create barriers to equal opportunity for Asian Americans.

Some of these factors arise out of the tendency of the general public and the media to stereotype Asian Americans. Most Americans have very little knowledge of the history and cultures of Asian Americans and very little awareness of the diversity among them. This ignorance leads many to lump together Asian Americans in a single group and to perceive them through stereotypes. Other factors that underlie discrimination against Asian Americans include the linguistic, cultural, and religious differences that exist between many Asian Americans, particularly recent immigrants, and the general public. These differences foster misunderstandings between Asian and non-Asian Americans and among different Asian ethnic groups themselves, impede Asian Americans' access to public services, and serve as serious barriers to the equal opportunity of Asians in the United States. Seven contributory factors are discussed below.

1) Viewing Asian Americans as a Model Minority—Whereas, in the past, Asians were often stereotyped as sneaky, obsequious, or inscrutable, perhaps foremost among today's stereotypes of Asian Americans is the "model minority" stereotype. According to this stereotype, which is based partly on uncritical reliance on statistics revealing the high average family incomes, educational attainment, and occupational status of Asian Americans, Asian Americans are hardworking, intelligent, and successful.[125] As complimentary as it might sound, this stereotype has damaging consequences. First, it leads people to ignore the very real social and economic problems faced by many segments of the Asian American population and may result in the needs of poorer, less successful Asian Americans being overlooked. Second, emphasis on the model minority stereotype may also divert public attention from the existence of discrimination even against more successful Asian Americans (e.g., "glass ceiling" in employment and discriminatory admissions policies in institutions of higher learning). Third, the model minority stereotype may result in undue pressure being put on young Asian Americans to succeed in school, particularly in mathematics and science classes, and in their careers. Too much pressure to succeed on young Asian Americans has been linked to mental health problems and even teen suicide.[126] Finally, the origin of this stereotype was an effort to discredit other minorities by arguing that if Asian Americans can succeed, so can blacks and Hispanics, and many Asian Americans resent being used in this fashion.[127]

This model minority stereotype is not a recent phenomenon. More than a decade ago, the misleading nature and damaging consequences of the stereotype had already been clearly pointed out. For instance, in 1978 the President's Commission on Mental Health noted:

There is widespread belief that Asian and Pacific Americans do not suffer the discrimination and disadvantages associated with other minority groups. The fact is that in spite of recent efforts to promote civil rights and equal opportunities for ethnic minorities in

---

125 For general discussions of the model minority stereotype, its validity, and its implications, see Ki-Taek Chun, "The Myth of Asian American Success and Its Educational Ramifications," *IRCD Bulletin*, vol. 15, no. 1-2 (Winter/Spring 1980), pp. 1-12, and Won Moo Hurh and Kwang Chung Kim, "The 'Success' Image of Asian Americans: Its Validity, and Its Practical and Theoretical Implications," *Ethnic and Racial Studies*, vol. 12, no. 4 (October 1989), pp. 512-38.

126 Joan E. Rigdon, "Exploding Myth—Asian-American Youth Suffer a Rising Toll from Heavy Pressures: Suicides and Distress Increase As They Face Stereotypes and Parents' Expectations," *Wall Street Journal*, July 10, 1991.

127 See *Asian America*, pp. 317-19, for a discussion of the origin of the term, "model minority."

19

the United States, Asian and Pacific Americans have been largely neglected and ignored. . . . [128]

In 1980, based on the analysis of all available evidence, the U.S. Commission on Civil Rights concluded:

The belief is widely held that Asian Americans are a successful minority who no longer suffer from disadvantage. This belief, however, is not supported by the facts. Many Asian Americans take issue with the "model minority" perspective. . . . [129]

and

Asian Americans as a group are not the successful minority that the prevailing stereotype suggests. Individual cases of success should not imply that the diverse peoples who make up the Asian American communities are uniformly successful. . . .Despite the problems Asian Americans encounter, the success stereotype appears to have led policy makers to ignore those truly in need. [130]

2) Perceiving Asian Americans as Foreigners—A second contributing factor is the perception that all Asians in this country are foreigners. It is perhaps this perception that led to American acceptance of the internment of Japanese Americans during World War II. The perception that all Asians are foreigners may also explain why Asian Americans whose families have been in the United States for generations or many Asian American youths who were born here are frequently the objects of such queries and comments as: "Where did you learn English?" and "You speak such good English."

More seriously, Asian Americans of all groups tend to suffer adverse consequences when international events cause tensions between the United States and Asian countries. For instance, as shall be seen in chapter 2, many Americans take out their frustrations about Japan's economic success on Asian Americans of all national origins. The 1982 killing of Vincent Chin was prompted by his killers' resentment of the Japanese for their automobile exports to the United States. [131] The perception of Asian Americans as foreigners may also impede their acceptance in all areas of their lives and contribute to subtle as well as overt forms of discrimination against them in education, employment, and other arenas. [132]

3) Stereotyping Asian Americans as Unaggressive and Lacking in Communications Skills—Asian Americans, while viewed as intelligent and talented at mathematics and science, are considered unaggressive and lacking in good communication skills. This stereotype may blind employers to the qualifications of individual Asian Americans and hence contribute to the glass ceiling that impedes Asian Americans' success in managerial careers. It may also lead teachers and counselors to discourage Asian American students from even pursuing nontechnical careers.

4) Limited English Proficiency—Many Asian Americans, recent immigrants in particular, have limited English proficiency, and some do not speak or understand English at all. Persons with limited English proficiency face a serious barrier to full participation in American society and our

---

128   President's Commission on Mental Health, Report of the Special Populations Subpanel on the Mental Health of Asian/Pacific Americans, *Task Force Panel Reports,* vol. 3 (1978), p. 785.

129   U.S. Commission on Civil Rights, *Success of Asian Americans: Fact or Fiction?* (Washington, DC: Government Printing Office, 1980), p. 19.

130   Ibid., p. 24.

131   See chap. 2 for an account of Vincent Chin's killing.

132   For a discussion of how the perception that Asian Americans are foreigners affects Japanese Americans, see Bill Hosokawa, "Accentuating the American in Japanese American," *Perspectives (The Civil Rights Quarterly),* vol. 14, no. 3 (Fall 1982), pp. 40-44.

economy. A person's ability to learn about and gain access to public services (such as education, police services, and health care), employment, and the larger American society are often severely hampered by limited English proficiency. Thus, providing Asian Americans with truly equal opportunity requires substantial efforts to bridge the gap in communication (e.g., providing interpretive services) and to facilitate the learning of English. However, partly as a result of the practical difficulty of servicing the diverse language needs of Asian Americans (i.e., several dialects of Chinese, Japanese, Tagalog, Vietnamese, Lao, Khmer, Thai, and others), limited-English-proficient Asian Americans are drastically underserved in the areas of interpretation and English instruction.

5) **Cultural Differences**—Asian immigrants come from societies that have very different cultures from the mainstream cultures in the United States. Cultural differences often lead to misunderstandings, which in turn can lead to discriminatory treatment or to intergroup tensions, as in the case of Korean American store owners and their customers who are members of minority groups. These tensions can erupt into full scale racial conflict. Bridging cultural gaps requires not only that new immigrants be given a real opportunity to acculturate, but also that all Americans acquire a greater awareness of other cultures.

6) **Religious Diversity**—Many Asian Americans adhere to religions that are not widely practiced in the United States, such as Buddhism, Hinduism, Islam, and Sikhism, to name a few. These religions are unfamiliar to most Americans educated in the Judeo-Christian tradition, and, despite the long tradition of religious tolerance, these religious differences generate hostility against Asian Americans. Not only do the religious differences between Asian Americans and the general public contribute to anti-Asian bigotry and violence, but they can at times cause other conflicts when the practices and requirements of non-Western religions are incompatible with long-established mainstream traditions.

7) **Preimmigration Trauma**—Another factor hampering some Asian Americans' access to equal opportunity arises out of the wartime ordeals they have endured, as well as negative experiences they have had with governmental officials in their home countries. The problems faced by many Asian Americans in acculturating to this country are exacerbated by their preimmigration experiences: many recent Asian immigrants, particularly the Vietnamese, Cambodians, Hmong, and Laotians, are refugees, who come from war-torn countries and have survived ordeals in their own countries and on their journeys to the United States. Many lost loved ones during the war and live in incomplete families in this country. Refugees often carry scars from psychological trauma and many suffer from post-traumatic stress disorder, which make it difficult for them to cope with day-to-day life, let alone face the challenge of adjusting to a new society. In addition, they may bring to this country an ingrained distrust of authority arising out of negative experiences they had with governmental officials in their countries of origin. This distrust may deter many from interactions with governmental agencies in the United States, such as the police, welfare offices, and so on. As a result, a gulf may arise between the police and the Asian American community, adversely affecting police-community relations. Because of their unwillingness to convey their needs forcefully, many Asian Americans may not receive many basic public services.

Chapter 2

Bigotry and Violence Against Asian Americans

Many Asian Americans are forced to endure anti-Asian bigotry, ranging from ignorant and insensitive remarks, to stereotypical portrayals of Asians in the media, to name-calling, on a regular basis. Asian Americans are also the frequent victims of hate crimes, including vandalism, assault, and sometimes even murder. Although incidents of bigotry and violence against Asian Americans are reflections of a broader national climate of ethnic, racial, and religious intolerance, they are also reprehensible outgrowths of ingrained anti-Asian feelings that reside to a greater or lesser extent among many members of American society.[1]

In 1986 the U.S. Commission on Civil Rights published a report on acts of bigotry and violence against Asian Americans.[2] The Commission report documented many examples of bias-related incidents against Asian Americans and noted some of the factors contributing to anti-Asian activities. That report concluded:

[A]nti-Asian activity in the form of violence, vandalism, harassment, and intimidation continues to occur across the Nation. Incidents were reported in every jurisdiction visited by Commission staff and in other parts of the country as well. . . .The United States is a multiracial, pluralistic society built on the principles of freedom, justice, and opportunity for all. We cannot allow these principles to be violated in the case of Asian Americans by anyone. Rather, we must ensure that persons of Asian descent are guaranteed the rights promised to residents and citizens of this Nation.[3]

More recently, the Civil Rights Commission issued a general statement on intimidation and violence in America.[4] The Commission statement identified several factors that contribute to racial intimidation and violence, including:

1) racial integration of neighborhoods leading to "move-in violence";
2) deep-seated racial hatred played upon by organized hate groups;
3) economic competition among racial and ethnic groups;
4) insensitive media coverage of minority groups; and
5) poor police response to hate crimes.[5]

All of these ingredients play a role in anti-Asian bigotry and violence. For instance, economic competition among racial and ethnic groups is undoubtedly one of the underlying

---

1   Bigotry and violence against Asian Americans was one of the major concerns voiced by participants of the Commission's Roundtable Conferences. (Michael Chou, Ning Chiu, Statements at the U.S. Commission on Civil Rights Roundtable Conference on Civil Rights, Houston, TX, May 27, 1989; Mini Liu, Tsiwen Law, and Carlton Sagara, Statements at the U.S. Commission on Civil Rights Roundtable Conference on Civil Rights, New York, NY, June 23, 1989; Francis Assisi and Karl Matushita, Statement at the U.S. Commission on Civil Rights Roundtable Conference on Civil Rights, San Francisco, CA, July 29, 1989.)

2   U.S. Commission on Civil Rights, *Recent Activities Against Citizens and Residents of Asian Descent* (Clearinghouse Publication 88, 1986) (hereafter cited as *Recent Activities Against Citizens and Residents of Asian Descent*).

3   Ibid., pp. 57, 58.

4   U.S. Commission on Civil Rights, *Intimidation and Violence: Racial and Religious Bigotry in America* (Clearinghouse Publication 96, September 1990).

5   Ibid., pp. 11-19.

causes of the tensions between Asian American businessmen and many of their customers across the country. Unbalanced media coverage, such as coverage that fosters the model minority stereotype, has also contributed to anti-Asian sentiments. Asian Americans, like other minorities, are increasingly becoming the targets of organized hate groups, as evidenced by the activities of anti-Indian Dotbusters in New Jersey and the recent killing by skinhead associates of a Vietnamese youth in Houston.[6]

Anti-Asian bigotry and violence also has its own unique causes and manifestations, however.[7] As noted in chapter 1, the United States has a long history of prejudice and discrimination against Asians. In recent years, underlying anti-Asian sentiments have been aggravated by the increased visibility of Asian Americans due to a large influx of immigrants and refugees from Asia. The Asian population grew from 1.5 percent to 2.9 percent of the United States population just in the decade between 1980 and 1990.[8] Since Asian Americans are heavily concentrated geographically, the increase in the Asian population in some communities has been much more dramatic. For example, in Lowell, Massachusetts, the Cambodian population increased from a negligible percentage to roughly 25 percent of the population after 1980.[9] Many California communities have been similarly affected by Asian immigration.

High rates of immigration have also magnified the linguistic, cultural, and religious differences between Asian Americans and others residing in their communities. As more and more new immigrants have arrived from Asia, the percentage of the Asian American population that is native born with native-born parents—who consequently are native speakers of English and are more easily assimilated into the broader American culture—has declined. Not only do most new immigrants have limited English proficiency, reducing the potential for communication between them and their non-Asian counterparts, but they bring with them cultures and religions that are unfamiliar to the American public. These differences often generate misunderstandings that contribute to anti-Asian sentiments.

Because of their limited English proficiency and/or because of difficulties in acquiring the credentials required to pursue their chosen professions in the United States,[10] many Asian immigrants are unable to find jobs in the professions for which they were trained in their countries of origin and turn instead to self-employment as a means of earning a living. For instance, 17 percent of foreign-born Korean men working in the United States in 1980 were self-employed.[11] Many Asian immigrants operate small retail stores or restaurants in economically depressed, predominantly minority neighborhoods. The entry of small businesses owned by Asian Americans into these neighborhoods and their apparent financial success often provokes resentment on the part of neighborhood residents, who wonder why the business does not hire locally and often suspect that the Asian

---

6   See below for details on these incidents.

7   For another discussion of the factors underlying bigotry and violence against Asian Americans, see Morrison G. Wong, "Rise in Hate Crimes Against Asians in the United States" (paper presented at the 86th Annual Meeting of the American Sociological Association, Cincinnati, OH, Aug. 23-27, 1991).

8   See chap. 1.

9   Lowell's Southeast Asian population began to decline somewhat in the late 1980s and Southeast Asians now consitute less than 11 percent of Lowell's total population. "Asians in America: 1990 Census, Classification by States," *Asian Week*, August 1991, p. 30.

10   See chap. 6 for a discussion of the certification of foreign-educated professionals.

11   U.S. Bureau of the Census, 1980 Census of Population, vol. 2, Subject Reports, *Asian and Pacific Islander Population in the United States: 1980*, table 45A. This compares with roughly 10 percent of white men. U.S. Bureau of the Census, 1980 Census of Population, vol. 1, Characteristics of the Population, *General Social and Economic Characteristics: United States Summary*, table 90.

businesses are receiving special government subsidies. Contrary to these misperceptions, however, most small Asian businesses are family-owned and operated and cannot afford to hire nonfamily members: all the workers are family members, who work long hours for low pay. Furthermore, beyond short-term welfare and training programs offered only to those who are refugees, Asian immigrants are given very little government aid that is not generally available to all Americans, and, with limited exceptions, the government does not give Asian immigrants or refugees special help in opening their businesses. Furthermore, they do not typically receive much bank financing: they usually raise the capital for their businesses by pooling the resources of family and friends. Aggravating the resentment of Asian business owners are cultural and linguistic differences between immigrant business owners and residents of the neighborhoods they serve that lead the residents to perceive Asian Americans as rude and unfriendly. The boycott of several Korean businesses in New York City discussed below as well as a recent boycott in Los Angeles are examples of how racial tensions surrounding immigrant businesses can affect entire communities.

The general tendency to view all Asians as alike and the stereotype of Asians as foreigners make Asian Americans particularly vulnerable to the vicissitudes of the United States relations with Asian countries. Over the past half-century, the United States has frequently been at war with Asian countries (e.g., Japan, North Korea, Vietnam, and the Cold War with China), fostering in many Americans resentment and hatred of Asian nationals that, for some, carried over to their attitudes towards Asian Americans. In recent years the public's resentment of Japan's economic success, seemingly at the expense of our own, has added to historic anti-Asian senti-

ments. Many in the American public associate all Asians, regardless of their national origin, residence, or citizenship, with Japan's economic success and resent them accordingly. The killing of Vincent Chin, discussed below, is an example of how this resentment can erupt into violence.

Finally, the common stereotype of Asian Americans as a "model minority" also leads to increased racial tensions. Although most Americans are familiar with the widely discussed academic and economic success of some Asian Americans, they are largely unaware of the social problems, poverty, and high school dropout rates affecting many other Asian Americans.[12] As in the case of Asian-owned businesses, apparent success, whether real or illusory, leads to resentment and aggravates any previously existing anti-Asian sentiments.

Thus, to a large extent, existing anti-Asian sentiments in this country have been compounded by a lack of knowledge about Asian Americans on the part of the general public. The inaccurate "model minority" and "foreigner" stereotypes, the misperception that Asian immigrants receive unfair subsidies from the government, and the public's unfamiliarity with the diverse histories, cultures, and socioeconomic circumstances of Asian Americans all contribute to anti-Asian feelings.

This chapter updates the 1986 Commission report by providing recent examples of anti-Asian incidents, including violent incidents against individuals, housing-related incidents, incidents targeted at places of worship, incidents targeted at Asian-owned businesses, racial harassment on college campuses, and anti-Asian slurs made by public figures. The chapter then reviews existing statistics on hate crimes against Asian Americans and discusses the recently enacted Hate Crimes Statistics Act.[13]

---

12   See chap. 4 for a discussion of high school dropout rates among Asian Americans.
13   28 U.S.C. 534.

Recent Incidents of Bigotry and Violence Against Asian Americans

This section documents recent cases in which anti-Asian bigotry led to violence, harassment, vandalism, intimidation, and racial slurs.

Violent Incidents

Two racially motivated murders of Asian Americans in the 1980s have been etched into the national consciousness as examples of racism against Asian Americans: the murder of Vincent Chin in 1982 and the murder of Jim (Ming Hai) Loo in 1989. These killings are prominent examples of racially motivated violence against Asian Americans, but they are not isolated incidents. Racially motivated violence leading to injury and sometimes to death occurs with disturbing frequency across the country and affects many different Asian groups. This section discusses five examples of anti-Asian violence: the murders of Vincent Chin, Jim Loo, Navroze Mody, and Hung Truong, and the mass killing of Indochinese school children in Stockton, California.

Vincent Chin—The racially motivated murder of Vincent Chin and the inability of the American judicial system to bring his murderers to justice became a vivid symbol and source of outrage during the mid-1980s. The facts of the case are as follows.

On the evening of June 19, 1982, Vincent Chin, a 27-year-old Chinese American, met with some friends in a Detroit bar to celebrate his upcoming wedding. He was accosted by Ronald Ebens and Michael Nitz, two white automobile factory workers, who reportedly called him a "Jap" and blamed him for the loss of jobs in the automobile industry. Ebens and Nitz chased Chin out of the bar, and, when they caught up with him, Nitz held Chin while Ebens beat him "numerous times in the knee, the chest, and the head"[14] with a baseball bat. Chin died of his injuries 4 days later.[15]

Ebens and Nitz were initially charged with second-degree murder but subsequently allowed to plead guilty to manslaughter.[16] In March 1983 the defendants were each sentenced to 3 years' probation and fined $3,780 by Wayne Circuit County Judge Charles Kaufman, who reasoned that the defendants had no previous history of violence and were unlikely to violate probation.[17]

The U.S. Department of Justice brought Federal civil rights charges against Ebens and Nitz to a Federal grand jury, which indicted them on November 2, 1982. On June 18, 1984, Ebens was found guilty of interfering with Chin's civil rights, and on September 18, 1984, he was sentenced to 25 years in prison. However, Nitz was acquitted of the Federal civil rights charges.[18]

Ebens' conviction was overturned by the Sixth Circuit Court of Appeals in September 1986 for technical reasons, including issues pertaining to the admissibility of audio tapes and prosecutor-

---

14   *Recent Activities Against Citizens and Residents of Asian Descent*, p. 43, quoting Indictment at 2, U.S. v. Ebens, No. 83-60629 (E.D. Mich. 1983).

15   Ibid., pp. 43-44, and Ronald Takaki, "Who Killed Vincent Chin?" pp. 23-29, in Grace Yun, ed., *A Look Beyond the Model Minority Image: Critical Issues in Asian America* (New York: Minority Rights Group, 1989).

16   Ebens actually pled *nolo contendere*, meaning that the defendant does not admit or deny the charges, though a fine or sentence may be imposed pursuant to the charges. Blacks Law Dictionary 945 (5th ed. 1979).

17   *Recent Activities Against Citizens and Residents of Asian Descent*, pp. 43-44. Under mandatory sentencing guidelines subsequently promulgated by Michigan's Supreme Court, Ebens and Nitz would have received much stiffer sentences. Jim Shimoura, Esq., telephone interview, Sept. 18, 1990.

18   Ibid.

ial misconduct (overzealousness) in preparing witnesses.[19] When Ebens came up for retrial in the Eastern District of Michigan, the defense moved for a change of venue on the grounds that Ebens could not get a fair trial in Detroit.[20] The defense motion was granted, and the trial was moved to Cincinnati. The case was retried during the month of April 1987, and this time Ebens was acquitted.[21]

The acquittal of Ebens in the second Federal trial means that neither Ebens nor Nitz ever went to prison for Vincent Chin's killing. Some have speculated that the main reason that the Cincinnati jury acquitted Ebens is that the jury could not comprehend the reality of anti-Asian bias as it existed in Detroit in the early 1980s. Whereas Detroit in the early 1980s was the scene of a massive media campaign against foreign imports, especially those from Japan, a campaign that inflamed anti-Asian sentiments in that city, there had not been the same type of campaign in Cincinnati. Also, there were very few Asians in Cincinnati, and anti-Asian sentiments were not widespread.[22]

Others contend that the Cincinnati jury's acquittal of Ebens reflects a fundamental problem with current Federal civil rights laws. Ebens was charged under Federal criminal civil rights law section 245(b),[23] which prohibits (among other things) the racially motivated interference by force or threat of force with a person's use of public facilities, such as restaurants and bars.[24] Some experts argue that the jury may have been confused about what had to be shown for there to be a civil rights violation under section 245(b): even though the jury may have felt that the attack was indeed racially motivated, it might not have thought that Ebens specifically intended to interfere with Chin's use of a public facility (the bar).[25]

Jim (Ming Hai) Loo—Seven years after Vincent Chin's killing, another Chinese American was killed in Raleigh, North Carolina under similar circumstances.

Jim (Ming Hai) Loo, 24, had immigrated to the United States from China 13 years before, was working in a Chinese restaurant, and was saving money so that he could attend college. On the evening of Saturday, July 29, 1989, during an altercation that began in a nearby pool hall, Loo was hit on the back of the head by a handgun held by Robert Piche. He fell onto a broken beer bottle, which pierced his eye and caused a bone fragment to enter his brain, resulting in his death on July 31.

Loo and several Vietnamese friends had been playing pool in the pool hall, when Robert Piche, 35, and his brother, Lloyd Piche, 29, began calling them "gooks" and "chinks" and blaming them for American deaths in Vietnam. Lloyd Piche said, "I don't like you because you're Vietnamese. Our brothers went over to Vietnam, and they never came back,"[26] and "I'm gonna finish you tonight."[27] Although the manager forced the Piche brothers to leave the pool hall, they waited outside for Loo and his friends,

19   United States v. Ebens, 800 F.2d 1422 (6th Cir. 1986).

20   United States v. Ebens, 654 F. Supp. 144 (E.D. Mich. 1987).

21   James Shimoura, Esq., telephone interview, Sept. 18, 1990.

22   Ibid.

23   18 U.S.C. §245(b)(2)(1988).

24   Hogan and Hartson, Washington, DC, Lawyer's Committee for Civil Rights Under Law, *Striking Back at Bigotry: Remedies Under Federal and State Law for Violence Motivated by Racial, Religious, and Ethnic Prejudice* (Baltimore: National Institute Against Prejudice and Violence, 1986), p. 18.

25   Jack Keeney, Statement before the U.S. Commission on Civil Rights, Nov. 17, 1989.

26   Seth Effron, "Racial Slaying Prompts Fear, Anger in Raleigh," *Greensboro News and Record,* Sept. 24, 1989.

27   "Asians in America: Old Stereotypes, Renewed Violence Confront The Country's Fastest-Growing Ethnic Population," *Klanwatch Intelligence Report* no. 50, June 1990.

and attacked them as they left the pool hall. Robert Piche and his brother first attacked one of Loo's friends, Lahn Tang, with a shotgun, but when Tang escaped, Robert swung a pistol at another of Loo's friends, Jim Ta. He missed his intended victim and hit Loo on the head instead.[28]

Although Lloyd Piche made most of the racial remarks, he did not strike the fatal blow. He was sentenced to 6 months in prison for disorderly conduct and simple assault (on Tang), both of which are misdemeanors.[29] In March 1990, Robert Piche was found guilty of second-degree murder and assault with a deadly weapon and sentenced to a total of 37 years in prison. He will be eligible for parole after serving $4\frac{1}{2}$ years. Although Judge Howard E. Manning Jr. gave Piche a stiff lecture, the sentence was less than he could have meted out: under North Carolina law, Piche could have been given life in prison.[30]

Many Asian American community leaders, struck by the similarities between Loo's murder and Chin's, pressed the U.S. Department of Justice to bring Federal civil rights charges against Robert and Lloyd Piche.[31] They were particularly anxious to see a prosecution of Lloyd Piche, who received a minimal sentence despite being the chief instigator of the incident.[32] After a lengthy investigation, the Justice Department announced on March 29, 1991,[33] that it had indicted Lloyd Piche on Federal civil rights charges, but it did not indict Robert Piche.[34] In making the announcement, Attorney General Thornburgh said:

This is a heinous crime committed against innocent patrons of a public facility. Such egregious behavior, especially with death resulting, cannot go unpunished.

This country was built on the freedom to enjoy life, liberty and the pursuit of happiness. When innocent patrons of a public facility are harassed and ultimately killed simply because of their race, religion or national origin, the government has a moral and legal obligation to step in and prosecute.[35]

---

28   Melinda Ruley, "A Letter From the Loo Trial," *The Independent Weekly,* Mar. 29, 1990.

29   "Asians in America: Old Stereotypes, Renewed Violence Confront The Country's Fastest-Growing Ethnic Population," *Klanwatch Intelligence Report,* no. 50, June 1990.

30   Ruley, "A Letter From the Loo Trial." *See* N.C. Gen. Stat. §§14-1.1, 14-17 (Supp. 1987).

31   Dennis Hayashi, "Network Pressures Justice Dept. On Loo Case Civil Rights Charges," *National Network on Anti-Asian Violence Bulletin,* July 1990, p. 1, and Arthur S. Hayes, "Asian Americans Go to Court to Fight Bias," *Wall Street Journal,* Sept. 3, 1991.

32   William C. Hou, Organization of Chinese Americans, Inc., liaison to the National Network Against Anti-Asian Violence, telephone interview, Jan. 29, 1991; and Dennis Hayashi, Asian Law Caucus, telephone interview, Jan. 30, 1991.

33   U.S. Department of Justice, "Raleigh, N.C., Man Indicted for Federal Civil Rights Violations," Press Release, Mar. 29, 1991 (hereafter cited as Justice Department Press Release).

34   According to a Department official (Suzanne Drouet, U.S. Attorney, telephone interviews, Sept. 12, 1990, and Jan. 30, 1991), the Justice Department follows guidelines spelled out in the United States Attorneys' Manual in deciding about whether or not to bring Federal charges in "dual prosecution cases," like the Loo case, in which the offenders have already undergone a State prosecution. (The specific section of the United States Attorneys' Manual containing the dual prosecution guidelines is sec. 9-2.142, "Dual Prosecution and Successive Federal Prosecution Policies," pp. 19-25.) The manual precludes dual prosecutions except in cases where a compelling Federal interest has not been vindicated in the State prosecution. The manual offers civil rights cases as an example of where a compelling Federal interest is likely to be served. It also states that "a dual or successive prosecution. . .normally would not be authorized unless an enhanced sentence in the subsequent Federal prosecution is anticipated." (U.S. Attorney's Manual, Oct. 1, 1988, p. 23.) This is probably the case for Robert Piche, who has already received a lengthy jail term. According to an example provided in the manual, dual prosecution is likely to be warranted when the State conviction was for a misdemeanor and the anticipated Federal conviction would be for a Federal felony, as is the case for Lloyd Piche.

35   Justice Department Press Release.

Lloyd Piche was indicted on eight counts of violating Federal civil rights laws.[36] On July 15, 1991, in a Federal district court in Wilmington, North Carolina, Lloyd Piche was found guilty on all eight counts.[37] On October 15, 1991, Lloyd Piche was sentenced to 4 years in prison and ordered to pay over $28,000 in restitution to the Loo family. Although the Justice Department had sought the maximum sentence under Federal sentencing guidelines, Piche's sentence was less than the minimum sentence (6 to 7½ years) under the Federal guidelines.[38]

There are many similarities between the Loo and the Chin murders. In each case, the victim was a young man spending an evening relaxing with friends in a public facility (a bar in Chin's case, a pool hall in Loo's). In each case, an altercation began inside the public facility, and violence leading to murder erupted outside of the facility. In each case, the victim was killed after being mistaken for or associated with Asians of other nationalities. In Chin's case, his killers were venting hostility against foreign Japanese, and in Loo's case, his murderers apparently mistook him for a Vietnamese.[39] Thus, both Chin and Loo became victims simply because they were of Asian descent.

Together, the Chin and Loo murders underscore the harsh reality of racially motivated violence against Asians. They also signal in differing ways the general public's lack of awareness of and to some extent indifference towards anti-Asian discrimination. The 3-year probation and almost nominal fines imposed by Judge Kaufman on Chin's murderers are suggestive of very little value being placed on an Asian American life. The ultimate failure of the American justice system to convict Ebens of civil rights charges, perhaps partly because of the Cincinnati jury's difficulty in believing in the existence of anti-Asian hatred, also implies that many Americans view racial hatred purely as a black-white problem and are unaware that Asian Americans are also frequently targets of hate crimes. Finally, neither murder was given much national prominence. Chin's killing did receive some national attention, but Loo's killing (in stark contrast to the murder of a young black man in Bensonhurst that occurred at roughly the same time) was hardly covered by the national media and raised no national sense of outrage.[40]

Unlike the Vincent Chin case, Loo's murder resulted in a successful Federal prosecution—the first ever successful Federal civil rights prosecution where the victim was Asian American. If given sufficient attention, the Federal civil rights trial of Lloyd Piche could do much to highlight the racial aspect of Loo's killing and will send a message that anti-Asian racism will not be tolerated by the United States Government.

Navroze Mody—The 1987 killing of Navroze Mody shows that Asians, like other minorities, are potential targets of organized hate campaigns and that anti-Asian violence can be the outcome of such campaigns.

In early September 1987 the *Jersey Journal* published a letter from a group, called the Dotbusters, whose avowed purpose was to rid Jersey City of Asian Indians. There followed numerous racial incidents against Asian Indians

---

36   Ibid.

37   Johnny Ng, "Conviction in Loo Slaying Trial," *Asian Week*, July 19, 1991, p. 19.

38   Organization of Chinese Americans, Inc., News Release, "Lloyd Piche Sentenced to 4 Years For Civil Rights Violation of Jim Loo and 6 Others," Oct. 15, 1991. The judge apparently gave Piche a lesser sentence out of pique at the Justice Department for not also bringing civil rights charges against his brother, Robert Piche. Ibid.

39   The friends Loo was with that evening were Vietnamese.

40   One observer commented: "Unlike most civil rights prosecutions, [Lloyd Piche's trial] passed virtually unnoticed, despite its being only the second Federal civil rights prosecution involving an Asian victim. Compare this lack of coverage to the steady flow of reports about Asian gangs, drugs and gambling." Helen Zia, "Another American Racism," *New York Times*, Sept. 12, 1991.

ranging from vandalism to assault. On September 27, 1987, Navroze Mody, an Indian, was "bludgeoned with bricks, punched, and kicked into a coma" by a gang of 11 youths, while his white friend remained unharmed.[41] In April 1989 three of his assailants were convicted of assault, and one was convicted of aggravated assault. Murder charges were not brought against any of the assailants.[42]

Although many in the New Jersey Indian community felt that the crime was racially motivated, no bias charges were brought, and prosecutors denied that Mody's killers were Dotbusters. There were reports, however, that two of the youths involved in the Mody killing had attacked some Indian students at Stevens Institute of Technology 2 weeks previously, but that the police had not filed a report in that incident.[43] Whether or not Mody's killing was racially motivated, coming as it did in the wake of an organized outbreak of bigotry and violence against Asian Indians in Jersey City, it added significantly to the fears of Asian Indians throughout the country. Anti-Indian incidents continued to occur frequently in the Jersey City area for at least a year after Mody's killing.[44]

Hung Truong—A more recent killing of a 15-year-old Vietnamese boy in Houston, Texas, illustrates the threat posed to Asian Americans along with other minorities by skinheads.[45]

Hung Truong moved to the Houston area from Vietnam with his father in 1980. His mother and three brothers remained in Vietnam.[46] On August 9, 1990 at 2 a.m., Truong was walking down the street with three friends, when they were accosted by persons in two cars that stopped alongside them. Several minutes later, one of the cars followed them, stopped, and two 18-year-old men, Derek Hilla and Kevin Michael Allison, came out of the car, one of them carrying a club. One of Truong's friends later testified that the two men had shouted "White Power."[47] They chased Truong, who became separated from his friends, and kicked and beat him with their feet and hands. Allison later testified that Truong had begged them to stop, saying, "God forgive me for coming to this country. I'm so sorry."[48] After Hilla and Allison had left the scene, Truong's friends caught up with Truong, finding him lying on the ground bleeding.[49] Truong's friends went for help, but when the paramedics arrived, Truong seemed okay, and they let him go home with a friend. The following morning at 7:15 a.m. paramedics were called to Truong's friend's apartment. Truong died shortly after arrival at the hospital.[50] Hilla and Allison were arrested and charged with Truong's murder the following day.[51]

Hilla was well known to have racist views and to have skinhead ties.[52] During the January 1991

41   "Jersey City Indians Protest Racist Attacks," *The CAAAV Voice* (Newsletter of the Committee Against Anti-Asian Violence), vol. 1., no. 1 (Fall 1988), pp. 1-2.

42   "Mody Killers Let Off With Aggravated Assault," *The CAAAV Voice* (Newsletter of the Committee Against Anti-Asian Violence), vol. 1, no. 2 (Spring 1989), pp. 1, 5.

43   Ibid.

44   Summary of news articles in the *Jersey Journal* provided by Stanley Mark.

45   The Asian Pacific American Coalition reports several other anti-Asian incidents perpetrated by skinheads during 1990, including attacks in Santa Rosa, CA, and in southern Maryland and anti-Asian graffiti in Quincy, MA. Asian Pacific American Coalition, U.S.A., *APAC Alert*, vol. 10, no. 10 (October 1990) (hereafter cited as *APAC Alert*).

46   Kelly Rucker, "We Just Came Here to Be Happy: Father Mourns Slain Asian Teen," *Houston Chronicle*, Aug. 13, 1990.

47   Robert Stanton, "Victim's Friend Says Before Attack, 2 Men Yelled 'White Power,'" *The Houston Post*, Jan. 17, 1991.

48   Rad Sallee, "Teen Shows How He Kicked Vietnamese," *Houston Chronicle*, Jan. 19, 1991.

49   Stanton, "Victim's Friend Says Before Attack."

50   Eric Hanson and Tara Parker Pope, "'Skinheads' Charged in Teen's Death," *Houston Chronicle*, Aug. 11, 1990.

51   Ibid.

trial, witnesses described him as a violent man.[53] Although denying that he was a racist, Allison admitted during the trial that he had participated in a couple of fights with skinhead friends and that his parents had kicked him out of the house when they discovered a swastika in his room. He also admitted that the only reason he and Hilla had attacked Truong was because he was Vietnamese.[54]

On January 23, 1991, a Houston jury convicted Hilla of murder and Allison of involuntary manslaughter in Truong's killing. The jury sentenced Hilla to 45 years in prison and gave him a $10,000 fine. The jury also found that Hilla had used his feet as a deadly weapon, which means that he will be required to serve at least one-fourth of his sentence before becoming eligible for parole. Allison was sentenced to 10 years in prison (the maximum allowable prison sentence for involuntary manslaughter) and also was assessed a $10,000 fine.[55]

Although the prosecutor presented the case as a racial killing, neither Hilla nor Allison was tried on a civil rights charge, because Texas law does not provide for additional penalties for racially motivated crimes against persons. Truong's killing has added momentum to a movement to pass legislation that would provide stronger sentencing provisions for hate crimes.[56]

Stockton Schoolyard Massacre—A chilling massacre of school children in Stockton, California, illustrates the tragic consequences of racial hatred.

On January 17, 1989, a gunman dressed in military garb entered the schoolyard at Cleveland Elementary School in Stockton and repeatedly fired an AK47 assault rifle, killing five Indochinese children and wounding 30 others. The gunman, Patrick Edward Purdy, then turned the rifle on himself. The children who died were identified as Raphanar Or, 9; Ram Chun, 8; Thuy Tran, 6; Sokhim An, 6; and Ocun Lim, 8. Four of the dead children were Cambodian, and one was Vietnamese. Almost 60 percent of the pupils at Cleveland Elementary were from Southeast Asian families.[57]

In the days following the massacre, news coverage focused in large part on the rifle used by Purdy, and the incident was a powerful force behind gun control initiatives across the country.[58] Purdy was described as a "deranged young man. . .who nursed an obsession with guns and the military."[59] The possibility that the killings were racially motivated was hardly addressed in the national press.[60] Almost 10 months later, how-

52   Tara Parker Pope, "Gentle Giant or Bully Boy? Youth Revealed Darker Side Espousing Racial Violence, Acquaintances Say," *Houston Chronicle,* Aug. 19, 1990.

53   Robert Stanton, "Jurors Convict 2 'Skinheads' in Teen's Death," *The Houston Post,* Jan. 24, 1991.

54   Rad Sallee, "Teen Shows How He Kicked Vietnamese," *Houston Chronicle,* Jan. 19, 1991.

55   Rad Sallee and Ruth Piller, "Two Alleged 'Skinheads' Convicted in Death of Vietnamese Teen," *Houston Chronicle,* Jan. 24, 1991 and Rad Sallee, "Skinheads Get Prison, Fines in Killing," *Houston Chronicle,* Jan. 25, 1991.

56   Robert W. Gee, Asian American Coalition, Houston, TX, telephone interview, Jan. 30, 1991, and "A Hatred for Hate: Skinhead's 45-Year Term Shows Community Revulsion," *Houston Post* editorial, Jan. 29, 1991. Although legislation was introduced and voted on favorably by the responsible committees in both houses of the Texas State Legislature in 1991, the legislature went into recess before the legislation could be considered by either house. Robert W. Gee, "Texas Hate Crime Update," *National Network Against Anti-Asian Violence Bulletin,* July 1991, p. 1.

57   This account is based on Jay Mathews and Matt Lait, "Rifleman Slays Five At School: 29 Pupils, Teacher Shot in California; Assailant Kills Self," *Washington Post,* Jan. 18, 1989, p. A1.

58   Jay Mathews, "Schoolyard Massacre Refuels Drive for Stricter Gun Control: Killer Purchased Assault Rifle, 5 Handguns Legally," *Washington Post,* Jan. 20, 1989, p. A3.

59   Robert Reinhold, "After Shooting, Horror But Few Answers," *New York Times,* Jan. 19, 1989.

60   See, e.g., Robert Reinhold, "Killer Depicted as Loner Full of Hate," *New York Times,* Jan. 20, 1991, and Tamara Jones and Bob

ever, California Attorney General John Van de Kamp issued a report[61] on the incident concluding that the killings were driven by a hatred of racial and ethnic minorities. The report observed, "Purdy was filled with hate and anger toward many groups of people, including virtually all identifiable ethnic minorities."[62] It then concluded:

It appears highly probable that Purdy deliberately chose Cleveland Elementary School as the location for his murderous assault in substantial part because it was heavily populated by Southeast Asian children. His frequent resentful comments about Southeast Asians indicate a particular animosity against them.[63]

Housing-Related Incidents

It is not only in public places, such as bars, pool halls, and city streets, that Asian Americans encounter acts of bigotry and violence. They often face harassment and vandalism in their own homes and also experience other forms of intimidation aimed at keeping them from living or working in a neighborhood.

There have been numerous incidents of racist flyers being distributed in neighborhoods where Asian Americans live or work, calling for Asians to go home or be expelled. As an example, anti-Asian flyers were distributed to mailboxes in the Bensonhurst and Gravesend neighborhoods of Brooklyn during the fall of 1987. The flyers urged boycotting Korean and Chinese businesses and real estate agents involved in selling property to Asians. Both the New York City Commission on Human Rights and the police department's antibias unit investigated the incidents.[64] A survey by the New York City Commission on Human Rights found that 90 percent of Asian-owned stores in the neighborhood experienced serious losses in business after the flyers were distributed, and two Bensonhurst real estate offices mentioned in the flyers were subsequently vandalized.[65] The person or persons responsible for the flyers were never found. In a more recent incident, anti-Asian flyers were distributed this year in Castro Valley/Hayward, California, by members of the White Aryan Resistance.[66]

As many Cambodian refugees moved into New England in the early 1980s, housing-related incidents against them multiplied. In 1981, shortly after he had moved into his new house in Portsmouth, Maine, a Cambodian man was hit on the head by a rock hidden in a snowball thrown by neighbors as he was playing in the snow with his children. When he approached his neighbors, one of them said, "Go back where you came from, gook."[67] Between 1983 and 1987 there were recurrent incidents of violence against Cambodians living in Revere, Massachusetts, and vandalism against their homes, including rocks thrown at windows and several fires that destroyed entire buildings. Similar incidents occurred elsewhere in Massachusetts, such as a fire set by arsonists which left 31 Cambodians homeless in Lynn, Massachusetts, in December 1988.[68]

Baker, "Drifter Had A Fondness For Firearms," *Los Angeles Times*, Jan. 18, 1989.

61   Nelson Kempsky, Chief Deputy Attorney General, State of California, *A Report to Attorney General John K. Van de Kamp on Patrick Edward Purdy and the Cleveland School Killings* (October 1989).

62   Ibid., p. 10.

63   Ibid., p. 12.

64   Rita Giordano, "Anti-Asian Fliers' Origin a Mystery," *Newsday*, Nov. 4, 1987.

65   Rita Giordano, "Bensonhurst: Anti-Asian Bias Linked to Incidents," *Newsday*, Dec. 15, 1987.

66   *APAC Alert.*

67   Maine Advisory Committee to the U.S. Commission on Civil Rights, *Civil Rights Issues in Maine* (May 1989), p. 39.

68   Earl C. Yen, "Flames Leave Massachusetts Cambodian Families Homeless," *Asian Week*, Dec. 2, 1988, as summarized in materials provided by Stanley Mark.

Such incidents are not unique to New England. In Richmond, California, for instance, following numerous incidents of egg throwing and BB gun shots, eight cars parked outside an apartment complex where several Laotian refugees lived were badly damaged in September of 1990.[69] Nor do they only affect Southeast Asians. In 1987, in Queens, New York, a Chinese family was the repeated target of a group of young people who threw eggs, drove a car into their front gate, and said things like "Why don't you move away?"[70]

Incidents Targeted at Places of Worship

Hate activities have also been directed against Asian Americans' places of worship. One participant in the Roundtable Conferences reported that out of 60 Hindu temples he had surveyed, 55 had experienced some form of harassment or vandalism in the previous 6 months.[71] In a recent example, vandals spray painted hateful messages, including "No Chinks, Go Home to China," on a Chinese American church in Chandler, Arizona, and fired five rounds of ammunition through the church's doors. The incident, which occurred on September 11, 1990, was the

second time the church had been attacked within 2 months. The first attack, which also involved spray-painted hate messages and shots, had occurred on August 7. The incident was very upsetting to the Phoenix's Asian American community, which has grown in recent years, and now is 3 to 4 percent of the Phoenix area.[72]

Incidents Targeted at Asian-Owned Businesses

As was documented in the 1986 Commission report on racially motivated violence against Asians, anti-Asian activities are often targeted at Asian-owned businesses.[73] Many Asian Americans, especially Koreans, own and operate small retail businesses, such as grocery stores, laundries, and restaurants, often in inner-city neighborhoods. The apparent success of these businesses occasionally provokes resentment among persons residing in the neighborhood, and resentment leads to harassment, vandalism, and sometimes violence. Two recent examples, one in California and the other in New York, reflect continuing anti-Asian activities directed against businesses owned by Asian Americans.

Castro Valley, California—On November 25, 1989, at about 10:30 p.m., a group of white teen-

---

69   *APAC Alert.*

70   "Summary of Incidents of Racist Violence, New York City Area," provided by Mini Liu.

71   Francis Assisi, Statement at the U.S. Commission on Civil Rights Roundtable Conference on Civil Rights, San Francisco, CA, July 29, 1989.

72   Keiko Ohnuma, "Racist Vandals Attack Arizona Chinese Church," *Asian Week*, Sept. 21, 1990. Another recent incident, in which nine people, including six monks, were shot to death in a Thai temple outside of Phoenix, provoked fear and anxiety among Asian Americans. Although robbery was seen by the police as the most likely motive for the killings, many were afraid that the incident was bias related. (Seth Mydans, "Phoenix Asking If Bias Played Role in 9 Killings," *New York Times*, Aug. 13, 1991.) The investigation of the massacre led to the arrest of two different sets of suspects and much confusion within Phoenix's Thai and Asian American communities. Although the first set of suspects—four men—initially confessed to the killings, they later recanted their confessions, and eventually all charges against them were dropped. As of November 21, 1991, prosecutors were intending to prosecute two teenagers, who have also confessed to the killings. (Jane Fritsch, "Sudden Surplus of Suspects Marks Case of Slain Monks: Arizona Officials Seek Links Between 2 Apparently Unconnected Sets of Possible Killers; Temple Security Has Been Increased," *Los Angeles Times*, Nov. 19, 1991, p. A5; and "Four Held in Deaths at Buddhist Temple Will Be Released," *Los Angeles Times*, Nov. 21, 1991, p. A33.) U.S. Commission on Civil Rights staff, along with concerned Thai and Asian American citizens from California, traveled to Phoenix on Nov. 6, 1991, to offer support and help facilitate communication between the Thai community and Arizona officials.

73   *Recent Activities Against Citizens and Residents of Asian Descent*, pp. 53-56.

agers both physically and verbally assaulted Asian American employees and an Asian American store owner at a shopping center in Castro Valley, California. In the midst of the scuffle, gun shots were fired, and one of the attackers was hit in the leg. According to sheriff's investigators, the incident was racially motivated and the youths had assaulted the workers "because they did not like Asians."[74] The details of the incident as obtained from newspaper accounts and staff interviews with the victims are as follows.[75]

A Korean American employee at the Laurel Liquors store had gone into an outdoor garbage disposal area to deposit garbage when several youths slammed the disposal site's door shut and locked it. They taunted him, using ethnic slurs, and then let him out and beat him before he ran back to the liquor store.

During this commotion, a Chinese American man, a U.S.-born college graduate, who was helping clean up the Choice Meat and Deli store owned by his father two doors down from the liquor store, came out to see what the problem was. He was attacked by the youths, who knocked him down and kicked him repeatedly. His father, Frank Toy, came out of the meat store carrying a broom handle and tried to help his son. The assailants wrested the broom handle from Mr. Toy, who then went back inside his store and returned with a rifle. Mr. Toy fired two warning shots in the hope that the assailants would disperse. Someone grabbed Mr. Toy and the rifle, knocking him down. The rifle went off a couple of times, and a bullet hit one of the youths in the leg. Mr. Toy managed to drag his son into the meat store and lock the doors, but the assailants kicked the doors in and beat both

men severely while hurling racial insults and slurs and claiming that Mr. Toy had shot their friend. The attackers fled moments later when the sirens of approaching sheriff's cars were heard.

The attackers had inflicted enough physical harm to both Mr. Toy and his son to require prolonged medical treatment. The district attorney's office decided not to press charges against Mr. Toy on the grounds that the elder Toy had acted in self-defense. One attacker was arrested and placed on probation by a juvenile court referee. In March 1991 the assailant was taken off probation.[76]

When the local newspaper reported that a lawsuit had been filed against the attackers in March 1990, the Toy family received a telephone death threat, and for several nights the son was followed home by a pickup truck. As a result of the suit and mounting community interest in the case, considerable publicity was generated in the local news media during early summer. In August 1990, some 9 months after the incident, another attacker was arrested. However, charges against this second attacker were later dismissed for insufficient evidence.[77]

The Toys continued to be harassed after the incident. Soon after the November incident, a white man came into the store asking for change. When he was told that there was not enough change, the man went to the Safeway grocery store next door, then came back to Mr. Toy's store, shouting, "See this change? We Americans help each other!" On more than several occasions, ice cream and soda were thrown against the store windows during the night.[78]

---

74   Dennis J. Oliver, "Teen Rampage Blamed On Racism: Authorities Charge 17-Year-Old With Violating Chinese Butchers' Rights," *The Korean Times San Francisco Edition,* Nov. (date unknown), 1989, p. 1.

75   This account is based on several sources: Andy Jokelson, "Asians Targets of Taunts, Assault," *The Oakland Tribune,* Nov. 28, 1989, p. A-11; Oliver, "Teen Rampage," p. 1; Frank Toy and Melvin Toy, personal interviews, Castro Valley, CA, Feb. 22, 1990.

76   John Poppas and John Billups, Alameda County District Attorney's Office, telephone interviews, Oct. 1, 1991.

77   Roger Patton, attorney representing the Toys, telephone interview, Oct. 1, 1991.

78   Frank Toy, staff interview, Castro Valley, CA, Feb. 22, 1990.

Mr. Toy also recalls that during the first 4 years of his 10-year ownership of the store, he had to endure a long series of harassing acts by county inspectors, which persisted until he hired an attorney and threatened to sue. The harassment included: 1) not allowing Mr. Toy to put up a neon sign similar to the one on the store next door, 2) telling Mr. Toy that promotional advertisements displayed inside the store were too big and had to be reduced, and 3) asking Mr. Toy to change the color of fluorescent lamps inside the meat compartment, when other stores were allowed to use the same ones as his.[79]

Concerned about the continuing undercurrent of anti-Asian prejudice in the area, declining sales, and most important, his wife's apprehension for the family's safety, Mr. Toy closed his store on June 29, 1990, incurring over a $100,000 loss, and found a part-time job at another grocery store in the same city.[80]

Boycott of Korean Grocers in Flatbush, Brooklyn, N.Y.—On January 18, 1990, a seemingly minor incident occurred at the Family Red Apple Market grocery store (hereafter the Red Apple grocery store) in the Flatbush section of Brooklyn. It quickly led to a year-long boycott by black residents of two Korean American-owned groceries. This boycott forced the owners to the brink of bankruptcy, brought about one of the largest mass rallies of Asian Americans in the history of New York City, and resulted in a flurry of accusations between the offices of the district attorney and the mayor. The handling of

the boycott led many Korean Americans to become disillusioned with the political process. The nature of the boycott remains controversial: a committee set up by Mayor Dinkins to investigate the incident (hereafter, Mayor's Committee) concluded it was "incident-based,"[81] although the city council's committee on general welfare flatly rejected this characterization and viewed it as racially motivated.[82] The city council committee also questioned the neutrality and credibility of the Mayor's Committee. The incident is a significant one because it illustrates a widespread pattern of racial tensions between immigrant small retail store owners and their minority clients.

The incident that led to the boycott occurred on January 18, 1990. At about 6:00 p.m., Ghislaine Felissaint, a Haitian American resident of Flatbush, was shopping for a few produce items at the Red Apple store. As she was leaving the store to go across the street to another store which seemed to have a shorter line, she was asked to open her bag, and she refused.[83] An altercation erupted between Ms. Felissaint and store employees, the police were called, and she was taken to a nearby hospital emergency room where "she was treated for superficial injuries and released several hours later."[84]

What took place during the altercation is not totally clear, for the two sides have given conflicting versions. According to Ms. Felissaint, the store employee grabbed her by the neck and slapped her. She fell to the floor, and another

---

79   Ibid.

80   Melvin Toy, telephone interview, Dec. 11, 1990.

81   New York City Mayor's Committee, *Report of the Mayor's Committee Investigating the Protest Against Two Korean-Owned Groceries on Church Avenue in Brooklyn* (Aug. 30, 1990), p. 3 of Executive Summary, and pp. 14-15 of text (hereafter cited as *Mayor's Committee Report*).

82   The Council of the City of New York, Committee on General Welfare, *An Analysis of the Report of the Mayor's Committee Investigating the Protest Against Two Korean-Owned Groceries as Church Avenue in Brooklyn* (December 1990), pp. 54-59 (hereafter cited as *An Analysis of the Mayor's Committee Report*).

83   Arnold H. Lubasch, "Woman Who Touched Off Boycott Describes Attack," *The New York Times*, Jan. 5, 1991.

84   *Mayor's Committee Report*, p. 20. The report stated that "Mme. Felissaint refused medical treatment at the scene on Church Avenue. She was treated for superficial injuries at Caledonia Hospital, where her attorney requested that she be admitted for observation. She was not admitted, however, and was released from the emergency room." Ibid.

employee kicked her on her left side and under her stomach.[85] Since the assault, she has had "frequent headaches, and has developed serious gynecological problems. She has not been able to work for five months."[86] At a January 26 meeting held at the police station, the attorney for Ms. Felissaint brought forth further allegations that "the female Oriental [cashier] was heard to say 'I'm tired of the f—-ing black people.'"[87] The police officer who interviewed Ms. Felissaint at the hospital stated that she did not "mention ethnic remarks. . .and the female cashier spoke little or no English."[88]

The store employees' version is somewhat different. According to them, when Ms. Felissaint arrived at the cash register, she had $3 worth of food, but presented only $2 to the cashier. While she looked in her bag for more money, the cashier began to wait on another customer because the line of customers was very long. She became angry, began yelling racial slurs, and then threw a hot pepper at the cashier. The cashier responded by throwing a pepper back at her. This squabble grew, with Ms. Felissaint knocking down boxes of hot pepper, and spitting in the cashier's face. The store manager intervened, appealing to her to calm down and asking her to forget about the $1. When he requested, with his "hands on her shoulders," that she leave the store, she "laid herself down on the floor." Customers began to take sides, some telling her that she should sue, and others advising her to get up and leave.[89]

When the police arrived, they called an ambulance for Ms. Felissaint and, at the insistence of the crowd, arrested Bong Jae Jang, who identified himself as the owner of the store, for committing a third-degree assault. At this point the crowd was becoming "somewhat violent, throwing rocks and bottles at the Koreans. The personnel quickly closed the store."[90]

A boycott of the store began shortly after the incident. According to the police record, at about 7:00 p.m. approximately 40 persons assembled in front of the store:

to protest the assault upon the Haitian woman by the Korean merchants, demanding that the store close permanently. Unidentified spokespersons voiced their opposition to the Korean-American treatment of customers in general, indicating that there have been a number of incidents in which customers have been manhandled and there is a lack of respect to all black customers. When [the store] closed at about 2000 hours the demonstrators moved across the street to 1826 Church Ave, another Korean-owned fruit and vegetable market [Church Fruits and Vegetables].[91]

After closing the Red Apple store, an employee "ran across the street to take refuge from the angry crowd" gathered outside the store. While crossing the street to the Church Fruits and Vegetables store, "he was hit by bottles, rocks and fruits."[92] It is because this employee took refuge in the Church Fruits and Vegetables store that the demonstrators followed him across the street. Although the two stores have been

---

85   *Mayor's Committee Report,* pp. 19-20.

86   Ibid., pp. 20-21.

87   Lt. Charles E. Monahan, Commanding Officer, 70 Squad, New York City Police Department, memorandum to the Commanding Officer entitled "Meeting with Representatives of the Haitian Community," Jan. 26, 1990, p. 1.

88   Ibid.

89   *Mayor's Committee Report,* pp. 21-22.

90   Ibid., p. 22.

91   Commanding Officer, 70th Precinct, New York City Police Department, "Chronology of Events Surrounding Haitian Demonstrations on Church Avenue," Feb. 6, 1990. p. 1 (hereafter cited as Commanding Officer Memorandum).

92   *Mayor's Committee Report,* p. 23.

competitors and are in no way connected to each other, a connection was established in the minds of the demonstrators, and Church Fruits and Vegetables also became a target of boycott.[93]

On the following day, there was a demonstration of about 25 persons in front of the Red Apple and the Church Fruits and Vegetables stores. The demonstrators "demanded that the store be closed permanently, claiming that a woman was beaten therein and is now in a coma."[94] The next day, approximately 150 protesters began demonstrating in front of the store, and the crowd grew to about 400 persons by the late afternoon. One demonstrator was arrested for disorderly conduct after knocking over fruit stands and pushing bystanders.[95]

In this manner, the boycott grew in size and gathered momentum. In the months that followed:

The boycott often became volatile and racially charged in tone, resulting in several instances of violence, as the demonstrators, using bull horns and positioning themselves in close proximity to the store entrances, exhorted, and, in certain instances, verbally abused shoppers in order to dissuade them from patronizing the boycotted stores.[96]

Racist leaflets were distributed, and an act of violence by a demonstrator resulted in the wife of one of the store owners undergoing a medical abortion,[97] leading one reporter to name the boycott the "'ugliest crack' in the gorgeous mosaic of racial harmony in the city."[98] The boycott was still continuing at least a year later. In early 1991 demonstrators appeared only on evenings and weekends, but they still were driving away some shoppers.[99]

Several specific developments that occurred subsequent to the January 18, 1990, incident are worthy of special mention:

1) On April 21, 1990, Mayor David N. Dinkins, who was elected on his campaign promise of racial harmony and assumed office 17 days before the start of the boycott, appointed a committee to investigate the circumstances of and climate surrounding the January 18th incident and to make recommendations on resolving the protest and boycott.[100]

2) Because of the continuing protest and its devastating effects on business, the store owners applied for and, on May 10, 1990, were granted injunctive relief by the Kings County Supreme Court. Balancing the protesters' rights to congregate and express their position and the store owners' rights to engage in commerce, the court issued an order that the demonstrators could continue their protest from a distance of not less than 50 feet from the store entrances and directed the New York City Police Department to enforce its provisions. The police department failed to enforce the May 10 order, however. Because of this failure and the continuing boycott's adverse commercial impact, on June 4, 1990, the store owners initiated a mandamus

93   Ibid.

94   Commanding Officer Memorandum, p. 2.

95   Ibid.

96   Boung Jae Jang v. Lee Brown, No. 90-02710 (Sup. Ct. N.Y. Sept. 17, 1990) at 2.

97   On Feb. 2, 1990, a female demonstrator came into Church Fruits and Vegetables "yelling and looking for a confrontation" and an altercation ensued with Mrs. Park, the storeowner's wife, who was 2 months pregnant. This demonstrator "took hold of Mrs. Park's face and neck and attempted to scratch her." Mrs. Park was hit during the scuffle and subsequently required a medical abortion. She has returned to Korea, "physically, emotionally, and financially exhausted." This account is based on the *Mayor's Committee Report*, pp. 23-24, and *An Analysis of the Mayor's Committee Report*, p. 14.

98   Laurie Goodstein, "Split Between Blacks, Koreans Widens in N.Y. Court," *Washington Post*, May 8, 1990.

99   Bethany Kandel, "Tensions Ease Year After NYC Grocery Boycott," *USA Today*, Jan. 4, 1991, p. 8A.

100   *Mayor's Committee Report*, p. 1.

proceeding to compel the police department to enforce the court order. On June 26, 1990, the court directed the police department to implement its May 10 order. The police department, however, arguing that law enforcement is a matter exclusively committed to the discretion of the police department and that public safety and community relations concerns strongly militated against enforcing the May 10 order, appealed the June 26 decision on several grounds.[101]

3) On September 17, 1990, the State appellate court unanimously concluded that the police department must enforce the lawful order of the court. Specifically, the court noted that the police assertion that to enforce the May 10 order would engender community resentment towards the police or exacerbate the intensity of the protest was unpersuasive. This assertion, the court reasoned, failed to recognize that the court prescribed the measures as reasonable and necessary after examining the relevant circumstances. Furthermore, the police are not "entitled to unilaterally conclude otherwise by, in essence, abrogating to themselves the ultimate authority to weigh the petitioners' entitlement to effective enforcement of the court's order. . .and state officials are not entitled to rely on community hostility as an excuse not to protect. . .the exercise of fundamental rights."[102]

4) On August 30, 1990, the Mayor's Committee issued its report (hereafter the Mayor's Committee Report). The report concluded that:

a) The boycott was "incident-based," not racially motivated.[103]

b) Although the New York City Police Department did a commendable job of keeping peace in the neighborhood, the police failed to inform the Bias Investigation Unit of the department, even though both sides claimed that racial insults were used, and the police treated the incident "in a light and superficial manner." None of the police officers spoke Korean, French, or Creole, and the police lost "crucial witnesses" because they were more intent on clearing the store than determining what had happened.[104]

c) The mainstream media coverage of the situation was "inflammatory and polarizing," "overly simplistic and in some cases blatantly racist," and did not assist the resolution process.[105]

d) The district attorney's office did not move the resulting court cases as expeditiously as it could have, thereby contributing to the erosion of public trust in the criminal justice system.[106]

5) On the same day that the Mayor's Committee Report was released, August 30, 1990, the District Attorney of Kings County issued a 14-page statement responding to the report, characterizing it as "flawed because of inaccuracy and an incomplete review of facts and circumstances."[107]

6) The New York City Council's Committee on General Welfare (Council Committee) held a public hearing on the report on September 12,

101   Boung Jae Jang v. Lee Brown, No. 90-02710 (Sup. Ct. N.Y., Sept. 17, 1990), at 3-4.

102   *Id.* at 6.

103   *Mayor's Committee Report,* pp. 15-16. This conclusion was drawn in spite of the committee's recognition that "openly racist remarks were made and leaflets with racist statements were distributed by some protesters" (p. 15) and its own assessment that "conflict between particular Korean merchants and particular Black shoppers is not a new phenomenon. In the past 5 years several difficult protest and boycott situations have erupted in New York City. Very similar conflicts have been seen in many major urban centers in the past decade." (p. 3)

104   Ibid., pp. 39-40.

105   Ibid., p. 3 (Executive Summary) and p. 31 (text).

106   Ibid., p. 34.

1990, and issued its findings and conclusions in December 1990. The Council Committee observed that the Mayor's Committee Report was "a disappointment to all participants in the situation and to the public who was hoping for a courageous moral stand from its leadership."[108] Specific conclusions were as follows:

a) "From the outset, the Mayor's Committee was apparently unwilling to evaluate critically the facts of the January 18 incident...and [its] failure to investigate the protest meaningfully appears to be purposeful." As evidence for this statement, the Council Committee cited the basic fact that the Mayor's Committee failed to interview the protestors themselves regarding their causes for the boycott.[109]

b) The Mayor's Committee failed to attribute racist behavior to the particular groups responsible for the distribution of racist literature. The Council Committee called this failure "baffling," since some of the racist literature was clearly identified with particular groups.[110]

c) "While the goal of resolving the boycott is laudable, it cannot be done at the expense of the constitutional rights of one of the parties, nor the abrogation of the function of the police [as law enforcement agents]."[111]

d) "The City's refusal to enforce the fifty-foot order [for demonstrators not to congregate within 50 feet from the stores] absent the specific direction of two courts is without defense....The Mayor's failure to direct the police to enforce [the court order] raises questions about his willingness to exercise his authority. The failure of the Committee to criticize this [aspect] is profoundly disturbing."[112]

e) The conclusion that "the protest is incident-based and not primarily racist is contradicted by the facts. This erroneous conclusion adversely affects the rationale behind the Committee's recommendations regarding resolution of the protest."[113]

7) The Mayor's Committee Report was also criticized by the media. For example, a *New York Times* editorial noted, "Cynics suggested the [appointment of the committee] was merely a device to diffuse responsibility for an intolerable display of racism. The report makes even the cynics look starry-eyed. ...The Flatbush boycott [is] racist. ...The report leaves Mayor Dinkins still seeming to excuse racial picketing. By doing so, he encourages the spread of this pernicious tactic."[114]

8) On September 18, 1990, Asian Americans (primarily, but not exclusively, Korean Americans) held a civil rights rally in front of the city

---

107   Charles J. Hynes, District Attorney of Kings County, NY, "Statement by Kings County District Attorney Charles J. Hynes in Response to Mayoral Committee Report," pp. 1 and 7-12.

108   *An Analysis of the Mayor's Committee Report,* p. 6.

109   Ibid., pp. 38, 40.

110   Ibid., p. 44. Copies of 14 different flyers distributed by demonstrators are shown in *An Analysis of the Mayor's Committee Report,* exhibit 10.

111   Ibid., p. 47-48.

112   Ibid., pp. 48, 50. The council committee also noted the importance of the fact that "since shortly after the City began enforcing the court order, the level of confrontation between the parties and the police has not increased, but diminished [contrary to the police forecast]. Shoppers have returned to the stores, apparently demonstrating that they were kept away—not by sympathy with the boycott—but by intimidation from the demonstrators." Ibid., p. 50.

113   Ibid., p. 54. For detailed discussion of this point, see pp. 54-59, *An Analysis of the Mayor's Committee Report.*

114   "These Boycotts Are Racist and Wrong," *New York Times,* Aug. 31, 1990.

hall. This peaceful rally, officially named by the organizers as "Peace Rally For Racial Harmony," drew a record crowd of near 10,000 persons, the largest rally of its kind in the city. It promoted themes of racial harmony, racial justice, and cultural pluralism. At this rally Mayor Dinkins announced that the city would enforce the court order barring demonstrators within 50 feet from the stores.[115]

9) After the appeals court decision, the police department started enforcing the 50-foot court order, arresting 13 persons for disorderly conduct. On September 21, 1990, Mayor Dinkins visited the two boycotted stores and shopped. His visit was characterized as "directly contradict[ing] his previous position on how to handle the protest. . .and adopted instead exactly the tactic that an array of other politicians and opinion-makers had urged on him for months."[116] After the mayor's visit, business at the two boycotted stores took a sharp upswing.[117] Over the following weekend, however, 19 gasoline bombs were discovered on the roof of the Red Apple store by police officers who were conducting a routine sweep of the building.[118] The police noted, "We don't know who did this or for what purpose, [but] because of the close proximity to the Korean grocery stores, there's a possibility it's connected."[119] Although there were no major boycott-related violence or incidents since the mayor's visit, demonstrators were still appearing on evenings and weekends, driving away some customers, even after one year.[120]

The year-long boycott exacerbated race relations in the Flatbush area and may have led to a violent attack on three Vietnamese American men by a large group of black youths who mistook them for Koreans.[121] In that incident, which took place early in the morning of Sunday, May 13, 1990, as many as 15 youths were gathered outside an apartment building in which the Vietnamese men lived. One of them threw a beer bottle, shattering a plate-glass window in the Vietnamese men's apartment. When the Vietnamese men came out to see what was going on, the youths attacked them with a baseball bat, knives, and bottles, shouting, "Koreans, what are you doing here?"[122] and other racial slurs. One of the Vietnamese men, Tuan Ana Cao, suffered a fractured skull and other severe injuries in that attack.[123] Despite the proximity of the attack to the location of the boycott and the anti-Korean remarks made by the attackers, the police commissioner maintained that the incident was not related to the grocery store boycott.[124]

115   Myong-sok Lee, "Developments Leading To the 9.18 Rally," *Korea Times New York*, Oct. 3, 1990. p. A5.

116   Todd S. Purdum, "Dinkins Supports Shunned Grocers," *New York Times*, Sept. 22, 1990.

117   One source described the positive impact of the mayor's visit as follows: "Despite cries of 'Boycott!' that were hurled at them, a stream of customers flowed through the steady rain past the demonstrators and shopped at both stores. Many said they had been afraid to cross the picket lines in past months, but were stirred to action by Mayor Dinkins's decision to shop at the stores on Friday." David Gonzalez, *New York Times*, Sept. 23, 1990.

118   David Gonzalez, "19 Firebombs Found on Roof of Grocery," *New York Times*, Sept. 24, 1990.

119   New York Daily News, "Police Find Firebombs Near Boycotted Stores," *Washington Post*, Sept. 24, 1990.

120   Bethany Kandel, "Tensions Ease Year After NYC Grocery Boycott," *USA Today*, Jan. 4, 1991, p. 8A.

121   The account of this incident is based on Robert D. McFadden, "Blacks Attack 3 Vietnamese; One Hurt Badly," *New York Times*, May 14, 1990 (hereafter cited as "Blacks Attack 3 Vietnamese").

122   Ibid.

123   The police arrested two of the black teenagers on May 14. ("2 Black Teens Arrested in N.Y. Racial Incident," *Washington Times*, May 15, 1990.) Police response may have been delayed because of difficulties in communicating with the Vietnamese victims, who had limited English proficiency. According to the *New York Times*, "[F]or hours after the attack, the police were unable to communicate with [Mr. Cao] effectively until a Vietnamese interpreter could be found." ("Blacks Attack 3 Vietnamese").

The Flatbush incident illustrates what can happen when racial tensions are unchecked and racial incidents mishandled by local governments. An incident that might have been managed in such a way as to improve racial relations in New York City instead ended up worsening racial relations and disillusioning many Korean Americans about the American political process.[125]

Harassment of Vietnamese Fishermen

The 1986 Commission report noted a general pattern of friction between Vietnamese fishermen and native fishermen in Florida, Texas, and California. The friction was caused by difficulties in communication, the Vietnamese fishermen's lack of awareness of local fishing regulations, and economic competition between established native fishermen and the Vietnamese newcomers. The report documented many incidents of vandalism and violence arising out of this friction, including Ku Klux Klan activity against Vietnamese fishermen in Texas. The report also pointed to a pattern of using State government action, such as restrictive laws and regulations, against Vietnamese fishermen.[126]

A more recent incident demonstrates that such acts of harassment were not an isolated episode. In 1989 Vietnamese fishermen charged that the U.S. Coast Guard's selective enforcement of a 200-year-old law was being used to harass them and drive them out of the fishing business in California. The Jones Act,[127] enacted in the late 1700s, effectively prohibits noncitizens from owning or operating large boats (heavier than 5 net tons) in U.S. waters. The original objective of the act was to ensure that such boats would be operated by persons predisposed to defend the United States in the event of war. The U.S. Coast Guard apparently began enforcing the Jones Act against Vietnamese fishermen in northern California waters in November of 1987. Most of the Vietnamese fishermen in northern California are permanent residents who have not yet met the waiting period for becoming citizens, and thus could not operate their fishing boats in certain waters under the law. Fines of $500 were levied against fishermen found violating the law, and the Coast Guard threatened to seize boats that were operated illegally. Several fishermen gave up fishing after that, while others continued.[128]

According to the Vietnamese fishermen, the law had not been enforced by the U.S. Coast Guard in recent years, and they believe it was being selectively enforced against Vietnamese fishermen. The U.S. Coast Guard, however, contends that "[h]ere in the San Francisco Bay Area, it has been enforced at the same level as far back as anybody can remember."[129] The

---

124   "2 Black Teens Arrested in N.Y. Racial Incident," *Washington Times*, May 15, 1990.

125   A special panel discussion, "Toward Racial Harmony: The Flatbush Incident," sponsored by the Korean American Journalist Association at the annual convention of the Asian American Journalists Association, New York, NY, Aug. 24, 1990.

     The Flatbush incident took on an international dimension when an influential monthly magazine in Korea carried an article on the Flatbush incident. The article contains extensive quotes from the store owners imparting the impression that New York's police are insensitive and unresponsive to the concerns of Korean American merchants, almost to the point of negligence. Similarly, the actions of city hall are also criticized severely. Jae-Myong Kim, "New York Produce Merchants Beleaguered By Black Boycotters: An Interview With Jae-Bong Jang of the Red Apple Store," *Wol-gan Joong-ang*, December 1990, pp. 510-17 (in Korean). Such coverage of racial incidents in the United States might serve to aggravate anti-American feelings worldwide and have an unintended ripple effect on our international relations.

126   *Recent Activities Against Citizens and Residents of Asian Descent*, pp. 50-53.

127   46 U.S.C. §§8103(a), 12102(a)(1), and 12110(d) (1988).

128   Susan Freinkel, "Livelihoods on the Line: 200-Year-Old Law Unconstitutional, Viet Fishermen Say," *The Recorder*, Sept. 28, 1989.

129   Ibid.

Vietnamese fishermen contend further that the Jones Act is unconstitutional, because there is no longer any overriding military need for the law, and its enforcement deprives the fishermen of their ability to earn a living.[130]

On September 27, 1989, the Vietnamese Fishermen Association of America and six individual fishermen brought a suit seeking an injunction to stop the Coast Guard from enforcing the law on the grounds that it is unconstitutional. The next day Judge Orrick of the United States District Court for the Northern District of California issued a temporary restraining order stopping the Coast Guard from enforcing the law while the issue was being litigated. On October 16, Judge Schwarzer, of the same court, denied application for a preliminary injunction on the grounds that the fishermen were unlikely to win their suit on the merits.[131] The fishermen appealed the denial of a preliminary injunction and at the same time filed an emergency motion for injunctive relief, which was granted on November 15, 1989.[132] At that point in time, it was agreed by the parties that the October 16 decision denying a preliminary injunction would be treated as a decision in favor of the Coast Guard, and on January 24, 1990, the fishermen appealed this decision. Arguments were heard on July 20, 1990.[133]

Before a decision was rendered, however, Congress passed and President Bush signed legislation sponsored by Representative Norman Mineta (D-CA) that would allow permanent resident aliens to operate fishing boats in excess of 5 tons in California coastal waters.[134]

Racial Harassment on College Campuses

Bigotry and violence against Asian Americans extends to college campuses,[135] where the way the incidents are handled reveals much about the underlying climate of the institution. An incident that took place at the University of Connecticut (UConn) at Storrs in December 1987 is illustrative.[136]

On the evening of December 3, 1987, at about 9:30, Marta Ho, Feona Lee, and six other students of Asian descent boarded a bus that was to take them to a semiformal Christmas dance sponsored by two University dorms at the Italian-American Club in the nearby town of Tolland. . . .Marta in a black-and-white, knee-length gown made of silk, which she had borrowed from her sister, and Feona in a full-length, blue silk gown that she had brought from her native Hong Kong. . . .The crowded bus held between 50 and 60 people—some of them drinking and yelling profanities. The group of eight Asian American students found seats scattered toward the rear of the bus. . . .While waiting on the bus parked in front of a dormitory, Feona felt something land in her hair. "At first I thought it was just water dripping from the bus. . . .Then I felt something warm and slimy hit me in the face." She realized it was spit. As she stood up and turned to face her attackers, she was hit again, this time in the eye. "Who did that?" she screamed, "Stop!". . . When Daniel Shan, one of the eight [Asian

---

130 Brief for Appellants in the case of Vietnamese Fishermen Association of America v. Paul Yost before the U.S. Court of Appeals for the 9th Circuit.

131 Vietnamese Fishermen Association of America v. Paul Yost, No. C 89-3522 WWS (N.D. Cal. Oct. 16, 1989) (1989 U.S. Dist. LEXIS 15075).

132 Ibid.

133 Ibid.

134 The law does not apply to all United States coastal waters. (See 46 U.S.C 59aa.) The Alaskan fishing industry had objected to having the law apply to Alaskan coastal waters for fear that Canadian fishermen could take advantage of the law. (Katherine Bishop, "For Vietnamese-Americans, a Victory in Congress," New York Times, Oct. 31, 1990.)

135 The problem of bigotry and violence against Asian Americans in our schools is discussed in chap. 4.

136 This account is excerpted from David Morse, "Prejudicial Studies: One Astounding Lesson From the University of Connecticut," Northeast/Hartford Courant, Nov. 26, 1989, pp. 10-32.

American] students, rushed over to see what was wrong, Feona was facing a group of half-dozen young men sitting in the back seats—drinking beer, some of them chewing tobacco—two of whom Shan recognized as football players. When Feona sat down, these two men spat on her, hitting [Shan] as well, and yelling slurs such as "Chinks!" "Gooks," and "Oriental faggots!" Shan and another man in the group, Ron Cheung, approached the two men, demanding they apologize. The two harassers invited them to fight, while one of the two threw a punch at Cheung and missed. Someone separated them, and the bus driver yelled at everyone to "Sit down and shut up!" No effort was made to put the spitters off the bus. . .By the time the bus pulled up to the Club, the harassment had lasted nearly 45 minutes.

The Asian American students tried to salvage the evening by dancing and staying on the opposite side of the room from their antagonists. But one of the two harassers followed them repeatedly elbowing Marta's dance partner, making "animal sounds" and screaming insults. According to one witness, this harasser dropped his sweatpants, mooning her and her partner, and then danced with his penis exposed. Later he urinated on a window and confronted Danny Shan in a stairway, apparently trying to get him to fight. . . .The victims complained to three Resident Assistants, upperclass students hired by the university as nominal authorities in the dormitories. But they were told "not to spoil a good time," otherwise they "would be written up." When they asked permission to leave the dance, they were told they could not because the RAs were responsible for the victims' safety. . . .Marta and Feona called the Vernon police by mistake instead of the Tolland police. . . .A little before midnight, a squad car drove up. Although the victims thought it was in response to their call, the squad car was responding to another call stemming from an unrelated fight. By this time the dance was coming to an end, and the first bus had arrived to take people home; without making a complaint to the trooper, the group got on the bus and rode back to the UConn campus. . . .A group photograph taken afterward at the dormitory shows the brown tobacco stains on Feona's blue gown and on her wrist.

At the insistence of Marta's sister, Maria Ho, the victims went to the campus police on Dec. 4, 1987 to report the incident. After listening to their story, the officer on duty conferred with his supervisor and told them there was nothing he could do because the incident had taken place in Tolland, outside UConn's jurisdiction, suggesting they take their complaint to state police and the campus affirmative action office. Only after he was confronted with the question, "Aren't you at least going to take a report?" he agreed to take a "miscellaneous" report for future reference.

It was nearly 10:00 p.m. that evening that the victims finally were able to talk to a state trooper in Tolland. The officer advised the victims to go back to campus police because the incident had begun on UConn property. According to the victims, the trooper's response upon being told of the incident was "to laugh." He also said something like, "Boy, this guy must have been drunk out of his mind." Furthermore, Feona recalls, "He asked me, did I see [the man] pull his pants down, and did I see his penis? I said I did, and he asked me, do I really know what a penis looks like?". . . It was 11:00 p.m. when the victims finally went home after being shunted back and forth all day.

The following Monday, December 7, Maria called the university's Office of Affirmative Action Programs and made an afternoon appointment. When the victims showed up, they were told the case lay outside the office's jurisdiction and referred to the Dean of Students. . . .When Maria called the Dean's office Tuesday, she learned the dean was out and his assistant offered to schedule them for later in the week. Maria then replied that if they did not receive prompt attention, they would tell their story to the newspapers. At that point the assistant invited the students to come to the office to give oral testimony. . . .

After Maria Ho's threat to bring the incident to the press, the pace of the university's response picked up. On Thursday, December 10, the two perpetrators were charged with violating the Student Conduct Code and a hearing was scheduled for the accused. In the meantime, the university's director of public safety determined that the actions that occurred while the bus was parked on UConn property were within his jurisdiction. The victims were summoned back to give sworn affidavits, and warrants were obtained for the arrest of the two accused students for disorderly conduct.[137] Eventually, one of the two accused was expelled from school for 1 year and the other, a star football player, was prohibited from living in the student dormitories but allowed to continue to play for the UConn football team.

To the Asian American community and students, the "administration's treatment of them was as bad as the original incident. Perhaps worse."[138] The frustration at the university's handling led to a protest fast of 8 days by an Asian American faculty member on the campus in the summer of 1988[139] and to the university senate's passage in September 1988 of a resolution mandating an investigation into the December 3, 1987, incident and the university's response.[140] The university senate's subcommittee on discriminatory harassment, in its report released in early April 1989, noted that the dean of students may have mishandled the disciplinary hearings on the December 1987 incident by violating procedural rules and possibly coercing the victims.[141] Based on this report, the college of liberal arts and sciences faculty passed a resolution requesting that "UConn President John Casteen investigate the allegations and if substantiated, the Dean and his assistant be suspended from participation in any hearing affecting College of Liberal Arts and Sciences students."[142] The subcommittee report also noted serious causes for concern at the Storrs campus: "deep-seated intolerance, a perceived absence of leadership at the top, an atmosphere 'altogether too permissive of harassing behavior,' and lack of trust in the administration."[143] The report found that "deep-seated prejudice at UConn has bred a climate in which harassment based on race, sex, ethnic background and sexual preference is tolerated by administrators, students, faculty and staff members."[144] Commenting on the report, one newspaper editorial noted that "without question, there are harassment problems on the campus. . . . Whether the problem is less or greater at UConn than at other universities of equal size is not known. What is known is there is a problem of apparent pervasive prejudice and harassment. The cure for the

---

137 Ibid., p. 19. This quickened pace provides a contrast with the university's allegedly sluggish response to its internal committee's recommendations on campus racism and student acts of bigotry. For example, at the time of the Tolland incident, the affirmative action advisory committee for the Greater Hartford campus was considering dissolving itself since "none of [its] proposals were acted upon" in spite of repeated recommendations. And its counterpart at Storrs was waiting for the university president's response to its recommendations submitted in July 1987. Ibid., p. 18.

138 Ibid., p. 25. Also note the following quotes echoing similar sentiments: "What was particularly distressing about the UConn incident, really, was the failure of the administration to respond in any meaningful way afterward." (Statement attributed to Peter Kiang, cited in ibid., p. 26); "The Asian-American victims have complained repeatedly and bitterly of the treatment given them by the UConn administration. When they appeared for help to the campus police, the Dean of Students, the residential life people, and the Office of Affirmative Action, they were first ignored, then given the 'run around.'" Paul Bock, "Institutionalized Racism at the University of Connecticut Continues: Recent Developments" (paper presented at the 1990 convention of the Association of Asian American Studies, Santa Barbara, CA, May 19, 1990), p. 3.

139 Jean Caldwell, "A Quiet Professor Turns Protester," *Boston Globe,* Aug. 19, 1988, p. 2, and "UConn Professor Ends 8-Day Fast Against Racism," *Boston Globe,* Aug. 20, 1988, p. 32.

140 Morse, "Prejudicial Studies," p. 28.

141 Katherine Farrish, "Investigation Sought Into UConn Hearings," *Hartford Courant,* Apr. 6, 1989, p. B1; Jim Amspacher, "Ardaiolo Criticized, Report Called Weak: Dean Said To Have Violated Conduct Code," *The Daily Campus* (The University of Connecticut, Storrs), Apr. 6, 1989, p. 1.

142 Amspacher, "Ardaiolo Criticized," p. 1.

143 Morse, "Prejudicial Studies," p. 28.

144 Katherine Farrish, "UConn Students Reflect on State of Race Relations," *Hartford Courant,* Apr. 16, 1989, p. B-1.

ailment is contained in the report if it is applied to the patient without delay."[145]

By nearly unanimous voice vote, the University of Connecticut's Faculty Senate voted on May 1, 1989, not to suspend the dean of students for his alleged mishandling of the December 3, 1987, incident.[146] Soon after the senate vote, University President Casteen announced that he found no evidence of wrongdoing by the dean of students[147] (who resigned in June 1989 to become vice president of student life at a college in South Carolina). At the same time he instituted two changes in the Student Conduct Code: 1) preventing students found guilty of harassment from playing sports or taking part in other activities for at least one semester, and 2) imposing suspension or expulsion as a possible punishment on every student accused of discriminatory harassment.[148] The president also acknowledged that he should have responded more quickly to the incident: "In hindsight, if I had known more of the incident, I would have or should have acted differently. I would have taken a fairly strong posture."[149]

Racial Slurs Made by Public Figures

When public figures make racial slurs against Asian Americans, they lend an aura of legiti-macy to the anti-Asian attitudes held by many in the public and indirectly encourage anti-Asian activities. In a much-publicized incident in 1990, Jimmy Breslin, a prominent columnist for *Newsday*, angered at criticism of one of his columns by a female colleague who is Korean American, publicly referred to her as a "yellow cur" and "slant-eyed."[150] *Newsday* management's apparent reluctance to discipline Breslin after he had made what to some seemed an inadequate apology, provoked accusations that they were operating under a double standard.[151] The situation was further aggravated when Breslin made light of the situation several days later, joking on the air, referring to his nephew's wedding to a Korean woman, "Now does this mean I can't go to the wedding?" The next day, *Newsday* management gave Breslin a 2-week suspension.[152]

Breslin's comment is by no means an isolated incident. In a much less publicized incident, Cliff Kincaid, a Washington, DC, radio personality, referred to CBS television anchor Connie Chung as "Connie Chink." Later, explaining himself, he said, "It's a slang term. It is not a vulgar term," and argued that it was not a term like "honky."[153] Yet, a handbook for journalists, sponsored by the National Conference of Christians and Jews, the Asian American Journalists Association, and the Association of Asian Pa-

---

145 Editorial, "Prejudice at UConn," *The Chronicle* (Willimantic, Conn.), Apr. 12, 1989, p. 8.

146 Katherine Farrish, "UConn Dean's Accusers Rebuffed," *Hartford Courant*, p. D-1. After this vote, one of the supporters of the rebuffed motion said, "Not taking step constitutes a glossing over of misdeeds, and a confirmation of the perception. . .that the violation of victims' rights goes unpunished." (Ibid.)

147 Morse, "Prejudicial Studies," p. 28.

148 Ibid.

149 Ibid.

150 Constance Hays, "Asian-American Groups Call for Breslin's Ouster Over Racial Slurs," *New York Times*, May 7, 1990.

151 A *Washington Times* editorial contrasted Breslin's treatment to that of CBS commentator, Andy Rooney, who was suspended for making antihomosexual remarks. ("Tabloid Backs Breslin, But Few Others Do," *Washington Times*, May 8, 1990.) Others pointed out that *Newsday* had previously ousted an editor who had been accused of making a racist remark about a black colleague. (Lee Michael Katz, "Columnist Under Fire: Outrage at Breslin's Ethnic Slur," *USA Today*, May 8, 1990.) New York City's former mayor, Ed Koch, was quoted as saying, "If he'd said the same thing about blacks they would have fired him." (Eleanor Randolph, "In N.Y., The Breslin Backlash: Asians Demand Ouster after Newsday Tirade," *Washington Post*, May 8, 1990.)

152 David Braaten, "A Jest Goes Sour; Breslin Gets Hook," *Washington Times*, May 10, 1990.

153 Jeffrey Horke, "On Radio, A Racial 'Joke': WNTR Host Takes on Connie Chung," *Washington Post*, (date unknown), 1990.

cific American Artists, defines the term "chink" as:

racial slur— A derogatory term for Chinese and Chinese Americans that some believe was derived from the Ch'ing Dynasty, which ruled during the period of the first major migration of Chinese immigrants. Avoid except in direct quotes and specific historical references.[154]

Kincaid's ignorance is illustrative of insensitivity in the media to Asian Americans.[155]

Racial remarks made by politicians can be even more damaging, because they suggest that the political process itself is racist. In January 1990, John Silber, candidate for the Democratic nomination for Governor of Massachusetts, called Massachusetts a "welfare magnet" that has "suddenly become popular for people who are accustomed to living in the tropical climate." He was also quoted as saying, "Why should Lowell [Massachusetts] be the Cambodian capital of America? Why should they all be concentrated in one place? This needs to be examined."[156] Cambodian community leaders in Lowell found these remarks demeaning and offensive. They considered Silber's remarks another reflection of the anti-Asian bias that had led to the "English-only" ordinance that had recently been passed by the Lowell City Council. Silber went on to win the Democratic nomination, but in November 1990 he narrowly lost his bid to become Governor of Massachusetts.

Statistics on Hate Crimes Against Asian Americans

A thorough understanding of hate crimes against Asians is required before effective measures to combat such crimes can be implemented. Whereas the study of individual incidents of violence provides insight into the nature of anti-Asian hate crimes, statistical data can help to assess the extent of the problem and to uncover patterns in these incidents. Unfortunately, an adequate source of comprehensive statistical information on hate crimes does not now exist. The Hate Crimes Statistics Act enacted in 1990 by Congress provides for collection of hate crimes statistics at the Federal level and offers hope that national data on hate crimes will become available within the next few years. For now, however, one must be content with the fragmentary evidence provided by local hate crimes statistics.

Local Hate Crime Statistics

A few cities and States across the Nation do collect statistics on hate crimes. Most of these data collection efforts were initiated within the last 2 or 3 years, and it is apparent that the inherent problems in collecting hate crime data have not yet been solved. One major problem in the collection of accurate hate crime data is that hate crimes are underreported by the victims of the crime. This is particularly true in the case of the Asian American community, especially recent immigrants, for a variety of reasons, including language problems, distrust of the police,[157]

154   Bill Sing, ed., *Asian Pacific Americans: A Handbook on How to Cover and Portray Our Nation's Fastest Growing Minority Group* (National Conference of Christians and Jews, Asian American Journalists Association, and Association of Asian Pacific American Artist, 1989), p. 49 (hereafter cited as *Asian Pacific Americans: A Handbook*).

155   In a Mar. 26, 1990, letter to Tom Krimsier, Vice President and General Manager of WNTR Radio, S.B. Woo, National President, and Melinda Yee, Executive Director, Organization for Chinese Americans, expressed outrage at Mr. Kincaid's remarks, explaining "The word 'Chink' is clearly derogatory and a racial slur, similar to words such as 'Nigger' or 'Spic.'" In response, Mr. Krimsier apologized for the incident, noted that Mr. Kincaid has also apologized on the air, expressed the belief that Mr. Kincaid's remarks were "unintentional on his part," and promised to prevent any reoccurrence. Tom Krimsier, letter to S.B. Woo and Melinda Yee, Mar. 30, 1989.

156   Constance L. Hays, "Remarks Inflame Massachusetts Contest," *New York Times,* Jan. 27, 1990.

the desire not to cause problems, and shame at becoming a victim of a crime. As a result, many hate crimes are never reported to the police. A second major problem in the collection of accurate hate crime data is that even when a racially motivated crime is reported to the police, the police often do not report the crime as a hate crime. For instance, a racially motivated incident that resulted in a mugging might be classified as a simple assault and battery. Police departments generally do not provide sufficient training to police officers on the beat on how to recognize hate crimes. Only some larger jurisdictions have formed special units whose mission it is to collect hate crime statistics and combat hate crimes.[158]

Because of these limitations, it is difficult to assess the representativeness of currently available data on hate crimes. It seems clear that these data are likely to reflect only a relatively small subset of racially motivated crimes. Nonetheless, local hate crimes statistics provide some basis for assessing the nature and extent of hate crimes against Asian Americans. A review of hate crimes statistics reports from cities across the country reveals that Asians are frequently victims of hate crimes.

Philadelphia—A 1988 Philadelphia Human Relations Commission report revealed that while Asians made up under 4 percent of Philadelphia's population, they were the victims in 20 percent of the city's hate crimes. Asians were more likely on a per capita basis to become victims of hate crimes than whites, blacks, Hispanics, or Jews.[159]

Los Angeles—The Los Angeles County Commission on Human Relations has been collecting data on crimes motivated by racial and religious bigotry in Los Angeles County since 1980. In 1990 the commission issued a report on trends in hate crimes over the decade of the 1980s. In the 9 years that the Commission had been tracking racially motivated hate crimes, 14.9 percent of the victims were Asian (compared with 62.0 percent black). Between 1986 and 1989, when the number of hate crimes reported was larger, presumably because of a better reporting system, 15.2 percent of hate crime victims were Asians.[160] An analysis of the individual crimes listed at the back of the 1988 and 1990 annual reports of the commission reveals that, of the 32 hate crimes against Asians in 1988 and 1989, 10 (or roughly one-third) were against businesses, 2 were in schools, 1 was against an ethnic church, and the remaining 19 (or roughly two-thirds) affected victims in their residences. Crimes ranged from graffiti and property vandalism, to hate literature, cross burning, and assault.[161]

Boston—An analysis of data on civil rights violations provided by the Community Disorders Unit of the Boston Police Department over the years 1983-87 found: "When compared to the population size of the various racial groups in the city of Boston, the Asian community in general, and the Vietnamese community in particular, suffer significantly higher rates of racial violence than other racial or ethnic groups in the city."[162] Out of 452 incidents, 104 involved Asian victims, of whom 53 were Vietnamese.[163]

---

157   See chap. 3 on police-community relations for a discussion of the distrust many Asian Americans feel for the police.

158   Examples are New York City and Boston.

159   Philadelphia Commission on Human Relations, *State of Intergroup Harmony: 1988,* pp. 53-55.

160   Los Angeles County Commission on Human Relations, *Hate Crime in the 1980's: A Decade of Bigotry*, A Report to the Los Angeles County Board of Supervisors (February 1990), p. 9.

161   Los Angeles County Commission on Human Relations, *Hate Crime in Los Angeles County, 1988,* and *Hate Crime in Los Angeles County, 1989.*

162   Jack McDevitt, "The Study of the Implementation of the Massachusetts Civil Rights Act," Jan. 25, 1989, p. 9.

163   Ibid., table I.

Asians were unlikely to be perpetrators of racial incidents.[164]

Chicago—The Chicago Commission on Human Relations reported only 9 bias crimes against Asians in 1989, out of 185 total.[165] However, an independent group, Asian Human Services, reported 30 bias crimes against Asians in 1989, up from 20 the previous year.[166] The discrepancy between the number of anti-Asian incidents reported to Chicago's Human Relations Commission and the number of incidents known to an Asian community support group illustrates the difficulty in obtaining reliable data on hate crimes.

New York—New York City's Police Department has a bias unit similar to Boston's, with 19 investigating officers. In 1988 the bias unit reported 550 hate crimes, of which 24 were against Asians.[167] In 1989 there were 13 hate crimes against Asian Americans, and in 1990 there were 28.[168]

The Hate Crimes Statistics Act of 1990

Because the absence of nationwide data on hate crimes severely hampers efforts to monitor activities against minority groups, the 1986 Commission report on anti-Asian activities concluded that these "limitations lead inescapably to the conclusion that there needs to be a mechanism to gather these statistics on a national basis."[169]

A mechanism for nationwide data collection was finally provided by the Hate Crimes Statistics Act, enacted on April 23, 1990.[170] The act calls for the Attorney General to collect nationwide data on "the incidence of criminal acts that manifest prejudice based on race, religion, homosexuality or heterosexuality, ethnicity, or such other characteristics as the Attorney General considers appropriate" for a period of 4 years and to publish annual reports analyzing the data.[171]

Plans for implementing the Hate Crimes Statistics Act were drawn up by the Uniform Crime Reporting Section of the Federal Bureau of Investigation, and nationwide data collection began on January 1, 1991.[172] The Uniform Crime Reporting Section prepared a pamphlet entitled "Hate Crime Data Collection Guidelines" to inform police departments about what data to collect and report. The guidelines define and give examples of hate crimes, require that all crimes be evaluated at two levels of review for whether or not they are motivated by bias, and specify the information police departments are to provide about each hate crime.[173] The section also developed a "Training Guide for Hate Crime Data Collection" and has sponsored

---

164   Ibid., p. 10.

165   Chicago Commission on Human Relations, *Bias Crime Report, 1989*, p. 3.

166   Michael Selinker, "Reports of Bias Crime Decline in 1989," *The Chicago Reporter*, vol. 19, no. 3 (March 1990), p. 6.

167   Howard Kurtz, "New York Measures Surge in Bias-Related Crime: Authorities See Violence Against Minorities, Gays as Symbolic of National Trend," *Washington Post*, Oct. 28, 1989.

168   Asian American Legal Defense and Education Fund, *Outlook* (date unknown).

169   *Recent Activities Against Citizens and Residents of Asian Descent*, p. 57.

170   28 U.S.C. 534.

171   *Id.*

172   Harper Wilson, Chief, Uniform Crime Reporting Section, Federal Bureau of Investigation, telephone interview, Jan. 31, 1991 (hereafter cited as Wilson interview).

173   The information required includes: the type of offense; the location; the bias motivation (racial—anti-white, anti-black, anti-American Indian/Alaska Native, anti-Asian/Pacific Islander, anti-Multi-Racial Group, ethnicity/national origin—anti-Arab, anti-Hispanic, and anti-Other Ethnicity, religious and sexual); victim type (individual, business, financial institution, government, religious organization, society/public, other, unknown); the number of offenders; and the race of the offenders. (U.S. Department of Justice, Federal Bureau of Investigation, Uniform Crime Reporting, "Hate Crime Data Collection Guidelines.")

six regional training conferences, which were to be completed by the end of October 1991.[174]

If the Hate Crimes Statistics Act is to be effective, however, it will be necessary to take additional measures to ensure that the data gathered under the act are accurate. Local communities that do gather statistics on hate crimes have experienced considerable difficulties in obtaining accurate information. For instance, a recent report evaluating Boston's hate crime statistics finds that victims of all races are unlikely to report racial incidents, are often reluctant to identify them as racially motivated, and even when they have reported them, are reluctant to cooperate with police investigations.[175] Furthermore, the report finds that officers on the scene are unlikely to recognize incidents as hate crimes: only 19 of the 452 hate incidents in the report's sample that were subsequently identified as hate crimes were initially categorized as civil rights violations by officers on the scene.[176] Underreporting of hate crimes by victims and difficulties encountered by police officers on the scene in identifying crimes that are racially motivated are not limited to Boston. These appear to be nationwide problems.[177]

The Boston report concludes that for hate crime data to be accurate, special police units with the responsibility of investigating and reporting hate crimes are necessary. As an example, the report cites Boston Police Department's Community Disorders Unit, which sorts through all police reports to identify potential racial incidents and then assigns officers to investigate the incidents.[178]

It is clear from the experiences of localities across the country that effective implementation of the Hate Crimes Statistics Act may require more than developing a national reporting system for hate crimes. Additional ingredients necessary for a successful implementation of the act include:

1) improved outreach to victim communities to encourage hate crime victims to recognize and report hate crimes;
2) improved police training so that officers on the beat can identify hate crimes;
3) the formation of new police units that specialize in identifying, investigating, and reporting hate crimes, as well as guiding community outreach and police training efforts.

To ensure that localities take the necessary measures to provide accurate hate crime data, the U.S. Department of Justice will need to provide guidance to local police departments. Thus, effective implementation of the Hate Crime Statistics Act will require more resources for local police departments and a significant Federal effort to ensure accurate data collection.

---

174   Wilson interview.

175   McDevitt, "The Study of the Implementation of the Massachusetts Civil Rights Act."

176   Ibid., p. 24.

177   For example, Jerry Chagala, Director of San Diego County's human relations commission, which compiles hate crime data for San Diego County, cited several examples where police officers incorrectly identified crimes as racially motivated, including a mother-son fight (mother and son were black) and a burglary of a Filipino woman's house. Jerry Chagala, interview, Mar. 5, 1990.)

178   McDevitt, "The Study of the Implementation of the Massachusetts Civil Rights Act."

Chapter 3

Police-Community Relations

There are serious fissures in the relationship between the Asian American community and the police that leave many Asian Americans without effective access to police protection and some with the fear that they themselves may become the victims of police misconduct. Most police departments are unable to meet the needs of the Asian American communities they serve. This inability stems from a variety of sources, ranging from insufficient resources and police ignorance of and insensitivity towards Asian cultures to outright police hostility towards Asian Americans. Although many police departments are making efforts to reach out to Asian Americans, these efforts are, with some exceptions, inadequate.

To provide a greater public awareness of the problems and encourage possible solutions, this chapter examines several aspects of police relations with the Asian American community. It first discusses major barriers to Asian Americans' access to police protection, particularly language barriers and underreporting of crime. It then addresses the problem of police misconduct, including harassment and mistreatment of Asian Americans, and considers the underrepresentation of Asian Americans among the police. Some police departments have made noteworthy efforts to reach out to Asian Americans, and a fourth section describes some of their approaches. The chapter concludes with a case study of police-community relations in one city: Lowell, Massachusetts.

Asian Americans' Access to Police Protection

For many Asian Americans, access to police protection is severely limited by their lack of English proficiency, by their reluctance to call upon the police for help, or by both. When Asian Americans come into contact with the police, language barriers produce gaps in communication that too often result in Asian Americans' being denied equal protection under the law. The first subsection below discusses the adequacy of the interpretive services used by the police and then gives examples of how Asian Americans suffer when the police fail to provide such services. Many Asian Americans, especially immigrants, are reluctant to seek police protection and tend not to report crimes. This constitutes another major barrier to Asian Americans' access to police protection, which is discussed in the second subsection below.

Language Barriers

Because many Asian Americans, recent immigrants in particular, have limited English proficiency, they need interpreters to communicate effectively with the police. Yet, staff research indicates that interpretive services provided by police departments are generally inadequate to meet the need. For instance, according to a survey of 20 California law enforcement jurisdictions carried out for the California Attorney General's Asian/Pacific Advisory Committee, "[h]alf of the agencies said they do not have sufficient interpreters and stated they could always use more."[1]

---

1   "Survey Analysis"—summary of the results of a telephone survey of 20 selected law enforcement jurisdictions in California carried

Even for those police departments using interpreters, the survey does not distinguish between untrained persons who volunteer their services from time to time and bilingual police officers or paid agency staff. Many police departments rely on local Asian American community organizations to supply interpretive services voluntarily on an emergency basis. Reliance on voluntary interpretive services can have serious drawbacks, however. Voluntary services are not always available when they are needed,[2] and community organizations often find their operations disrupted and their own missions difficult to fulfill because of interruptions occasioned when they supply interpreters to the police and other agencies, such as local government, the courts, and health facilities.[3] Indeed, discussing the Philadelphia Police Department's use of volunteer interpreters, the Philadelphia Mayor's Asian American Advisory Board cautioned that police reliance on volunteer interpreters, in addition to placing undue strain on the volunteers, may result in inaccurate information and poses problems of confidentiality.[4]

Even when police departments do have paid interpreters and/or bilingual officers, they often do not have enough of them or do not use them effectively. Even where police departments have staff interpreters for some Asian languages, they typically do not have interpreters who can collectively cover all Asian languages. Concerning the paucity of interpreter service, the California Attorney General's Asian and Pacific American Advisory Committee stated that, in California:

[o]fficers with bilingual/bicultural skills in Southeast Asian cultures were rare, even in larger police and sheriff's departments whose jurisdictions include substantial refugee populations. The survey indicated that among sworn officers, their language and cultural skills were predominantly in Chinese and Japanese, rather than in languages of those least acculturated.[5]

The San Diego Police Department, among the best, has 5 officers who speak Southeast Asian languages, 18 who speak Tagalog, and 2 who speak Japanese.[6]

Furthermore, some departments, although they may have arranged to provide interpretive services, have not fully informed police officers on the street or the Asian American community about the availability of these services. For instance, in Philadelphia, the Mayor's Asian American Advisory Board found:

The Police Department. . .claims that all Police officers are instructed to contact specific bilingual Police personnel for assistance. In fact, the Board receives reports from private citizens who are routinely called by Police officers for interpretive services even when the Police Department has personnel who are hired to translate in the relevant language; moreover, the Police officers deny knowledge of such bilingual per-

---

out by the Division of Law Enforcement, California Department of Justice, for the Attorney General's Asian/Pacific Advisory Committee, provided by Barbara Takei, committee consultant.

2   In San Diego, for instance, according to a police deputy, "[v]arious Asian community groups also offer help with interpreters on an emergency basis, but it can take an hour to get one to the scene of a crime or emergency." Gregory Gross, "In Multilingual Times, Cops Scramble to Cope," *San Diego Union,* Aug. 14, 1989.

3   Margaret Penrose, Union of Pan Asian Communities, San Diego, interview, Mar. 5, 1990.

4   The advisory committee's report states: "Private citizens who may be willing to act as interpreters in emergencies report that they are routinely called upon, without regard to time of day or availability of City interpreters. These volunteers quickly become overutilized, putting a strain on their own employment and personal lives. In addition, the use of volunteers, although valuable and sometimes necessary, presents problems of confidentiality and accuracy." City of Philadelphia, *Report of the Mayor's Asian American Advisory Board* (Sept. 7, 1989), p. 3 (hereafter cited as *Philadelphia Report.*)

5   State of California, Attorney General's Asian Pacific Advisory Committee, *Final Report* (December 1988), p. 64 (hereafter cited as *Attorney General's Report.*)

6   Gross, "In Multilingual Times."

sonnel and when informed often persist in seeking assistance from private citizens.[7]

Access to interpretive services is particularly critical in emergency situations, and it is in emergencies when they are the least available. It is extremely rare for 911 operators to speak an Asian language. Philadelphia and other cities have attempted to cope with emergency situations by using the services provided by a private organization in Monterey, California, which provides interpretation over the telephone.[8] In Philadelphia the service works as follows.

When a non-English 911 call comes in, if it is in Spanish, it is taken by one of the Spanish-speaking 911 operators working for the police department. If the call is not in Spanish, the 911 operator receiving the call speed dials the supervisor's station, and the supervisor speed dials the Monterey number. The caller, the operator, and Monterey then talk on a conference call. The Monterey service determines the language spoken by the caller and provides an interpreter.[9]

A police department spokesman said that the delay in responding to the caller is at most a minute and usually much less. Only a very small proportion of the city of Philadelphia's 911 calls uses the Monterey service. As an example, in 1 month, Philadelphia had a total of 230,000 911 calls, of which 60 used the Monterey service.[10] The Philadelphia Mayor's Asian American Advisory Board observed, however, that not all Asian-language 911 callers were offered the Monterey interpretive service:

[T]he Police Department has repeatedly assured the Board that persons of limited English proficiency who call the emergency 911 number are automatically connected with an interpretive service that will identify the caller's language and provide assistance by a college-educated interpreter. In fact, the Board continues to receive reports of persons who call 911 and who are told that they cannot be helped because they do not speak English.[11]

The cost of using the Monterey interpretive service is relatively modest,[12] but despite the low cost, most police departments do not subscribe to the service.

In addition to the Monterey interpretive service, some police departments have adopted other approaches to providing emergency services to Asian-speaking 911 callers. In San Diego, for instance, the police department is teaching the residents of Southeast Asian ancestry to dial 911, say "Help, help, help," and leave the phone off the hook. The police trace the call and automatically dispatch an officer to the scene.[13] This approach has the drawback of not

---

7   *Philadelphia Report,* p. 3.

8   The service is provided by AT&T Language Line, 171 Lower Ragsdale Drive, Monterey, CA 93940. The AT&T Language operates both for-profit and not-for-profit services. Not-for-profit services are offered to public agencies, such as police departments, government agencies, schools, and hospitals. Their services are used by hundreds of law enforcement agencies besides the Philadelphia Police Department, including the California Highway Patrol, New York City's 911 services, and the Miami Police Department. They hire staff to meet the anticipated needs of their clients. Staff are usually native speakers of the foreign language and fluent English speakers, are college educated, and have passed a rigorous telephone interpretation test. Harry Moedinger, National Sales Manager, AT&T Language Line, telephone interview, Feb. 27, 1991 (hereafter cited as Moedinger interview).

9   Capt. Howard Farkas, Philadelphia Police Department, telephone interview, Feb. 7, 1990.

10   Ibid.

11   *Philadelphia Report,* p. 3.

12   The not-for-profit fees for AT&T Language Line are: a one-time $1,000 sign-on fee, and $1.94 per minute of service, with a minimum monthly fee of $20. Moedinger interview.

13   Donald K. Abbott, Indochinese Liaison Officer, San Diego Police Department, telephone interview, Jan. 31, 1990 (hereafter cited as Abbott interview).

permitting the caller to receive help immediately over the phone, nor does it help to ensure that the police officers dispatched to the scene will be able to speak the caller's language.

A serious consequence of the general inadequacy of police interpretive services is that when Asian Americans with limited English proficiency are involved in incidents that require police intervention, they often have difficulty getting the police to understand their side of the story. It is rare for the police to use official interpreters in minor incidents, although sometimes they enlist the help of persons on the scene.[14] Sometimes, lacking immediate access to interpreters, the police do not even attempt to take information from limited-English-proficient Asian Americans involved in an incident. Other times, they misinterpret the innocent silence or attempts of Asian Americans to make themselves understood as an admission of guilt or misconstrue faltering English and agitated behavior as indicating hostility or defiance. Staff heard of many instances, ranging from traffic accidents to physical altercations, in which the police, based on only the partial information obtained from English-speaking witnesses, cited or arrested allegedly innocent limited-English-proficient Asian Americans and let English-speaking parties go free. The California Attorney General's Asian and Pacific Islander Advisory Committee observed that when Asian Americans are victims, "communication barriers between the police and the victim can create major problems. One of the most commonly repeated experiences is one in which the perpetrator is allowed to go free and the victim is arrested."[15] These problems are not limited to California. In Philadelphia, the Mayor's Asian American Advisory Board identified "the failure of the Police to solicit or record the testimony of Asian Americans in interracial conflicts" as an issue of concern in the Asian American community.[16] To illustrate this problem, we describe below several examples of situations in which barriers to communications resulted in the miscarriage of justice.

● In January 1987 Mr. Huang, a Chinese American who spoke no English, was given a ticket for double parking. According to a newspaper account of the incident provided by the Coalition Against Anti-Asian Violence, he tried to explain himself, and then sat in the car to wait for the officer to give him his ticket. The officer not only gave him the original ticket for double parking, but also gave him a second ticket and then walked away with Mr. Huang's driver's license. Mr. Huang followed the police officer to ask for the return of his license, at which point the officer handcuffed him, shoved him around, and took him to the police station. Mr. Huang was charged with traffic violations, resisting arrest, and harassing a police officer.[17]

● In 1989 a Cambodian was rear-ended by a motorcyclist in Stockton, California. When the police arrived on the scene, they listened only to the motorcyclist, who was white, and then began to rough up the Cambodian driver and pushed him against his car.[18]

---

14   Asian-language speakers on the scene are not always unbiased observers. For instance, as discussed in greater detail in chap. 7, the husbands of battered Asian American wives with limited English proficiency are often used as interpreters by the police even when the Asian wives have called to seek police protection. Moreover, even when the Asian-language speakers do speak English, they themselves may have limited English proficiency, and they may not be familiar with specialized police terms or the terms necessary to describe an accident or other incident. Thus they are often of limited value for police officers who need effective two-way communication with witnesses.

15   *Attorney General's Report,* p. 61.

16   *Philadelphia Report,* p. 6.

17   "Huang Jin Bao Update—*Centre Daily News* Interview Reveals More Details," *New York Nichibei,* Apr. 9, 1987.

18   Boon Heuang Khoonsrivong, Executive Director, Refugee Resource Center of the Lao Khmer Association, interview in Stockton,

- In a similar incident in Fresno, California, the car driven by a Hmong man was rear-ended by a car driven by a white woman. When the police arrived on the scene, they talked only to the white woman and then issued the Hmong man a citation for rear-ending the white woman.[19]

- In a Southern California shopping center, a white man provoked a fight with a Vietnamese man. The Vietnamese man called the police. When the police arrived, they asked the white man to explain what had happened, but did not ask the Vietnamese man for his side of the story. The Vietnamese man was arrested, charged, and he later pleaded guilty to disorderly conduct.[20]

- On January 31, 1991, New York City traffic police severely beat Zhong Guoqing, a Chinese immigrant, whom they had pulled over for allegedly running a red light. Mr. Zhong apparently did not understand the police officer's request for his registration and got out of his car instead. The police officer became angry and asked him, "Are you a wise guy?" and then pushed him against the car, handcuffed him, and beat him severely about the head. Mr. Zhong was charged with assaulting police, resisting arrest and obstructing governmental administration. He spent the night in the hospital recovering from his wounds, and he may have lost partial vision in one eye. He may bring police brutality charges against the city.[21]

Underreporting of Crime

For a variety of reasons, including the difficulties in communicating with the police cited above, many Asian Americans, especially immigrants, are reluctant to seek police protection and do not report crimes when they occur. In California, for instance, most police departments estimate that only 40-50 percent of crimes against Asian Americans are reported to the police, and several jurisdictions estimate that the percentage of crimes reported is as low as 10 percent.[22] This underreporting of crime constitutes a major barrier to police access by Asian Americans.

An often-cited reason for why Asian Americans seldom seek police protection is that Asians are distrustful of the police. Many immigrant Asians bring with them a legacy of distrust of authority resulting from their unfortunate experiences with governmental or law enforcement agencies in their countries of origin. This distrust is aggravated by poor communications with the police, due not only to the language barriers discussed above, but also to difficulties in bridging the cultural gap that exists between many Asian Americans and the police. Few police officers across the country have been given sufficient training about Asian cultures, and as a result, many Asian Americans receive culturally insensitive treatment from police officers. For instance, when police officers are uninformed about the traditional Hmong healing practice of "coining" their children, which leaves bruises and red marks on the children's skin, they may treat the parents as child abusers. Asian Americans' distrust of the police is enhanced when they hear of or encounter instances of police misconduct such as those discussed in the next section. Finally, Asian Americans may feel alienated from and frustrated by the unresponsiveness of local authorities at all levels, as in the case of Lowell, Massachusetts, detailed below. Whatever the reasons for Asian Americans' distrust of the police, for Asian Americans to have full access to police protection, that distrust must be dispelled.

CA, Feb. 27, 1990.

19   Ibid.

20   Interview with members of the Santa Ana Vietnamese community, Santa Ana, CA, Mar. 2, 1990.

21   Asian American Legal Defense Fund, "Chinese Charge Police Brutality," *Outlook* (date unknown).

22   *Attorney General's Report,* p. 62.

Other factors also contribute to the underreporting of crime by Asian Americans. One of these is immigrant Asians' ignorance of their rights under the American judicial system. Most new immigrants arrive in this country with very little knowledge of our laws and civil rights tradition. They may not know what is and what is not against the law, how to report a crime, what their rights as victims are, and how to pursue recourse when their rights are violated. Additional factors that may contribute to the underreporting of crime by Asian Americans are feelings of shame at having become victims, fear of retribution by the perpetrator (coupled with a lack of confidence in police ability to protect them from such retaliation), and reluctance to undertake the time-consuming and stressful process of dealing with the police at a time when their lives are already complicated by the stresses and strains of adjusting to a new homeland. Enhanced efforts on the part of police departments, local governments, and community groups to inform Asian Americans of their rights, to describe police procedures, to dispel Asian American distrust of the police, and to reach out to Asian Americans in general would help to resolve the problem of underreporting.

Police Misconduct

Police misconduct towards Asian Americans fuels the Asian American community's distrust of the police and contributes to Asian Americans' feeling that they are treated as second-class citizens. Staff learned about instances of police misconduct in various parts of the country, ranging from harassment to cases of serious brutality against Asian Americans.

Police Harassment—There have been incidents across the country of police harassment of Asian Americans, especially Asian American youth. In the absence of systematic monitoring or data gathering, it is not possible to assess the extent of police harassment of Asian American youth. However, community leaders and civil rights advocates across the country have advised Commission staff that undue police harassment of Asian American youth is a common occurrence. Over the past few years Asian youth gangs have increasingly been terrorizing Asian communities across the country. As a result, in many jurisdictions, police believe that Asian American teenagers are heavily involved in gang activities, and it is alleged that they occasionally use this presumption as a justification for stopping young Asians in an apparently random fashion and asking intrusive questions or detaining them.

The following is a summary of an incident that took place in Hercules, California, in August 1989.[23]

Historically a small, predominantly white town of 1,000 residents, Hercules has mushroomed in recent years to 17,000 residents, 25 percent of whom are Filipino.[24] At the time of the incident in question, there had been a general pattern of harassment of Filipino youngsters by Hercules and Pinole (a neighboring city) police. Allegedly, the police frequently stopped young Filipinos for no apparent reason, searched their car trunks, and asked them if they were members of gangs, and occasionally the police broke up group activities, such as basketball games, on public property. Until the incident in August, the parents of the Filipino teenagers

---

23 For more details on the incident and its resolution as described by the city manager of Hercules, see Marilyn E. Leuck, City Manager, city of Hercules (CA), letter to James S. Cunningham, Assistant Staff Director for Programs, Policy, and Research, U.S. Commission on Civil Rights, re Comment on Draft Report: Civil Rights Issues Facing Asian Americans in the 1990s, Oct. 4, 1991, in the appendix.

24 1990 Census data provided by Marilyn Leuck, City Manager, Hercules, CA, and Johnny Ng, "Filipinos Charge Bias Against Hercules Cops," *Asian Week*, Dec. 22, 1989.

were unaware of the situation, because their children were afraid to tell their parents.[25]

According to a complaint filed on November 17, 1989, with the Hercules Police Chief on behalf of 11 Hercules teenagers and their parents, on August 28, Hercules police, responding to a complaint that a fight was taking place, arrested 18 youths who were in the vicinity of the fight, all of whom were Filipino, Latino, or black, and charged them with disturbing the peace and trespassing. White youth who were in the vicinity were allegedly not detained and told by the officers to go home. The complaint charged that the arrested youth, some of whom were unnecessarily handcuffed, were driven to the police station and detained for "from two to five hours";[26] that the youths were photographed and fingerprinted; that several of the youths were refused permission to call their parents; and that one girl was refused permission to use the bathroom for over an hour and a half. The complaint charged further that the arresting officers used excessive force and had sought to intimidate the youths, including threatening to hurt them.[27]

Responding to the allegations, the Hercules city manager denied that the Hercules police had selected minority youth for detention, pointing out that they had detained "only those individuals who the officer had reasonable cause to believe had violated the law. . ."[28] The city manager also said that the longest any of the youths

had been held was 3 hours and 45 minutes;[29] that photographing and fingerprinting was warranted under the circumstances;[30] that it had been too noisy in the booking room for the youths to call their parents, but that officers had contacted the parents instead;[31] and the reason one girl had been refused permission to use the bathroom was that there was no female officer to accompany her.[32] The city manager further said that there was no evidence that the police officers had used excessive force or sought to intimidate the youths.[33]

The youths' parents reached a settlement with the city of Hercules at the end of 1990. The city agreed to modify its procedures to allow detained youth to phone home and to give them privacy in bathrooms. Furthermore, there have been no reports of police harassment in Hercules since the complaint was filed in November 1989.[34] Tensions may have been further eased following a Contra Costa Human Rights Commission Hearing on unfair treatment of minority youth by school and law enforcement officials held on February 10, 1990, at which the Filipino parents and students (along with other minorities) testified.[35]

A serious incident of police harassment of Asian Americans in Revere, Massachusetts, which has a large Southeast Asian (largely Cambodian) population, is recounted below.[36]

25   William Tamayo, Esq., Asian Law Caucus, telephone interview, Jan. 22, 1990.

26   William R. Tamayo, Esq, Asian Law Caucus, and Mark Morodomi, Esq., and John M. Crew, Esq., American Civil Liberties Union of Northern California, letter to Hercules Chief of Police Russell S. Quinn, Re Complaint of Police Misconduct and Request for Administrative Investigation, Nov. 17, 1989, p. 4.

27   Ibid.

28   Marilyn Leuck, City Manager, Hercules (CA), letter to Mark Morodomi, William Tamayo, and John Crew Re City of Hercules' Response to Complaints of Police Misconduct on Aug. 28, 1989, Feb. 13, 1990, p. 4 (hereafter cited as Hercules response).

29   Ibid., p. 8.

30   Ibid., pp. 6-7.

31   Ibid., p. 7.

32   Ibid., p. 10.

33   Ibid., pp. 6, 9-10.

34   William Tamayo, Asian Law Caucus, telephone interview, Jan. 9, 1991.

35   Contra Costa County (CA) Human Relations Commission, *Report of the Hearing on Youth in Contra Costa County* (Feb. 10, 1990).

On June 1, 1991, a young Italian American man who had recently moved to Revere was murdered. Witnesses said that he was brutally beaten and stabbed repeatedly by a group of Asian men. The Revere Police Department, which has no Asian American police officers and has no access to interpreters, was unable to solve the case and apprehend the murderers quickly and came under increasing criticism from the victim's family.

On July 1, in an attempt to force information about the murder to the surface, a team of 40 Revere police officers, along with representatives of the Immigration and Naturalization Service, made a 2-hour sweep through a Cambodian neighborhood in search of persons with outstanding warrants and possible illegal aliens. "We wanted to break open a case,"[37] said one of the police officers involved in the sweep. Cambodian Americans living in Revere were frightened and angered by the police sweep.

Staff were also told about incidents of police harassment in Lowell, Massachusetts, and San Diego. In Lowell there was an alleged pattern of Massachusetts State police officers randomly stopping Cambodian youth driving on State roads and searching their cars for weapons.[38] A couple of years ago, police in San Diego allegedly entered a cafe frequented by Asian youth, strip-searched everyone on the premises, and took pictures of the Asians for their gang files. San Diego Police apparently stopped this type of behavior when threatened with a lawsuit.[39]

Police Brutality—Commission staff have learned of a number of incidents of police brutality against Asian Americans across the country, yet these incidents received little national publicity. Furthermore, it appears that the police officers involved in these incidents are not always disciplined, in part because of the reluctance of many Asian Americans to file a complaint against the police. Some illustrative examples are described below.

● One morning in early January 1987, New York City police arrived at the door of the Chinatown apartment of a Chinese couple named Wong to follow up on a complaint by a cable-television serviceman that the Wongs were illegally using cable service and had threatened him with a knife. When the Wongs answered the door, they asked to see a warrant. The police allegedly responded by beating down the door and hitting both of the Wongs (Mrs. Wong was hit by handcuffs and subsequently required 12 stitches in the face). The Wongs and two relatives, named Woo, who were also in the apartment, were all arrested. According to the Wongs, the police asked them, "Why don't you Chinese go back to China?" The Wongs and the Woos were charged with second-degree assault, resisting arrest, and obstructing governmental administration. They were not released until the following afternoon. Although the charges against the Wongs and the Woos were later dropped for insufficient evidence, no disciplinary action was brought against the police officers involved. The police department stated that the Wongs themselves had become violent and hit the police officers. The Wongs filed a lawsuit against the New York City Police Department, and in 1989 the suit was settled for $90,000.[40]

---

36 The following account is based on Amy Sessler, "Revere Slaying, Police Probe Reveal Raw Ethnic, Racial Nerves," *Boston Globe,* June 16, 1991, p. 30, and Chris Block, "Sweep Upsets Asians in Revere," *Boston Globe,* July 3, 1991.

37 Lt. Col. Thomas Spartichino, Massachusetts State Police, as quoted in Block, "Sweep Upsets Asians."

38 Sam Bok Sok, Coalition for a Better Acre, interview in Lowell, MA, Feb. 12, 1990.

39 Margaret Penrose, Union of Pan Asian Communities, interview in San Diego, CA, Mar. 5, 1990.

40 "Chinatown, NY—Alleged Police Brutality Against Chinese American Family," *New York Nichibei,* Jan. 29, 1987; Elaine Rivera, "Barriers Often Conceal Prejudice Against Asians," *Newsday,* Jan. 30, 1987; Elaine Rivera, "DA Drops Assault Charges In Chinatown Brutality Case," *Newsday,* Apr. 2, 1987; Barbara Lippman, "Chinatown Brouhaha: Family Claims Brutality, Sues Police,"

- In September 1987 a Korean student was stopped in Manhattan for a traffic violation he committed while on his bicycle. According to a newspaper account, witnesses saw him being forced off his bicycle onto the ground by the police, who proceeded to beat his head against the pavement. The student was then arrested for traffic violations, disorderly conduct, and obstructing governmental administration. The witnesses followed the student to the police station, where, they claim, the police made a reference to the student's "Asian nose."[41]

- In July 1989 a Philadelphia grand jury indicted a police officer for illegally arresting a Southeast Asian man to "appease his neighbors," who did not want him living in the neighborhood. The officer was charged with falsely arresting Mr. Phomsaath inside his home on charges of public intoxication, handcuffing him and beating him with a nightstick. The officer booked the man at the police station under the name "Mao Tse-Dung."[42]

- In San Jose, California, a Vietnamese man was stopped by police officers as he was walking home from work. A white police officer reportedly threatened him with a knife while asking questions. Eventually he was let go unharmed. He never reported the incident, but it became widely known in the San Jose Vietnamese community and was cited to staff as an example of a pattern of frequent police harassment of Asians in San Jose.[43]

Representation of Asian Americans Among the Police

Asian Americans are noticeably underrepresented among police officers in most law enforcement jurisdictions across the country. For instance, only 1.7 percent of officers in the California State Highway Patrol are Asian Americans, and in Los Angeles, where Asians constitute roughly 10 percent of the population, only 1.8 percent of city police officers are Asian.[44] The problem of underrepresentation is particularly severe for new immigrant groups from Southeast Asia and elsewhere. As an example, Lowell, Massachusetts, a city whose population is roughly one-quarter Cambodian, has no Cambodian police officers. This lack of representation may severely restrict police access to information about crime in Asian American communities, which in turn may hamper police efforts to protect these communities from growing criminal activity.

In interviews with many Asian American community leaders across the country, staff learned that the dearth of Asian police officers is a common source of frustration for members of Asian American communities in all parts of the country. Typically, Asian Americans, especially those belonging to immigrant communities, feel that the police are not interested in recruiting Asian police officers. They cite lack of efforts to inform Asian Americans about vacancies in police departments or about the procedures for applying for police positions, failure to relax arbitrarily restrictive requirements for becoming a police officer, and the lack of affirmative plans to recruit Asian, particularly Southeast Asian, police officers as evidence that police departments are not truly interested in increasing Asian American representation. They also cite the length of time required between initial application and acceptance into police training as a

New York Daily News, July 29, 1987; and Helen Thorpe, "Chinese Family's Suit Alleging Police Brutality Ends in $90,000 Settlement," *The New York Observer,* Aug. 14, 1989.

41 Howard W. French, "Bicyclist Says Officers Beat Him As They Held Him in Traffic Case," *New York Times,* Sept. 6, 1987, and Coalition Against Anti-Asian Violence, "Police Brutality: Incident Summaries," provided by Mini Liu.

42 Christopher Hepp, "Officer Accused of Beating Asian," *Philadelphia Inquirer,* July 21, 1989.

43 Me Le Ho, Ray Lou, Cal H. B. Nguyen, Zoon Nguyen, and Vu-Duc Vuong, group interview in San Jose, CA, Feb. 21, 1990.

44 *Attorney General's Report,* p. 74.

major barrier for many Asian Americans seeking to become police officers.

Police, on the other hand, cite the difficulty of attracting Asian Americans, who allegedly prefer other careers or do not have the requisite qualifications. One Asian American police officer, who was in charge of Asian gang enforcement for his department, told staff that many Asian parents do not want their children to become police officers, because they have negative experiences with or impressions of the police, because the job is too dangerous, or because the pay and prestige are too low. He also claimed that many Asian Americans, especially new immigrants, are not sufficiently aggressive to do the job. He said that his police department had been unable to attract a Vietnamese police officer, because there were too few qualified Vietnamese and because his department was in competition with every other law enforcement agency in California.[45]

It is not at all evident, however, that Asian Americans do not want to become police officers. Asian community members dispute this contention.[46] In virtually every Asian community visited by Commission staff, community leaders were able to cite examples of Asian Americans who had sought to become police officers but who had either been discouraged from applying or had not been accepted. Furthermore, there is a pervasive stereotype that Asians are not sufficiently aggressive to be police officers. As pointed out in the California Attorney General's report, this stereotype works to the disadvantage of Asian Americans seeking to become police officers, since it likely colors the perceptions of those who evaluate Asian American candidates.

The stereotype of Asian/Pacific Islander Americans as subservient, unassertive, and lacking communications skills can create institutional bias that makes it more difficult for Asians to pass the subjective portions of the screening process.[47]

The report continues:

Asian/Pacific Islander Americans may be eliminated by psychological evaluation, because they are defined as lacking the desirable psychological characteristics for the rigors of the job. The definition of the desirable psychological characteristics for an officer is an issue that has yet to be resolved, and care must be taken to insure that such criteria [do]. . .not unfairly impact Asian/Pacific Islander Americans.[48]

For those from Southeast Asia and other recent immigrants, two major barriers to employment as police officers appear to be lack of citizenship status and lack of English-language proficiency. Since most Southeast Asians who are old enough to be police officers are immigrants who came to this country in the 1980s, very few have lived in the United States long enough to become citizens. Most police departments require all police officers to be United States citizens, and thus many Southeast Asians are automatically disqualified. Given that good police-community relations depend in large part upon group representation within the police force, it is important for police departments to reexamine the necessity of any requirement, such as citizenship status, that automatically excludes a large proportion of a group that is seriously underrepresented among police officers. Indeed, some police departments have relaxed the citizenship requirement in an effort to increase the representation of immigrant Asians in their police forces.[49]

---

45   Ignatius Chinn, Northern California Asian Police Officer's Association, telephone interview, Feb. 20, 1990.

46   *Attorney General's Report,* p. 75.

47   Ibid., p. 76.

48   Ibid., p. 77.

49   Ibid., p. 76.

For Asian immigrants who seek to become police officers, limited English-language proficiency is a barrier that is extremely difficult to overcome and hence requires special remedies. In most jurisdictions across the country, to be accepted for police training, applicants are required to pass a battery of tests, including tests that measure the applicant's fluency in speaking and writing English. Many police officers contend that good written English ability is necessary to write a police report. They also contend that good spoken English is necessary for the police officer to communicate over the radio. According to one police officer, "[i]t doesn't do us any good if they're fluent in their native language but they can't handle English well enough to use the radio or take a report."[50] A San Diego police officer told staff of a Southeast Asian probationary police officer who finally was not accepted into the police force because he could not make himself understood over the radio.[51] Police departments can help overcome the language barrier by offering special English classes to candidates. Furthermore, efforts to establish precisely what level of English proficiency is necessary for the job and to develop appropriate tests of English proficiency could help to eliminate the suspicion that the language requirements for Asian American police officers are set arbitrarily high.

In San Francisco, the police department was sued because of the underrepresentation of Asians on its police force. The suit resulted in a 1979 consent decree that "established specific goals and timetables for hiring persons bilingual in Chinese."[52] In most other cities, however, Asian Americans have not been included in lawsuits to increase minority representation among the police. When they are under court order to increase the representations of women and non-Asian minorities in their forces, police departments have much less incentive to increase the number of Asian police officers.[53]

Police Department Asian American Outreach Approaches

Police misconduct toward Asian Americans and the underrepresentation of Asian Americans on police forces across the country are compounding the problem of poor police-community relations caused by language barriers and underreporting of crime by Asian Americans. To improve their relationship with Asian Americans, some police departments are experimenting with alternative ways of reaching out to the Asian American communities in their cities. As part of a new trend in police departments across the country, commonly referred to as "community policing," many police departments are trying two approaches. The first approach entails hiring Asian American community service officers (CSOs) to help regular police officers in their dealings with Asian American communities, while the second approach involves setting up Asian American police advisory boards.

The CSOs, hired under the first approach, are noncommissioned police officers who take on

---

50   Gross, "In Multilingual Times."

51   Abbott interview.

52   *Attorney General's Report*, p. 75.

53   The Los Angeles Police Department, for instance, is under a court order to increase its representation of women, blacks, and Hispanics, but not Asians. Staff were told that Asians were hesitant to sue to be included in the consent decree, because they feared that in the wake of the Supreme Court's *Martin v. Wilks* decision (109 S.Ct. 2180 (1989)), the entire decree could unravel if they sought to be included in it. Staff interview with Stewart Kwoh and Kathryn Imahara, Asian Pacific American Legal Center, Mar. 1, 1990. The U.S. Commission on Civil Rights has endorsed proposed legislation, the Civil Rights Act of 1990, now called the Civil Rights Act of 1991 (H.R. 1, 102nd Cong., 1st Sess.), which would undo the effects of the *Wilks* decision. U.S. Commission on Civil Rights, *Report on the Civil Rights Act of 1990* (July 1990).

many, but not all of the police officers' duties. A good example of a police department using this approach is San Diego, which has 12 CSOs serving San Diego's Indochinese communities. In San Diego, CSOs wear uniforms and carry badges but do not have guns. They work out of a storefront office located in a heavily Indochinese neighborhood. They take reports in their storefront office, and they are also sent out to take reports in the field. In addition to taking reports, San Diego's CSOs are involved in proactive activities, such as attending community gatherings, juvenile counseling, helping battered women get temporary restraining orders, and making Asian-language videos. They also help the police force gather information on crimes and gang activity within the Asian community by recruiting paid and volunteer informants. They are given training in cardiopulmonary resuscitation (CPR) and disaster preparedness.[54]

A second example of a police department using this approach is the Los Angeles Police Department:

The Los Angeles Police Department has two storefronts serving Asian/Pacific Islander communities, one located in a Korean neighborhood; the other in a Chinese neighborhood. Both storefronts are the result of organized community demand for such operations, and subsequent donations from individuals and organizations within the community helped provide space and needed materials. The storefronts are staffed by a police officer and a bilingual community person whose salary is paid by community donations and the police department.[55]

Although CSOs are potentially an extremely valuable way of reaching out to Asian communities, their use may have some unintended consequences. There are some reports that CSOs are treated as second-class citizens within many police departments.[56] There also might be a tendency for police departments to rely on CSOs rather than intensifying their efforts to recruit Asians as regular police officers.

The second common "community policing" approach is to set up Asian American police advisory boards. These boards consist of representatives of the Asian American community who meet regularly with the police to voice the concerns of the Asian American community and who help gain community support for police investigations of criminal activity within the Asian American community. An example of such a board is San Diego's Southeast Asian Refugee-Police Advisory Task Force, set up in November 1989.[57] A similar advisory committee operates in Oakland. Oakland's Asian Advisory Committee:

---

54   Abbott interview. Requirements for becoming a CSO in San Diego are fairly rigorous. CSOs must have a high school diploma, California driver's license, and a green card or I94 form. Before being accepted, applicants must also take a written exam, fill out background packages, undergo a background investigation and a psychological profile, take polygraph exams, and finally submit to an oral interview. CSOs in San Diego are full-time employees. Starting pay is $17,500, and the pay rises to $24,500 after 2 years.

55   *Attorney General's Report*, p. 65. Los Angeles also has an Asian Task Force, which is staffed with 10 police officers who speak Korean, Japanese, Chinese, Thai, and Tagalog, to provide expertise to police investigations.

56   Steven Thom, U.S. Department of Justice, Community Relations Service, San Francisco Office, telephone interview, Feb. 20, 1990.

57   San Diego Police Department, *Introducing the Southeast Asian Refugee-Police Advisory Task Force* (Nov. 27, 1989). The proposed functions for the task force are given as follows:

"1) To channel information from the Southeast Asian Refugee communities to the Chief of Police.

"2) To serve as a conduit for information from the Police Department to the Southeast Asian refugee communities.

"3) To provide backup assistance for translation and intervention where language and cultural differences impede police work.

"4) To enhance the image of the Police Department and community visibility through jointly sponsored intercultural events.

"5) To develop rapport with the Southeast Asian business community. The business community is a critical component in refugee communities. Business owners provide leadership, funds, and general contact within the communities. In the course of doing business they encounter public safety issues and need to consult with the police. The police also need to consult with the business lead-

[deals] with issues ranging from affirmative action in the Oakland Police department to its recent emphasis on responding to the criminal justice needs of the local Southeast Asian population.

The Asian Advisory Committee is currently working on resolving crime problems related to language and culture differences, including the reluctance of recent immigrants and refugees to report crime. As a result of cooperation among Committee representatives and Asian/Pacific Islander communities, the Oakland Police Department established four outreach offices, located and staffed to serve respective Laotian, Vietnamese, Cambodian, and Chinese communities.[58]

For such advisory boards to work well, however, there needs to be a real commitment on the part of both the police department and the Asian community to make them work. Otherwise, there is a danger that the advisory boards will become tokens that the police can point to as evidence that they are making efforts to reach out to the Asian community, when in fact their outreach efforts are wholly inadequate.

Efforts are underway across the country to encourage innovative approaches to providing police protection to ethnic communities. For instance, on April 2-4, 1991, the Office of Refugee Resettlement and the Family Support Administration of the U.S. Department of Health and Human Services sponsored a joint conference with the Community Relations Service of the U.S. Department of Justice, entitled "Building Bridges: National Southeast Asian Refugee/Law Enforcement Conference," which brought together law enforcement officials and Southeast Asian community leaders from across the country to exchange ideas and information about ways to improve the relations between Southeast Asians and the police. Participants at this conference generally agreed that a broad approach to improved relations was needed, including attacking problems at their roots rather

than adopting the traditional police posture of responding to symptoms (i.e., taking steps necessary to ward off criminal activity rather than concentrating only on arresting perpetrators after a crime has taken place.) As examples, participants advocated police and community efforts to reach out to Southeast Asian youth in schools and community centers, to help facilitate the transition of new immigrants into this country, and to help deal with the breakdown of the traditional Asian family structure that often occurs among Southeast Asian refugee families and leaves Southeast Asian youth lost and without guidance.

Lowell, Massachusetts: A Case Study of Police-Community Relations

Relations between minorities and the police usually mirror the relations between minorities and the community at large. They cannot be fully understood in isolation from the broader context of the local political and economic climate and interracial/ethnic relations. The following discussion of police-community relations in Lowell, Massachusetts, is embedded in the larger context of interracial/ethnic relations in Lowell. The case study of Lowell demonstrates the strains on those intergroup relations that can occur when a small community is transformed overnight by a large influx of immigrants and refugees, many of whom are limited English proficient, who require extensive commitments of social service and other resources to help them integrate into the community.

Lowell was established in 1826 and grew with the booming textile industry along the Merrimack River, attracting successive waves of immigrants. By the 1890s, when the textile industry reached its peak, Lowell was widely recognized as a city built by immigrants working in textile

---

ers over these same issues."

58   *Attorney General's Report*, pp. 65-66.

mills. For about five decades starting in the 1920s, Lowell endured a long period of economic depression. In the mid-1970s, however, benefiting from a statewide economic turnaround, Lowell experienced an economic revitalization. The city's vacant industrial land area diminished from 100 acres in 1978 to none in 1987, and over the same period its unemployment rate dropped from 13.8 to 3 percent.[59]

Lowell's economic opportunities attracted Southeast Asian immigrants and refugees to the city in large numbers during the early 1980s. In 1980 the size of the Southeast Asian population in Lowell was less than 100, but it had increased three-hundred-fold to roughly 30,000 by the mid-1980s. Then, Southeast Asians made up 30 percent of Lowell's population (Cambodians at 25 percent, and Laotians and Vietnamese at 5 percent).[60] The phenomenal growth of Lowell's Southeast Asian population during the early 1980s posed two serious dilemmas for the city of Lowell: how to educate Southeast Asian children, most of whom had limited English proficiency, and how to provide adequate police protection to Southeast Asian residents. Lowell's failure to solve the problem of educating Southeast Asian children serves as a backdrop for understanding the subsequent breakdown of police-community relations.

By 1987 the proportion of Lowell's school children who were minorities had grown to 40 percent. Faced with a massive influx of students, the Lowell School Committee set up makeshift classrooms in nonschool buildings, often resulting in substandard, unsafe conditions for students (e.g., a basement boiler room, an auditorium storage area, and a converted bathroom with a toilet stall in it). Incoming minority students were generally assigned either to the makeshift classrooms or to specific schools. As a result, Lowell's public schools became highly segregated. For example, in 1986 one school was 100 percent minority, and other schools had 74, 72, 55, and 53 percent minority enrollment, respectively, while a few schools had minority enrollment as low as 4.2 percent and 3.6 percent.[61] The Lowell school system had also failed to build necessary teaching personnel to implement much-needed bilingual/bicultural education programs in the Lowell public schools.[62]

Concerned with high dropout rates among Lowell's language-minority students as well as the substandard educational environment and insufficient teaching personnel in Lowell's schools, minority parents and community leaders made repeated attempts to improve the situation, consulting and pleading with city and school officials, but to no avail. In one of the meetings with the Lowell School Committee, parents of language-minority students requested interpreters, since at least half of the 100 or more people present, mostly parents of Hispanic and Southeast Asian students, could not speak or understand English. Yet one committee member left the meeting saying he would not attend a school committee meeting that was not conducted in English. His departure broke the quorum, touching off an "explosive racial confrontation."[63] During the ensuing melee, this committee member was quoted as saying, "I've seen enough of you on the streets" to an angry Hispanic parent.[64]

---

59   This account is drawn from Peter Nien-chu Kiang, "Southeast Asian Parent Empowerment: The Challenge of Changing Demographics in Lowell, MA," *Asian American Policy Review,* vol. 1, no. 1 (1990).

60   Since the mid-1980s the Southeast Asian population in Lowell has declined, and Asians currently constitute less than 11 percent of Lowell's population. "Asians in America: 1990 Census, Classification by States," *Asian Week,* August 1991, p. 30.

61   Hispanic Parents Advisory Council v. Kouleharas, Civ. Action No. 87-1968-MA (D.Mass., 1987), at 18.

62   *Id.* at 22.

63   Nancy Costello, "Committeeman Sparks Racial Clash at Meeting," *Lowell Sun,* May 7, 1987, p. 1.

64   Ibid.

In addition to such incidents of outright racial hostility, advocates of minority students' education encountered an entrenched barrier preventing the hiring of bilingual/ESL (English as a Second Language) teachers: the city and the school committee required that candidates for bilingual/ESL teaching positions pass the National Teachers Examination (NTE). Many of the candidates, for whom English was a second language, were unable to pass this exam, which had not been validated for language-minority test takers. Under State law, however, Lowell and the school committee are "free to abandon reliance on the NTE and substitute a more equitable measure for hiring bilingual/ESL teachers, but they have deliberately refused to do so."[65] Because of this requirement, most of the candidates for bilingual/ESL positions were effectively barred from attaining eligibility for permanent employee status. They were forced to work instead as temporary teacher aides, which meant lower pay and fewer fringe benefits.

The city and school system's apparent intransigence in providing for the needs of minority students and the occasional incidents of racial hostility, in addition to the deprivation of equal educational opportunity for the city's minority students, finally prompted concerned parents to file a suit with the Federal district court against the Lowell School Committee in 1987.[66] The suit resulted in a consent decree designed to implement a long series of comprehensive remedial programs providing relief for the concerns of the Hispanic and Southeast Asian parents.[67]

Aggravating this already poor situation was a series of events that took place over the past few years that added to the concern, worry, and apprehension in Lowell's Southeast Asian community. These events are briefly described below:

● A few years ago, a proposal for the construction in the city park of a 12.5-foot concrete statue as a symbol of the Southeast Asian contribution in Lowell was turned down by the city council. One council member allegedly said, "I fought in the Vietnam War, and I don't want that stuff in our city park."[68]

● On September 15, 1987, an 11-year-old white student accosted Vandy Phorng, a 13-year-old Cambodian student, while Vandy and his brothers were walking along the canal near their home. After making racial comments about Vandy's background, the white youth punched Vandy in the face, dragged him down a flight of stairs to the canal, and pushed him into the water. Vandy was carried away by the strong current and drowned.[69]

● On May 12, 1989, a male University of Lowell student harassed a female board member of the Cambodian Mutual Assistance Association. He blocked the Southeast Asian woman from entering a Burger King restaurant in Lowell, saying, "What do you think—you own this country? Go back to your f—ing country or I will kill you." On May 13, she received a phone call from a man saying, "If you don't go back to your f—ing country, I will kill you." She recognized the voice as that of her harasser. On June 1 he was arrested on a criminal warrant for assault and battery, threatening to kill, and a civil rights violation.[70]

---

65   Ibid., at 23.

66   Hispanic Parents Advisory Council v. Kouleharas, Civ. Action No. 87-1968 (D.Mass. 1987).

67   Lowell Public Schools, *Voluntary Compliance Plan Pursuant to Title VI of the Civil Rights Act of 1964* (Nov. 9, 1988). For further details on this suit, see chap. 4 of this report.

68   Sam Bok Sok, Coalition for a Better Acre, interview, Feb. 12, 1990.

69   Doris Sue Wong, "Day of Fishing Ends in Violent Death for Lowell Boy," *Boston Globe,* Sept. 23, 1987; L. Kim Tan, "Family Demands Justice in Teen's Slaying," *Boston Herald,* Sept. 23, 1987, cited in Kiang, "Southeast Asian Parent Empowerment."

70   Nancy Costello, "ULowell Student Charged in Racial Threat, Assault on S.E. Asian Leader," *Lowell Sun,* June 9, 1989, p. 13;

• In the November 1989 election, voters in Lowell endorsed a nonbinding referendum declaring English as the city's official language by a margin of 3 to 1 in one of the largest turnouts in recent years. The sponsor of this referendum was the same school committee member who had allegedly manifested racist behavior in the past and precipitated a racial clash by refusing to allow interpreters for parents with limited English proficiency (see above). This person publicly stated his intention to force the issue at the State and Federal levels. Southeast Asians and Hispanics interpreted the outcome of the referendum as a reflection of underlying antiminority sentiment. The Southeast Asian opponents of the English-only movement fear that "it will inspire and legitimize discrimination."[71]

• As previously recounted in chapter 2, in January 1990, John Silber, then the candidate for the Democratic nomination for Governor of Massachusetts (and eventually the Democratic nominee) was widely quoted as making anti-Cambodian remarks. He called Massachusetts "a welfare magnet" that had "suddenly become popular for people who are accustomed to living in the tropical climate," and he said, "Why should Lowell be the Cambodian capital of America? It is extraordinary. Why should they all be concentrated in one place? This needs to be examined."[72]

These events added to Southeast Asians' distrust of and isolation from the broader Lowell community. Sensing anti-Asian hostility in the outside world and burdened with the struggle of surviving in a strange country, most Southeast Asians lived secluded lives within their ethnic communities. An effective bridge of communication did not exist between Southeast Asians and the city of Lowell. Thus, when Southeast Asians increasingly became the victims of robberies and attacks by community youth gangs, they became fearful for their physical safety, but they were reluctant to turn to the police for help. The vulnerability of Southeast Asians in Lowell and the inability of Lowell police to protect them is underscored in the following incident.

At 10:00 p.m. on June 28, 1990, two masked gunmen pumped four bullets into Chhoeung Ley, a Cambodian man, inside his home. Robbery by a Southeast Asian youth gang was suspected by the police. The police investigation of the murder did not make meaningful progress, and the police appealed to the Southeast Asian community to come forward with pertinent information. The police appeal for murder clues was met with unresponsive reticence on the part of the community, however. Southeast Asian community leaders feel that the lackluster response to the police appeal for information arose out of a general perception in the Southeast Asian community that the Lowell police as a whole[73] are insensitive to and neglectful of Southeast Asian concerns and that the police make overtures to the community only when they desperately need the help of the Southeast Asian community. More significantly, the police are viewed neither as worthy of community trust nor as capable of protecting informants against possible retaliation by the perpetrators.[74] The

Nancy Costello, "Judge Bars Student from Thai Activist," *Lowell Sun,* July 15, 1989, p. 1; Jessie Yuan and J. Shiao, "Dr. Prem Suksawat, Victim of Racial Harassment in Lowell," *The [Asian American Resource Workshop] Newsletter,* August 1989, p. 1.

71 Jules Crittenden, "City Campaign May Spawn Statewide Ballot Battle," *Lowell Sun,* Oct. 26, 1989, p. 1; Jules Crittenden "Lowell Voters Say 'Yes' to English Referendum," *Lowell Sun,* Nov. 8, 1989, p. 1.

72 Constance L. Hays, "Remarks Inflame Massachusetts Contest," *New York Times,* Jan. 27, 1990.

73 In general, community leaders thought that Officer Jeffrey Davidson, who has served as the one-man, part-time community relations officer in Lowell, has done his best within limited resources.

74 Vera Godley, Executive Director, Cambodian Mutual Assistance Association of Greater Lowell, Inc., telephone interview, Oct. 17, 1990 (hereafter cited as Godley interview, Oct. 17, 1990). In her official capacity, Ms. Godley was conveying the general sense of

Ley murder case remains unsolved after 15 months.[75]

The Ley murder surfaced the ordeal of fear and intimidation many Southeast Asians have been forced to live under and also revealed the inadequacy of police protection in Lowell, as well as police inability to penetrate ethnic communities. A few days after the murder, Lowell's mayor appealed to the Southeast Asian community to come forward with information regarding the case and agreed with community leaders on the urgent need to recruit Southeast Asian police officers.[76] However, the mayor's recruitment pledge was received by most Southeast Asians in Lowell as an empty political gesture necessitated by the emergency at hand. Fifteen months after the mayor's pledge, the Lowell police were still without Southeast Asian police officers.[77]

The Ley murder was only one of a series of crimes by Southeast Asian youth gangs and others against members of Lowell's Southeast Asian communities, and most of these crimes were not resolved by the police. According to a police source, in the past 3 years there have been approximately 40 cases of shooting, armed home invasion, robbery, and extortion against Southeast Asians in Lowell, and police have cleared between 30 percent and 40 percent of the cases.[78] On the average, then, every month at least one crime committed against the Southeast Asian community is reported to the police, and two cases out of three go unsolved. This fact alone would explain why, as alleged by community leaders, Southeast Asians in Lowell feel vulnerable and unprotected by the police.[79] Moreover, many community leaders suspect that Southeast Asians in Lowell seriously underreport crimes committed against themselves, particularly when crimes appear to be committed by other Asian Americans.[80] Thus, the actual frequency of crimes and the rate of unresolved cases may be much higher than apparent from police records.

The seriousness of this situation invites inquiry as to why there are no Southeast Asian police officers on the city police force and how the police can offer equal protection to Southeast Asian citizens without Southeast Asian representation on the force. At a February 1990 meeting with Commission staff,[81] city officials

---

the board members of the association.

75   As of Oct. 1, 1991, 15 months after the murder, police had made no arrest, and the murder was still under active investigation. John Guilfoyle, Inspector, Lowell Police Department, telephone interview, Oct. 1, 1991 (hereafter cited as Guilfoyle interview).

76   Melissa Franks and Patrick Cook, "Police Link Gang to Murder: Community Leaders 'Frustrated' With Rash of Violence," *Lowell Sun*, July 1, 1990, p. 1; Doug Pizzi, "Police Appeal for Murder Clues: Community Lives in Fear of Gangs," *Lowell Sun*, July 2, 1990, p. 1; Patrick Cook, "Police Appeal For Murder Clues: Murder Investigation Hitting Roadblocks," *Lowell Sun*, July 2, 1990, p. 1.

77   Jeffrey Davidson, Community Relations Officer, Lowell Police Department, telephone interview, Oct. 1, 1991.

78   Guilfoyle interview. For a chronological summary account of the prominent cases, see Patrick Cook, "Chronology of Crime in Asian Community," *Lowell Sun*, July 3, 1990, p. 27.

79   In 1991 there were two gang-related murder cases in Lowell involving Southeast Asian youths (the To Ky murder and the drive-by shooting at a playground) and several incidents of home invasion of Southeast Asian families. In all of these cases, however, suspects have been arrested and are being duly processed by the judicial system. (Guilfoyle interview.) Southeast Asian community leaders also sense a positive change in the general climate of police community relations. The district attorney's office has shown interest in Southeast Asian community issues, and Lowell police have become responsive to the concerns of the Southeast Asian communities. (Vera Godley, Executive Director, Cambodian Mutual Assistance Association of Greater Lowell, Inc. (CMAA), telephone interview, Oct. 7, 1991; Charinthy Uong, President, CMAA, telephone interview, Oct. 8, 1991 (hereafter cited as Uong interview).)

80   Godley interview, Oct. 17, 1990.

81   City officials present at the meeting held on Feb. 12, 1990, included the mayor, city manager, city affirmative action officer, and po-

stated that they were fully aware of the need to recruit police officers of Southeast Asian ancestry, but that their good faith efforts in recruitment had not succeeded. The officials gave several reasons for their recruitment failure: 1) Southeast Asians do not take statewide qualifying examinations (i.e., they do not seem interested in becoming police officers); 2) U.S. citizenship is required to be a police officer, but most Southeast Asians in Lowell have not earned their citizenship yet; and 3) many Southeast Asians in Lowell are limited in English proficiency and lack necessary understanding of the workings of U.S. society and its culture. The officials further claimed that the city is prohibited from requesting waivers of the statewide examination for Southeast Asian candidates because of an earlier court order regarding black and Hispanic hires in the police force.[82]

Contradicting the city officials' contention that Southeast Asians were not interested in joining the police force and that most were not qualified, community leaders, at a separate meeting in February 1990, cited specific individuals who had tried to become police officers in Lowell and asserted that, with effectively targeted promotion, more Southeast Asians would consider law enforcement as a career, and with proper coaching and training, many would pass necessary examinations. City officials expressed their desire to hire a Southeast Asian police officer, but they had not requested the State department of personnel to exempt the city of Lowell from State requirements for Southeast Asian candidates.[83]

In this connection it is also instructive to review some events that took place after the Ley murder of June 1990. In anticipation of the State qualifying examination for police officers scheduled for October 1990 and in response to the mayor's pledge to recruit Southeast Asian police officers, the Cambodian Mutual Assistance Association (CMAA) of Lowell volunteered to advertise orientation/training workshops and offer bilingual interpretation service for the workshops, and city officials agreed to arrange such workshops.[84] Although a great deal of interest was generated in the Southeast Asian community, the promised workshops were never held, and the aspiring Southeast Asians were once more let down. This failure was due to a breakdown in communications between the city of Lowell and the State agency responsible for conducting such workshops, i.e., Lowell was overlooked as one of the high-priority workshop sites, and workshops could not be arranged in time for the examination. Even this fact of slippage and oversight, however, was discovered only when the CMAA took the initiative of inquiring why there was no notice of the planned workshops. Although there may be a good explanation for the breakdown in communication, it is clear that the urgency of the situation was not conveyed to the State agencies with sufficient intensity. As a result, Southeast Asian candidates now have to wait for another 2 years to take the statewide examination. In the meantime, the Southeast Asian community must continue to suffer from inadequate police protection[85] and cope with the overwhelming sense of fear and vulnerability.[86]

---

lice community relations officer (hereafter cited as Lowell officials interview).

82   Castro v. Beecher, [Civ. No. unavailable] (D.Mass. Jan. 7, 1975), Consent Decree, No. 70-1220-W (Jun. 27, 1975).

83   The city of Lowell has not requested any special waivers for Southeast Asian police candidates, and the city is silent as to why no request was ever made. Lowell officials interview.

84   Vera Godley, Executive Director, Cambodian Mutual Assistance Association of Greater Lowell, Inc., letter to Diane McLeod, Affirmative Action Officer, City of Lowell, MA, Sept. 4, 1990.

85   The city of Lowell has requested the State department of personnel to be allowed to hire two Southeast Asian-language-speaking candidates, although they are not at the top of the candidate list. Diane McLeod, Affirmative Action Officer, City of Lowell, MA,

The general situation in Lowell is largely the result of a severe shortage of resources available to provide essential services to help immigrant and refugee newcomers integrate into the community. When large numbers of Southeast Asian refugees arrived in Lowell almost overnight in the early 1980s, Lowell was unable to cope with the strains on its public schools and social service agencies which were unprepared to cope with the sudden increase and to provide necessary educational services to Southeast Asian students and adults with limited proficiency in English. As Lowell struggled to deal with this situation, Massachusetts' economic miracle turned into an economic debacle, and special State funds that had been available to help localities provide basic services to Southeast Asian refugees dried up.[87] At the same time, funding provided to Lowell by the Federal Government, although never adequate to meet the need, also began to decline. Although Lowell has received special annual grants from the Office of Refugee Resettlement (ORR) to address the impact of secondary migrants on the Lowell school system, the amount of these grants was cut in half in 1991, to $225,000.[88] The total amount allocated to Massachusetts for cash and medical assistance by ORR also declined dramatically, although the number of refugees arriving in Massachusetts increased.[89] Also, the Lowell school district was hit with a $4 million budget cut in 1991, making it even more difficult for Lowell to provide for the needs of Southeast Asian students out of its own resources.[90] According to the Massachusetts State refugee coordinator, most of the rest of ORR funding available to Lowell can only be used to provide for employment training of those refugees who have been in the country for less than 8 months, and none of it can be used for refugees who have been in the country for more than 3 years. Since most of Lowell's Southeast population arrived in the United States more than 3 years ago, they are not eligible to receive ORR funds.[91]

The difficulties encountered by Lowell in trying to provide basic services to Southeast Asian newcomers may be typical of the situation faced by small communities across the country. In the State of California, for instance, only the 13 most affected communities (based on the number of refugees) receive any Federal funds, and an official of the California Department of Social Services, Policy and Systems Branch, which is responsible for allocating the Federal funds, was adamant in his contention that the Federal funds were inadequate to meet the needs of the refugees.[92] There is a clear need for more Federal and State aid to help communities provide essential services to Southeast Asian and other immigrants and refugees.

telephone interview, Oct. 24, 1990.

86   As of early October 1991, no Southeast Asian person was in the Lowell City Hall or the Lowell Police Department, and citizens of Southeast Asian ancestry in Lowell continued to encounter barriers in accessing the city hall and the police department. Uong interview.

87   Regina Lee, State Refugee Coordinator, Massachusetts Office for Refugees and Immigrants, telephone interview, Nov. 20, 1991 (hereafter cited as Lee Nov. 20 interview).

88   Richard Howe, Mayor, Lowell, MA, telephone interview, Nov. 20, 1991. In addition to the $225,000 grant, Lowell received $59,000 for outreach by the police department to the Cambodian community. Only a small fraction of this amount was allowed for interpreters, however, far less than necessary for effective police work in Lowell's Southeast Asian community. Stevens interview.

89   Regina Lee, State Refugee Coordinator, Massachusetts Office for Refugees and Immigrants, telephone interview, Nov. 26, 1991.

90   George N. Tsapatsaris, Superintendent, Lowell School District, telephone interview, Nov. 20, 1991.

91   Lee Nov. 20 interview.

92   Frank Rondis, California Department of Social Services, Policy and Systems Branch, telephone interview, Nov. 22, 1991.

Chapter 4

Access to Educational Opportunity: Asian American Immigrant Children in Primary and Secondary Schools

Over the past two decades the United States has experienced a major influx of refugees and immigrants from Asia. This influx has brought with it a new generation of Asian American children who are either themselves immigrants or refugees or who are the American-born children of recently arrived immigrants or refugees. Many of these children enter our schools unfamiliar with mainstream American culture and knowing little or no English. This chapter focuses on the problems that confront this new generation of Asian American children as they enter our public primary and secondary school system.[1]

The chapter begins by describing the condition of Asian American immigrant children[2] in our schools and by assessing their academic performance levels and goes on to examine the educational services these children are receiving in our schools. It then describes the legal protections available to these children under Federal civil rights laws and outlines the recent history of Federal enforcement of these protections. Next, the chapter turns to examining the effects of racial tensions on Asian American immigrant students. Finally, it looks at promising avenues for improving the educational opportunities for Asian American students in our public schools.

Asian American Immigrant Students in American Schools

The Condition of Asian American Immigrant Students

Asian American immigrant children, particularly those who come from families at the bottom of the socioeconomic scale, face a multitude of learning and adjustment challenges that mainstream students do not confront. The recognition that they live in two very different worlds, that of the family and that of the mainstream society, may be a step to realizing what they have to undergo as they enter our nation's schools.

The family situations of Asian American immigrant students are typically very different from those of their fellow students. Often, their parents do not speak English and are having great difficulty in making the transition into American society. Their family is likely to be living below the poverty level,[3] with their parents either working extremely long hours to make ends meet or unable to find jobs at all. Because the immigrant students, although often themselves limited English proficient (LEP), are frequently more familiar with the English language and

---

1   The chapter addresses only tangentially issues related to the educational opportunity of native-born Asian American students whose parents were born in this country or who arrived many years ago.

2   In this chapter, the term "immigrant children" refers to children who are either immigrants or refugees themselves or who are the U.S.-born children of recently arrived immigrants and refugees. Many immigrant Asian American children are limited English proficient or formerly limited English proficient.

3   For instance, over 75 percent of Southeast Asian students in San Diego City public schools live below the poverty line. Ruben G. Rumbaut, "Immigrant Students in California Public Schools: A Summary of Current Knowledge," October 1989, table 6 (hereafter cited as "Immigrant Students").

American customs and culture than their parents are, they are often forced to take on the role of go-between or interpreter between their parents and society at large.

At quite an early age. . .children serve as interpreters for their parents and help their families confront many adult tasks. For example, if their tenement has no heat in the winter, the school child who knows English might be the one to place a telephone call. . .these immigrant children face much more responsibility and pressure than the average American school child.[4]

This role reversal undermines parental authority, sometimes leading to tensions within Asian American immigrant families.

For children from Southeast Asia, an unusual dimension of their life experience needs to be recognized. Because of the political turmoil in Southeast Asia, most Southeast Asian children carry scars from the ordeal of surviving the extreme hardship of the battlefields and refugee detention camps or arduous boat rides to freedom. Still vivid and alive are their memories of starvation, violence, torture, cruelty, and even witnessing the rape and murder of their parents, siblings, or relatives. Indeed, post-traumatic stress syndrome (which includes such symptoms as depression, severe insomnia, nightmares, reliving war experiences, isolation, and suicide) is common among refugee children.[5] These children often cannot turn to their families for comfort and support. Many live in families that have been torn apart by the violence in Southeast Asia: for instance, less than half of the Cambodian students in San Diego live in two-parent households (many live with their widowed mothers).[6] The adults they live with also have extremely high rates of post-traumatic stress syndrome and are having immense difficulty coping with everyday life. They often have little or no emotional or physical energy left over to give to their children. In addition to the devastating effects of the war itself on these families, the dislocation from non-Western societies and the extremely low education levels of many adult refugees (especially women)[7] leave many Southeast Asian parents ill-prepared to cope in American society and with little background for helping their children in school or even understanding what they are doing there.

During the schoolday, Asian American immigrant children are transported into a different world. They are Americans—trying to become like their peers and belong to the mainstream; and they are outsiders—trying to fit into a foreign land with a foreign tongue. Instead of encountering a supportive school environment, Asian American immigrant students all too often find schools that are unprepared to deal with diversity, teachers who do not know their languages and culture and are insensitive to their needs, and an atmosphere that is unfriendly and frequently charged with racial hostility. On the playground, other students may ridicule them for their accent, demeanor, or look. They may call them names or shout at them, "Go back where you belong!" Older students may be physically harassed and even provoked into physical fights, sometimes involving weapons. Quickly, Asian American immigrant children are made to feel like outsiders in our schools, which detracts from

---

4   Ying Chen, cited in John Willshire Carrera, *New Voices: Immigrant Students in U.S. Public Schools* (Boston, MA: National Coalition of Advocates for Students, 1988), p. 21 (hereafter cited as *New Voices*).

5   Ibid., p. 24, and Laurie Olsen, *Crossing the Schoolhouse Border: Immigrant Students and the California Public Schools* (San Francisco: California Tomorrow, 1988), p. 23 (hereafter cited as *Crossing the Border*).

6   "Immigrant Students," p. 22.

7   The average education levels of the parents of Southeast Asian students in San Diego city schools range from 8.9 years for the Vietnamese to 1.3 years for Hmong students. On the average, the English literacy rates of Southeast Asian mothers was poor. "Immigrant Students," table 6.

their ability to concentrate on school work and often has devastating consequences for their self-esteem.

Thus, Asian American immigrant children find themselves torn between the conflicting values of home, on the one hand, and peer group and school, on the other hand. According to the testimony of an 11th grade Cambodian girl:

My family has such set values and they hold to them strongly. They hold onto the old ways. It is very difficult to explain something to them about my life now. We end up always arguing—about school, religion, how I dress, what I can and can't do. They even get mad at me for arguing. They say I shouldn't talk back. I hate my family. We fight all the time.[8]

All these factors contribute to the undermining of traditional Asian family life, which too often leaves Asian American LEP students without meaningful parental support or authority at a time when they desperately need them.[9]

The Academic Performance of Asian American Immigrant Students

Because of the language and cultural barriers they face, Asian American immigrant students are at risk of low achievement in our schools. English competence is known to be an important predictor of academic success.[10] "Nothing more effectively separates students from the mainstream of school experience than the inability to speak English and to communicate with others."[11] When students feel like outsiders in the school environment, do not have a sense of belonging, have few friends involved in school, and are not integrated into the social or academic life of their school, they become likely candidates for academic failure.

Unfortunately, the lack of adequate data critically hampers efforts to evaluate the academic performance of Asian American immigrant students. No comprehensive data on the academic achievement of Asian American immigrant students are available.[12] What data do exist provide a mixed picture of how these children are doing in school. By some measures, they appear to be succeeding academically, but other indicators suggest that there are some serious problems as well. In particular, the most recent wave of immigrant and refugee children from Asia seems to be encountering more educational difficulties than earlier waves.[13]

The following discussion examines what existing data on grades, test scores, dropout rates,

---

8   11th grade Cambodian girl, as quoted in *Crossing the Border*, p. 31.

9   Two valuable ethnographic case studies examine the school and family situations facing immigrant Asian American children in detail: Henry T. Trueba, Lila Jacobs, and Elizabeth Kirton, *Cultural Conflict and Adaptation: The Case of Hmong Children in American Society* (New York: Falmer Press, 1990), and Margaret A. Gibson, *Accommodation Without Assimilation: Sikh Immigrants in an American High School* (Ithaca, NY: Cornell University Press, 1988).

10   Joan Baratz-Snowden, Donald Rock, Judith Pollack, and Gita Wilder, *The Educational Progress of Language Minority Children: Findings from the NAEP 1985-1986 Special Study* (Princeton, NJ: Educational Testing Service, May 1988), p. 174 (hereafter cited as *1988 NAEP Report*).

11   Patricia Gandara, California Assembly Office of Research, Sacramento, CA. Cited in *New Voices*, p. 66.

12   Council of Chief State School Officers, *School Success for Limited English Proficient Students: The Challenge and State Response* (February 1990), p. 15 (hereafter cited as *School Success of LEP Students*). For example, this report notes that: "the most overarching conclusion to be drawn from the surveys is that lack of adequate data poses a serious barrier to enlightened, effective program development and service delivery. We do know that there are significant numbers of LEP children who are not receiving services that they need in school. But we found it difficult, if not impossible, to even ascertain how many LEP children there are, where they are, and whether they are being served." Ibid., pp. 20-21.

13   Ibid., p. 15. Huynh Dinh Te, "Southeast Asian Students: Facing the Language Challenge," *Equity News*, April 1988 (two-page document; pages unnumbered).

70

and post-school aspirations reveal about the academic achievement levels of Asian American immigrant students.

Grades and Test Scores—Grades and test scores are a primary measure of how well students are doing in school. Considerable information exists documenting the high average grades and test scores of Asian American students as a group. However, since the Asian American population is so heterogeneous with respect to ethnicity, length of time in the United States, and socioeconomic status, such group average information is unlikely to reflect the grades and test scores of Asian American immigrant children. A few studies offer a partial glance at the grades and test scores of Asian American immigrant children.

In the mid-1980s, the Educational Testing Service conducted a national study of the educational achievement of language-minority children as part of the National Assessment of Educational Progress (NAEP), an ongoing congressionally mandated project to conduct surveys on the educational attainment of American children.[14] The NAEP study compared the educational achievement of language-minority and non-language-minority children by race and ethnicity, where "language-minority" children were defined as children who lived in a home where the language spoken by most family members was not English. The study found that 11th grade Asian American language-minority children read significantly less well than their non-language-minority counterparts, although little difference was found in grades 4 and 8.[15] Only one-fifth of Asian American language-minority 11th graders were at an adept or advanced reading level, compared with roughly one-half of both their Asian American and white non-language-minority counterparts.[16]

The NAEP sample, however, excluded children whose English proficiency was deemed by their schools to be too low for them to take the NAEP Reading Assessment test. Roughly 11-13 percent of Asian children were excluded from the sample.[17] If they had been incorporated in the study, the difference in reading performance between language-minority and non-language-minority children would have undoubtedly been much greater, because the reading scores of the least English proficient would have been very low. Thus, in all likelihood, the NAEP study seriously overestimates the educational achievement of language-minority Asian American children.

A second potentially valuable resource for studying the educational attainment of Asian American children nationally is the National Education Longitudinal Survey (NELS), which began studying eighth graders in 1988 and had 1,501 Asian students in its sample. NELS includes a host of information about these students, including information about their English proficiency. Unfortunately, this study has the same drawback as the NAEP study: NELS systematically excludes persons with very low English proficiency from its sample. To date, there has been only one study of NELS that concentrates on Asian American children.[18] Unfortunately, this study does not distinguish between recent immigrants and children whose families have been in the United States for generations.

---

14   Joan C. Baratz-Snowden and Richard Duran, *The Educational Progress of Language Minority Students: Findings from the 1983-1984 NAEP Reading Survey* (Princeton, NJ: Educational Testing Service, January 1987) (hereafter cited as *1987 NAEP Report*).

15   Ibid., p. 59, table 21.

16   Ibid., p. 64, table 22.

17   *1987 NAEP Report*, p. 20, table 2.

18   Samuel S. Peng and Ralph M. Lee, "Diversity of Asian American Students and Its Implications for Education: A Study of the 1988 Eighth Graders" (paper presented at the annual conference of the National Association for Bilingual Education, Washington, DC, Jan. 11, 1991).

The study does show reading and math achievement scores separately for each Asian group, however, revealing considerable heterogeneity in achievement within the Asian American student population. For instance, the composite reading and math achievement scores of Chinese, Japanese, Korean, and South and West Asian children were well above the national average, but the composite scores of Southeast Asian and Filipino children were average, and the scores of Pacific Islander children were well below average. Children from all Asian groups had higher math scores than reading scores.[19]

State and local studies provide additional information on the educational achievement of Asian American immigrant children. An analysis of the performance of language-minority children on the California Assessment Program (CAP) exams concluded: "With few exceptions. . . , most immigrant language groups scored below the norm in all subject areas. Southeast Asian and Hispanic immigrant students appeared most at risk on the basis of these test scores."[20] The study also noted that the data not only demonstrated the heterogeneity of the Asian American immigrant population, but also dispelled the model minority myth:

The CAP test scores reveal that when results for all Asian groups are combined, the higher achievement of some obscures the need of certain other Asian language subgroups, such as the Southeast Asians. And the relatively lower reading and writing scores of all immigrant Asians shatters the myth that all Asian students excel and need little in the way of language assistance and support.[21]

Finally, the study found that self-reported grade point averages and teacher comments indicated that, despite low test scores, Asian language-minority children received very high grades.

One local study analyzed the school records of all Southeast Asian children in the city of San Diego schools and also matched the school records with family information for a subsample of the children.[22] That study found that the cumulative grade point averages (GPAs) of Southeast Asian 11th and 12th graders in San Diego was 2.52, higher than the white GPA of 2.33.[23] The average GPA of Southeast Asian students who were classified as LEP was somewhat lower than that of those who were not, but was not lower than the average GPA of native-born white students.[24] Among Southeast Asians, Vietnamese and ethnic Chinese students had the highest GPAs, and Hmong students had intermediate GPAs (but still higher than those of white students). Laotian and Cambodian students had GPAs at or below those of whites.[25]

The San Diego study found, however, that despite their average or above-average GPAs, Southeast Asian 11th and 12th graders performed less well than white students on reading and math achievement tests administered by San Diego city schools.[26] The reading scores of Southeast Asian students were lower than those of all other groups in the city, except for Samoan students, and well below the national norm.[27]

19   Ibid., table 3.

20   *Crossing the Border*, p. 86.

21   Ibid., p. 87.

22   Ruben G. Rumbaut and Kenji Ima, *The Adaptation of Southeast Asian Refugee Youth: A Comparative Study,* Final Report to the Office of Refugee Resettlement (January 1988) (hereafter cited as *Adaptation of Youth*).

23   Ibid., p. 21a, fig. 3.5. The study found that (other) Asian and Filipino students also had grade point averages above the white average, but that Pacific Islanders and Samoans had grade point averages far below the white average (2.01 and 1.76, respectively). The Samoan GPA was lower than that for any other group. Ibid.

24   Ibid., p. 21c, fig. 3-7.

25   Ibid.

26   The tests used by San Diego city schools are the Comprehensive Tests of Basic Skills.

The math scores of Southeast Asian students, although slightly below those of white San Diego students, were somewhat above the national norm. It should also be noted, however, that the scores reported in the study do not reflect the achievement of students with the lowest English proficiency, because the tests are not administered to LEP students until their English proficiency is deemed minimally adequate to take the test.[28]

The San Diego study's finding that Southeast Asian students have higher grade point averages than other groups, but lower achievement scores, especially in the area of reading confirms the similar finding of the California-wide analysis cited above. The discrepancy between the test scores and grades of Asian American immigrant students may be indicative of the hard work many Southeast Asian students put in to overcome the barriers they face; the difficulties limited-English-proficient students may have with time-constrained exams as compared with the type of learning that goes on in the classroom; or students choosing to specialize in courses, such as mathematics and science courses, where reading achievement is less fundamental. On the other hand, it may also indicate that Southeast Asian students are being given higher grades because they work hard, attend regularly and turn in their assignments, or because teachers stereotype all Asian students as high achievers, and not necessarily because they are really learning something.[29]

Dropout Rates—The language and cultural barriers faced by Asian American immigrant children make them prime candidates for dropping out of school. Previous research has found that language-minority students have dropout rates that are twice as high as the dropout rates of non-language-minority students.[30] "Limited proficiency in English is a significant factor contributing to students dropping out at all levels of education."[31] There are some indications that some groups of Asian American immigrant students may have high dropout rates. An examination of the attrition rates of California school districts with high concentrations of LEP students showed that "the highest average attrition rate (48 percent) was for the schools with large concentrations of Southeast Asians."[32] High dropout rates have also been reported for subgroups of Asian Americans: 46.1 percent for Filipino school students[33] and 60 percent for Samoans[34] in California. In Lowell, Massachusetts, where approximately 33 percent of the public school population are Southeast Asians, during the 1986-1987 school year "over half of the Laotian students who started out the school year in the Lowell High School dropped out due to the absence of Lao-speaking staff there to provide school instruction or counseling."[35]

There is very little firm data on the dropout rates of Asian American students, however. The NAEP study cited above looked at the proportion of language-minority students nationwide who were older than average for their grade level and who most likely had repeated grades.

27   Ibid., p. 34a, fig. 3.18.

28   Ibid., p. 34.

29   See *Crossing the Border*, p. 87.

30   Ibid., p. 90.

31   California State University, Curriculum and Assessment Cluster Committee, *California's Limited English Language Students: An Intersegmental Agenda* (September 1989), p. 1.

32   Ibid., p. 88.

33   Lisa Javier, Executive Director, Search to Involve Filipino Americans, Los Angeles, CA. Cited in *New Voices*, p. 66.

34   Audrey Yamayaki-Noji, Commissioner, Orange County Human Relations Department. Cited in *New Voices*, p. 66.

35   Hispanic Parents Advisory Council v. Kouleharas, Civ. Action No. 87-1968-MA (D. Mass., July 31, 1987) at 24.

Since grade repetition has long been considered predictive of subsequent school dropout, these data provide some indications about the dropout risks for Asian American language-minority students. The study found that the incidence of above-grade ages among fourth and eighth grade Asian American language-minority students was comparable to that of Asian American non-language-minority students and to that of white students and lower than those of Hispanic and black students. Among 11th graders, however, only 61 percent of Asian American language-minority children were at or below the age of 17 (the modal age for 11th graders), far less than the roughly 84 percent of both white and Asian non-language-minority children who were 17 or younger. Furthermore, 16 percent of Asian language-minority students were 19 or older, more than four times the percentage for Asian American non-language-minority students and 10 times the percentage for white students. This percentage was also considerably higher than the percentages for Hispanic language-minority children (12 percent) and for black students (7 percent).[36] These data could reflect a large incidence of grade repetition among Asian American immigrant students in high school, or alternatively they could indicate that recently arrived Asian students are placed below their grade level in high school to allow them time to catch up.

The NAEP study's question of 4th, 8th, and 11th grade students about whether they expected to graduate from high school provides additional evidence on the dropout rates of Asian American immigrant students. The NAEP study found that in eighth grade, virtually all Asian American language-minority students expected to graduate from high school.[37] In 11th grade, however, 8 percent of Asian American language-minority students did not expect to graduate, a larger percentage than for any other group.[38] The study cautions, however, that because of the small sample size, the differences across groups are not statistically significant.[39]

The study of San Diego high school students cited above looks at dropout rates directly. That study found a high degree of variation among Asian American groups in their rates of dropout. Pacific Islanders had the highest dropout rate[40] (17 percent) among all the groups in the city, and Cambodian students in San Diego had the third highest (after Hispanics) dropout rate (14 percent); the Vietnamese dropout rate (11 percent) was slightly higher than the white rate (10 percent). The other Asian American groups had dropout rates well below that of white students, with Hmong students having the lowest dropout rate (5 percent) of all the groups in the city.[41]

The NAEP and San Diego studies are not adequate in and of themselves as indicators of the dropout rates of Asian American immigrant students, and much more research needs to be done before the dropout patterns of Asian American immigrant students are known with any confidence. However, these indications of high dropout rates are disturbing because they suggest that schools are failing to meet the

---

36   *1987 NAEP Report*, p. 31, table 7.

37   Ibid., p. 33, table 8. Roughly one-fifth to one-quarter of fourth graders of all groups say that they do not expect to graduate from high school. Their responses are unlikely to be sufficiently reliable to warrant serious analysis. Ibid.

38   Ibid.

39   Ibid., p. 32.

40   The dropout rates were measured as the percentage of 10th-12th graders in the school system who dropped out during the 1985-86 academic year. A student was classified as a dropout if he or she left school and no request from another school system for the student's transcript was received within 45 school days of the student's departure. *Adaptation of Youth*, p. 53.

41   Ibid., p. 53a, fig. 5-1. This variation in dropout rates among Asian American groups may be accounted for in part by such variables as length of stay in the United States, native language, and educational attainment of parents.

needs of a large number of immigrant Asian children. Many of these children become frustrated over their lack of academic accomplishment, feel abandoned by the schools, and turn instead to youth gangs and criminal activities.[42] In San Diego, for instance, there has been a notable growth recently in the number of Cambodian gang members, some of whom were involved in a drive-by shooting that killed a Hmong soldier who had recently returned from the Gulf War, and in Sacramento, Vietnamese gang members recently participated in a shopping mall shootout that killed six people.[43]

Post-High School Aspirations—The post-high school aspirations of Asian American immigrant students may be indicative of how well they feel they are doing in school. The NAEP study asked 11th grade students about their plans after high school. A higher percentage (56 percent) of Asian American language minority 11th graders planned to enter college than for any other group except for non-language-minority Asian students.[44]

The San Diego study documents similarly high aspirations for some Asian groups but finds that others have below-average aspirations. Students in San Diego city schools are asked in 10th grade what their two top career choices are. The San Diego study's analysis of their responses reveals that Vietnamese and Hmong students are more likely to aspire to professional jobs and less likely to aspire to low-status jobs[45] than any other group. On the other hand, Laotian and Cambodian students were the least likely to aspire to professional careers and the most likely to aspire to low-status jobs of all the groups in the city.[46] Furthermore, when San Diego city schools did a followup study to see what became of its high school graduates 3 years after graduation, although many Southeast Asian students had gone on to college, many others were not in school and were unemployed or out of the labor force.[47]

Existing data sources do not provide an adequate basis for reaching firm conclusions about the educational achievement of Asian American immigrant students. They suffer from critical design flaws (the exclusion of many limited-English-proficient students from their samples) and small sample sizes, and they do not always collect enough information to provide a context or explanation for their findings. Regardless, on balance, the data suggest that Asian American immigrant students, although performing well by some measures, are leaving our public schools with some serious deficiencies, particularly in the areas of reading and writing, and that some subgroups have high dropout rates. Furthermore, the San Diego study's finding of important differences in achievement among Southeast Asian groups underscores the importance of studying Asian groups separately. Relying on average data is likely to provide misleading evidence about the nature of the educational problems facing Asian American youth.

---

42 Kenji Ima, Professor of Sociology, San Diego State University, comments on July 31 Draft Report, pp. 1-2 (hereafter cited as Ima Comments).

43 Ibid.

44 *1987 NAEP Report*, p. 33, table 9. Seventy percent of Asian American non-language-minority students planned to go to college. For comparison, 45 percent of white, 36 percent of black, and 36 percent of Hispanic non-language-minority students and 32 percent of language-minority Hispanics planned to go to college. Ibid.

45 The San Diego study defined clerical jobs, personal service jobs, police, fire, and military jobs, and blue-collar and agricultural occupations to be "low-status" jobs. *Adaptation of Youth*, p. 47.

46 Ibid., p. 47c, fig. 4-3.

47 Ima Comments, p. 2.

The Provision of Educational Programs for Asian American LEP Students

Nationwide, there are 3.6 million school-aged LEP children.[48] The number of LEP students has grown considerably in recent years and is expected to continue growing during the coming decade. One estimate projected a 35 percent increase in the number of LEP students between 1976 and 2000,[49] although this is likely to be a serious underestimate.[50] Meeting the needs of our nation's LEP children is one of the most serious challenges to our educational system in the coming decades.

A large proportion of Asian American LEP students are recently arrived refugee/immigrant children from Southeast Asia.[51] Because Southeast Asians in the U.S. have a much lower mean age than other immigrant groups, including those from Central America,[52] and Southeast Asian women in the U.S. have fertility rates several times higher than that of white women,[53] the proportion of the Nation's LEP student population who are Asian Americans is likely to rise considerably in coming years. Even now,

---

48 In 1982 the U.S. Department of Education reported that there were approximately 3.6 million school-aged language-minority children who were limited in the English-language skills needed to succeed in an English-medium school. U.S. Department of Education, *The Condition of Bilingual Education in the Nation, 1982: A Report from the Secretary of Education to the President and the Congress* (1982), p. 2. Subsequently, in 1987 the Department of Education revised this figure to 1.75 million. U.S. Department of Education, Office of Planning, Budget and Evaluation, "Numbers of Limited English Proficient Children: National, State, and Language-Specific Estimates," April 1987, pp. 7-8.

 Although estimates vary, the figure of 3.5 million is used by school officials. For example, the Council of Chief State School Officers notes that "approximately 3.5 million children are eligible for special language-related instruction either in English or in the native language." Council of Chief State School Officers, *School Success for Limited English Proficient Students: The Challenge and State Response*, February 1990, p. 15.

49 Rebecca Oxford-Carpenter, Louis Pol, David Lopez, Paul Stupp, Murray Gendell, and Samuel Peng, *Demographic Projections of Non-English-Language-Background and Limited-English-Proficient Persons* (Rosslyn, VA: InterAmerica Research Associates, 1984), pp. 19, 68.

50 Since the projection used 1976 and 1978 data, it did not take into account the influx of refugees from Southeast Asia and the large number of immigrants who arrived in the United States in the late 1970s and during the 1980s, particularly those from Asian countries. As a result, the projection was bound to be an underestimate.

 The projection for the State of California illustrates the point. The 1990 projection for California was 712,900 (see Oxford-Carpenter, *Demographic Projections*, p. 70), but the 1989-1990 school year State survey of students shows the actual number to be much higher: 825,500. James A. Fulton, Administrator, Educational Demographics Unit, California State Department of Education, telephone interview, Aug. 2, 1990 (hereafter cited as Fulton interview).

51 As of Sept. 30, 1989, approximately 920,000 refugees from Southeast Asia had been admitted to the U.S. since 1975. The school-age population (6-17) was about 24 percent of the total and an additional 19 percent were young adults aged 18-24. U.S. Department of Health and Human Services, Office of Refugee Resettlement, *Report to the Congress: Refugee Resettlement Program* (Jan. 31, 1990), pp. 6, 76, and A-1.

 In California, 53 percent of LEP students of Asian origin are from Southeast Asia, with most of the remainder coming from East Asia and the Philippines ("Immigrant Students," fig. 2.), and more than half of Southeast Asian students in San Diego city schools are classified as LEP. *Adaptation of Youth*, p. 19c, fig. 3-3.

52 The mean ages for Southeast Asian groups in the United States are 13 for Hmongs, 18 for Cambodians, 19 for Laotians, and 21 for Vietnamese, respectively. The mean ages for Latin American groups (23 years for Mexicans, 26 years for Dominicans, and 27 years for Jamaicans) are much closer to the U.S. national mean age of 30. *New Voices*, p. 5.

53 Current U.S. fertility rates are: 1.7 children per lifetime for white women, 2.4 for black women, and 2.9 for Mexican American women, compared with 3.4 for Vietnamese women, 4.6 for Laotian women, 7.6 for Cambodian women, and 11.9 for Hmong women. *New Voices*, pp. 6-7.

one out of every three LEP students in California is an Asian American.[54] Thus, the education of LEP students is a national challenge that will continue to increase in its scope and magnitude, particularly for Asian Americans.

Providing equal educational opportunity to Asian American LEP students requires sound student assessment procedures and programs orienting them and their parents to American society and American schools. Asian American LEP students need bilingual education and English as a Second Language programs staffed by trained teachers to enable them to learn English and at the same time to keep up in school. They need professional bilingual/bicultural counseling services to help them in their personal, social, and academic development. This section examines whether these needs are being met by our public schools.

There is no national data source showing how well served Asian American LEP students are by English as a Second Language (ESL) and bilingual education programs and other educational services. A proxy for the extent to which Asian American students are served by bilingual education programs is the frequency with which they are taught by Asian American teachers. The nationwide NAEP study discussed above found that an extremely small proportion of Asian American language-minority students are taught by Asian American teachers: 4.7 percent of 4th graders, 3.3 percent of 8th graders, and 0.4 percent of 11th graders. As a point of reference, it should be noted that much higher percentages of Hispanic language-minority students are taught by Hispanic teachers (21.0 percent of the 4th graders, 15.9 percent of the 8th graders, and 23.7 percent of the 11th graders).[55] Furthermore, Asian American immigrant students who

do have Asian American teachers may have teachers of a different national origin and/or teachers who do not speak their language.

State and local statistics confirm that Asian American LEP students across the country are underserved by ESL and bilingual education programs. A 1987 State of California study found that Southeast Asians were dramatically underserved by bilingual education. For example, there was a need for 217 Cambodian bilingual teachers statewide, but there were no certified Cambodian bilingual teachers in the State, and only 77 percent of the need was met by bilingual teachers for whom State-mandated teacher certification requirements had been waived. The situation was even worse for Hmong and Mien students, for whom there also were no certified bilingual teachers, and for whom only 39 and 11 percent, respectively, of the need was filled by teachers on waiver. The situation for Vietnamese and Laotian students was slightly better, with virtually all of their needs being met by teachers on waiver.[56] A similar situation prevailed in Massachusetts, where there were no certified bilingual teachers to serve 2,356 Cambodian and 2,604 Thai LEP students. There were three certified bilingual teachers to serve 276 Laotian LEP students and eight certified bilingual teachers to serve 833 Vietnamese LEP students. There were one Cambodian guidance counselor, two Vietnamese guidance counselors, and no Laotian or Thai guidance counselors in the entire State.[57]

Not only are Asian American LEP students underserved by bilingual teachers in California, but the situation has deteriorated in recent years. The number of Asian-language bilingual teachers declined by 10 percent and the number of Asian language teachers in training declined

---

54   Approximately 255,000 of the 825,500 LEP students in California are Asian Americans. Fulton interview.

55   These figures are for reading and English courses. *1987 NAEP Report*, p. 51, table 17.

56   California State Department of Education Data Bical Report No. 87-9C, cited in "Southeast Asian Students: Facing the Language Challenge."

57   Tables provided by Dr. Juan Rodriguez, Program Director, Bilingual/ESL, College of Education, University of Lowell, Lowell, MA.

by 58 percent between 1988 and 1990.[58] A recent report to the California Department of Education concluded:

On the whole, the number of fully certificated Asian language bilingual teachers has decreased from 1985 to 1990. Both waivered teachers and classroom aides had stepped into the breech, a less than desirable situation. Many waivered teachers were not knowledgeable of the child's primary language, and the aides are not, for the most part, professionally trained. In 1988, waivered teachers were eliminated and their place taken by "English language development teachers"; and in 1990, they were joined by monolingual English speaking teachers who were added to the primary language "teacher in training.". . .In effect, Asian primary language teachers have declined and are being replaced by monolingual English speakers and primary language aides. This means a deterioration of the teaching force capacity to provide Asian primary language instructions.[59]

Local statistics show a similar picture. An analysis of 1987 data on instruction of LEP students in the Los Angeles Unified School District (LAUSD) found:

[I]n 1987 only 7 of the 81 languages spoken by LEP students were served by bilingual teachers, and district-wide the LAUSD had only one bilingual teacher for every 100 LEP students. Of the 1,478 bilingual elementary teachers in the LAUSD in 1987. . . .1,409 (95%) spoke only Spanish as their second language. The remaining bilingual teachers consisted of 33 Cantonese speakers, 28 Korean, 4 Japanese, 2 Armenian, and one Pilipino and Vietnamese each. There were about 6,000 LEP students speaking 74 other languages for whom not a single bilingual teacher was available.[60]

The study noted that LAUSD's 967 Cambodian students, who had no bilingual teachers available to them, were among the slowest to be transferred to all-English curricula because of their generally deprived socioeconomic backgrounds.[61]

In the Fresno (California) Unified School District, roughly 19 percent of the students enrolled in the 1990-91 school year, or 12,659 students, were Asian Americans.[62] Approximately 80 percent of Fresno's Asian American students were classified as LEP, and 99 percent of Fresno's LEP Asian American students were Southeast Asian.[63] During this school year, however, there were no Southeast Asian bilingual teachers in the district and no Southeast Asian was in training to become a certified bilingual teacher.[64] Thus, nearly 10,000 Southeast Asian LEP students spent the entire school year without a single Southeast Asian bilingual teacher.

Like Fresno, the Stockton (California) area had a large influx of refugees from Southeast Asia in the 1980s, and the situation of the Stockton Unified School District parallels that of Fresno. Of Stockton's total student enrollment in the 1990-91 school year, 28 percent were Asian Americans, 68 percent of whom are counted as LEP.[65] Of the Asian American LEP students, 84 percent, or 5,606 students, were Southeast Asians.[66] Yet there were no South-

58   Kenji Ima, *What Do We Know About Asian and Pacific Islander Language Minority Students?* Report to the Bilingual Education Office, California Department of Education (1991), table 12.

59   Ibid., pp. 25-26.

60   "Immigrant Students," p. 10.

61   Ibid.

62   Richard Diaz, consultant, California State Department of Education, Office of Program Evaluation and Research, Educational Demographics Unit, telephone interview, Oct. 8, 1991 (hereafter cited as Diaz interview).

63   Judy Lambert, bilingual education consultant, California State Department of Education, Office of Bilingual Education, telephone interview, Oct. 8, 1991 (hereafter cited as Lambert interview).

64   Ibid.

65   Diaz interview.

east Asian certified bilingual teachers in the entire district.[67]

In the Providence (Rhode Island) school district, as of October 1990, 12 percent of the students enrolled were Asian Americans, but teachers of Asian American ancestry constituted less than 1 percent of the teachers in the district.[68] Approximately 96 percent of the Asian American students were Southeast Asians, about 60 percent of whom were LEP students (i.e., approximately 1,450 students are Southeast Asian LEP students).[69] Across the entire district, however, there was not one Southeast Asian teacher in ESL/bilingual classes.[70] And in spite of the large number of Southeast Asian LEP students, not even one counselor was either Southeast Asian or spoke or understood their language.[71]

In October 1990 the Lowell (Massachusetts) school district had about 3,300 Southeast Asian (largely Cambodian) students, constituting 26 percent of the total enrollment, but only 37 teachers, or 4 percent of all teachers, of Southeast Asian ancestry.[72]

A recent assessment of the educational services provided to LEP students in California schools concluded that they were generally inadequate, and there are no indications that California does not typify the Nation as a whole:

In many districts a critical shortage of trained bilingual teachers, counselors and aides has made bilingual programs difficult to implement and has drastically upset the success of bilingual programs and the students who need them. This is the most universally reported problem throughout the state. To provide the primary language support needed by immigrant students at all levels, specially credentialed staff are desperately needed, but in district after district where we did our research, we found that need going unmet. . . .This shortage is particularly acute for Indochinese languages, even with the great majority of teachers for these groups on waiver.[73]

The study also found that school orientation programs for newcomers were in most cases nonexistent.[74]

The quality of programs intended for LEP students is as important as the presence of bilingual teachers and counselors. A review of a few selected districts shows that existing programs are generally inadequate. For example, a 1989 compliance review of the LEP programs of the Providence school district identified serious deficiencies, which included:

1) Identification of LEP students and information on them were inaccurate. A review of 3,000 LEP census forms revealed 1,200 errors.[75]

2) The assessment and placement decisions regarding LEP students were made without consulting teachers and district staff,[76]

---

66   Lambert interview.

67   Ibid. The situation may improve in the future since 30 Southeast Asian (20 Cambodian, 4 Lao, and 6 Vietnamese) teachers were in training to become certified bilingual teachers in the 1990-91 school year. Ibid.

68   Paul Vorro, Assistant Superintendent for Personnel, Providence School District, RI, telephone interview, Oct. 8, 1991.

69   Fran Mossberg, Supervisor, ESL/Bilingual Programs, Providence (RI) School District, telephone interview, Oct. 8, 1991.

70   Ibid.

71   Ibid.

72   George N. Tsapatsaris, Superintendent, Lowell School District, telephone interview, Oct. 8, 1991. In the past 2 years, the number of Southeast Asian teachers has increased from 20 to 37. Efforts are being made to increase the number of Southeast Asian teachers further. Ibid.

73   *Crossing the Border*, pp. 59-60.

74   Ibid., p. 71.

75   Rhode Island State Department of Education, *Basic Education Program Monitoring Report, Part a, 1987-1988* (1989), p. b.

3) The quality of English as a second language instruction was hampered by the large numbers of students and their varying levels of English proficiency.[77]

4) Teachers were not following curriculum parallel to that of the English monolingual students in all the academic areas.

An ethnographic study of Hmong students attending school in La Playa, California, reveals an even more dire situation for limited-English-proficient students.[78] The authors of this study found that some Hmong students, rather than being given adequate language instruction, were placed in programs for learning disabled children, in large part because of their limited English proficiency:

To confirm teachers' suspicion that children's "disabilities" and academic failures were always a personal characteristic, the. . .children were tested by the school psychologist,. . .and. . .were officially declared "handicapped. . . ." It did not matter that the testing took place in English, a language the children did not understand, or that the information leading to teacher referral was not accurate, or that the child's performance in domains such as art or mathematics was above average.[79]

Rather than making educational progress in the learning disabled program, the children became increasingly isolated, disengaged from the classroom, and depressed. The authors found:

The most disturbing finding in our research was that some Indochinese children have stopped trying to learn and have accepted and internalized their "disabilities" as their own personal attribute. . . .The overall decrease in participation in classroom activities and the documented deterioration of reading and writing skills show that some of these children did not see much hope of ever improving their performance.[80]

School personnel exhibited prejudice against Indochinese students:

Racial prejudice about the ability of Indochinese children in La Playa, whether conscious or unconscious, is deeply rooted in the misperception by mainstream teachers and peers that these children are academically incompetent because they have an inferior intelligence or an inferior culture, not because they have a different set of experiences leading to different values and cognitive system.[81]

And they were insensitive to the cultural barriers facing their students:

There is a serious ignorance and pervasive insensitivity by school personnel and textbook writers regarding the inherent inaccessibility and confusion for minorities reading text written with mainstream middle-class American children in mind. Such insensitivity to the obvious cultural and linguistic gap between minority home cultures and mainstream cultures paves the way for school personnel to stereotype and underestimate minority children's learning potential.[82]

Thus, the school did not even begin to meet the educational needs of the LEP Hmong children studied by these authors.

---

76   Ibid., p. 246b.
77   Ibid., p. 247b.
78   Trueba, Jacobs, and Kirton, *Cultural Conflict and Adaptation: The Case of Hmong in Children in American Society.*
79·   Ibid., pp. 104-05.
80   Ibid., p. 104.
81   Ibid., pp. 103-04.
82   Ibid., pp. 105-06.

Equal Educational Opportunity for LEP Students: Legal Protections and Federal Enforcement

It is a violation of Federal civil rights laws to deny a meaningful opportunity for limited-English-proficient (LEP) students to participate in a public educational program, and school systems are required to take affirmative steps to rectify the language deficiency of LEP students.[83] This section discusses how a crucial Supreme Court case brought by Chinese American students and their parents helped to shape the law protecting all LEP students, reviews the recent history of Federal enforcement of the rights of LEP students,[84] and describes two recent court cases involving Asian American LEP students.

The Lau Decision

In the early 1970s, frustrated by the persistent inattention to their needs by school officials, non-English-speaking students of Chinese ancestry enrolled in the San Francisco Unified School District brought a class action suit against officials of the school district. In this landmark suit the plaintiffs sought relief against alleged unequal educational opportunities resulting from the officials' failure to establish a program to rectify the students' language problem. The U.S. District Court for the Northern District of California denied the relief sought by the plaintiffs.[85]

The Ninth Circuit Court of Appeals affirmed the district court's denial of the relief, citing the lower court's reasoning: that the students' rights to an education and to equal educational opportunities had been satisfied because they received "the same education made available on the same terms and conditions to the other tens of thousands of students in the San Francisco Unified School District."[86] The court held that the school district had no duty "to rectify appellants' special deficiencies, as long as they provided these students with access to the same educational system made available to all other students."[87]

Thus, the court of appeals rejected the argument that the school district had an affirmative

---

83   Title VI of the Civil Rights Act of 1964 bans discrimination based on race, color, and national origin by any program receiving Federal financial assistance, which includes the nation's public schools. It states: "No person in the United States shall, on the ground of race, color, or national origin, be excluded from participation in, be denied the benefits of, or be subjected to discrimination under any program or activity receiving Federal financial assistance." (42 U.S.C. §2000c.) Title VI has been interpreted to require schools to take affirmative steps to provide instruction to LEP students. (Lau v. Nichols, 414 U.S. 563 (1974).) See below for a detailed discussion of the *Lau* decision.

      The Equal Education Opportunity Act (EEOA) of 1974 also provides a statutory basis for protecting the equal educational opportunity rights of LEP students. It specifically states:

      "No State shall deny equal educational opportunity to an individual on account of his or her race, color, sex, or national origin, by—

        "(f) the failure by an educational agency to take appropriate action to overcome language barriers that impede equal participation by its students in its instructional programs." (20 U.S.C. §1703.)

84   For a thorough review of the Federal enforcement during the Reagan years and before of laws dealing with language-minority students, including a discussion of the enforcement of both civil rights laws and the Bilingual Education Act, which provides Federal funds for the education of language-minority students to school districts, see Elliot M. Mincberg, Naomi Cahn, Marcia R. Isaacson, and James J. Lyons, "The Problems of Segregation and Inequality of Educational Opportunity," chap. 7, pp. 88-127, in Citizens' Commission on Civil Rights, *One Nation Indivisible: The Civil Rights Challenge of the 1990s* (1988) (hereafter cited as *Citizens' Commission Report*).

85   483 F.2d 791 (1973).

86   *Id.* at 793.

87   *Id.*

duty to provide language instruction to compensate for students' language handicaps.[88] The court also concluded that the school district's failure to give non-English-speaking students special attention "does not amount to a 'denial'. . .of educational opportunities"[89] and its responsibility "extends no further than to provide them with the same facilities, textbooks, teachers and curriculum as is provided to other children in the district."[90] The dissenting judge, however, pointed out that:

> when [a student] cannot understand the language employed in the school, he cannot be said to have an educational opportunity in any sense. . . .His educational opportunity is manifestly unequal even though there is an illusion of equality since the facilities, books, and teachers made available are the same as those made available to the rest of the students. . .A pupil knowing only a foreign language cannot be said to have an educational opportunity equal to his fellow students unless and until he acquires some minimal facility in the English language.[91]

In 1974 the U.S. Supreme Court, in *Lau v. Nichols,* unanimously overturned the lower court's decision, finding that the San Francisco Unified School District had violated Title VI of the Civil Rights Act of 1964.[92] The Supreme Court held that the school district's failure to provide English-language instruction denied a meaningful opportunity for LEP students to participate in the public educational program[93] and that "there is no equality of treatment merely by providing students with the same facilities, textbooks, teachers, and curriculum."[94] The Court further pointed out that since the California Education Code requires proficiency in English as a prerequisite for graduation, and basic English skills are at the core of what public schools teach, it makes a "mockery of public education" to require that a child must already have acquired those basic skills in order to participate effectively in the educational program.[95] Thus, in *Lau v. Nichols* the Supreme Court made it clear that under Title VI school districts' obligation to provide equal educational opportunity for all children includes the responsibility to take affirmative steps "to rectify the language deficiency in order to open" programs to LEP children.[96]

Federal Enforcement of Title VI After Lau

Development of Guidelines for Compliance with the Lau Decision—The enforcement and compliance oversight responsibility for Title VI lay originally with the Office for Civil Rights in the Department of Health, Education, and Welfare (OCR/HEW), and when the Department of Education was formed, it fell to the Office for Civil Rights in the Department of Education (OCR).[97]

---

88   *Id.* at 797.

89   *Id.* at 797.

90   *Id.* at 799.

91   *Id.* at 801.

92   414 U.S. 563 (1974).

93   *Id.* at 568.

94   *Id.* at 566.

95   *Id.*

96   *Id.* at 570, *quoting* 45 C.F.R. §80.3 *et seq.* (Stewart, J., concurring).

97   In addition to Title VI of the Civil Rights Act of 1964 (42 U.S.C. §2000d *et seq.*), OCR is responsible for enforcing the following Federal civil rights laws prohibiting discrimination in federally assisted education programs and activities:

      1) Title IX of the Education Amendments of 1972, which prohibits discrimination on the basis of sex (20 U.S.C. §1681 *et seq.*);

      2) sec. 504 of the Rehabilitation Act of 1973, which prohibits discrimination on the basis of physical and mental handicap (29

Since the *Lau* Court did not address what kind of special instruction schools should provide to LEP students, it became necessary for OCR/HEW to develop guidelines to help school districts understand their responsibilities to language-minority students under Title VI as interpreted in the *Lau* decision. The guidelines, usually referred to as the "*Lau* Remedies" or "*Lau* Guidelines"[98] were issued in August 1975 and widely circulated in memorandum form to school officials and the public. Although the *Lau* Remedies were neither published in the *Federal Register* nor promulgated as formal regulations, they quickly evolved into the de facto standards that the OCR/HEW staff applied to assess school districts' compliance with Title VI under *Lau*.[99] In subsequent years, several court decisions were based on whether or not the Lau Remedies had been followed.[100] In 1978, however, the Northwest Arctic School District in Alaska filed a suit challenging OCR/HEW's use of the *Lau* Remedies as the basis for determining Title VI compliance on the grounds that the Remedies had never been published in the *Federal Register* or promulgated as formal regulations. In a consent decree, OCR/HEW agreed to publish formal Title VI *Lau* compliance guidelines at the earliest practical date.[101] In August 1980, in compliance with the consent decree, the newly formed Department of Education published in the *Federal Register* a Notice of Proposed Rulemaking (NPRM), which required school districts receiving Federal assistance to provide special instruction to all LEP students.[102]

The NPRM was widely criticized as too prescriptive,[103] however, and it was officially withdrawn in the early days of the first Reagan administration (February 1981). Subsequently, on December 3, 1985, OCR issued a new set of Title VI compliance procedures.[104] Like the 1975 *Lau* Remedies, the 1985 compliance procedures were never published in the *Federal Register*, but they remain OCR's stated policy. The 1985 procedures reaffirm that school districts serving LEP students must "take affirmative steps" to open their instructional programs to language-minority students.[105] In determining whether a school district has taken appropriate steps, they are not prescriptive, however:

In providing educational services to language minority students, school districts may use any method or program that has proven successful, or may implement any sound educational program that promises to be successful. Districts are expected to carry out their programs, evaluate the results to make sure the programs are working as anticipated, and modify programs that do not meet these expectations.[106]

U.S.C. §794); and

   3) the Age Discrimination Act of 1975, which prohibits discrimination on the basis of age (42 U.S.C. §6101 *et seq.*)

98   Officially entitled "Task Force Findings Specifying Remedies Available for Eliminating Past Educational Practices Ruled Unlawful Under Lau v. Nichols."

99   U.S. Department of Education, "The Office for Civil Rights' Title VI Language Minority Compliance Procedures," issued Dec. 3, 1985, reissued Apr. 6, 1990, p. 2 (hereafter cited as "Title VI Compliance Procedures").

100   For example, see Serna v. Portales Municipal Schools, 499 F.2d 1147 (10th Cir. 1974); Cintron v. Brentwood Union Free School Districts, 455 F. Supp. 57 (E.D.N.Y. 1976); and Rios v. Reed, 480 F. Supp. 14 (E.D.N.Y 1978).

101   Northwest Arctic School District v. Califano, No. A-77-216 (D. Alaska Sept. 29, 1978). Cited in James J. Lyons, *Legal Responsibilities of Education Agencies Serving National Origin Language Minority Students* (Washington, DC: Mid-Atlantic Equity Center, American University, 1988).

102   45 Fed. Reg. 52,052 (1980).

103   Lyons, *Legal Responsibilities of Education Agencies*, p. 19.

104   "Title VI Compliance Procedures."

105   Ibid., p. 2.

OCR Enforcement of the Rights of Language-Minority Students—In recent years OCR has received substantial criticism for its alleged failure to enforce Title VI requirements aggressively. In 1988, for instance, a Citizens' Commission on Civil Rights analysis of OCR's enforcement activities came to the following conclusion: "With respect to ensuring equal educational opportunity for limited-English-proficient students,. . ., OCR [has] failed to fulfill [its] responsibilities over the last eight years."[107] Similar charges of OCR's nonenforcement of its obligations were made repeatedly at congressional oversight hearings held in 1982, 1985, and 1987.[108]

In 1985 Congress requested OCR to compile data on its enforcement activities.[109] These data revealed that during the period from 1981 through 1985 school districts were nine times less likely to be scheduled for a compliance review than during the previous 5-year period.[110] During this same period, OCR conducted only 95 compliance reviews covering 65 districts, compared with 573 districts reviewed between 1976 and 1980.[111] When violators agreed to take corrective action, OCR officials rarely made site visits to see whether corrective actions had been taken as agreed.[112] An *Education Week* analysis of the data found that:

[o]f the 78 plans negotiated or renegotiated under the Reagan Administration, only 6 have been the targets of subsequent monitoring or compliance reviews. From 1981 to 1983, 44 districts failed compliance reviews and agreed to make changes. But OCR returned to only two of these for later review or monitoring.[113]

Other oversight functions of OCR such as complaint investigation and monitoring visits also declined sharply.[114] In the 202 reviews OCR had conducted since 1981, it found a 58 percent rate of compliance violation with Title VI.[115]

The steady and mounting criticism of OCR led to a 1988 congressional investigation of OCR enforcement activities.[116] This investigation concluded that "the agency has adamantly failed to enforce the civil rights laws according to its mandate"[117] and that "the history of OCR is a history of lethargy, defiance, and unwillingness to enforce the law."[118] Some of the major findings of this report were:

---

106   Ibid., p. 3.

107   *Citizens' Commission Report*, p. 123.

108   U.S. House of Representatives, Committee on Education and Labor, *A Report on the Investigation of the Civil Rights Enforcement Activities of the Office for Civil Rights, U.S Department of Education*, H.R. Serial No. 100-FF, 100th Cong., 2nd Sess. (1989), pp. 20-21 (hereafter cited as *Investigation of OCR*).

109   In December 1985 the House Education and Labor Committee, the Judiciary Subcommittee on Civil and Constitutional Rights, and the Government Operations' Subcommittee on Human Resources and Intergovernmental Relations requested enforcement data from OCR, which was then analyzed by *Education Week*, resulting in a report. James Crawford, "U.S. Enforcement of Bilingual Plans Declines Sharply," *Education Week*, vol. V, no. 37 (June 4, 1986), p. 1.

110   Crawford, "Enforcement of Bilingual Plans Declines," p. 1.

111   Ibid., p. 14.

112   Ibid., p. 1.

113   Ibid., p. 15.

114   Ibid., p. 1.

115   *Investigation of OCR*, p. 2.

116   Ibid.

117   Ibid., p. 1.

118   Ibid., p. 20.

1) OCR "has not vigorously enforced laws protecting the rights of women and minorities in education since 1981."[119]

2) "There was a clear perception among the [OCR] regional office staff that certain issues were 'off limits' and could not be investigated. Most of the issues involved race discrimination. Among such issues were: discrimination involving disciplinary actions and the placement of black students in special education programs."[120]

3) "The National Office made it virtually impossible to find a violation of the civil rights laws because the standard of proof required to establish a violation was a stringent 'intent' standard, which many regional staff interviewed believed was not required by the courts."[121]

At a House Committee on Education and Labor oversight hearing on November 28, 1989, then-Acting Assistant Secretary for Civil Rights William L. Smith made a point-by-point response to the findings of the 1989 report.[122] Regarding the specific findings listed above, Smith responded as follows:

1) In response to the first finding, Smith noted that the finding was based on statistical evidence on the types of complaints OCR had investigated and on the number of complaints it had found to be justified, and he argued that "OCR has no control over the kinds of complaints it receives or the merits of those complaints."[123]

2) In response to the second "off limits" finding, Smith stated "except for those issues over which OCR has no jurisdiction, no issues are 'off limits' to OCR. All issues that arise through the complaint process are treated equally, and investigations are carried out as necessary to resolve any issues raised by the complaint allegations."[124]

3) In response to the allegation that OCR's national office had adopted an "intent" standard of proof, Smith stated that "the regulations do not require proof of intent to discriminate to find a violation of Title VI. . . .The regional offices have never been told that a violation of Title VI will be found only if the regional offices can obtain evidence of intent to discriminate. All evidence gathered in an investigation, including any evidence of an intent to discriminate, is evaluated under the pertinent regulations to determine whether the recipients are in compliance."[125]

Faced with continuing allegations of OCR's neglect of its oversight responsibility and the lack of evidence of visible improvement, Con-

119   Of the 9,768 complaints investigations initiated by OCR during FYs 1981-1988, only 3 percent was related to national origin discrimination allegations, 15 percent to race discrimination, and 17 percent to gender discrimination. Of the 1,378 compliance reviews initiated, only 46 related to national origin discrimination issues and 162 to race discrimination. Ibid., p. 2.

120   Ibid., p. 4.

121   Ibid., p. 5.

122   William L. Smith, Acting Assistant Secretary for Civil Rights, U.S. Department of Education, "Office for Civil Rights Response to the Committee on Education and Labor Staff Report Entitled Investigation of the Civil Rights Enforcement Activities of the Office for Civil Rights, U.S. Department of Education," pp. 302-271 in U.S. House of Representatives, Committee on Education and Labor, *Hearing on the Federal Enforcement of Equal Educational Opportunity Laws*, H.R. Serial No. 101-73, 101st Cong., 1st Sess. (1990).

123   Ibid., p. 311.

124   Ibid., p. 333.

125   Ibid., p. 334.

gress requested the General Accounting Office (GAO) to conduct an investigation of OCR activities. In July 1991, GAO released a report on OCR's enforcement activities with respect to within-school discrimination which found that the number of compliance reviews conducted by OCR in this area declined between 1987 and 1990, that OCR had not issued much internal policy guidance on how to conduct compliance reviews on this topic, and OCR had not adequately monitored districts' corrective actions.[126] In response to GAO's findings, Assistant Secretary for Civil Rights Michael L. Williams noted that the number of compliance reviews had declined in all areas because of a dramatic increase in the number of complaint investigations OCR needed to undertake, that OCR had already prepared a draft of the written policy guidance on how to conduct within-school-discrimination compliance investigations, and OCR had recently made monitoring compliance a top priority.[127]

OCR made "Equal Educational Opportunities for National-Origin Minority and Native-American Students Who are Limited-English Proficient" its number one priority issue for fiscal year 1991.[128] OCR is planning to increase the number of compliance reviews it undertakes in this and other high priority areas.[129] In September 1991 Assistant Secretary Williams issued a policy update on schools' obligations under Lau, and OCR also has provided guidance and training to its regional staff on procedures for investigations involving charges of noncompliance with Title VI as interpreted by the Lau Court.[130]

Two Recent Court Cases

In recent years, two successful lawsuits have been filed on behalf of Asian American LEP students. In each case, school officials agreed to take affirmative steps to remedy the language deficiency of students to bring the defendant school district into compliance with Title VI under Lau. One of these suits was in Philadelphia, Pennsylvania, and the other in Lowell, Massachusetts.

Y.S. v. School District of Philadelphia— More than 20,000 refugees from Southeast Asia settled in Philadelphia after 1975, and in the early 1980s it became apparent that Asian LEP students were failing in large numbers at the junior and senior high schools, and that their educational needs were not being met in significant ways. Informal negotiations with district officials failed to produce any results. In December 1985 a lawsuit[131] was filed against the Philadelphia School District by the Education Law Center, a public interest law firm, on behalf of Asian LEP students. It was the first Federal lawsuit concerning the affirmative obligation of a school district toward its LEP students since the Supreme Court's Lau decision in 1974.[132] The suit

---

126   U.S. General Accounting Office, *Within-School Discrimination: Inadequate Title VI Enforcement by the Office for Civil Rights* (Washington, DC: Government Printing Office, 1991), pp. 4-5.

127   Michael L. Williams, Assistant Secretary for Civil Rights, letter to Franklin Frazier, Director, Education and Employment Issues, U.S. General Accounting Office, May 10, 1991, as printed in ibid., pp. 73-77.

128   Michael Williams, Assistant Secretary for Civil Rights, "National Enforcement Strategy, Office for Civil Rights: FYs 1991-1992," Dec. 11, 1990.

129   In fiscal year 1991, OCR initiated 12 Title VI *Lau* compliance reviews out of a total of 40 reviews initiated. OCR is planning to increase the number of *Lau* compliance reviews still further in fiscal year 1992. Michael L. Williams, Assistant Secretary for Civil Rights, U.S. Department of Education, letter to Wilfredo J. Gonzalez, Staff Director, U.S. Commission on Civil Rights, Oct. 16, 1991, p. 1.

130   Ibid, p. 2.

131   Y.S. v. School District of Philadelphia, C.A. No. 85-6924 (E.D. Pa., 1985).

132   Len Rieser, *A Short History of Y.S. v. School District of Philadelphia* (Education Law Center: July 1990), pp. 1-2.

alleged that the school district had failed to take sufficient steps to address the problems stemming from LEP students' and their parents' language handicaps, and that as a result the students were without adequate counseling services, bilingual instruction, and special education. It further alleged that the students' parents were denied meaningful notice and an opportunity to be heard with respect to decisions about their children's education.[133]

Plaintiffs' efforts to interest the district in reaching an out-of-court settlement drew no substantive response until the court began the process of scheduling a trial date in late 1987. As the trial became imminent, the district indicated that it would consider a settlement.[134] The resulting negotiations eventually produced an "Interim Remedial Agreement," which was approved and entered by the court on May 4, 1988.[135] In the agreement, the district "recognizes and accepts its obligation to facilitate the linguistic, academic, and cultural transition of language minority students in the public school system. Additionally, the intent of [this plan is] to facilitate and support such transition while maintaining and fostering an appreciation and respect for the cultures and languages of language minority students."[136] Under the agreement, the district was to undertake a set of immediate remedies and appoint a cabinet-level officer who would develop and implement a long-range remedial plan to be implemented under the court supervision. The court has retained jurisdiction of *Y.S.* at least through mid-1993, and has demonstrated an interest in ensuring that its orders are carried out.[137]

Hispanic Parents Advisory Council v. Kouleharas—On July 31, 1987, a lawsuit was filed against the Lowell School Committee on behalf of Hispanic, Southeast Asian, and other language-minority students alleging unconstitutional segregation and denial of educational opportunities to students of limited English proficiency.[138] The minority enrollment in the Lowell Public Schools had been approximately 4 percent in 1975, but, with the heavy influx of Southeast Asian refugees starting in the late 1970s, it had reached 40 percent by 1987.[139] In the 1986-1987 school year, one-half of all minority students were enrolled in bilingual/bicultural educational programs, and about 60 percent of the enrollees were Southeast Asian students.[140] These minority students were concentrated in several schools[141] with substandard facilities. The suit charged that:

---

133 Ibid., pp. 1-2.

134 Ibid., p. 4.

135 Y.S. v. School District of Philadelphia, C.A. 85-6924, Interim Remedial Agreement, entered E.D. Pa., May 4, 1988.

136 School District of Philadelphia, Office of Curriculum, *Proposed Remedial Plan for Services to Asian LEP Students* (December 1988), p. 4.

137 Quarterly reports, which are reviewed and countersigned by the plaintiffs, are submitted to the court for review. Plaintiffs seem to be reasonably satisfied with the progresses made by the school district. For example, see Leonard Rieser, "Fourth Quarterly Report to the Court for Y.S., et al., v. School District of Philadelphia, C.A. No. 85-6924," Apr. 16, 1990.

138 Hispanic Parents Advisory Council v. Kouleharas, Civ. Action No. 87-1968-MA.

139 Peter Nien-chu Kiang, "Southeast Asian Parent Empowerment: The Challenge of Changing Demographics in Lowell, Massachusetts," *Asian American Policy Review*, vol. 1, no. 1 (1990). With 25,000 Cambodian residents, Lowell now has the second largest community of Cambodian refugees in the country after Long Beach, CA. In addition, Lowell has approximately 5,000 residents from other Southeast Asian countries. Ibid.

140 Hispanic Parents Advisory Council v. Kouleharas, at 18-19.

141 For example, in 1986, the Ames School and the Moore Street School had 73.9 percent and 72.1 percent minority students, respectively. The adoption of the Boys Club as a school resulted in 100 percent minority enrollment. (*Id.* at 18.) During the 1989 school year, when Southeast Asian students made up roughly 23 percent of Lowell's total enrollment, there was one school that was 64 per-

1) Bilingual students are unlawfully segregated and housed in "inappropriate, overcrowded, substandard,. . .unsafe facilities."[142]

2) There is an "insufficient number of personnel to implement the bilingual/bicultural education programs."[143] and

3) Defendants created an employment barrier to hiring linguistic minority candidates by "deliberately refus[ing]" to abandon the passing of the National Teachers Examination test as a prerequisite.[144]

The suit resulted in a settlement under which the Lowell Public Schools adopted a Voluntary *Lau* Compliance Plan,[145] which was characterized as a model "pointing a direction in which the tide can be turned."[146] This plan contained specific remedial provisions regarding equitable student assignment,[147] increasing qualified bilingual staff personnel,[148] better identification of LEP students, and prompt service to them.[149] Also contained in the plan was a dropout prevention and recovery program,[150] a noteworthy feature that responded to the high dropout rate of LEP students in Lowell.[151] Since its inception, 30 students have graduated from the program with a high school diploma, and there are approximately 80 students participating in the program at any one time.[152] Among those monitoring the implementation of the plan, there is a shared sense of some progress.[153]

Racial Tensions in Public Schools

Public high school campuses throughout the Nation are confronted with a high level of racial tension and are often marred by incidents of bigotry and violence. Several recent studies[154] on immigrant/refugee students in public schools

---

cent Southeast Asian and four other schools with Southeast Asian percentages above 40 percent. It also had four schools that were 5 percent or less Southeast Asian. (Materials provided by Dr. Juan Rodriguez, Program Director, Bilingual/ESL, College of Education, University of Lowell, Lowell, MA.)

142 Ibid., p. 20.

143 Ibid., p. 22.

144 Ibid., p. 23.

145 Lowell Public Schools, Lowell, MA, *Voluntary Lau Compliance Plan* (Oct. 28, 1988).

146 Camilo Perez-Bustillo, Chief Counsel for Plaintiffs, cited in Deborah L. Gold, "Legal Settlement in Bilingual Case Hailed as Model," *Education Week*, vol. VIII, no. 16 (Jan. 11, 1989).

147 Consent Agreement at 1-2.

148 *Id.* at 13-19.

149 *Id.* at 22-24.

150 *Id.* at 26-28. The program is conducted at a community college instead of at the Lowell High School so that the dropout students do not have to come back to the same setting that they decided to leave. Courses are taught by the teachers from the Lowell High School to ensure program quality, and counseling services are offered through interpreters or bilingual counselors. James T. Foye, Director of Guidance, Lowell (MA) School District, telephone interview, Aug. 21, 1990 (hereafter cited as Foye interview).

151 "Hispanic, Cambodian, and Laotian linguistic minority students have dropped out of the Lowell Public Schools at a disproportionate rate throughout the period of time that the Lowell Public Schools have failed to comply with federal law respecting treatment of these students. . . .During the 1986-1987 school year, over half of the Laotian students who started out the school year in the Lowell High School dropped out due to the absence of Lao-speaking staff there to provide school instruction or counseling." Hispanic Parents Advisory Council v. Kouleharas, at 24.

152 Foye interview.

153 Roger Rice, Director, Multicultural Educational Training Advocacy (META), Summerville, MA, telephone interview, July 12, 1990.

154 These studies are:

offer a distressing portrait of the unfriendly, often hostile school environment in which many Asian American students, especially immigrant children, find themselves. One study summarized the school climate facing immigrant children as follows:

If they come to schools seeking a social safe haven, a place to recapture some of a lost childhood, and a place to begin building for a better future, they are often bitterly disappointed.

It was distressing to hear so many young newcomers describe the hatred, prejudice and violence which too often awaits them in U.S. schools. Young immigrants told [us] at length about the insensitivity — often bordering on outright racism — directed toward them by American students, and sometimes by teachers. "What have we done to be treated this way?" they asked, over and over again.!155

A similar characterization is given by another study:

Racial and ethnic hostility, violence and prejudice clearly are an integral part of the social fabric on most school campuses and in many communities. This is of humanitarian concern because of the effects on the children who are its victims. But it is also of concern because of what it says about our society. Native U.S. born children are given little help, through the school curricula and programs or in their community role models, in understanding the newcomers in their midst. Fear, intolerance, ethnocentrism and prejudice prevent a democracy from thriving, and make a pluralistic society unworkable. The majority of the immigrant students in our research believe that Americans feel negatively and unwelcoming towards them. Comments like, "they look down on us," "they are afraid we are going to take over," "they wish we'd go back where we came from," or "they think we are taking their jobs and money" were most common. . . .

Almost every student in our sample reported the first school year included incidents of being called names, pushed or spat upon, deliberately tricked, teased and laughed at because of their race, language difficulties, accent or foreign dress.

A third study, the indepth investigation of the adaptation of refugee students in the San Diego city school system cited above, reveals a similar picture. The authors conclude:

[R]efugee students were affected by the racism shown by other students and staff toward [them]. The pervasiveness of name-calling and even physical confrontations based on ethnic-racial grounds was discussed by many [of] our respondents. . . .Almost all of the respondents have experienced some form of racism in the U.S., and many have been affected deeply by it, [leading one Khmer respondent to conclude] that no one who is not white can ever really become an

---

John Willshire Carrera, *New Voices: Immigrant Students in U.S. Public Schools* (Boston: National Coalition of Advocates for Students, 1988) (hereafter cited as *New Voices*). This study was based in part on 1) 180 structured interviews and 24 case studies; 2) five public hearings in which approximately 150 witnesses participated; and 3) interviews with Federal, State, local, and school personnel familiar with the school experiences of immigrant children. *New Voices*, p. 133.

Laurie Olsen, *Crossing the Schoolhouse Border: Immigrant Students and the California Public Schools* (San Francisco: California Tomorrow, 1988) (hereafter cited as *Crossing the Border*). This study incorporates findings from 1) 360 indepth interviews with recently arrived immigrant students; 2) interviews with close to 200 community advocates, agency staff, teachers, and researchers; 3) a study of 29 school districts; and 4) public hearings at which 55 witnesses presented testimony. *Crossing the Border*, p. 112.

Ruben G. Rumbaut and Kenji Ima, *The Adaptation of Southeast Asian Refugee Youth: A Comparative Study, Final Report to the U.S. Department of Health and Human Services, Office of Refugee Resettlement* (January 1988) (hereafter cited as *Adaptation of Youth*). This report relied on several data sources, including official records from the San Diego city schools containing demographic and educational performance information on 24,666 students, dropout data on 2,691 students, and suspension data on 8,102 students. For further details on other data sources used in the report, see *Adaptation of Youth*, pp. 12-18.

155   *New Voices*, p. 59.
156   *Crossing the Border*, p. 35.

"American.". . .It is clear that Southeast Asian refugee students have been subjected in recent years to pervasive racial prejudice within the public schools, reflecting more general anti-Asian attitudes in the wider society, and that this is a factor which exacerbates the problems of their adjustment.[157]

The personal testimony of a female student who immigrated to this country from China offers vivid details:

[When I came to America,] working extremely hard didn't make us feel sad, facing challenges didn't make us feel sad, but some of the Americans' attitudes towards us did break our hearts. Before I came to America I had a beautiful dream about this country. At that time I didn't know that the first word I learned in this country would be a dirty word. American students always picked on us, frightened us, made fun of us and laughed at our English. They broke our lockers, threw food on us in cafeteria, said dirty words to us, pushed us on the campus. Many times they shouted at me "Get out of here, you chink, go back to your country." Many times they pushed me and yell on me. I've been pushed, I had gum thrown on my hair. I've been hit by stones, I've been shot by air-gun. I've been insulted by all the dirty words in English. All this really made me frustrated and sad. I often asked myself, "Why do they pick on me?"[158]

This portrait of the racially hostile environment encountered by Asian American students in our schools is consistent with what Commission staff has learned from site visits and interviews. For instance, one participant at our New York Roundtable Conference cited racial harassment of Asian American students by other students as her top concern and gave several chilling examples of students who had been physically assaulted in racial incidents in New York City schools.[159]

School teachers and staff may themselves add to the hostile climate. Many Asian American children perceive their teachers and school officials to be prejudiced against them. For instance, in San Diego, it was found that Vietnamese students felt that they were not treated fairly by their teachers:

[One] student said that a teacher told them to shut up and then made a negative reference to Vietnam. Others identified certain teachers as imposing what they felt was unfair punishment on Vietnamese students. They feel little can be done to correct such incidents, accepting the advice of older refugees about "not making waves," yet they also feel that non-refugee students get help for their problems.[160]

It also appears that school officials often fail to take adequate steps to deal with this racially charged environment. Teachers and administrators apparently frequently minimize or overlook the seriousness of anti-Asian sentiments in public schools. Even when racial tensions are called to the attention of school officials, it is alleged, they often brush aside the problem or explain it away in a glib manner. When Asian American students get involved in disputes or fights with other students, teachers and administrators are said to come down harder and impose harsher disciplinary actions on the Asian students. A New York Roundtable Conference participant gave several examples of unequal discipline in New York City schools and cited Korean American parents as saying:

We just don't understand. In Korea, two people talk in classroom, both will be punished. We don't understand. There is a new rule in America. If two people talk in the classroom, only one kid is punished, and it will be the Korean kid.[161]

---

157 *Adaptation of Youth*, pp. 96-97.

158 *Crossing the Border*, p. 34.

159 Theresa Ying Hsu, Director, Asian American Communications, Statement at the U.S. Commission on Civil Rights Roundtable Conference on Asian American Civil Rights Issues for the 1990s, New York, NY, June 12, 1989 (hereafter cited as Hsu Statement).

160 *Adaptation of Youth*, p. 61.

School officials' failure to recognize the serious ramifications of racial incidents and their inability to intervene effectively results in their losing credibility as a reliable source of impartial adjudication. As a result, some students take matters into their own hands in resolving what they consider unjust situations. These interrelated factors are said to contribute to and in a way be responsible for the outbreak of interracial incidents, sometimes involving deadly arms.

Even when school officials recognize the seriousness of the situation, they may receive little support from district administrators. As an example, in an incident brought to the attention of the Commission at the Houston Roundtable Conference,[162] the parents of students who were responsible for sending hate literature to an Asian American teacher and who initially were severely punished by their high school principal were able to persuade district officials to undo the punishment. For several years prior to the incident, Sharpstown Senior High School in Houston had been the scene of mounting racial tensions as the school's minority population increased rapidly.[163] The situation became so extreme that a new principal was assigned to the school specifically to control the racial problems. The new principal clamped down hard on racist behavior, instituting a policy of suspending for the rest of the year students caught fighting. The school climate appeared to be improving when Betty Waki, an Asian American teacher who was the advisor to the yearbook, received an application to be on the yearbook staff that was filled with racist parody and anti-Asian remarks. The principal suspended the two honor students responsible for the racist application for 3 days. When the students' parents appealed, the district superintendent reversed the principal's decision, instead placing the students on detention for 4 hours and assigning them to write a 300-word essay. The reversal of the principal's decision undermined his authority and resulted in students taking his efforts to combat racism in the schools less seriously. Participants at the Commission's Houston Roundtable Conference alleged that the district superintendent's decision was only one example of a long history of insensitivity to Asian American concerns by the Houston Independent School District.[164]

Described below are several other specific incidents illustrating the generic situation depicted in the foregoing pages. Of these incidents, the story of Chol-Soo Lee's high school years is typical of the ordeal that many Asian Americans, particularly immigrant or LEP students, have to endure. At age 13 he was already confined in a juvenile hall, and at age 20 he was a convicted murderer serving a life sentence (which was overturned later, setting him free.) An account of how he initially got into trouble with the law is illustrative:[165]

At the age of 12, Chol-Soo came to the United States from Korea to join his mother after 2 years of separation. By the time he joined his mother, she had already left her abusive GI husband and had come to San Francisco with her 4-year-old daughter. For 2 years she had been working 16 hours a day, seven days a week, as a motel maid during daytime hours and as bar-

161   Anonymous Korean American parents, as cited in Hsu Statement.

162   Glenda Kay Joe, Statement at the U.S. Commission on Civil Rights Roundtable Conference on Asian Civil Rights Issues for the 1990s, Houston, TX, May 27, 1989 (hereafter cited as Glenda Joe Statement).

163   The following account of the incident is based on Barbara Karkabi, "Betty Waki: Sharpstown Teacher Devoted to Easing School's Racial Tension," *Houston Chronicle*, Apr. 24, 1989, p. D1.

164   Glenda Joe Statement and Michael Chou, Statement at the U.S. Commission on Civil Rights Roundtable Conference on Asian Civil Rights Issues for the 1990s, Houston, TX, May 27, 1989.

165   This account is a summary based on K.W. Lee, "Lost in a Strange Culture: The Americanization of Chol-Soo Lee," *Sacramento Union*, Jan. 29, 1979.

maid at night to save money for Chol-Soo to travel to the States.

Within a year of his arrival, he was confined to a juvenile hall following a fight with a student and a shoving incident involving three school teachers, including his vice principal. Several key players described the precipitating incident as follows.

According to his mother, "One day I was in shower. The school principal say 'you hurry and come down to school.' Chol-Soo was already gone to juvenile hall. Police took him. I go to the school board. What kind of school is this? He speaks no English, and they take him to juvenile hall. . . .I was so ashamed and sad. I talk to my son in Korean. What happen? He say 'I walk in line with boys. A boy bump into me. He hit me. I hit him. He hit me again. I hit him back.' Why? 'The boy call Korean boy stupid, stupid. Teachers say I am wrong. I am crazy boy.'. . .They say my boy kick principal. My boy say three teachers hold him tight. 'I try to get away from them, so I kick up. They call police.'"[166]

According to the vice principal's report of the incident, "Lee and another boy had a fight in which Lee had deliberately attacked the other boy. The principal called Lee into his office and while he was talking to him, Lee ran out to the class and brought the boy back. The principal talked to the other boy and excused him. As the other boy walked out, Lee leaped up and ran after and attacked him. The principal and other teachers dragged Lee off while the boy was swearing and kicking. The principal believed Lee was quite disturbed."[167]

According to Chol-Soo himself, as narrated to a reporter, "Some guy bumped into me in the hallway and looked toward me as if it was my fault. He started the fight, so I fought him back. During the fight a teacher grabbed and started taking me down to school principal's office and let the guy I was fighting with go to his class. I couldn't understand what the teacher told the principal, but he said he was calling my mother to let her know I was suspended from school again. So I tried to explain to the principal I was not at fault in the fight and couldn't succeed because of my English. So I thought if I brought the other boy he will tell the truth so I can be saved from being suspended, but when the guy was telling what happened, I understood enough to know that he was telling a lie. So I tried to tell he was lying, but the principal didn't believe or couldn't understand what I was saying. I was so angry I started fighting the guy. The principal grabbed me and the guy ran out. The principal and other teachers held me until police came."[168]

The probation officer's report on the incident stated, "The boy admits he had been fighting another boy but it was his contention that it was the other boy's fault. He says that the principal didn't listen to what he was trying to tell him, and he became very angry and shoved the principal. . .It should be understood that he is new to American culture since he came to the United States only a year ago. In this writer's opinion, intense counseling either through the school department or through the children's hospital should now be employed to hasten his adjustment to the American way of life. It may take another year or more for him to become entirely assimilated, but with professional assistance, this writer is confident the lad will eventually come through okay."[169]

In the following episode the anger caused by harassment and the desire to avenge and do justice erupted into violence involving deadly weapons:

---

166   Ibid., p. 2.
167   Ibid.
168   Ibid., p. 5.
169   Ibid., p. 4.

During a lunch break on Jan. 16, 1990, two youths opened fire on a group of students outside Central High School, Providence, Rhode Island, missing their target but striking two bystanders. The two gunmen, a Cambodian student at Central and his Cambodian friend from Lowell, Massachusetts, were arrested minutes after the shooting. They told the police that they were aiming at one of several white youths who had been harassing Cambodian students. According to these students, Southeast Asian students (largely Cambodians) are constantly harassed by a "group of white students" and called names. "The name-calling erupted into a fight with sticks, pipes and bottles last fall and has been festering since. The problem escalated last week, including a fight in which one Cambodian student reportedly suffered a broken arm." One of the two youths at Central High School decided to fight back and enlisted assistance from his friend in Lowell.[170]

The next episode shows the erosion in the trust between Asian American students and school officials:

In early February 1990, a Cambodian girl at Central High School in Providence, Rhode Island, got into a fight with other girls and got suspended for a week although the other two girls she fought against were not. After the fight, the Cambodian girl armed herself with a dart because of continuing harassment and abuse, as well as fear of physical attack.[171]

When she was suspended, the girl came with her parents to the Cambodian community service center, puzzled as to why the teachers had not listened to both sides of the story. They wanted to know why the other girls did not get suspended. This episode presented hardly anything new to the center staff; they had heard of similar incidents many times before. Although the center staff did not attempt to clarify the circumstances of suspension with school officials,[172] the incident nevertheless shows how Cambodian students and their parents come to believe that school officials are biased against Cambodians and hand out disparate disciplinary actions.

Racial harassment, if left unchecked, can escalate into intimidation and open violence. The following incident shows how audacious the harassers can be:

In April 1989 a Cambodian social worker was driving by Central High School in Providence and saw a Cambodian girl who was just getting out of school being harassed and chased by a group of students. The woman shouted at the girl to get into her car quickly because she was afraid physical harm might be done to the girl. When the girl jumped into the car, the harassers started throwing rocks and broke all the windows. The damage was over $1,000. This type of harassment, intimidation, and terrorizing is said to be not unusual.[173]

In December 1989 a school parking lot gunfight involving Korean American students occurred in California. Here again, the incident shows that the injury to a student's pride suffered as a result of racial insults and harassment can easily erupt into open violence if it is left to fester without being resolved by appropriate authorities:

A female student of Korean descent at Calabasas High School in a suburb of Los Angeles had been racially harassed by a white male student. She asked a female friend to help with the situation, and her friend in turn alerted some Korean American male students from another high school. Several Korean American male stu-

170   Laura Meade, "2 Wounded in Central Shooting: 2 youths held; Racial Tension Blamed For Midday Attack," *Providence Journal-Bulletin*, Jan. 17, 1990.

171   Staff of the Socio-Economic Development Center for Southeast Asians, Providence, RI, interview, Apr. 18, 1990.

172   Ibid.

173   Rhode Island Advisory Committee to the U.S. Commission on Civil Rights, *Bigotry and Violence in Rhode Island*, April 1990, p. 17.

dents came to Calabasas, a scuffle with some white students ensued, and one of the visitors was beaten with a baseball bat. The following week, six Korean American male students returned to Calabasas High's parking lot in three vehicles to seek retaliation for the beating of their friend. Upon noticing the parked car of a sheriff, who had been alerted by the school administration of a possible fight, they tried to drive out of the parking lot. At this point the same student who had wielded the baseball bat the week before aimed his revolver at one of the fleeing cars and fired several rounds. Fortunately, no one was hit.[174]

Although several students at a closed school board meeting spoke in support of the Korean American student's allegation of racial tension on campus, the principal denied that there was any racial tension on campus involving Korean American students.[175] No action had been taken against the alleged harasser because, according to the principal, "we have no proof of what he's done."[176] The student's explanation as to why she did not go to school officials is revealing: "If you bring it to the principal, all they could do is talk to the person, suspend the person: next time, he would get revenge on you. It could only get worse."[177]

A strikingly similar incident took place in Long Beach, California, this time involving Crystal, a ninth grader who came to the U.S. from Cambodia at the age of 2:[178]

While waiting for a ride on the curbside, Crystal got into an argument with another girl, as had happened many times before. This time, however, a male student who was standing nearby started pushing Crystal. At about this time,

Crystal's older brother arrived to pick her up. Seeing his sister being pushed around by a male student, he got out of his car and challenged the pusher, "That is my sister, if you have to push her why don't you push me." A scuffle began. Although the school vice principal was standing nearby all through the commotion, he did absolutely nothing until the situation began to get out of hand. The scuffle was finally broken up and the crowd dispersed. Upon returning home, Crystal and her brother were severely scolded by their father because the principal had already called and given a distorted account of the incident.

The following day Crystal and her brother went to school to complain to officials for having given a distorted account to their father without hearing their side of the story. When they challenged the vice principal to give his account of what he had seen at the scene, he shouted back saying, "Shut up before I put you on the boat."

At about this time, there was a noisy disturbance outside the building, near where they had parked their car. Dashing outside, they found that a group of students were kicking and rocking their car with their cousin inside. There was a lot of pushing, and soon Crystal's brother and cousin were in the midst of a fight with other Caucasian students. School officials came to the scene and found a gun in her brother's hand. The police were called, and the situation was brought under control. Crystal's brother and cousin were spared from being arrested when Crystal's father negotiated an agreement with the principal that Crystal would withdraw from school voluntarily.[179]

---

174   This account is a condensed version based on Sophia Kyung Kim, "Calabasas Student May Face Expulsion From High School: Korean Teen Says She Was Victim of Racial Slurs," *Korea Times* (Los Angeles Edition), Jan. 19, 1990.

175   Ibid.

176   Ibid.

177   Ibid.

178   The following account is based on information provided by Crystal Hul. Crystal Hul, telephone interview, Nov. 28, 1990 (hereafter cited as Crystal Hul interview).

According to Crystal, on several previous occasions Cambodian students had told the vice principal about incidents of racial harassment, but he had done nothing. Refugee students from Cambodia generally do not go to school officials with their interracial problems for two reasons: 1) they are not confident with English; and 2) they do not think it would help their situation.[180]

To this day, Crystal's father remains convinced that his children were sufficiently provoked and that the incident simply reflected underlying racial tensions that school officials refused to acknowledge. Although he believed that school officials were responsible for not addressing the real cause of the whole problem and that his children were victims of the officials' inattention rather than instigators of the incident, he did not think he could effectively argue and win the case. To protect his children's future from the adverse consequences of expulsion and police records, he decided to withdraw his daughter. He is certain that he was able to negotiate this much because he was a widely known Cambodian community leader and had some credibility with police and school officials. He suspects that other refugees with a poor command of English would have fared far worse than he and his children.[181]

Anti-Asian harassment and slurs on middle and high school campuses are neither limited to children from Southeast Asia, nor a recent phenomenon. In late 1989 a Chinese American man and his son were assaulted by a group of six white youths in their meat store in Castro Valley, California, which they had owned and operated for the past 10 years. (See above for further details on this episode.) In recounting this episode to Commission staff, the son of the Chinese American store owner, who is U.S. born and a college graduate, recalls that "anti-Asian prejudice and atmosphere are not new; they were there when I was going to junior and senior high schools here in Castro Valley. Kids routinely used to tease us by mimicking slanted eyes, and taunted and harassed us with racial remarks."[182] According to him, they were not violent; the racial incidents he had experienced in school were more or less contained but unmistakably there. Asian American kids were "sort of resigned," made the most of the situation, and did not talk about it at all. Now things are much more open and violent, "it seems that the social constraint that existed is no longer with us."[183]

There are indications that racial incidents occur among much younger children and have been out there for a long time. Here is an example:

Soon after Mrs. Kwak's 8-year-old son started attending a public school in a predominantly white neighborhood in the late 1960s, she received a phone call from the principal saying that her son, David, had pushed a girl on the school bus. After some discussion, she and the principal agreed that David should be required to walk to school for a week as punishment. She naturally gave David a long lecture that he should not hit or push little girls on the school bus and that not being able to ride the school bus was his punishment. A day or two later she received a call from a neighborhood friend, saying, "I saw David walking to school." This friend

---

179   Crystal Hul graduated from another public high school in Long Beach in 1990. (Crystal Hul interview.) The principal and vice principal of the high school who were involved in Crystal's case are no longer with the school. In the past several years, there have been no expulsions of Asian American students on account of interracial incidents. (Sue McKee, Principal, Hills Jr. High School, telephone interview, Nov. 30, 1990.)

180   Crystal Hul interview.

181   Nil Hul, Executive Director, Cambodian Association of America, Nov. 28, 1990.

182   Melvin Toy, personal interview, Castro Valley, CA, Feb. 22, 1990.

183   Ibid.

was quite amazed that Mrs. Kwak did not know and had not asked why David had pushed the girl. The neighborhood friend said that her son, who also rode the same bus as David, had seen the girl making fun of David for his Chinese appearance and the situation escalating into a shoving match. The mother immediately called the principal and reinstated David's privilege to ride the school bus, and she protested his premature account of the incident, that is, for not having looked into how the pushing got started and for having given her a prejudicial account.

Although her anger at the principal dissipated long ago, Mrs. Kwak still feels bothered by one aspect of this incident. When she confronted David later over why he had not explained that the girl had made him angry by making fun of him, he said, "Mom, I didn't want to lie or anything. She started the whole thing, but I didn't want you to feel hurt by what she said." It pains her, the mother says, to think that a young child had not only to be afflicted by an insult, but also to suppress his outrage at authority figures and accept what must have appeared an unfair punishment in order to shield his mother. She remains apprehensive that minority children leave our public schools thinking that school officials do not care to understand their concerns.[184]

A U.S.-born journalist recalls growing up in New York City as a Chinese American boy in the 1960s. His painful memories include the following facets:

I was reminded constantly that I was different. I recall how quickly my schoolmates could turn on me with taunts of "Ching, Chong, Chinaman.". . .I tried to fit in, though at times it seemed impossible, especially on the rare days when Chinese New Year or "exotic" Asia was mentioned in school. Reflexively, the entire class would turn to stare at me at the mere mention of any Asian country. "I am not from China," I would say to myself. "I'm from New York. I don't know anything about China." During recess, some students would mimic Chinese speech. Others would pull back their eyes in a squint. Behind a mask of smiles and laughs, I would try to hide my pain. . . .Racism was inescapable. Once, while I was walking home with my father, the doorman at a nearby building yelled, "Hey, China-man." My father paused momentarily, then continued walking, dragging me along behind him. There was fury in his step.[185]

One serious consequence of racial tensions in the schools has been that Asian American youth join gangs to defend themselves and become involved in criminal activities. In San Diego, for instance, after a high school riot during which Asian American students were beaten by black, Latino, and white students, the number of Cambodian gang members increased dramatically. The violent activities of Asian youth gangs in turn reinforce existing stereotypes and escalate racial tensions.[186]

Experiencing incidents such as those illustrated in the foregoing pages is likely to engender in Asian American children the feeling that they are unwelcome outsiders and a sense of societal victimization and injustice, and may cause them to become self-defensive. There are signs that some Asian Americans carry with them unhealed wounds from the racial incidents of high school days. Although such wounds are often concealed, they can remain active psychologically, hindering effective developmental growth in post-secondary education years. An Asian American counselor at a prestigious college[187] observes that many Asian American students on his campus, particularly those in their freshmen and sophomore years, are not interact-

---

184   Katherine Kwak, interview in Washington, DC, Sept. 25, 1990.

185   Steven A. Chin, "Searching for Eastern Roots: 'Hollow Bamboo' Seeks To Be Filled," *Washington Times*, May 29, 1990, p. E5. This
          story originally ran in the *San Francisco Examiner*, May 6, 1990.

186   Ima Comments, p. 3.

187   Tommy Lee Woon, Assistant Dean and Director of Asian American affairs, Oberlin College, telephone interview, Dec. 15, 1989.

ing with fellow students as actively as their non-Asian American counterparts. He sees in them an element of apprehensive caution, a deliberate withdrawal while they appraise the situation, as if they want to see if other students' openness is genuine and also if the open liberal atmosphere of the campus is authentic. He recalls one particular case:

Throughout the entire year of counseling, the student has been doing reasonably well academically, but his social life was not up to par for a freshman. He had a tendency to be withdrawn, he was very hesitant in reaching out to other students, he did not participate in many campus activities. He was tentative in style and cautious in approach. It seemed he was withholding quite a lot within and couldn't decide whether he should open up. . . .It was toward the end of the year-long counseling that he gradually let himself go and opened up. During his high school years he was an object of frequent racial harassment and ridicule – he was not strong enough to fight back and put his harassers in place. He withdrew into himself and just concentrated on school work. He did well in school and his parents and teachers thought he was doing O.K., but he did not enjoy his school life. Deep inside, he wanted to graduate and get away from school. He did not have a good feeling of belonging to any group, and he was keenly aware of his inner sense of estrangement. Years of alienation made it difficult for him to trust his peers.[188]

The counselor was the first person with whom he shared his debilitating sense of isolation and loneliness.

The pervasive anti-Asian climate and the frequent acts of bigotry and violence in our schools not only inflict hidden injuries and lasting damage, but also create barriers to the educational attainment of the Asian American student victims, such as suspension from school and dropping out of school. An analysis of suspensions in San Diego city schools by race and ethnicity offers valuable information about how the racially charged climate in our schools may cause some students to engage in behavior that results in school suspension. The San Diego study cited above found that although Asian students of all groups had lower overall suspension rates during the 1984-85 school year than black, Hispanic, and white students, a far larger percentage of their suspensions was for fighting (as opposed to defiance or substance abuse).[189] The suspension rates for black, Hispanic, and white students were 13.9, 7.5, and 6.3 percent, respectively, whereas the suspension rates for Filipino and Southeast Asian students ranged from a high of 4.8 percent for Vietnamese students to a low of 1.0 percent for Hmong students.[190] Yet the proportion of all suspensions that were for fighting were much higher for Filipino and Southeast Asian students than for other groups: ranging from 67 percent of all suspensions for Hmong students to 45 percent of suspensions for Vietnamese students (compared to 25, 36, and 43 percent of suspensions for white, Hispanic, and black students, respectively).[191] Furthermore, although the number of suspensions had fallen sharply for all other groups since the previous school year, the number of suspensions of Asian students had increased by 22 percent, and the number of suspensions for Southeast Asian students had increased by the large figure of 47 percent.[192]

---

188   Ibid.

189   *Adaptation of Youth*, pp. 55-58b.

190   Ibid., p. 55a, fig. 5-2.

191   Ibid., p. 57c, fig. 5-6.

192   Although the number of suspensions for Asian students could have increased merely because of an increase in their numbers in the school system, there is evidence that this is not the case. A San Diego school district report found that the number of suspensions increased by a far larger percentage than the number of Asian students between the 1983-84 and the 1984-85 academic years. San Diego City Schools, Planning, Research, and Evaluation Division, *Report on 1984-85 Student Suspensions* (May 27, 1986) p. A-4,

Citing a San Diego city schools report (Schools Report), the San Diego study attributed the large percentage of Southeast Asian and Filipino student suspensions that were for physical fighting and the large 1-year increase in the number of their suspensions to racial tensions in the schools. The Schools Report had found evidence of "linguistic, racial and social barriers [facing] Indochinese students" in the schools, including "increasing prejudice toward all Asians, particularly the Indochinese."[193] The report had also noted that, "Both schools and community report increased physical retaliation by Indochinese students in response to verbal and physical abuse from other students."[194] Finally, the Schools Report had observed that:

Concerns regarding the problems faced by Indochinese students have increased dramatically within the past year. There is increased community dissatisfaction over the Asian "model minority" success stereotype as well as the name-calling and physical abuse between Indochinese and other students. Staff and students demonstrate a lack of understanding of particular Indochinese behaviors and values. Increase of gang influence is also noted within the Indochinese community.[195]

The San Diego study found that, in contrast to Hmong students, who apparently keep themselves distant from other students, and Cambodian students, who tend to be concerned with getting along,[196] Vietnamese and the Laotian students, in particular, appear to be "conflict-oriented and aggressively preoccupied with 'saving face' (and ethnic pride), and are more easily drawn into racial confrontations in the U.S. when provoked by non-refugee students."[197] The report adds that:

Some Vietnamese students (particularly males),. . .told us that they will not respond at the first insult from an American student, would take notice of a second insult from the same provocateur, and will "blow up" and get into a fight in response to a third or subsequent provocation.[198]

The San Diego study found further that racial incidents begin in the elementary grades, dramatically increasing in the middle years, and peaking at the about the 10th or 11th grade,[199] and that for some students, racial tensions led to gang-style activities.

For some youths, especially the Vietnamese and the Lao, confrontations result in a search for companions who can thus help protect themselves from aggressive non-refugee classmates. In some of the cases we found in the Probations Department data, juveniles reported joining peer groups initially for protection, but once in those groups a switch in interests occurred away from school toward peer preoccupations for fun and material indulgences. Parentless youths are the most susceptible for such "gang" involvements, though it should be noted that the majority of those troubled youths come from homes with one or both parents.[200]

Racial tensions may also cause some Asian American students to drop out of school. Another study of immigrant students found that one out of four immigrant students had considered dropping out of school and the "most-

---

    table 2.

193   San Diego City Schools, Community Relations and Integration Services Division report (1985), cited in *Adaptation of Youth*, p. 58.
194   Ibid.
195   Ibid.
196   *Adaptation of Youth*, p. 55.
197   Ibid., p. 56.
198   Ibid.
199   Ibid., p. 97.
200   Ibid.

echoed reasons given" by them included "hostility and prejudice felt in the school environment."[201] A Southeast Asian social worker in Stockton reports that in an average week he sees or hears of four Indochinese students dropping out of school. According to him, reasons for dropping out varies, but one prominent reason is the hostile school environment and loss of interest in school.[202]

Racial confrontations, thus, affect youths by diverting them away from an academic focus to a peer-group preoccupation. Some react by fighting, others by withdrawing from their peers. Probable consequences are marred acculturation, lowered academic achievement, trouble with the law, and even higher school dropouts. These consequences forebode a high price that not only the individuals involved but also our society as a whole are bound to pay in the future.[203]

Improving the Education of Asian American Immigrant Children: Barriers and Promising Avenues

The education of Asian American immigrant children in our public schools is beset with serious problems. Schools face critical shortages of bilingual and English as a Second Language (ESL) teachers and counselors for most Asian immigrant groups. Racial tensions are festering in schools, and little is being done about them. Many Asian American students are leaving our schools with below-average English proficiency. This section examines some of the barriers to improving the educational services provided to Asian American students and discusses some promising avenues for overcoming them.

Teacher Certification Requirements

Teacher certification requirements are a major barrier to the recruitment of the bilingual teachers and counselors so critically needed to educate Asian American immigrant children. Across the country very few Southeast Asian immigrants or refugees have become certified teachers.

Documenting Previous Education and Experience—A barrier facing adult refugees from Southeast Asia in particular is that they are unable to obtain transcripts and references showing their educational attainment or their experience as teachers or professors in their home countries. In the absence of such documentation, these refugees are unable to meet teacher certification requirements without duplicating years of education and training they already had in their home countries. For instance, Hoa Truong, a refugee who escaped from Vietnam on a boat, had taught English in Vietnam for 12 years. When she arrived in Massachusetts, she was given a waiver that allowed her to teach temporarily, but the State required that she go back to school and go through the entire teacher training program to become a certified teacher.[204] Many potential teachers choose to take other jobs rather than repeating educational programs they have already completed and thus are lost as educators for Asian American children.

The University of Lowell and the State of Massachusetts developed an innovative and apparently unique program to help Southeast Asian refugees document their previous education and employment. This program was prompted by a critical shortage of Southeast Asian teachers and a court order requiring Low-

201   *Crossing the Border*, p. 88.

202   Ky Hoang, Youth Program Coordinator, Vietnamese Voluntary Foundation, Stockton, CA, personal interview, Feb. 28, 1990.

203   Ibid., p. 97.

204   William Freebairn, "State Will Certify S.E. Asia Teachers," *Union-News*, Jan. 4, 1990, p. 3.

ell, Massachusetts, schools to improve the education of Southeast Asian and other language-minority students. Under the program, the Academic Credentials Committee for Undocumented Educators, made up of prominent Southeast Asians who are very familiar with the education systems of their native countries before the Communist takeover, interviews prospective teachers intensively about their home country background and certifies their U.S.-equivalent levels of education. The State of Massachusetts accepts the findings of the committee in determining whether or not an interviewed candidate has met the requirements to become a teacher. If certified by the committee, candidates are exempted from repeating educational programs the committee determines they have already completed in their home country. A pilot program for the Vietnamese community began in 1989, and subsequently an ongoing program was instituted for Cambodians, Laotians, and Vietnamese. In June 1990, 38 Cambodians, 7 Laotians, and 11 Vietnamese were interviewed and their academic credentials reconstructed.[205] Programs such as the one in Massachusetts are urgently needed in other States to meet the need for bilingual teachers and counselors.

Teacher Certification Examinations—A second problem is that in many States, teachers need to pass a written examination to be certified. Asian American immigrants, even those who appear to have the basic qualifications nec-

essary for becoming teachers, generally have very high failure rates on these tests and do poorly on those sections of the test requiring high levels of English proficiency. For instance, since 1983 teacher certification in California has required a passing score on the California Basic Educational Skills Test (CBEST), which is made up of three subtests: mathematics, writing, and reading.[206] On average, Asian candidates had significantly lower CBEST pass rates than whites, although their pass rates were higher than those of Hispanic and black test takers.[207]

A recent study of Southeast Asian test takers in San Diego shows how the CBEST has become an almost insurmountable barrier to teacher certification for Southeast Asians.[208] By 1980 the city of San Diego was faced with a critical shortage of Southeast Asian teachers. To help fill this gap, San Diego State University and the city of San Diego jointly created an Indochinese Teaching Intern Program to give Southeast Asian professionals the skills and credentials needed to become certified teachers. The program initially enrolled 47 interns. When the interns took the CBEST test in 1983, not one of them passed. By 1987 only 7 of the interns had passed the test. Interns who failed the exam were initially allowed to teach under certification waivers, but these waivers expired in 1985, and by 1987 only 3 of the 47 interns were full-time teachers, and one was a substitute teacher. This study of the interns found that

---

205   Frank E. Markarewicz, "Getting the Past on Paper: Untangling the Red Tape For Southeast Asians," *University of Lowell Magazine*, vol. 5, no. 1 (Spring 1990), pp. 8-9, and materials provided by Dr. Juan Rodriguez, Program Director, Bilingual/ESL, College of Education, University of Lowell, Lowell, MA.

206   Each of the subtests is scored on a scale of 20 to 80. To pass the CBEST test, candidates must have a total score of 123 (an average of 41 on each subtest) and must score no lower than 37 on any of the subtests. Educational Testing Service, "California Basic Educational Skills Test, Information Bulletin, October 1989-August 1990," pp. 7-8.

207   Li-Rong Lilly Cheng and Kenji Ima, "The California Basic Educational Skills Test (CBEST) and Indochinese Teacher Interns: A Case of a Cultural Barrier to Foreign-Born Asian Professionals?" chap. 10 in Gary Y. Okihiro, Shirley Hune, Arthur A, Hansen, and John M. Liu, eds., *Reflections on Shattered Windows: Promises and Prospects for Asian American Studies* (Pullman, WA: Washington State University Press, 1988). Of course, the average pass rates for Asian test takers includes the scores of all Asian Americans in the State of California, not just immigrant Asians.

208   Ibid.

"[a]lthough ten of the original forty-seven interns dropped out or resigned [before taking the CBEST exam], the majority of the remaining interns have not become teachers because of the CBEST requirement."[209] In recent years, additional requirements for teacher certification have been instituted, making it more difficult for Southeast Asian teachers to become certified. These additional requirements include oral English-language fluency and demonstrated classroom management skills.[210]

The study also analyzed the problems the interns had taking the CBEST exam. It found that the interns had a higher than average pass rate for the mathematics subtest of the exam, but exceedingly low pass rates for the writing and reading subtests. Among 19 interns for whom the study had complete records, the average score on the mathematics exam was 51.6 (well above the passing score of 41), whereas the average scores on the reading and writing subtests were 26.7 and 32.1, respectively.[211] A closer analysis of four of the most successful interns is revealing. All of these interns had graduated from American universities and been involved with the San Diego city schools for years. Yet, they had problems with the cultural content and the abstract nature of the writing assignments typical in the CBEST exam, and they had difficulties with the inferential thinking needed to answer questions in the reading portion of the CBEST exam correctly.[212]

The difficulty that Southeast Asians have encountered in passing the CBEST exam appears to be having a chilling effect not only on teacher recruitment from among older Southeast Asian refugees, but also on the enrollment of Southeast Asian college students in teacher training programs. Commission staff were told by Cambodian students at California State University at Long Beach, some of whom were teacher aides in the Long Beach schools, that they were hesitant to take the education courses and train to become teachers because they were afraid they would not be able to pass the exam. Despite the urgent need in California for Cambodian-speaking bilingual teachers, these students did not know of any Cambodian students who were training to become teachers.[213]

Waivers and Teacher's Aides—Schools have adopted two main approaches to dealing with the shortage of certified bilingual teachers and counselors: waiving teacher certification requirements and hiring other bilingual personnel, such as teacher's aides, to help in the classroom. Waiving teacher certification requirements allows schools and school districts to bring bilingual personnel into the classrooms to fill immediate needs when there are insufficient certified bilingual personnel. Usually, the waivers expire after a few years unless the teacher either passes the relevant test or shows progress towards acquiring the necessary credentials for teacher certification.[214] Furthermore, teachers on waiver do not always receive the same pay and benefits as regular teachers.

Many school systems have resorted to hiring bilingual teacher's aides to help in the classroom and/or to communicate with the parents of language-minority students as an alternative to hiring credentialed bilingual and ESL teachers. Hiring teacher's aides may help to fill the gap created by the shortage of credentialed teachers. Unless accompanied by active teacher recruit-

---

209   Ibid., p. 69.

210   Ima Comments.

211   Ibid., p. 71.

212   Ibid.

213   Interview with students at California State University at Long Beach, Mar. 3, 1990 (hereafter cited as College students interview).

214   Interviews with Dr. Juan Rodriguez, Program Director, Bilingual/ESL, College of Education, University of Lowell, Lowell, MA, Feb. 12, 1990, and Profs. Ruben Rumbaut and Kenji Ima, San Diego State University, San Diego, CA, Mar. 5, 1990.

ment and training programs, however, hiring teacher's aides may become a mere token response to the needs of Southeast Asian students. As an example, Cambodian college students at California State University at Long Beach who were part-time teacher's aides in a local school district told Civil Rights Commission staff that they had received no training for their positions and maintained that in many cases the teachers they were working for gave them routine tasks, such as grading homework, to perform rather than having them interact with and help Cambodian children.[215]

States and localities need to continue to explore alternatives to rigid teacher certification requirements when urgent needs for teachers are not being met. They also need to put more resources into recruiting and training Asian American bilingual teachers.

Other Barriers and Avenues for Overcoming Them

Many Asian American immigrant students and their parents arrive in this country with little background to help them understand American public school systems. Many have very little previous education, and what formal education they have received has been in a very different setting and in schools with a completely different structure and culture from those they find in America. Too often these students are dumped in our classrooms with little or no preparation, and their parents are given no help in understanding how our school system works and little opportunity to participate in making decisions about their children's education. Asian American immigrant students and their parents need comprehensive orientation programs to help them understand and adjust to American schools and to help assess each student's individual educational and emotional needs before the student is placed in the classroom. Once the orientation and assessment has been completed, the students need ongoing programs that help them bridge their two cultures, deal with their social and emotional needs, and prepare them to become successful students in American schools, while their parents need ongoing programs to keep them informed.

Asian American immigrant students usually encounter fellow students, teachers, and administrators who know little or nothing about their cultures and histories. Frequently, school officials do not understand their new students and are unprepared to help them cope with their transition into American schools, and their fellow students have no background to help them appreciate why their new classmates are so different and are likely to react to them with hostility. For Asian American students to realize their full potential to learn, they need school environments that are understanding and supportive, not insensitive and hostile. Aggressive programs to educate school personnel and students about Asian (and other) cultures and histories and to combat racism in our schools are urgently needed.

A summary of the educational needs of immigrant students in California's public schools and a compilation of programs across the State that are helping to meet those needs can be found in a 1989 California Tomorrow report.[216] The report finds that immigrant students need orientation and assessment programs; programs to help students bridge their cultural differences; programs to improve intercultural relations in our schools and to teach mainstream teachers about their needs and cultures; educa-

---

215   College students interview. These students were teacher aides for the Long Beach Unified School District, Long Beach, CA.

216   Laurie Olsen, *Bridges: Promising Programs For the Education of Immigrant Children* (San Francisco: California Tomorrow, 1989).

tional curricula that are sensitive to the multi-cultural makeup of our classrooms; and academic support and outreach efforts to keep their parents informed about and get them involved in the schools.[217] These recommendations are relevant to the entire country, not just the State of California.

---

217   Ibid.

Chapter 5

Access to Educational Opportunity: Higher Education

The Commission's Roundtable Conferences and staff followup investigations revealed a number of concerns in the Asian American community related to higher education. Foremost among these concerns were alleged discriminatory admissions policies against Asian American applicants to elite colleges and universities, which is the subject of the present chapter. A number of other concerns are not covered here but are also worthy of attention. These include allegations of inequitable awarding of financial aid to Asian American students; inadequate academic and other supplementary services for language-minority students of Asian ancestry; underrepresentation of Asian Americans among faculty and administrators (particularly at the higher ranks); and the failure of colleges to incorporate the experiences and contributions of Asian Americans into the mainstream curriculum.

The allegation that our most prestigious colleges and universities use discriminatory admissions policies against Asian American applicants was first made on several college campuses in the early 1980s. At issue was whether elite colleges and universities, in the face of increasing numbers of Asian American applications, were placing ceilings on the number of Asian Americans they would admit. More generally, the issue was whether Asian American applicants were less likely to be accepted at elite colleges and universities than white applicants with comparable characteristics. The admissions discrimination controversy quickly became a highly visible national issue leading to Federal Government intervention, including the introduction of a congressional resolution condemning any use of admissions quotas against Asian Americans. During the past decade, the Department of Education's Office for Civil Rights (OCR) undertook multiyear investigations of the admissions procedures of several institutions of higher education. In 1990, OCR released reports on its investigations of Harvard University and the University of California at Los Angeles, and OCR investigations of other institutions are in progress. Meanwhile, the central issue, whether or not there is or has been admissions discrimination against Asian American applicants, became clouded as the admissions discrimination issue became associated with the continuing national debate on affirmative action.

This chapter provides an overview of the controversy to help the public develop an informed understanding of the key issues involved. It first discusses how the controversy has unfolded and, in doing so, identifies the central issues. It then relates how the controversy played out on three different campuses—Brown University, the University of California at Berkeley, and Harvard University.

The Controversy

The allegation of discriminatory admissions policies against Asian Americans was first raised in 1983 with a statement issued by the Asian American Students Association at Brown University.[1] "After four frustrating years" of unpublicized discussion and negotiation with

---

1   Asian American Students Association of Brown University, *Asian American Admission At Brown University* (Oct. 11, 1983) (hereafter cited as *Asian American Admission At Brown*).

university officials regarding the low admit rate of Asian American applicants in comparison to other applicants to Brown, Asian American students at Brown decided to "document and publicize. . .a prima facie case of racial discrimination against Asian Americans in the Brown University admission process."[2] Their main contention was that although Asian American applicants as a group have one of the highest academic standings among all subgroups and the number of Asian American applicants increased eight and a half times between 1975 and 1983,[3] the number of Asian American students admitted did not "reflect this increase in any significant way."[4] The number of Asian American applicants admitted to Brown rose from 74 in 1975 to 140 in 1983, less than a twofold increase.[5]

In 1983 the East Coast Asian Student Union (ECASU) released a study that revealed a similar pattern in other East Coast institutions. This study surveyed 25 schools in the East Coast and found that in most schools the number of Asian American applicants admitted had barely increased during the 1970s and early 1980s, although the number of Asian American applicants had increased dramatically. The result was lower admit rates for Asian American applicants in comparison to other groups, including whites. The ECASU report concluded that the higher rejection rates of qualified Asian American applicants were the result of low personal ratings by admissions officers who considered that Asian American students were overrepresented and presumed that they had narrow career interests and passive personality.[6]

The issue erupted again in 1984, this time at the University of California at Berkeley. In spite of the university's earlier projection of an increased enrollment of Asian American students,[7] the number of newly enrolled Asian American students at Berkeley fell by 21 percent between 1983 and 1984, in comparison to a decline of 11 percent for white students over the same period. The admit rate for Asian American students fell from 48 percent in 1983 to 34 percent in 1984.[8] Alarmed by this development, Asian American civil rights groups and community representatives formed the Asian American Task Force on University of California Admissions (hereafter referred to as the Task Force) to determine the causes of the sudden decline and to study the effect of a set of new admissions criteria on Asian American applicants.[9] The Task Force report, released in June 1985 after 6 months of intensive study, concluded that the "sharp decline. . .in Fall 1984 resulted from unilateral, undisclosed changes in freshman admission policies."[10]

The issue of whether Asian American applicants are treated fairly at the Nation's top institutions of higher education began to receive national attention in 1985 when the *New York Times* and the *Washington Post* printed articles on this topic.[11] The *New York Times* article

2   Ibid., p. 1.

3   The numbers of applicants to Brown University are shown below in table 5.1 (of this report).

4   Ibid., p. 2.

5   Ibid., table 2a.

6   Jayjia Hsia, *Asian Americans in Higher Education and at Work* (Hillsdale, NJ: Lawrence Erlbaum, 1988), pp. 93-94.

7   Asian American Task Force on University of California Admissions, *Asian American Struggle For Fairness in Higher Education, Highlights of ATFUA 1984-1988* (undated), p. 7 (hereafter cited as Task Force Highlights).

8   Asian American Task Force on University of California Admissions, *Task Force Report* (June 17, 1985), pp. 6-7 (hereafter cited as *Task Force Report*).

9   *Task Force Report*, p. 1.

10   Task Force Highlights, pp. 7-8.

11   Michael Winerip, "Asian-Americans Question Ivy League's Entry Policies," *New York Times*, May 30, 1985, pp. B1, B4; "The Super

started with the experience of one faculty member who served on a Princeton admissions committee: "We were going over the applicant list and we came to a clearly qualified Asian American student. And one committee member said, 'We have enough of them.' And someone else turned to me and said, 'You have to admit, there are a lot.'"[12] The article went on to say, "This year at Princeton 17 percent of all applicants and 14 percent of Asian-American applicants were accepted. At Harvard, 15.9 percent of all applicants and 12.5 percent of Asian-Americans were accepted. At Yale 18 percent of all applicants and 16.7 percent of Asian-Americans were accepted."[13] As for the academic qualifications of Asian American applicants, the same Princeton faculty member was quoted as saying, "My hunch is if you look at the top 20 percent of the Asian-Americans being rejected at Ivy League schools, they are better qualified academically than the bottom part of the class that is accepted."[14] The article also described how difficult it had been for concerned Princeton students and alumni to get admissions-related statistics from the university.

In the next few years numerous articles in professional journals[15] and in magazines and newspapers[16] drew the Nation's attention to the question of restrictive admissions policies against Asian Americans. By 1988 the sustained attention of the print media and researchers had transformed what had started out as a local matter at several colleges into a highly visible national issue. The core concern was whether the Nation's elite institutions of higher education, faced with an increasing number of qualified Asian American applicants, were placing a ceiling on the number of Asian American students they would admit. Phrased differently, the issue was whether higher standards of admission were being applied to Asian American candidates as a means of reducing or containing the number of Asian American students.

Although based on scattered data for different colleges for different years, the cumulative literature of this period showed a pattern of lower admit rates for Asian American students than for white students. At most selective colleges, the enrollment of Asian American students did not rise in proportion to the rapidly increasing number of Asian American applicants. At such prestigious colleges[17] as Harvard, Brown, Princeton, Yale, Stanford, and the University of California at Berkeley and Los Ange-

---

Students," *Washington Post* (editorial), Nov. 16, 1985, p. A22.

12 Winerip, "Ivy League's Entry Policies," p. B1. Although this particular quote was in reference to a graduate school admissions committee, it reflected a widespread suspicion as to what might be happening behind the closed doors.

13 Ibid., p. B4.

14 Ibid.

15 John H. Bunzel and Jeffrey K.D. Au, "Diversity or Discrimination?—Asian Americans in College," *The Public Interest*, no. 87 (Spring 1987), pp. 49-62; John H. Bunzel, "Affirmative Action Admissions: How It 'Works' at UC Berkeley," *The Public Interest*, no. 93 (Fall 1988), pp. 111-28; Jayjia Hsia, "Limits of Affirmative Action: Asian American Access to Higher Education," *Educational Policy*, vol. 2, no. 2 (1988), pp. 119-36; Don T. Nakanishi, "Asian Pacific Americans and Selective Undergraduate Admissions," *Journal of College Admissions*, vol. 118 (Winter 1988), pp. 17-26; L. Ling-chi Wang, "Meritocracy and Diversity in Higher Education: Discrimination Against Asian Americans in the Post-Bakke Era," *The Urban Review*, vol. 20, no. 3 (1988), pp. 183-209.

16 For example, see: Winerip, "Ivy League's Entry Policies"; "The Super Students," *Washington Post* (editorial), Nov. 16, 1985, p. A22; Lawrence Biemiller, "Asian Students Fear Top Colleges Use Quota Systems: Acceptances Haven't Kept Pace With Increases in Applications," *Chronicle of Higher Education*, Nov. 19, 1986, p. 1; Dorothy Gilliam, "A New Restrictive Racial Quota," *Washington Post*, Feb. 5, 1987, p. D3; Eloise Salholz and Shawn Doherty, "Do Colleges Set Asian Quotas? Enrollments Are Up, But They Could Be Higher Still," *Newsweek*, Feb. 9, 1987, p. 60; "The Specter of Quotas," *Washington Post* (editorial), Dec. 17, 1988, p. A18; Robin Wilson, "U.S. Studies Policies at Harvard, UCLA on Admitting Asians: Public Concern Over Quotas Cited; Universities Vehemently Deny Bias," *Chronicle of Higher Education*, Nov. 30, 1988, p. A1.

les, Asian American applicants were admitted at a lower rate than white applicants at one point or another in the 1980s, although Asian American applicants had academic qualifications comparable to those of white applicants.[18] In 1988 the issue of admissions discrimination against Asian Americans began to receive Federal Government attention. In January and June of 1988, the U.S. Department of Education's Office for Civil Rights informed the University of California at Los Angeles and Harvard University, respectively, of its plan to conduct compliance reviews of their admissions policies.[19] On May 3, 1988, then-President Reagan spoke in opposition to Asian quotas in college admissions.[20] On November 30, 1988, Senators Thomas A. Daschle (D-SD) and Paul Simon (D-IL) hosted a congressional seminar on the "alleged anti-Asian bias in university admissions."[21]

The year 1988 also marked a turning point in the development of the admissions discrimination controversy. Until 1988 the controversy had

---

17   Although it was most telling among prestigious private colleges, the low admissions rate for Asian American applicants was also observed at 4-year public institutions. According to a 1985 national survey of 4-year undergraduate institutions, the Asian American admit rate to public institutions was 92 percent of the total admit rate (i.e., 66 percent vs. 72 percent), while the Asian American admit rate to private institutions was 77 percent of the total admit rate (i.e., 49 percent vs. 62 percent). Hunter M. Breland, Gita Wilder, and Nancy J. Robertson, *Demographics, Standards, and Equity: Challenges in College Admissions* (AACRAO, ACT, The College Board, Educational Testing Service, and NACAC, 1986), cited in Jayjia Hsia, "Limits of Affirmative Action: Asian American Access to Higher Education," *Educational Policy*, vol. 2, no. 2 (1988), p. 122.

18   Among those who monitored and researched the issue, the simple facts of the disparate admit rate and the slow increases in the numbers of Asian Americans enrolled were undisputed, but their interpretive context differed. While some researchers merely deplored the lack of access to the kind of data and decisionmaking information necessary to support or refute the allegation, others saw the controversy as "another manifestation of a very old anti-Asian racism." Notice a distinct contrast in the following quotes:
"It should be emphasized that we have not found any definitive evidence that numerical limits on Asian American admissions might be in effect. . . .But it is equally important. . .that. . .we have not been given the kind of access to data and decision-making information that would permit us to support or refute conclusively [the allegation of numerical limits]. . . .The possibility of numerical limits on Asian Americans operating in the college admissions process. . .cannot be rejected out of hand." (Bunzel and Au, "Asian Americans in College," p. 61.)
"To maintain their privileged status and to perpetuate their domination. . .[the nation's elite colleges and universities] have been forced in the 1980s to modify their admissions criteria in order to slow down the Asian American 'invasion,' much like what these same institutions had to do from 1918 to 1947 when they discovered the 'Jewish problem.' To these elite institutions, Asian American students constitute a 'New Yellow Peril'. . . .The current efforts to limit Asian American access to high-quality education is in fact another manifestation of a very old anti-Asian racism deeply woven into the fabric of our society and embedded in our culture and national consciousness." [Wang, "Discrimination Against Asian Americans, pp. 201, 205."]

19   U.S. Department of Education, Office for Civil Rights, "Chronology of OCR Asian Quota Compliance Review," by Gary Curran, Jan. 23, 1989, p. 1 (hereafter cited as OCR Chronology). Prior to the announcement, OCR began receiving individual complaints about Asian American discrimination in college admissions. On July 13, 1987, the OCR regional offices were instructed to select for compliance reviews higher education institutions where there were suggestions of using quotas to deny admission to qualified Asian American applicants. Ibid.

20   On the occasion of signing the Asian/Pacific American Heritage Week Proclamation, then-President Reagan said: "I know there's a growing concern that some universities may be discriminating against citizens of Asian and Pacific heritage. . .despite their academic qualifications. To deny any individual access to higher education when it has been won on the basis of merit is a repudiation of everything America stands for. Let everyone be clear. . .that the use of informal exclusionary racial quotas, or any practice of racial discrimination against any individual violates the law, is morally wrong, and will not be tolerated." *Public Papers of the Presidents of the United States, Ronald Reagan*, 1988, Book I, p. 546 (Washington, DC: Government Printing Office, 1990).

21   Congressional Record-Senate, S. 1135, Feb. 2, 1989. In May 1989, ABC's TV program "20/20" covered the issue, further directing the national attention to the controversy. ABC-TV, "20/20 Program," May 5, 1989, 10:00-11:00 PM (EST).

been uncomplicated. It centered around the simple empirical question of whether or not the Nation's prestigious colleges and universities treated Asian American applicants fairly in comparison to white applicants. The question was clearly amenable to resolution. It would have required comparing the admit rates of Asian American and white candidates after adjusting for pertinent characteristics and qualifications. Such an analysis would have been relatively straightforward if the admissions data had been made available to researchers.[22] Admissions-related data for selective colleges and universities were extremely difficult to obtain,[23] however, preventing the kind of systematic investigation that could have provided a factual basis for resolving the controversy[24] and creating in some observers the suspicion of a possible coverup by college administrators.

Starting in 1988 the controversy took on a new twist as it became embroiled in the national debate on affirmative action. The admissions discrimination issue was embraced by those who have traditionally opposed affirmative action policies, who argued that the restrictive admissions policies against Asian Americans are both symptomatic of a larger problem, affirmative action in university admissions,[25] and an inevitable outcome of affirmative action programs. This casting of the controversy as part of the national debate on affirmative action deflected attention from the core issue, whether or not elite colleges and universities had instituted discriminatory admissions practices against Asian American students.

At this stage in the controversy, late in 1990, OCR released its long-awaited civil rights compliance reviews of Harvard's undergraduate and the University of California at Los Angeles' (UCLA) graduate programs. OCR, in a report that is discussed in some detail below, found Harvard free of any discriminatory admissions policy against Asian American applicants,[26] but concluded that one graduate program at UCLA had discriminated against Asian American applicants in violation of civil rights laws.[27] Several

---

22   Writing on the larger picture of the controversy, Nakanishi observed that "the admissions debate might not have become so explosive if there had been a body of empirical knowledge that all parties to the dispute could have used to test or verify their largely unfounded assumptions and assertions about Asian American students." Don T. Nakanishi, "A Quota on Excellence? The Asian American Admissions Debate," *Change* (November/December 1989), p. 40.

23   Researchers have generally been unable to obtain pertinent data. For example, Dr. Dana Takagi of the University of California at Santa Cruz, who is working on a book on this controversy, and Ms. Lai-Wan Wong of Wesleyan University, who is working on her thesis, recounted a similar experience regarding access to critical admissions data at selective campuses. Dana Takagi, telephone interview, Feb. 7, 1991; Lai-Wan Wong, telephone interview, Mar. 4, 1991. Requests for admissions data by Commission staff have encountered similar difficulties with selective institutions.

24   Many researchers have deplored the inaccessibility of pertinent data, which inhibited objective appraisal of the controversy. Note such comments as "Because of numerous and, in our view, often questionable policies of confidentiality, it has been extremely difficult to collect official and comprehensive admissions data." Bunzel and Au, "Asian Americans in College," p. 53. "It is. . .important to note. . .that with the exception of Brown, we have not been given the kind of access to data and decision-making information that would permit us to support or refute [the allegation of numerical limits on Asian American admissions]." Ibid. "The scope of this study is severely limited by the closely guarded data and documents available to date." Wang, "Discrimination Against Asian Americans," p. 190.

25   Dana Y. Takagi, "From Discrimination to Affirmative Action: Facts in the Asian American Admissions Controversy," *Social Problems*, vol. 37, no. 4 (1990), p. 578.

26   Thomas J. Hibino, Acting Regional Director, Region 1, U.S. Department of Education, Office for Civil Rights, letter to Derek Bok, President, Harvard University, entitled "Compliance Review No. 01-88-6009," Oct. 4, 1990, p. 1 (hereafter cited as OCR Letter). U.S. Department of Education, Office for Civil Rights, "Statement of Findings, Compliance Review No. 01-88-6009" (on Harvard University), Oct. 4, 1990 (hereafter cited as OCR Findings).

other colleges were under review by OCR as of September 1991.[28]

Given the politically charged environment engulfing the controversy, it is important for the public not to lose sight of the central issue of the controversy: Do institutions of higher education, particularly the elite ones, treat Asian American applicants unfairly compared to whites?

Three Case Studies

The remainder of this chapter offers descriptions of how three institutions—Brown, the University of California at Berkeley, and Harvard—coped with the admissions discrimination issue. These institutions are selected for attention because their admissions policies and processes have undergone intense scrutiny and the outcomes of these investigations are publicly available. Furthermore, these three universities provide instructive contrasts in the manner in which controversy was handled.

Brown University

Brown University's Asian American community became concerned about possible admissions discrimination against Asian Americans when the Asian American admit rate, which had historically been higher than the overall Brown admit rate, became equal to and then fell below the overall admit rate during the 4-year period

between 1980 and 1983 (see table 5.1).[29] They sought to resolve the issue without making it public by talking with the Brown administration and the admissions office. When 4 years of efforts "resulted in little, if any, change in admission policy vis a vis Asian Americans and no substantial increase in the number of Asian Americans admitted,"[30] the Asian American Students Association of Brown University (AASA) decided to "document and publicize the prima facie case of racial discrimination against Asian Americans in the Brown University admissions process"[31] by releasing a report in October 1983.

Table 5.1 shows the admissions data contained in the AASA report for the classes of 1979-87 and also updated admissions data for the classes of 1989-93. Based on an analysis of the admissions data for the classes of 1979-87, the AASA report found that:

1) Between the classes of 1982 and 1983 the admit rate for Asian American students fell dramatically, from 46 percent to 26 percent. In comparison, the overall admit rate declined only slightly, from 27 percent to 24 percent.

2) There were 235 more Asian American applicants for the class of 1983 than for the class of 1982, but the number of Asian American applicants accepted declined by one, from 141 to 140.

---

27   John E. Palomino, Director, Region IX, U.S. Department of Education, Office for Civil Rights, letter to Charles E. Young, Chancellor, University of California at Los Angeles, "Statement of Findings, Compliance Review No. 09-89-6004," Oct. 1, 1990, p. 2. OCR also imposed a recordkeeping requirement on several other UCLA graduate programs that had not kept sufficient data on their admissions processes for OCR to be able to reach a determination about whether or not they were in compliance with Title VI. Ibid.

28   As of October 1991, the following colleges were under compliance review or complaint investigation regarding the admissions of Asian American students: the University of California at Berkeley (undergraduate programs); the University of California at Los Angeles (undergraduate programs); Boalt Hall School of Law at the University of California at Berkeley; and the School of Optometry at the University of California at Berkeley. Lillian Dorka, Attorney Advisor to the Assistant Secretary for Civil Rights, U.S. Department of Education, Office for Civil Rights, telephone interview, Oct. 15, 1991.

29   *Asian American Admission at Brown*, p. 1.

30   Ibid.

31   Ibid.

TABLE 5.1
Admissions Data: Brown University, Classes 1979–1993

	1979	1980	1981	1982	1983	1984	1985	1986	1987	1989	1990	1991	1992	1993
Total freshman class														
Applicants	8,635	9,125	9,156	10,565	11,298	11,901	11,817	11,746	13,278	13,707	13,081	12,486	12,731	11,720
Admits	2,856	2,830	3,016	2,846	2,673	2,559	2,593	2,604	2,624	2,637	2,627	2,788	2,701	2,869
Admit rate (%)	33	31	33	27	24	22	22	22	20	19	20	22	21	24
Asian Americans														
Applicants	168	265	224	307	542	679	868	1,006	1,425	1,539	1,627	1,703	1,564	1,783
Admits	74	101	106	141	140	153	156	188	204	256	245	324	303	424
Admit rate (%)	44	38	47	46	26	23	18	19	14	17	15	19	19	24
Asian American admits as % of total freshman admits	2.6	3.6	3.5	5.0	5.2	6.0	6.0	7.2	7.8	9.7	9.3	11.6	11.2	**14.8**

Source: Information for classes 1979-89 was obtained from tables 2a and 2b, the Asian American Students Association at Brown Report (1984). Information for the classes of 1989-93 was provided by the Office of the Dean of Admissions, Brown University. Information for the class of 1988 was not available.

3) After the dramatic decline between 1982 and 1983, the Asian American admit rate continued to fall, from 26 percent to 14 percent, for the classes of 1984-87 although the class-wide admit rate remained almost constant over this period. Starting with the class of 1985 the Asian American admit rate was below the classwide admit rate.

4) Although the number of Asian American applicants to Brown University increased steadily between the classes of 1979 and 1987, the number of students admitted seemed to plateau between the classes of 1982 and 1983 and between the classes of 1984 and 1985.

AASA's inquiry concerning the causes of the disparity in admissions rates led it to two conclusions:

1) Asian American and white applicants were comparable in their academic qualifications, and the academic profile of the Asian American applicant pool had not changed sufficiently to "justify such a drastic decrease in the admit rate."[32]

2) The acceptance of the "model minority" myth of Asian Americans by university administrators and admissions officers led to inattention to, and disparate efforts in, recruiting Asian Americans.[33]

Finding the explanations offered by Brown insufficient, AASA recommended that the admit rate for Asian American applicants be made "at least equal to the all-college admit rate,"[34] that a greater number of socioeconomically disadvantaged Asian Americans be recruited,[35] and that more information on Asian American applicants and acceptances be gathered and made available for analysis.[36]

Four months after the AASA report, the Brown University Corporation Committee on Minority Affairs (hereafter referred to as Corporation Committee) issued a forthright report[37] admitting the existence of "an extremely serious situation,"[38] concurring that "Asian American applicants have been treated unfairly in the admissions process,"[39] and calling for "immediate remedial measures."[40] The report specifically stated:

---

32   Ibid., p. 7 and table 6.

33   Ibid., pp. 8-13. Specific illustrations cited in the AASA report include:

    1) "no letters [of recruitment] were sent to Asian American students in California, New York, Pennsylvania. . .because [they] were 'self-recruiting,' and [admissions officers argued that] Brown need not make any special effort to recruit Asians." (Ibid., p. 10.)

    2) The "model minority myth especially hurts Asians from lower income families. Inner-city and economically disadvantaged Asian students need extra consideration and affirmative action to compete. . .with the more affluent and assimilated suburban Asian students." (Ibid., p. 11.)

    3) Funding was cut off by the admissions office, preventing student representatives from attending a College Day in New York's Chinatown along with representatives from other schools on the East Coast. Funding was restored after AASA's strong opposition. (Ibid., p. 11.)

    4) Asian American students' efforts to meet with individual admissions officers informally to discuss Asian American admissions were thwarted. The associate director of minority recruitment asked admissions officers not to meet with the Asian American students and also tried to discourage AASA from carrying out its plans. (Ibid., p. 12.)

34   Ibid., p. 26.

35   Ibid.

36   Ibid., p. 27.

37   Brown University Corporation Committee on Minority Affairs, "Report to the Corporation Committee on Minority Affairs From Its Subcommittee on Asian American Admissions," Feb. 10, 1984.

38   Ibid., p. 2.

While. . .we do not claim intentionally unfair treatment on the part of individuals or in the stated admission policies of the University, the admission practices used to implement these policies have resulted in such unfair treatment [of Asian American candidates that]. If left unrectified, the combination of policies and practices would make the resulting inequities intentional.[41]

The report uncovered several factors contributing to the differential treatment of Asian American applicants. Two of these factors are of interest here. The first involves the use of historical benchmark figures as enrollment goals, which had resulted in limiting the number of Asian American admits:

When the Asian American admits closely approximated its historical benchmark number, the admission process is curtailed without regard to the total number of Asian American applicants for the current year or their academic qualifications.[42]

The second factor was the subjective nature of rating nonacademic or personal characteristics. The Corporation Committee was forthright in pointing out:

It was clearly stated by all admission staff to whom we spoke that Asian American applicants receive comparatively low non-academic ratings. These unjustified low ratings are due to the cultural biases and stereotypes which prevail in the admission office.[43]

Based on its findings, the Corporation Committee made five remedial recommendations. These recommendations included: 1) the admit rate for each minority subgroup of applicants with qualifications equal or comparable to those of nonminority applicants "should be *at least* equal to the admit rate of non-minority applicants,"[44] and 2) statistical information concerning admissions and financial aid should be made available on request to legitimate university groups with an interest in these areas.[45] The Corporation Committee also urged the president of Brown to proclaim its recommendations as part of the official university policy on admissions.[46] The Corporation Committee report and its recommendations were subsequently adopted by the university, and the administration as a whole embraced the Corporation Committee's underlying spirit of open self-criticism.[47] As shown in table 5.1, the admit rate of Asian American applicants improved gradually starting with the class of 1989, and, for the class of 1993, it became identical to the admit rate of the total freshman class.

---

39   Ibid.

40   Ibid.

41   Ibid.

42   Ibid., p. 3.

43   Ibid., p. 4.

44   Ibid., p. 5, italics in original.

45   Ibid., p. 7.

46   Ibid.

47   An example of the spirit of open self-criticism is the report submitted by the Visiting Committee on Minority Life and Education at Brown University, entitled "The American University and the Pluralist Ideal." Impressed by the intense desire of both students and administration officials to "see [Brown] measure up to higher standards of ethnic sensitivity and racial civility," this committee noted: "the existence of the Visiting Committee illustrates the point. The President and the Board of Fellows invited this critique. . . .We have admired the open, candid, and sharing attitudes encountered as we went about our inquiry." Brown University, *The American University and the Pluralist Ideal: A Report of the Visiting Committee on Minority Life and Education at Brown University* (May 1986). Quotes are from pp. 3 and xi, respectively.

The University of California at Berkeley

The Asian American Task Force on University of California Admissions (hereafter Task Force),[48] formed in fall 1984 in response to the precipitous decline in Asian American freshman enrollment, released its report in June 1985.[49] According to the Task Force report, several factors caused the number of Asian Americans admitted at Berkeley to decline. Specifically, the report stated that UC-Berkeley:

1) imposed a minimum 400 score on SAT verbal test to deny admission to eligible Asian American immigrant freshman student applicants;

2) unexpectedly ceased freshman admission consideration for low-income, first-generation-collegiate Asian American applicants; . . .redirected them to other UC campuses; these low-income Asian American students did not enroll in significant numbers at other UC campuses because of the economic barriers in attending a campus far from home;

3) did not include Asian American faculty and staff members in the discussion, adoption and implementation of freshman admission policies; did not publicize to affected Asian American applicants changes in freshman admission policies.[50]

Throughout 1985 and 1986, there were many exchanges between the Task Force and university officials, who disputed the Task Force findings. In particular, the university officials flatly denied the Task Force's contention that Berkeley had imposed a minimum SAT-verbal score requirement. During these years, Asian American community leaders and the Task Force also made their concerns known to the press and the State legislature. In 1987 several developments occurred: California State Assembly Speaker Willie Brown announced his support for greater legislative oversight involvement to resolve the controversy over the alleged admissions quotas; California State Senate President Pro Tempore David Roberti requested the State auditor general to conduct an audit of the UC-Berkeley freshman admissions policies and procedures as they affected Asian American and white applicants; and the UC-Berkeley Academic Senate appointed the Special Committee on Asian American Admissions to review the allegations of the Task Force.[51]

The State auditor general's report,[52] released in October 1987, reached the following conclusions regarding Asian American applicants, while noting that gaining admission to Berkeley had become increasingly more difficult for both Asian American and white candidates between 1981 and 1987:

1) of the 49 separate admission rates comparing Asian American with white applicants across different colleges and programs for the seven-year period between 1981 and 1987, Asian American applicants were admitted at a lower rate in 37 instances and at a higher rate in 12;[53]

2) during the same period, the average high school grade point average (GPA) of Asian American applicants rose from 3.20 to 3.72, while the average GPA for whites rose from 3.27 to 3.62;[54]

---

48   The Task Force was co-chaired by San Francisco Municipal Court Judge Lillian Sing and Alameda County Superior Court Judge Ken Kawaichi.

49   *Task Force Report.*

50   Task Force Highlights, p. 8.

51   Ibid., p. 9.

52   Auditor General of California, *A Review of First-Year Admissions of Asians and Caucasians at the University of California at Berkeley* (October 1987) (hereafter cited as Auditor General's Report).

53   Ibid., p. S-4.

54   Ibid.

3) in the College of Letters and Sciences, the decision made by the university to redirect economically disadvantaged candidates to other campuses was a major factor explaining the drop in the number of Asian American freshman admitted in the fall of 1984.[55]

In February 1989 the Academic Senate's Special Committee on Asian American Admissions (hereafter Special Committee) released its report.[56] The report, which is based on examination of university documents, interviews with university staff, and other information,[57] is important because it represents a thorough investigation of the controversy and because it paved the way for an eventual agreement between the Asian American community and the university to develop new procedures and policies that would ensure fairness and provide reassurance to the Asian community.[58] The following pages discuss three important findings of the report in detail.

Economic Disadvantage Removed From Protected Category

A comparison of the admit rates of Asian American and white applicants for the years 1981 to 1987 showed that in 2 years, 1984 and 1987, "the campus should have admitted approximately 50 more Asian Americans [if Asian Americans had been admitted at the same rate as whites with the same academic qualifications], or about 1.1 percent of the campus-wide admit pool."[59] The Special Committee found that the university's decision to cease guaranteeing admission to applicants who qualified for the educational opportunity program (EOP) but not for affirmative action (i.e., applicants who came from an economically disadvantaged background but were not members of underrepresented groups) was the major reason for the 1984 drop in Asian American enrollment.[60] The committee estimated that in 1984 the dropping of EOP as a protected category resulted in denying admission to 146 EOP applicants, about 90 percent of whom were Asian Americans.[61]

---

55   Ibid., p. 48. The report found that "if Asian and Caucasian EOP [Educational Opportunity] applicants had been admitted to the College of Letters and Science at the same rate as they were in 1983, then the difference in the overall 1984 admission rates of the two groups (51.9 percent for Asians and 59.5 percent for Caucasians) would have been 2.1 percentage points—58.0 percent for Asians and 60.1 percent for Caucasians." Ibid.

56   University of California, Berkeley, *Report of the Special Committee on Asian American Admissions of the Berkeley Division of the Academic Senate* (February 1989), p. 4 (hereafter cited as *Shack Report*, as it is commonly referred to after the committee's chairman Prof. W.A. Shack).

57   The Special Committee examined relevant documents and interviewed persons involved in shaping and implementing admissions policies as well as the Task Force members. The committee also evaluated the auditor general's report, other statistical information, and Berkeley's admission policies as a whole. Ibid., p. 4-5.

58   "A Joint Statement by Judges Ken Kawaichi and Lillian Sing, Co-chairs of the Asian American Task Force on University Admissions, and Chancellor Ira Michael Heyman of the University of California at Berkeley," Apr. 6, 1989 (hereafter cited as Joint Statement).

59   *Shack Report*, p. 23.

60   Ibid., p. 6.

61   Ibid., p. 30. This committee finding was consistent with the finding by the State auditor general discussed above. The committee finding that the EOP decision led to roughly 130 fewer Asian American applicants being admitted in 1984 when only 50 more Asian American students needed to be admitted to reach parity with whites suggests that other factors were also at work, but that the EOP decision, by itself, could more than explain the entire Asian American deficit in 1984.

In the process of evaluating the university's reasons for changing its policy on EOP applicants, the Special Committee was made aware of and became "troubled" by the allegation of one Asian American administration staff member that "administrators and staff have expressed the view that there are 'too many Asians' at Berkeley"[62] and by the "perception of another staff person that some of the participants in a December 1983 admissions meeting 'seemed to be deliberately searching for a standard which could be used to exclude Asian immigrant applicants.'"[63] Given these indications of anti-Asian bias within the Berkeley administration, the committee acknowledged the possibility that anti-Asian bias might have contributed to the decision to change the policy on EOP applicants:

It is possible that some or all of the decision-makers were motivated, in whole or in part, by a desire to reduce the enrollment of Asian Americans—a group that represented, as they surely knew, the largest percentage of the Non-AA [affirmative action] EOP applicants. There is some second-hand evidence, or at least internal allegations, that some people in the Campus Administration were thinking this way.[64]

However, the committee concluded that the policy change was most likely based on legitimate considerations and not anti-Asian bias:

While these allegations are troubling, they are impressionistic charges that cannot outweigh, in our opinion, the substantial evidence that the decision to redirect non-AA EOP applicants was based on legitimate considerations. The legitimate reasons for the decision, as described above, were plausible, substantial, and plainly at work. . . .We therefore think it unlikely that the decision to end protection for non-AA EOP applicants reflected intentional bias against Asian Americans.[65]

In concluding that the policy change was based upon legitimate reasons,[66] the committee believed that because the policy change was widely reviewed and accepted by many within the Berkeley administration, any anti-Asian motivation for the policy change would have been detected and the policy would not have been adopted had its motivation been anti-Asian bias.[67] As a result, the committee did not consider whether these legitimate reasons might have been pretexts for reducing the number of Asian American students on campus. Given the information presented to the committee[68] suggesting that at least some university administrators at some staff meetings expressed and shared their concern that there were too many Asian American students on the Berkeley campus, the committee could have investigated further to determine whether and to what extent anti-Asian bias played a role in the EOP policy change.

---

62   *Shack Report*, p. 7.

63   Ibid., p. 7.

64   Ibid., p. 31.

65   Ibid., p. 32.

66   Two legitimate reasons for the policy change were cited by the committee. These were: 1) The number of EOP students was becoming "too large," and the admission guarantee to EOP students was beginning to interfere with the admission of affirmative action students; and 2) EOP students were "having considerable difficulties with the English language," imposing both academic and financial costs on the university. Ibid., p. 31.

67   The committee stated: "[T]he number and variety of the persons and groups participating in the decision. . .make it in our view unlikely that an improper purpose of limiting Asian enrollment would either have eluded all these decision-makers or been shared by all of them. We therefore think it unlikely that the decision to end protection for non-AA EOP applicants reflected intentional bias against Asian Americans." (Ibid., p. 32.)

68   Patrick S. Hayashi, Assistant to the Chancellor, letter to Prof. William Shack, Chair, Special Committee on Asian American Admissions, Academic Senate, Apr. 7, 1988, pp. 1-2 (hereafter cited as Hayashi letter).

Furthermore, since the policy change was likely to have a disparate impact on a minority group, it should have been evaluated to determine: 1) whether the purpose it is designed to accomplish is necessary; 2) whether the policy change in fact would accomplish that purpose; and 3) whether there exist other measures that could accomplish that purpose without a disparate impact. Such scrutiny would constitute an important safeguard against the adoption of discriminatory admissions policies. It is not clear from the Special Committee report that the EOP-redirection decision was ever given such scrutiny, nor does the report attempt to address this issue.

Raising Required Minimum on GPA, But Not on Entrance Tests

Faced with a surge of applications to the College of Letters and Science (L and S) for the fall of 1984, the administration decided to raise the minimum grade point average (GPA), but did not raise the required minimum scores on college entrance tests, that would guarantee admission. At that time Berkeley guaranteed admission to candidates who met either a minimum GPA threshold or a minimum score on college entrance tests.[69] Asian American applicants were more likely to be admitted on the strength of their GPA, whereas white applicants were more likely to be admitted on the strength of test scores (especially English tests). Thus, raising only the minimum GPA threshold had the effect of disadvantaging Asian American applicants relative to white applicants.[70]

Regarding this policy change the committee concluded:

We do not know why L and S decided, or who in L and S decided, to respond to the surge in applications by raising the GPA threshold but not by raising the test-score threshold as well. We cannot rule out the possibility that this decision had the purpose, at least in part, of limiting the number of Asian Americans admitted relative to the number of whites. But neither can we confirm that possibility.[71]

Considering the serious nature of this possibility, it would have been legitimate for the committee to have investigated further the process and circumstances leading to the GPA decision with a view to determining more definitively 1) the extent to which the decision was motivated by a desire to reduce the number of Asian American students on campus and 2) whether the decision was given the thorough scrutiny warranted for policies that are likely to have a disparate impact.

Directive For Setting Minimum SAT-Verbal Score

On December 28, 1983, the director of the Office of Admissions and Records announced that applicants of "permanent aliens" status not meeting a minimum SAT-verbal score[72] would be redirected to other campuses.[73] The directive (hereafter referred to as the Bailey directive) was rescinded in early January 1984, however, about 10 days after it was issued and before it had an adverse effect on any applicant to Berkeley.

---

69   This policy has been abandoned since then in favor the Academic Index Score, which is now in use.

70   *Shack Report*, pp. 5, 24.

71   Ibid., p. 24.

72   A score of less than 400 for those applicants in the upper 50 percent of the applicant pool and a score of less than 450 for those in the lower 50 percent of the pool. *Shack Report*, p. 34.

73   Robert L. Bailey, memorandum "Permanent Aliens—Fall 1984," to Vice Chancellor Watson M. Laetsch, Dec. 28, 1983 (reproduced as app. II-C in the Shack Report) (hereafter cited as Bailey directive).

Since the directive affected Asian American immigrant applicants more than any other group,[74] the directive naturally became one of the focal points of the 1985 Task Force report. As noted earlier, however, the existence of the directive was repeatedly denied by the university administration,[75] creating a tense atmosphere filled with anger, distrust, and accusation. Finally, in early 1988, the California State Assembly Subcommittee on Higher Education released two internal memoranda (dated December 28, 1983, and January 4, 1984) written by the director of admissions at UC-Berkeley establishing a minimum score of 400 on the SAT-verbal test for immigrant applicants only. At the subcommittee hearing at which the Bailey directive was released, the UC-Berkeley chancellor apologized publicly to the Asian American community for the insensitive manner in which Berkeley administration officials had handled and responded to their concerns about freshman admissions quotas against Asian American applicants.[76]

The following pages offer a brief account of the events surrounding the issuance of the directive. Faced with a 25 percent increase in applications for fall 1984, the director of the Office of Admissions and Records (OAR) was advised that some action was needed to avoid a potential overenrollment crisis. In early December 1983 the university held a meeting at which ways to reduce the number of new freshmen admitted were discussed. During the course of this meeting, someone suggested establishing a minimum SAT-verbal score requirement of 400 for immigrant students. This suggestion met with strenuous objections for its adverse impact on Asian Americans and its discriminatory intent, and the meeting ended without any decision.[77]

---

74   *Shack Report*, p. 38.

75   In responding to the Task Force, the university claimed that "the Campus never instituted a minimum verbal SAT score of 400. . . .In fact, of freshmen entering in Fall 1984, 9 percent (and 14 percent of Asian freshmen) scored below 400 on the verbal scale." B. Thomas Travers, Assistant Vice Chancellor for Undergraduate Affairs, letter to Ken Kawaichi and Lillian K. Sing, Co-chairs, Asian American Task Force on UC Admissions, July 26, 1985, p. 6 (hereafter cited as Travers letter).

76   "In this regard, first I would like to say I wish I had been more sensitive to the underlying concerns at issue. While they did not manifest themselves as neatly as I now see them, Berkeley could have reacted more openly and less defensively than we did. Because the anxieties were elevated, I apologize for this. I really do believe, that regardless of the occasional hostilities between the Task Force and the campus, that the Task Force has performed a very good service in opening up all of these issues for a vote, for viewing and for debate.

"Second, I believe that there is no systematic bias against Asian-Americans in our admissions system, that no verbal SAT became operative in '84 and that the removal of Asians from blanket EOP protection was done in good faith. I want to be sure of the correctness of these conclusions and the fairness of the results. The Academic Senate at Berkeley has set up a special committee to investigate these matters." Chancellor Ira Michael Heyman, Statement at the hearing of the California State Assembly Subcommittee on Higher Education, chaired by Tom Hayden, *Asian-American Admissions at the University of California: Excerpts from a Legislative Hearing*, Jan. 26, 1988, pp. 4-5.

77   The written statement of one person who participated at this meeting is worth quoting because it illustrates the dynamics that prevailed at the meeting:

"In early December 1983, Assistant Vice Chancellor Travers asked that I attend a meeting to discuss admissions. I normally did not attend meetings on admissions and I do not know why I was invited to attend this meeting. . . .At that meeting, we discussed ways to reduce the number of new freshmen admitted for Fall, 1984. . . .Someone suggested that OAR (Office of Admissions and Records) establish a minimum SAT-Verbal score requirement of 400 for immigrant students. The stated rationale was that there was a great deal of concern about the number of Asian immigrants who were coming to Berkeley who had difficulty writing or speaking English well.

"I objected to this proposal on the grounds that, if implemented, it would clearly discriminate against Asians. Someone countered by saying that the proposed minimum standard was not discriminatory in that it would be applied to everyone equally. I stated that it would not be applied equally to everyone, that it would be applied only to 'immigrants.' Someone stated that it would be applied

On December 28, 1983, however, the OAR director issued the controversial Bailey directive implementing the policy of a minimum SAT-verbal score. At an Undergraduate Affairs staff retreat held on January 8-10, 1984, an Asian American staff person, who had been present at the early December meeting and had raised objections to the proposal at that time, spoke with vice chancellor for Undergraduate Affairs. The Asian American staff person repeated his objections to the SAT-verbal minimum requirement, whereupon the vice chancellor "agreed with [his] concerns and immediately ordered the policy be revoked."[78] The Special Committee determined that, although a dozen or so Asian American applicants were to be affected by the directive, the rescission of the directive came in time to stop the mailing of rejection letters and instead accept those applicants.[79]

Two of the committee's findings regarding the Bailey directive merit comment. First, the committee stated:

The Bailey directive of December 28, 1983, was improper. . . .On its face the directive discriminated against aliens living permanently in the United States.

. . .Such discrimination against resident aliens may well be illegal or unconstitutional; in any event, it violates [the] University policy [of not treating immigrants or refugees any differently from citizens in its admission process].[80]

Nonetheless, the committee did not conclude that the directive was necessarily motivated by a desire to reduce the number of Asian students on campus:

Whether the Bailey directive also represented discrimination "against Asians" is a more difficult question. Bailey and the other policy-makers involved surely knew that the largest number of applicants excluded by the directive would be Asian immigrants. It does not necessarily follow, however, that the directive was intended to exclude these applicants because they were Asians, or that it reflected a desire to reduce the number of Asians at Berkeley.[81]

As these quotes demonstrate, the committee report dismisses the argument that imposing a minimum SAT-verbal score for immigrant students represented intentional discrimination against Asians. This dismissal, however, needs to be weighed against several facts: 1) the policy

---

to all immigrants. I said that even that statement was false in that Hispanic immigrants would be protected under affirmative action policy. I said that it was clear that the vast majority of students who would be impacted would be Asians. I pointed out that. . .one must also look at projected impact. . . .I also stated that any change of policy of this sort should be made in consultation with the appropriate Academic Senate committees and not by administrators alone.

"I further argued that the proposed policy was discriminatory in intent in that some of the people present seemed to be deliberately searching for a standard which could be used to exclude Asian immigrant applicants. Finally, I stated that if Berkeley established an SAT-Verbal minimum requirement for immigrants, members of the Asian American community would object strongly. Someone opined that because there are so many Asian students at Berkeley nobody would notice the change. . . .I said that they were 'fools' if they through they could get away with this change in policy. Someone asked how. . .anyone else would learn of the change. I responded by saying, 'I'll tell them personally.'

"After the Christmas holiday, I spoke with Director Bailey and learned that the policy had been implemented. I informed AVC Travers that I had learned that the SAT-Verbal minimum requirement had been implemented and repeated my objections." Hiyashi letter.

78 *Shack Report*, p. 36. Although the Bailey directive was in the form of a memorandum addressed to Laetsch, Laetsch was not aware of it until the retreat because he had been away from Berkeley over the holidays and had stopped back in Berkeley for only 1 day before going to the retreat. "On learning of the directive," Laetsch said, "he immediately rescinded it." Ibid., p. 36-37.

79 Ibid., pp. 37-38.

80 Ibid., p. 38.

81 Ibid.

change affected only one specific population group (i.e., immigrant applicants), and a large majority of that population group was known to be Asian American; 2) the inevitable effect of the policy change on the number of Asian American students admitted had been pointed out in no uncertain terms at the December meeting;[82] 3) alternatives to the policy were not discussed at the December meeting, nor were other objectives mentioned that would have been achieved by the SAT-verbal minimum score.[83] Given these facts, some could draw the conclusion that the policy change was indeed motivated by a desire to reduce the number of Asian American students, or at least was intended to exclude certain applicants because they were Asians. It would have been helpful if the committee had elaborated its conclusions more fully.[84]

Second, the committee stated:

We also find troubling the claim by the Campus administration over a prolonged period that it could not find this memorandum. As best we can determine, the memorandum was not produced by the Administration until January 1988. Such conduct casts doubt on the University's good faith and naturally arouses suspicions among the communities interested in the University's admissions policy. . . .[85]

[One must also consider,] not only the issuance of the directive in the first place, and the likelihood that the improper judgement it reflected was not Bailey's alone, but also the prolonged footdragging of the Berkeley Administration in producing the key document.[86]

However, the committee's investigation does not explain adequately how the directive came to be issued in spite of the strong objections voiced at the early December meeting. Considering the possibility that the improper judgment reflected in the directive was "not Bailey's alone," and that indeed other decision-makers were implicated, it would have been legitimate for the committee to have undertaken a more comprehensive investigation of how the decision was made and to have developed recommendations for measures that would protect against a future recurrence.[87]

The prolonged controversy at Berkeley was finally resolved in April 1989 when the Task Force and the university issued a joint statement

---

82   Hayashi letter.

83   Hayashi letter, pp. 1-2, and *Shack Report*, pp. 34-7.

84   Moreover, the committee failed to point out that the internal process should have had built-in safeguards to ensure that policy changes with a disparate impact never be made without careful examination of whether or not they are necessary. Instead, the committee appears to be satisfied with the internal process at Berkeley because the Bailey directive was revoked before any damage was done: "Indeed, it might be said that the internal processes of Berkeley Administration showed healthy capacities of self-correction in this case. An improper directive was issued, but it was met by prompt and vigorous internal criticism, criticism that came from subordinate officials. . .as well as persons in other offices. As a result the directive was retracted two weeks later, before it could have any impact." Ibid., p. 40.

85   Ibid., p. 38.

86   Ibid., p. 40.

87   As for the university's "footdragging," some of the facts of the situation call into question the university's claim that it could not find the directive. In particular, an assistant vice chancellor was present at the early December 1983 meeting (Hayashi letter, p. 1), and the directive was carbon-copied to him on Dec. 28, 1983 (Bailey directive, p. 1). In addition, he was also informed of the directive's implementation after the 1983 winter break (Hayashi letter, p. 2). Yet, this official claimed in July 1985 that "the Campus never instituted a minimum Verbal-SAT score of 400" (Travers letter, p. 6). Although there may be some ambiguity as to whether the university ever "instituted" a minimum verbal SAT for immigrant students since the policy never actually affected any applicants, the university was clearly less than forthcoming in its denial. Had the university adopted a more candid approach, the issue might have been resolved much sooner.

promising mutual cooperation. The joint statement said, "We are here today to put the past in perspective and move forward together to ensure that the admissions process at Berkeley guarantees fairness to all groups and is based on full public understanding."[88] This joint statement officially ended an era of tense confrontation between the Asian American community and the university, marking the beginning of a forward-looking spirit of cooperation.

Harvard University

In 1988, in response both to questions about Harvard's admissions process raised by Asian American organizations and by media and research reports and to specific concerns brought directly to the U.S. Department of Education,[89] OCR initiated a compliance review of Harvard University to determine whether Harvard discriminated against Asian American applicants to its undergraduate program in violation of Title VI of the Civil Rights Act of 1964.[90] After 2 years of intensive investigation, OCR released its report on October 5, 1990,[91] concluding:

Harvard has not violated Title VI with respect to the admission of Asian American applicants to the undergraduate program. Over the last ten years Asian American applicants have been admitted at a significantly lower rate than white applicants; however, . . .this disparity is not the result of discriminatory policies or procedures. We found no evidence of the existence or use of quotas, nor did we find that Asian Americans were treated differently than white applicants in the implementation of the admissions process. . . .We determined that the primary cause of the disparity was the preference given to children of alumni and recruited athletes. . .and that [the preferences] were legitimate and not a pretext for discrimination.[92]

The OCR report on Harvard presents the results of the first thorough, outside investigation of the admissions discrimination issue at one of the country's top private universities. The report unveils, for the first time, some of the well-guarded institutional proprietary information about Harvard's admissions procedures.[93] More importantly, it provides a factual basis for evaluating the admissions discrimination controversy on its merits. Because of its historical importance, the OCR report merits careful consideration.[94]

OCR's findings are based on three separate components of its analysis: 1) an analysis of the overall admissions picture at Harvard; 2) a statistical analysis comparing the admit rates of white and Asian American applicants after adjusting for qualifications; and 3) a detailed study of Harvard's admissions process, including interviews with staff and an examination of a large number of applicant folders. The following

88   "A Joint Statement by Judges Ken Kawaichi and Lillian Sing, Co-Chairs of the Asian American Task Force on University Admissions, and Chancellor Ira Michael Heyman of the University of California at Berkeley," Apr. 6, 1989, p. 1.

89   U.S. Department of Education, Office for Civil Rights, "Statement of Findings" (for Compliance Review No. 01-88-6009 on Harvard University), Oct. 4, 1990, p. 2 (hereafter cited as OCR Findings).

90   OCR Letter.

91   U.S. Department of Education, "Harvard Cleared of Asian-American Discrimination Charges," Press Release, Oct. 5, 1990 (hereafter cited as OCR Press Release).

92   OCR Letter, p. 1.

93   Although there have been a number of historical studies of who attended Harvard and what influence Harvard graduates exert, few studies have empirically investigated who gets admitted to Harvard and on what basis. David Karen, "Who Gets Into Harvard? Selection and Exclusion at An Elite College" (Ph.D. diss., Harvard University, 1985), p. 4.

94   Some Asian American researchers have charged that the OCR report is flawed and have called for an independent evaluation of the OCR investigation. Scott Jaschik, "Doubts Are Raised About U.S. Inquiry on Harvard Policies," *Chronicle of Higher Education*, Feb. 6, 1991, p. A19.

TABLE 5.2
Admissions Data: Harvard University, Classes 1983–1992

	1983	1984	1985	1986	1987	1988	1989	1990	1991	1992
Whites										
Applicants	10,344	10,708	9,849	9,715	8,855	9,219	9,561	9,196	9,270	9,157
Admits	1,744	1,642	1,609	1,755	1,707	1,629	1,596	1,623	1,474	1,453
Admit rate (%)	16.9	15.4	16.3	18.1	19.3	17.7	16.7	17.6	15.9	15.9
Asian Americans										
Applicants	784	1,015	1,161	1,351	1,391	1,605	1,731	2,054	2,168	2,263
Admits	118	153	167	180	199	204	220	232	267	291
Admit rate (%)	15.1	15.1	14.4	13.3	14.3	12.7	12.7	11.3	12.3	12.9
Asian American admit rate as % of total freshman admits	5.5	7.5	8.5	8.5	9.6	10.4	10.9	11.5	12.9	14.2

Source: U.S. Department of Education, Office for Civil Rights, *Statement of Findings*, Compliance Review 01-88-6009, 1990, tables 1, 2, and 3.

pages review these three components of OCR's investigation and offer general comments on Harvard's admissions policy vis a vis Asian American students and on OCR's conclusion that Harvard's policy giving admissions preferences to children of alumni does not violate Title VI.

Analysis of Harvard's Overall Admissions Picture

Table 5.2 shows the overall admissions picture for Asian American and white applicants to Harvard for the classes of 1983-92. The admit rate of Asian American applicants was lower than that of white applicants in the last 7 years of the 10-year period (classes of 1986-92). However, the number of Asian American applicants admitted to Harvard during the 1980s increased both in absolute number and as a percentage of the class along with the increase in the number of Asian American applicants. Specifically, the number of Asian American applicants admitted increased steadily from 118 to 291, while the number of Asian American admits as a percentage of the total class showed a parallel increase from 5.5 to 14.2 percent, without any apparent sign of reaching a plateau or ceiling. These statistics, along with the absence of contrary evidence un-

covered through its investigation, led OCR to conclude that Harvard had not placed a limit or "quota" or ceiling on the number or percentage of Asian American applicants admitted.[95]

Statistical Analysis of Admit Rates

Although the overall admissions picture led OCR to conclude that Harvard had not set an Asian American "quota," it did not help to resolve the broader issue of whether equally qualified Asian American and white applicants had equal chances of being admitted to Harvard. Therefore, OCR sought to address this issue by undertaking a statistical analysis of Harvard's admission decisions. The following summary of OCR's statistical analysis is based in part on OCR's report and in part on a statistical appendix[96] made available to Commission staff by OCR.

At the heart of OCR's statistical analysis is the estimation of logistic regressions predicting admission for Asian American and white candidates for the classes of 1983-92 based on their measured qualifications.[97] This analysis was designed to allow comparison of the admit rates of Asian American applicants and white applicants after controlling for differences in their qualifications.[98] The statistical analysis was carried out

---

95   OCR Findings, pp. 5-6.

96   U.S. Department of Education, Office for Civil Rights, "Harvard Discriminant, Logistic Regression, and Odds Ratio Analyses," May 10, 1990 (hereafter cited as OCR Statistical Appendix).

97   OCR estimated separate logistic regressions for Asian American and white applicants to Harvard. The dependent (or criterion) variable in these regressions was the admit/reject decision for the applicant, and the independent (or predictor) variables included measures of the applicant's qualifications (e.g., test scores, grades, teacher ratings, extracurricular activities, interview ratings, etc). (Ibid., pp. 33-34.) OCR's findings were also based in part on the results of another type of statistical analysis (i.e., an odds ratio analysis)—described in OCR's statistical appendix, but not mentioned in the OCR report—that further supports OCR's finding that when athletes and legacies are removed from consideration similarly qualified Asian American and white candidates are almost equally likely to be admitted. (OCR Statistical Appendix, pp. 8-12.)

98   With respect to the relative qualifications of Asian American applicants, OCR reported two major findings: "i) Asian American applicants had significantly higher scores than whites on academic rating, SAT math, class rank, and teacher rating. White applicants, on the other hand, were higher on athletic rating, personal rating, and SAT verbal" (ibid., p. 33); and "ii) eight of the ten criterion variables relevant to the admissions decision significantly differentiated the two groups (with the exception of SAT verbal, Asian American applicants were higher on academic scores while white applicants were higher on non-academic scores)" (OCR Findings, p. 34). Judging that the "magnitude of the difference between the two groups was small," however, OCR concluded that

in two stages. In the first stage, OCR analyzed the admit rates of all applicants[99] and found that there were significant differences between the factors influencing the admit/reject decisions for Asian American and white candidates. In the second stage, because Harvard asserted that the preferences given to children of alumni (legacies) and recruited athlete applicants explained the admit rate disparity,[100] OCR repeated the analysis without these two preference groups. Upon removing legacies and athletes from its analysis, OCR found that "all of these race effects [i.e., group differences between Asian Americans and whites] disappeared, with the exception that one variable, the reader academic rating, continued to have a small adverse effect on Asian Americans."[101] This finding means that once legacies and athletes were removed from consideration, Asian American and white candidates with the same measured qualifications had similar admit rates. Indeed, even the raw or uncontrolled difference between the admit rates of Asian American and white candidates largely disappeared when legacies and athletes were removed from the sample: OCR states that the "disparity in admit rates [not controlling for qualifications] is virtually eliminated over the ten year period when removing legacies and recruited athletes from the sample."[102] These findings led OCR to conclude that the lower admit rate for Asian American applicants could be explained, as Harvard had contended, by their lower representation among legacies and athletes and was not the result of differential treatment of Asian American candidates.[103]

OCR made the appropriate decision to base its conclusions in large part on statistical analysis. However, several comments on OCR's statistical analysis and its presentation are in order. First, OCR's logistic regression analysis has several methodological problems that if corrected could potentially produce different results. Among these problems are OCR's specification of the independent variables,[104] OCR's decision to use a stepwise logistic regression procedure rather than including all relevant variables in the regressions,[105] and OCR's decisions about when and when not to aggregate different classes into one data set.[106] Second, given that the central legal question to be answered was whether *simi-*

"[the two groups] appear overall to be comparably qualified when viewing their means." (Ibid., p. 33.)

99   Those applicants for whom there were incomplete data were excluded from the analysis. As a result, slightly more than three-quarters of the applicants to Harvard over the period 1983-92 were ruled out from the statistical analysis. OCR Statistical Appendix, p. 4.

100   OCR Findings, p. 2.

101   Ibid., p. 34.

102   Ibid., p. 36.

103   Ibid., p. 40.

104   For instance, variables such as academic rating on which applicants were given a score from 1 to 5 by Harvard admissions staff were entered as continuous variables in the logistic regression analysis, when a more appropriate specification would have been to enter them as categorical variables. There is even evidence from OCR's odds ratio analysis to support the view that Asian Americans with the highest academic rating had much better relative chances of being admitted than Asian Americans with midlevel academic rating scores. (OCR Statistical Appendix, pp. 10-1.)

105   The stepwise procedure ends up discarding some variables, making it nearly it impossible to arrive at a straightforward interpretation of OCR's results. For instance, in some instances the dummy variable for race was excluded, while interaction terms between that dummy variable and other variables were kept (see, e.g., OCR Statistical Appendix, table 14.) In these situations it is difficult to interpret the coefficients on the interaction terms.

106   OCR's decision to aggregate 10 classes into one data set rather than estimating separate regressions for each year may have had the effect of masking discriminatory effects existing only in 1 or 2 years during the 10-year period. An incident of noncompliance (e.g., treating Asian American applicants in a discriminatory manner) in 1 year, if mixed together with the data from the other 9 years,

larly qualified Asian American and white candidates had the same chances of being admitted by Harvard (and not whether Asian American and white candidates as a group have the same admit rates), the most important statistical findings are those that compare Asian American and white admit rates after controlling for differences in qualifications—i.e., the logistic regressions. Yet the OCR report gives too little prominence to its discussion of the logistic regressions that control for differences in qualifications[107] and as a result may leave the casual reader with little understanding of the basis for OCR's statistical findings.

In addition, it should be noted that there is an inherent limitation in the ability of statistical analysis alone to resolve the issue of whether Asian American candidates receive discriminatory treatment in the admission process. This limitation is related to the subjective nature of some of the variables measuring the qualifications of the applicants. For example, one of the variables used in the OCR's regression analysis to measure an applicant's qualifications is a numerical rating of the applicant's "personal" characteristics given by admissions staff based on his or her application folder. Such subjective ratings are likely to be influenced by any biases and stereotypes subscribed to by Harvard's admissions staff. Thus, Asian American applicants may be given lower personal ratings than equally qualified white applicants depending on the reader's biases. Until it is known that the personal ratings given Asian American candidates do not incorporate such bias, the statistical results showing that the admit rates of Asian American and white candidates with equal measured qualifications were the same do not necessarily indicate that Asian American candidates did not face discrimination at Harvard. Partly because of these limitations, OCR undertook a careful review of Harvard's admissions process and Harvard's treatment of Asian Americans' file folders in addition to a statistical analysis.

Examination of Harvard's Admissions Process

OCR interviewed admissions staff to gain an understanding of the process, reviewed 400 applicant file folders to determine whether Asian American and white applicants were evaluated differently, and looked at reader summary sheets for an additional 2,000 applicant files.[108] Al-

---

may not be powerful enough to show its effects above and beyond what may have happened in other years. Thus, unless prohibited by practical considerations, such as small sample sizes, statistical analysis should be conducted on each class separately. OCT explained to Commission staff that small sample sizes were one of the considerations that prevented them from performing year-by-year logistic regressions. Furthermore, OCR states, "We believed that a statistical discrepancy found for a single year, but not present in later years or the current year, would have limited value in making a compliance determination." (Office for Civil Rights, "Comments and Concerns on Draft Report, Harvard Compliance Review," p. 2, accompanying Michael Williams, Assistant Secretary for Civil Rights, U.S. Department of Education, letter to Wilfredo J. Gonzalez, Staff Director, U.S. Commission on Civil Rights, Oct. 17, 1991 (hereafter cited as OCR Comments).

On the other hand, in comparing the admit rates of Asian American and white legacies, OCT chose to examine each class separately. OCR found that Asian American legacies had lower admit rates than white legacies, but that the differences were not significant. (OCR Findings, table 11, p. 38.) Had OCR aggregated the data to obtain a larger sample size, it might have found that the difference in Asian American and white legacy admit rates was signficant.

107   The OCR report devotes one paragraph to discussing the logistic regressions. (Ibid., pp. 34-35.) In contrast, the report gives considerable visibility to table 8, which shows the mean admit rates of Asian American and white candidates for all applicants and for nonathlete, nonlegacy applicants only—both with and with legacies and athletes. (Ibid., p. 36.) Because table 8 does not control for the qualifications of the applicants, it says little about how Harvard treats similarly qualified Asian American and white candidates. In addition, neither the OCR report nor the statistical appendix provided by OCR provides sufficient information for an outside observer to determine exactly what OCR did in its statistical analysis.

though OCR's indepth examination of Harvard's admissions process found several potential sources of discrimination, overall OCR did not find evidence that the admissions process was biased against Asian Americans. OCR's investigation did bring to light several issues worth examining. These issues are the ethnic read Harvard says it gives Asian American applicants and stereotyping comments made about Asian American applicants by Harvard's admissions staff.

Asian American Ethnic Read—Harvard explained to OCR investigators that it uses ethnic readers for Asian American (as well as black, Hispanic, and Native American) applicants to:

provide an additional or different sensitivity to the review of the application. The ethnic read is designed to ensure that no special cultural or ethnic factors are overlooked which might prevent an Asian American applicant's background from being fully understood.[109]

Furthermore, "[a]ccording to the Dean of Admissions, the Asian American reader reviews folders of Asian American applicants who 'have a chance,' perhaps 80 percent of the applicants."[110] Yet, contrary to this claim, OCR found that only 19 percent of Asian American applications were read by the Asian American ethnic reader. Moreover, the Asian American reader read most of these cases, not as an extra ethnic reader, but as the first reader who was assigned to read cases as other first readers would read their assignments.[111] In spite of Harvard's claim that nearly all of the Vietnamese and Filipino applicants were read by an ethnic reader, OCR found that for several applicants noted as being of Vietnamese or Filipino heritage, "there was no evidence of the ethnic read."[112] When confronted with this finding by OCR, Harvard asserted that:

the Asian American ethnic reader was assigned to dockets and sits on subcommittees which included over half of all Asian American applicants. Consequently, . . .in addition to those files in which OCR found evidence of the Asian American read, the Asian ethnic reader reviews files and participates in discussions at subcommittee and full committee meetings on many more Asian American applicants.[113]

Nonetheless, the OCR report found that "our file review did not support Harvard's assertion that the Asian American ethnic reader reviews 'most' or all files of Asian American applicants who 'have a chance.'"[114]

Based on its indepth review of Asian American and white candidates' file folders, OCR "could not conclude that the lack of an ethnic read put Asian American candidates at a disadvantage,"[115] but noted that "the possibility exists that some ethnically-related factors might be overlooked."[116] Nonetheless, OCR did not find that Harvard's failure to provide an ethnic read to many Asian American candidates was in violation of Title VI.[117]

---

108   OCR Findings, p. 19.

109   Ibid., p. 14.

110   Ibid.

111   Ibid., p. 23.

112   Ibid.

113   Ibid.

114   Ibid., p. 24.

115   Ibid.

116   Ibid.

117   In elaborating on this finding, OCR asserts that Harvard is not required by Title VI to provide an ethnic read to Asian American candidates, and thus Harvard's failure to do so does not constitute a violation of Title VI. (OCR Comments, p. 4.) However, if

In another apparent inconsistency between Harvard's stated policy and its procedures, although Harvard states that race and ethnicity are positive factors in the admissions decision,[118] OCR "found *no* readers' comments which suggested that an applicant's Asian ethnicity was a significant factor in deciding to admit the applicant in the same way that being a legacy or recruited athlete was instrumental."[119] Indeed, OCR observed:

None of those interviewed could think of, or remember a single case in which an applicant's Asian American ethnicity was cited as the "tip" which resulted in the applicant being admitted over a substantially equal white applicant.[120]

Thus, it is not clear whether Harvard has a well-articulated, consistent policy about whether Asian Americans should be given preference in admissions. In fact, there was considerable disagreement among file readers interviewed by OCR as to whether being Asian was likely to help an applicant in the admissions process.[121] Even though these discrepancies between Harvard's stated admissions policy and Harvard's procedures may not be in violation of Title VI, it is important for Harvard to clarify its admissions policy vis a vis Asian Americans to allay apprehensions about unfair treatment among the Asian American community.

Stereotyping Comments on Asian American Applicants—Out of concern for the potential stereotyping of Asian American applicants and its impact on the admissions decision, OCR reviewed reader comments on applicant folders for negative characterizations. OCR found several examples of readers making generalizations about Asian Americans. For example, consider the remark, "[the applicant's] scores and application seem so typical of other Asian applications I've read: extraordinarily gifted in math with the opposite extreme in English"[122] and references to a "classic V.N. [Vietnamese] bootstrap case"[123] and to "a classic BC/NC [blue collar/noncollege background] Asian American from the inner-city."[124] Furthermore, OCR found that "quite often"[125] and "in a number of cases"[126] Asian American applicants were described as being science/math oriented, quiet, shy, reserved, self-contained, and soft spoken. Interestingly enough, "these characteristics were underlined for added emphasis by the reader."[127] OCR further noted that while white applicants were similarly described, such descriptions were ascribed to Asian American applicants more frequently.[128] These comments suggest that Harvard's admissions staff may have been influenced by the stereotype of Asian Americans as achieving academic excellence at the expense of a balanced overall personal development. Based on its review of applicant file

---

OCR had found evidence that Asian American applicants were given discriminatory treatment as a result of the lack of an ethnic read, then the failure to provide an ethnic read would indeed have been a violation of Title VI.

118   OCR Findings, p. 8.

119   Ibid., p. 28, italics in original.

120   Ibid., p. 29.

121   Ibid., pp. 14-15.

122   Ibid., p. 25.

123   Ibid.

124   Ibid.

125   Ibid., p. 24.

126   Ibid.

127   Ibid.

128   Ibid.

folders, however, OCR found that "while some reader comments could be construed to negatively affect the case of Asian American applicants, the ratings given to the applicants, where these comments did occur, did not reflect a lower than expected score."[129] Therefore, OCR concluded that the stereotyping comments "could not be shown to have negatively impacted the ratings given to these applicants."[130]

Legacy Tips and Their Legitimacy

OCR concluded that Harvard's policy of giving preferential consideration to children of alumni (i.e., "legacies") does not violate Title VI.[131] This conclusion rests on three considerations. First, OCR noted that there was "no evidence to suggest that these preferences were instituted intentionally or deliberately to limit the number of Asian Americans at Harvard,"[132] since these preferences had been in place long before the number of Asian American applicants increased significantly. Second, OCR determined that Harvard's alumni preference policy was designed to serve the legitimate institutional goal of obtaining financial and volunteer support for the university from alumni, and that there were no viable alternative policies that would accomplish the same goal.[133] Finally, OCR argued that existing case law does not suggest that legacy preferences are illegal.[134]

In determining that alumni preferences serve a legitimate institutional goal, OCR accepted Harvard's explanation that:

[Harvard's alumni] are naturally, very interested in the college choices of their own children. If their children are rejected by Harvard, their affection for and interest in the college may decline; if their children are admitted, their involvement with the College is renewed. Having children share the parent's college affiliation stimulates those three aspects of contribution: of service, of money, and of community relations.[135]

OCR also accepted the evidence provided by Harvard that alumni contribute both financially and through service to the university. In addition, OCR asked Harvard whether it had considered alternative ways of achieving its goals that might have a less severe impact on Asian American applicants.[136] OCR accepted Harvard's response that "in our judgment, and in the judgment of our fellow institutions, tips for lineage. . .could not be eliminated without a severe effect on the strength and vitality of the institutions and their ability to achieve their educational objectives."[137] Given the importance of this issue, rather than merely accepting Harvard's assertion, OCR might have asked for supporting evidence that alumni support would indeed drop off substantially if legacy preferences were no longer given and that there were no reasonable alternative sources for such support.

OCR noted that although there is no case law addressing the legitimacy of a private university's admissions preferences to children of alumni, there is one case (*Rosenstock v. Board of Governors of University of North Carolina*)[138] in which

---

129   Ibid., p. 26.

130   Ibid.

131   Ibid., p. 43.

132   Ibid., p. 40.

133   Ibid., pp. 40, 43.

134   Ibid., p. 42.

135   Ibid., p. 40.

136   Ibid., p. 40.

137   Ibid., p. 41.

138   423 F. Supp. 1321 (1976).

a Federal district court was willing "to recognize the legitimacy of a link between a University's economic interests and admissions preference to alumni children based on the fact alumni donate large sums of money to the University."[139] Based on these considerations, OCR concluded that "there is no definitive authority to suggest that such preferences are unlawful in and of themselves."[140]

Although OCR is correct in its determination that legacy preferences are not clearly illegal under Title VI, it should be noted that the issue of the legality of alumni preferences under Title VI remains unresolved. As noted by OCR, the pertinence of *Rosenstock* to the legitimacy of Harvard's legacy preferences is open to question. It is true that the court in *Rosenstock* stated that since alumni provide substantial monetary support for the university, providing a preference to the children of alumni is rationally related to the legitimate objective of continuing that alumni support.[141] However, *Rosenstock* may not necessarily be controlling in the Harvard context for two reasons. First, no "suspect class," such as Asian Americans, was involved in the *Rosenstock* case, meaning that the university in that case only needed to meet the "rational relation" test rather than the stronger "strict scrutiny" test that would have been required had a suspect class been involved. Second, in *Rosenstock* the plaintiff's challenge was that the university (a public university) violated the equal protection and due process clauses of the 14th

amendment of the Constitution. Since Harvard

is a private university, it cannot be sued on these constitutional grounds and would instead be challenged for violating Title VI of the Civil Rights Act of 1964, and Title VI law, not constitutional law, would be controlling. OCR could make a valuable contribution to the resolution of this issue by issuing guidelines specifying in what circumstances alumni preferences are allowed under Title VI.

The issue of legacy tips is an important issue with far-reaching ramifications not only for the immediate question of Asian American admissions, but also for the general issue of equal opportunity in higher education. Although the practice of legacy tips was in place before Asian American applicants increased in number, its use will continue to affect Asian Americans and other minorities adversely to the extent that they are underrepresented among alumni of elite colleges and universities. It is too important an issue to grant legitimacy so readily based on "one Federal district court's willingness to recognize a link"[142] between an institution's economic interests and alumni contributions. It deserves to be debated and articulated by the larger community of legal scholars and civil rights advocates against the broader context of civil rights advancement.

It was in recognition of this broad national context and its profound ramifications that Senate Minority Leader Robert J. Dole (R-KA) wrote to Secretary of Education Lamar Alexander upon his nomination urging him to "re-ex-

amine the Department's. . .endorsement of the

---

139   OCR Findings, p. 42.

140   Ibid., p. 42.

141   423 F. Supp. 1322.

142   Ibid.

so-called 'legacy preference.'"[143] He was concerned that the practice of legacy preference "serves only to discourage the aspirations of those students who are not fortunate enough to come from privileged backgrounds."[144] He also observed that the practice "calls into question. . .the very assumptions undergirding our society (that 'the rules of the game are fair to all' and that 'merit will prevail')."[145]

143　Sen. Robert J. Dole (R-KA), letter to Secretary of Education nominee Lamar Alexander, Dec. 18, 1990, p. 1.

144　Ibid., p. 2.

145　Ibid.

Chapter 6

Employment Discrimination

Asian Americans face a number of barriers to equal participation in the labor market. Many of these barriers are encountered to a greater degree by the foreign born, who often confront linguistic and cultural barriers to finding employment commensurate with their education and experience, but even third- or fourth-generation Asian Americans find their employment prospects diminished because employers have stereotypical views of Asians and prejudice against citizens of Asian ancestry. Employment discrimination, to varying degrees, is a problem facing all Asian Americans. As will be seen in the succeeding pages, employment discrimination against Asian Americans ranges from discrimination based on accent or language, to discrimination caused by our nation's immigration control laws, to artificial barriers preventing many Asian Americans from rising to management positions for which they are qualified.

This chapter details several types of employment discrimination that are frequently experienced by Asian Americans and examines the legal protections available to victims of discrimination. The chapter covers five employment discrimination issues in detail: the glass ceiling, language rights in the workplace, the certification of foreign-educated professionals, discrimination caused by the Immigration Reform and Control Act, anti-Asian discrimination in construction unions, and employment discrimination against Asian American women. Resource limitations prevent the chapter from providing detailed coverage of other important issues, including several serious specific allegations of employment discrimination received by the Commission. These allegations include:

1) Participants at the Commission's New York and San Francisco Roundtable Conferences alleged that recently arrived Asian immigrants are exploited by firms who take advantage of their ignorance of their rights and their need for jobs. They spoke of employers of immigrant Asians who violated labor laws with unsafe working conditions, low pay, and long hours of work.[1]

2) Cambodians in Lowell, Massachusetts, alleged that there were some industrial employers in the area who resorted to numerous pretexts for discrimination—including pretending that they had run out of application forms and setting arbitrarily high job requirements (such as a high school diploma requirement for an unskilled job or extremely high English-proficiency requirements)—to avoid hiring Cambodian job applicants.[2]

Employment discrimination on the basis of race or national origin is prohibited under section 1981 of the Civil Rights Act of 1866,[3] which

---

1   May Ying Chen and Jackson Chin, Statement at the U.S. Commission on Civil Rights Roundtable Conference on Asian American Civil Rights Issues for the 1990s, New York, NY, June 23, 1989; Andy Anh, Statement at the U.S. Commission on Civil Rights Roundtable Conference on Asian American Civil Rights Issues for the 1990s, San Francisco, CA, July 29, 1989.

2   Vera Godley, Project Director, and Cambodian American staff members, Cambodian Mutual Assistance Association, interview, Lowell, MA, Feb. 12, 1990.

3   42 U.S.C. §1981.

prohibits racial discrimination in contracts (and has been interpreted to apply to national origin discrimination as well), and Title VII of the Civil Rights Act of 1964,[4] which prohibits employment discrimination on the basis of race, color, religion, sex, or national origin. Several recent Supreme Court decisions interpreting section 1981 and Title VII have had a negative effect on Asian Americans' ability to obtain legal redress for discrimination against them, however. In particular, the 1989 decision, *Patterson v. Mclean Credit Union,*[5] which limited the types of employer behavior that are illegal under section 1981, means that Asian Americans can no longer sue for damages when their employers racially harass them on the job. For example, as a direct result of the *Patterson* decision, a case brought by a Hawaiian woman of Asian descent against her employer was dismissed by the court, even though the court acknowledged that:

It is undisputed that [the woman's supervisor] McDonough made many derogatory and discriminatory remarks about various ethnic groups. . .McDonough referred to a Japanese person as a "Jap" and compared local people to "the spics in New York," stating that locals are "not capable of being supervisors" and are "incompetent". . . .McDonough told her. . ."in a contemptuous way" that "I have to have the only secretary who does the hula. . . ." McDonough adopted a rude and aggressive behavior with [the woman], yelling at her frequently and demeaning her in front of the other employees.[6]

Also, as noted elsewhere,[7] the Supreme Court's *Martin v. Wilks*[8] decision, which allows consent decrees to be challenged in court after they have been entered, has made it more difficult for Asian Americans to seek to be included in consent decrees requiring affirmative action in municipal and State government employment, while the *Wards Cove Packing Co. v. Atonio* decision[9] made it more difficult for Asian Americans and others who face artificial barriers to employment to prove their case in court. The U.S. Commission on Civil Rights has supported the Civil Rights Act of 1990 passed by Congress, but subsequently vetoed by President Bush, which would undo the effects of these three decisions.[10] Although the Civil Rights Act of 1990 was not enacted, in 1991, after exhaustive debate, Congress passed and President Bush signed into law a compromise bill, the Civil Rights Act of 1991,[11] containing most of the provisions of the Civil Rights Act of 1990.

Glass Ceiling

The perception that there is a "glass ceiling" barring most Asian Americans from attaining management positions (especially upper level management positions) for which they are qualified was perhaps the concern most frequently voiced by Asian American participants in the Commission's Roundtable Conferences[12] and by other Asian American individuals and advocacy groups across the country. Most felt that Asian

---

4   42 U.S.C. §2000.

5   491 U.S. 164 (1989).

6   Leong v. Hilton Hotels, 50 FEP Cas. 738 (D. Hawaii 1989), cited in NAACP Legal Defense and Education Fund, "The Impact of Patterson v. McLean Credit Union," Nov. 20, 1989.

7   See chap. 3, n. 53.

8   490 U.S. 755 (1989).

9   490 U.S. 642 (1989).

10   In June 1990 the Commissioners voted to endorse the Civil Rights Act of 1990 and released a report on the proposed legislation. U.S. Commission on Civil Rights, *Report on the Civil Rights Act of 1990* (July 1990). Similar legislation has been passed by the House of Representatives this year and is currently before the Senate.

11   Pub. L. 102-106.

12   The glass ceiling issue was raised by Romesh Divan, New York Roundtable Conference; Harry Gee, Theresa Chang, Martha Wong,

Americans are unfairly stereotyped as being un-aggressive, having poor communications skills and limited English proficiency, and being too technical to become managers, and that Asian Americans were excluded from networks necessary for promotions.

The following statement illustrates the depth and the nature of the concerns.

I am of the opinion that most Asian Americans are facing an insurmountable glass wall in the corporate world. As a matter of fact, most of us have given up hope of advancing up the corporate ladder. The more we think about it, the more frustrated, discouraged, and depressed we become. . . .

Within my company there are about 800 to 1,000 research and engineering professional staff members. About 60 of them are of Asian origin. We think that there are altogether about 200 management and management track positions in the company. There are no Asians in management positions and only one Asian in a management track position. . . .

I suspect that the minds of many corporate managers and the senior staff members who have direct control. . .are still in the 1960s. As a consequence, for most of them we Asians are a suspect class, and we usually have to prove that we are better in order to be equal. . . .

Even after we pass a certain test or a certain set of tests, the rules or penalties are much harsher against us if we ever make any mistake. . . .

Many of us feel that our Asian accent is a major stumbling block in our career path. . . .There is no doubt that communication skills are very important. However, adopting a standard that is unreasonably high may be tantamount to allowing an employment practice that is prejudicial against foreign-born Asian American employees. . . .

Most of us have proved our technical capability. However, many major corporations tend to overlook the non-technical side of many Asian Americans. Corporations pick pigeon holes for us. And what is worse, they believe that we are quite content staying in those technologically airtight pigeon holes.[13]

The perception among Asian Americans that discrimination is the root cause of their underrepresentation among higher managerial ranks is widespread. Thus, in a survey of 308 Asian American professionals and managers in the San Francisco Bay area, over two-thirds of the Chinese Americans, one-half of the Japanese Americans, and three-quarters of the Filipino Americans felt that racism was a very significant factor limiting their upward mobility.[14] Respondents also pointed to difficulties in networking, the lack of mentors, management insensitivity, and corporate culture as barriers to upper mobility.[15]

There exists some statistical evidence at the national level supporting the view that a glass ceiling exists for Asian Americans as well as for other minorities and women. A recent survey of highly successful executives in Fortune 500 companies shows that only 0.3 percent of senior ex-

Edward Chen, Chiang Cho, Wayne Liauh, William Chang, Albert Wang, Rong-Tai Ho, and Mark Chang, Houston Roundtable Conference; and Henry Der, Raj Prasad, Paul Wong, Vinod Patwardhan, and Virginia Barrientes, San Francisco Roundtable Conference.

13   Wayne Liauh, Statement at the U.S. Commission on Civil Rights Roundtable Conference on Asian American Civil Rights Issues for the 1990s, May 27, 1989.

14   Amado Cabezas, Tse Ming Tam, Brenda M. Lowe, Anna Wong, and Kathy Owyang Turner, "Empirical Study of Barriers to Upward Mobility of Asian Americans in the San Francisco Bay Area," in Gail M. Nomura, Russell Endo, Stephen H. Sumida, and Russell C. Leong, eds., *Frontiers of Asian American Studies: Writing, Research and Commentary* (Pullman, WA: Washington State University Press, 1989), p. 93.

15   Ibid.

ecutives in the United States are of Asian descent.[16] Thus, the representation of Asian Americans among senior executives is just one-tenth their representation in the population as a whole,[17] despite the high education levels of many Asian Americans. Not only are Asian Americans underrepresented at the highest levels of management, Asian Americans are underrepresented in managerial occupations in general. A recent Commission study showed that U.S.-born Asian American men were between 7 and 11 percent less likely to be in managerial occupations than non-Hispanic white men with the same measured characteristics.[18] It should be noted that since the analysis only includes U.S.-born Asian American men (and in addition adjusts for English-language proficiency), it is unlikely that English-language deficiencies or cultural barriers could be responsible for the finding of Asian underrepresentation among managers.

There also exist a number of local studies and studies of individual occupations or industries that suggest that there is indeed a glass ceiling for Asian Americans.[19] For instance, a recent study of Asian American engineers found that they were significantly less likely to be in managerial positions or to be promoted to managerial positions than white engineers with the same measured qualifications (e.g., educational attainment, years of experience) and other characteristics (e.g., field within engineering, region of residence, other demographic factors).[20] This finding held for U.S.-born Asian Americans as well as for immigrants. A report on the city of San Francisco's civil service by Chinese for Affirmative Action, an Asian American civil rights organization, concluded that "Asian professionals are clustered in technical jobs," "there is a serious deficit of Asian administrators," and "Asian professionals face the worst promotional opportunities of all groups."[21] The report also found that Asian American professional employees were considerably overrepresented in finance and operations, while they were largely unrepresented in public safety and judicial services.[22] In addition, the ratio of administrators to professionals was lower for Asians than for any

---

16   Korn/Ferry International, *Korn/Ferry's International Executive Profile: A Decade of Change in Corporate Leadership* (1990), table 61, p. 23.

17   According to newly released figures from the U.S. Bureau of the Census, persons of Asian descent made up 2.9 percent of the U.S. population in 1990. Barbara Vobejda, "Asians, Hispanics Giving Nation More Diversity," *Washington Post*, June 12, 1991.

18   U.S. Commission on Civil Rights, *The Economic Status of Americans of Asian Descent: An Exploratory Investigation* (Clearinghouse Publication 95, October 1988), pp. 72-75. The characteristics controlled for in the Civil Rights Commission analysis are: education, work experience, English ability, region, location, marital status, disability, and industry of work. Ibid., table 7.7, p. 75.

19   See chap. 7 for discussions related to the glass ceilings in journalism and in the legal profession.

20   Joyce Tang, "Asian American Engineers: Earnings, Occupational Status, and Promotions" (paper presented at the 86th annual meeting of the American Sociological Association, Cincinnati, OH, Aug. 23-27, 1991).

21   Henry Der and Colleen Lye, *The Broken Ladder '89: Asian Americans in City Government* (San Francisco: Chinese for Affirmative Action, 1989), p. 5.

22   Ibid, pp. 14-15. The occupational clustering of Asian Americans, although it does not bear directly on the issue of the glass ceiling (which applies, essentially, to promotions within occupations), may indicate the existence of other forms of employment discrimination against Asian Americans. For articles arguing that Asian Americans, especially immigrants, earn less than their white counterparts and are often forced into the "secondary labor market" (or the lower tier of the "primary labor market") or "peripheral" jobs, see Amado Cabezas and Gary Kawaguchi, "Empirical Evidence for Continuing Asian American Income Inequality: The Human Capital Model and Labor Market Segmentation," pp. 144-64 in Gary Y. Okihiro, Shirley Hume, Arthur A. Hansen, and John M. Liu, eds., *Reflections on Shattered Windows: Promises and Prospects for Asian American Studies* (Pullman, WA: Washington State University Press, 1988) and Eui Hang Shin and Kyung-Sup Chang, "Peripherization of Immigrant Professionals: Korean Physicians in the United States," *International Migration Review*, vol. 22, no. 4, pp. 609-26.

other group. Thus, 28 percent of the city's professionals but only 11 percent of the city's administrators were Asian American, whereas blacks and Hispanics had roughly the same representation among professionals as among administrators, and whites were more heavily represented among administrators than among professionals.[23]

A General Accounting Office (GAO) study of the aerospace industry also provides data suggesting that Asian Americans have difficulties moving from professional to managerial jobs in that industry.[24] An analysis of the data reported in the GAO study shows that although a higher percentage of aerospace professionals are Asian American than are either black or Hispanic, the reverse was true for managers: blacks and Hispanics both had higher percentages among managers than did Asian Americans.[25] Thus Asian Americans may be less successful in moving from professional to managerial jobs in the aerospace industry than other minority groups.[26]

The stories of those who have experienced the glass ceiling are compelling. Not only do these stories help to document the existence of a glass ceiling against Asian Americans, but they help to show that the glass ceiling is at least partially caused by sometimes subtle and sometimes overt discrimination against Asian Americans. Three such stories are told below.

● An Asian American sales professional with an MBA in marketing and sales had worked with the same Fortune 500 company for well over a decade and received many sales achievement awards when he was promoted to the regional sales manager for the San Francisco Bay area. He had been working in that position for 3 years when a new management group came in. His new boss frequently used racial slurs against him. For instance, one time, when he was speaking to his boss, his boss said, "Slow down, I cannot write as fast as a Chinaman." Eventually he was demoted and transferred to a sales territory. When he asked his boss why he had been demoted, his boss told him that it was his "gut feeling" that he [the sales professional] was not a good manager and that he did not exhibit leadership qualities. The man subsequently filed a discrimination suit against his employer at the California Fair Employment and Housing Commission and was issued a right to sue letter. The suit was eventually settled out of court. He still works for the same company, but he has not been reinstated to his old position.[27]

● A woman of Asian Indian descent was hired as the personnel manager for a midwestern city. She was the first woman and the first minority ever to be hired in a managerial position by that city. As soon as she arrived at her job, she began encountering resistance from her staff, and when she brought their behavior to the attention of her boss, he told her that her staff was insubordinate because she was a woman of color. Almost a year after she started the job, despite receiving an above-average performance appraisal, she was abruptly fired without severance pay. A subsequent investigation by the city's human relations commission found that "Substantial Evidence exists to show that the Complainant was discriminated against be-

---

23   Ibid., p. 20.

24   U.S. General Accounting Office, *Equal Employment Opportunity: Women and Minority Aerospace Managers and Professionals, 1979-86* (Oct. 26, 1989).

25   Ibid, p. 30. The GAO study does not provide information on white professionals and managers in the aerospace industry.

26   Without further information, it remains possible that the black and Hispanic managers in the aerospace industry did not move up from professional jobs but were placed in low-level administrative/management jobs that did not require professional aerospace expertise.

27   This summary is based on information provided by the Asian American sales professional, who requested anonymity in a telephone interview on Oct. 1, 1991.

cause of her sex, female, and her race, Asian; her national origin, India; and her color, non-white, in the manner in which she was terminated/suspended and in the conditions under which she performed her job." Despite the human relations commission finding, the city did nothing to rectify the situation. In fact, city employees repeatedly told the woman's professional colleagues and others who called that she was under suspension for not performing up to par. As a result, the woman could not find another comparable job, suffered considerable mental anguish, and did not have the financial resources necessary to pursue her case in court.[28]

• In early 1988, Angelo Tom, a fifth-generation Chinese American who had worked at the U.S. Department of Housing and Urban Development's (HUD) San Francisco Regional office for 9 years and become nationally recognized as the leading community planning and development analyst in the Bay area was turned down for promotion to the position of supervisor of his unit. The woman chosen to fill the job had less experience than Mr. Tom. At the time of Mr. Tom's rejection there were only three Asian Americans in middle-management positions at HUD's San Francisco office and none in upper management, and several qualified Asian Americans had repeatedly been rejected for management positions. After Mr. Tom filed a complaint, a HUD investigation found that he had been rejected for the position because he did not have leadership or interpersonal skills and was too technical for the job. Mr. Tom then requested and received a formal hearing in front of the U.S. Equal Employment Opportunity Commission (EEOC). At that hearing, witnesses refuted the HUD contention that he had poor

leadership and interpersonal skills, and the EEOC administrative law judge agreed. He also held that a white man who was highly technically skilled would have been promoted with the confidence that he could develop the general outlook necessary to perform the management job. Mr. Tom was awarded backpay, a retroactive promotion, and attorney's fees.[29]

Because the choice of whom to put in a management position is usually a highly subjective decision, Asian Americans are vulnerable to managers who subscribe to stereotypical views of Asian Americans as not having the qualities that make a good manager. In addition, the subjective nature of promotion decisions usually makes it very difficult to prove that the reason for an adverse employment decision was a discriminatory one. Although limited resources prevented the Commission on Civil Rights from undertaking in this report a thorough investigation of the glass ceiling as it affects Asian Americans, the Commission is convinced that the problem is a serious one and that it pervades both private corporations and government agencies. The issue merits considerable further research and increased enforcement efforts on the part of Federal, State, and local antidiscrimination agencies.

The glass ceiling has begun to capture the national spotlight as an important barrier to equal opportunity for Asian Americans, for other minorities, and for women. The Federal Government has recently taken several steps to deal with the glass ceiling problem. The U.S. Department of Labor and the Equal Employment Opportunity Commission have each recently made the glass ceiling issue one of their top priorities. In March 1990, EEOC Chairman Evan Kemp, Jr., announced that the EEOC would concen-

---

28   The woman requested anonymity. This account of her experience is based on materials she provided to Commission staff, including a copy of the city human relations commission report.

29   Johnny Ng, "Asian Wins EEOC decision in 'Glass Ceiling' Case," *Asian Week*, Nov. 3, 1989; Angelo Tom, memorandum to Phillip Savage, Director, Public Employment Division, ECCP Office of HUD Program Compliance, re Discrimination Complaint, May 27, 1988; and materials supplied by Dale Minami, plaintiff's attorney.

trate efforts on bringing and trying to win glass ceiling cases, although he acknowledged that such cases were often very difficult to prove.[30] In August 1990 then-Secretary of Labor Elizabeth Dole announced that the glass ceiling was her top priority,[31] and shortly thereafter the Department of Labor's Office of Federal Contract Compliance Programs (OFCCP) undertook a glass ceiling initiative under which "federal compliance officers will focus for the first time on examining succession plans in corporations—how individuals are selected for key high-level jobs."[32] As a first step, the OFCCP began a thorough study of the promotion systems used at nine Fortune 500 companies. The purpose of the study was to provide background information necessary to guide them in restructuring their compliance review system to target enforcement efforts on upper echelon jobs.[33] In 1991 the Department of Labor issued a report based on that study, finding that:

● Women and minorities do not reach the top of the corporate ladder, and minorities generaly plateau at lower levels than women.

● Corporations do not have in place crucial procedures for assessing and ensuring progress towards eliminating barriers to the career advancement of women and minorities. In particular, senior-level managers were not held accountable for equal employment opportunity responsibilities.

● Corporations used word-of-mouth and employee referral to fill vacancies and did not make training and other career advancement opportunities as available to women and minorities.[34]

Congress has also begun to address glass ceiling issues. In February 1990 Senator Robert Dole (R-KS) and U.S. Representative Susan Molinari (R-NY) introduced legislation entitled "The Women's Equal Opportunity Act of 1991" that would establish a Federal Glass Ceiling Commission to study the problem and recommend remedies.[35] A similar provision was included in the revised Civil Rights and Women's Equity in Employment Act of 1991,[36] passed by the House of Representatives in June 1991. Lastly, in May 1991, the Senate Governmental Affairs Committee held a hearing on the glass ceiling in Federal employment.[37]

Language Rights in the Workplace

The wave of Asian immigration beginning in 1965 and accelerating through most of the 1970s and early 1980s has brought to our shores a large number of Asian American workers with varying degrees of English-language proficiency. Some Asian American immigrants have very little command of the English language; others speak English well but are more at ease speaking in their native languages; and still others speak English fluently but retain recognizable accents. As the Asian American immigrant population has increased, language rights in the workplace have thus become a pressing civil rights issue for many Asian Americans.

Language rights in the workplace are governed by two Federal statutes that ban employment discrimination based on national origin: Title VII of the 1964 Civil Rights Act[38] and sec-

30 *Fair Employment Report*, vol. 28, no. 7, Mar. 28, 1990, p. 49.

31 *Fair Employment Report*, vol. 28, no. 18, Aug. 29, 1990, p. 137.

32 Bureau of National Affairs, *Daily Labor Report*, no. 52 (1990), p. A-1.

33 Bureau of National Affairs, *Daily Labor Report*, no. 177, Sep. 12, 1990, p. A-3.

34 U.S. Department of Labor, *A Report on the Glass Ceiling Initiative*, 1991, p. 5.

35 Bureau of National Affairs, *Daily Labor Report*, no. 36, Feb. 22, 1991, p. A-6.

36 H.R. 1, 102nd Cong., 1st Sess. (1991).

37 Bureau of National Affairs, *Daily Labor Report*, no. 96, May 17, 1991, pp. A-9—A-11.

38 42 U.S.C. §2000.

tion 1981 of the Civil Rights Act of 1866.[39] Because of the link between national origin and language, the ban on national origin discrimination in these two statutes has been interpreted to restrict employers' ability to discriminate based on workers' English-language proficiency, accent, or desire to speak another language. This section discusses the rights of non-native English speakers in the workplace and gives examples of cases when these rights have been infringed for Asian Americans. In particular, the section addresses three employment practices that frequently affect Asian Americans adversely: discrimination based on accent, the use of employment tests for non-native speakers of English, and English-only policies in the workplace.

Discrimination Based on Accent

The Federal courts have held that not giving a person a job or a promotion because of his or her accent violates Title VII of the Civil Rights Act of 1964's prohibition of national origin discrimination except in cases where the accent significantly impairs the individual's ability to perform the job in question. The issue of whether discrimination based on accent is national origin discrimination was decided in *Carino v. University of Oklahoma Board of Regents*,[40] a case in which a U.S. citizen of Filipino origin charged that he had been demoted from his supervisory position in a university dental laboratory because of his accent.

The plaintiff, Mr. Carino, had been hired in the position of supervisor of dental laboratory technology at the University of Oklahoma, but his position was later reclassified without his knowledge to senior dental laboratory technician. Neither his pay nor the duties he performed were affected by the reclassification of his position. When the dental laboratory expanded, a white man was hired to fill the position of dental laboratory supervisor. Mr. Carino had never been informed that he was no longer supervisor nor was he given an opportunity to apply for the position when it was filled. At about this time, Mr. Carino was reduced to performing general laboratory work because the University of Oklahoma no longer had a faculty member who required maxillofacial products, his specialty.[41]

Responding to discrimination charges made by Mr. Carino in a lawsuit, his employers argued that they were justified in demoting him from his supervisorial position because his accent hampered his work as a supervisor.[42] The district court hearing the case concluded, however, that Mr. Carino's accent did not affect his ability to perform his job:

It is the Court's opinion from the evidence and the observation of the plaintiff's speech at trial that his accent did not impair his ability to communicate or prevent him from performing any tasks required of the supervisor of the old dental laboratory.[43]

Furthermore, the court held that denial of employment opportunities because of a person's accent is national origin discrimination:

The Fifth Circuit court of Appeals reasoned in Garcia v. Gloor[44] that a trait related to national origin must be of an immutable nature in order to come within Title VII protections. . . .An accent would appear to approach that sort of immutable characteristic. . . .Although not as permanent as race or color, an accent is not easily changed for a person who was born and

---

39   42 U.S.C. §1981.

40   26 EPD ¶31,974 (W.D. Okla. 1981), *aff'd* 750 F.2d. 815, 35 EPD ¶34,850 (10th Cir. 1984).

41   *Id.*

42   *Id.* at 21,390.

43   *Id.* at 21,391.

44   Refers to Garcia v. Gloor [23 EPD ¶ 30,964] 618 F.2d 264 (5th Cir. 1980), *cert. denied*, [24 EPD ¶31,478], 449 U.S. 1113 (1981).

lived in a foreign country for a good length of time. This Court cannot give legal cognizance to adverse employment decisions made simply because a person speaks with a foreign accent. The court would recognize that in some instances a foreign accent may actually prevent a person from performing tasks required for employment or promotion, . . .; but otherwise an employer should not make adverse employment decisions simply because a person possesses an accent resulting from birth and life in a foreign country.[45]

Agreeing that accent alone was not a justification for an adverse employment decision, the Tenth Circuit upheld the district court's decision.[46]

Based partly on the *Carino* decision, the Equal Employment Opportunity Commission issued a policy statement holding that an adverse employment decision based on a person's accent is unlawful national origin discrimination:

Title VII case law establishes that denial of an employment opportunity because of manner of speaking or accent is unlawful discrimination on the basis of national origin provided that the employer cannot show a legitimate nondiscriminatory reason for the alleged discrimination. . . .A foreign accent that interferes with an employee's ability to perform a task may also constitute a legitimate nondiscriminatory reason for an adverse employment decision.[47]

A more recent case provides an example of when a person's foreign accent can be considered an acceptable justification for an adverse employment decision. In *Fragante v. City & County of Honolulu,*[48] the Ninth Circuit held that the Honolulu Division of Motor Vehicles could legitimately deny a Filipino American with a heavy accent a job as a clerk, a position that required the incumbent to communicate with the public over the telephone and at an information counter. The court held:

An adverse employment decision may be predicated upon an individual's accent when — but only when — it interferes materially with job performance. There is nothing improper about an employer making an *honest* assessment of the oral communications skills of a candidate for a job when such skills are reasonably related to job performance.[49]

The court cautioned, however:

Accent and national origin are obviously inextricably intertwined in many cases. It would therefore be an easy refuge in this context for an employer unlawfully discriminating against someone based on national origin to state falsely that it was not the person's national origin that caused the employment or promotion problem, but the candidate's inability to measure up to the communications skills demanded by the job. We encourage a very searching look by the district courts at such a claim.[50]

Yet, despite the illegality of discrimination based on accent, Asian Americans continue to be denied employment opportunities simply because they speak English with a foreign accent.[51]

---

45   *Carino* at 21,391.

46   The circuit court held that "[a] foreign accent that does not interfere with a Title VII claimant's ability to perform duties of the position he has been denied is not a legitimate justification for adverse employment decisions." Carino v. University of Oklahoma Bd. of Regents, 750 F.2d 815, 819 (1984).

47   U.S. Equal Employment Opportunity Commission, Office of Legal Counsel, "Policy Statement: Discrimination Based on Manner of Speaking or Accent," August 1986, pp. 51-53.

48   888 F.2d 591 (9th Cir. 1989), *cert denied*, 110 S. Ct. 1811 (1990).

49   *Id.* at 596-97.

50   *Id.* at 596.

51   Even when Asian Americans are not actually denied opportunities because of their accents, they may find themselves being forced to respond to complaints about their accents. For instance, in the mid-1980s, responding to complaints by students that many of their foreign-born teachers were difficult to understand, the Florida State Legislature set up a hotline to which University of Flor-

The following example may be typical of a situation that occurs regularly across the country:

A Japanese American woman who speaks English fluently but with a very slight accent was hired as a temporary receptionist in the human resources department of a southern California city. Her job was to respond to inquiries about posted jobs and to refer callers to the appropriate offices. She worked in the job as a temporary employee for 3 months and then was hired as a permanent from a field of three applicants. Six months later, although she had received no complaints about her accent, she was discharged from her job by a superior who told her to take English lessons and that she did not fit. She recently filed a complaint with the Equal Employment Opportunity Commission.[52]

Employment Tests

The potential for employer misuse of employment tests[53] in selecting employees is an emerging civil rights issue for Asian Americans, particularly when the tests are given to those who are not native speakers of English. A participant in the Commission's Houston Roundtable Conference raised specific concerns regarding the procedures for administering the General Aptitude Test Battery (GATB) in that State and regarding the use of honesty tests in hiring Asian American job applicants.[54] (Elsewhere, this report gives evidence suggesting that the use of tests for teacher certification and police officer selection may also have an adverse and unfair effect on Asian Americans.[55]) This subsection first discusses the general legal framework surrounding the use of employment tests for non-native speakers of English and then considers the use of the GATB and honesty tests in particular.

Title VII prohibits employers from using tests in the process of employee selection if they have an adverse impact on the basis of race, color, religion, sex, or national origin and they are not justified by business necessity.[56] If a test has an adverse impact,[57] then the employer must demonstrate that the test is a reasonable measure of success on the job: the test must be valid (i.e., its scores are appropriate and meaningful and, usually, equally meaningful for various races, sexes, and ethnic groups) and job related. Thus, the use of any test could be judged discriminatory if it requires knowledge or understanding of English beyond the job-related skill that the test is intended to measure and it has an adverse impact. Tests of English-language profi-

---

ida students could report teachers they felt did not speak English adequately. One of the first teachers reported was a first-year assistant professor of Indian origin, who was a native English speaker but who had a slight Indian accent. The professor was requested to meet with high university officials about the complaint, but in the end no adverse employment action was taken.

52 Kathryn Imahara, Director, Language Rights Project, Asian Pacific American Legal Center of Southern California, telephone interview, Jan. 28, 1991.

53 The discussion in this section is in large part extracted from an Apr. 3, 1990, internal Commission memorandum from Eileen E. Rudert, director of the Commission's project, "The Validity of Testing in Education and Employment," to James S. Cunningham, Director, Office of Programs, Policy, and Research. The information contained in the April 3 memorandum was updated based on a second memorandum dated Mar. 1, 1991.

54 Gordon Quan, Statement at the United States Commission on Civil Rights Roundtable Conference on Asian Civil Rights Issues for the 1990s, Houston, TX, May 27, 1989 (hereafter cited as Quan Statement).

55 See chap. 4 for a discussion of teacher certification tests and chap. 3 for a discussion of tests and police officer selection.

56 Precedents of what tests or test uses may be construed as discriminatory have been established in law cases, starting with the Supreme Court's landmark Griggs v. Duke Power Company (401 U.S. 424 (1971)) decision in 1971. Furthermore, the EEOC has published specific guidelines on employment selection procedures, including tests, entitled "Uniform Guidelines on Employment Selection Procedures." (29 C.F.R. 1607.)

57 The Uniform Guidelines define an adverse impact as a "selection rate for any race, sex, or ethnic group which is less than four-fifths (4/5) (or eighty percent) of the rate for the group with the highest rate." 29 C.F.R. 1607.4 D.

ciency may be used, however, when English is a skill necessary for success in the job.

Therefore, when English proficiency is critical to performing well on a test used in job selection, the test needs to be carefully scrutinized for job relatedness. Two specific examples where test practice may not conform with Title VII requirements are given below.

The GATB Exam—The General Aptitude Test Battery (GATB) is an employment test sponsored by the Department of Labor that is used widely across the country to match job seekers to employers' requests for job applicants. The GATB consists of 12 separately timed subtests[58] that are combined to form various aptitude scores. The GATB scores on four aptitudes (General Aptitude, Verbal and Numerical Aptitudes, and Clerical Perception) are affected by performance on the three subtests that use familiarity with or knowledge of English and thus are likely to be lower for persons with limited English proficiency.

A recent study of the GATB by the National Academy of Sciences observed that:

Foreign-born applicants, whose command of the English (or perhaps any written) language is marginal, cannot be reasonably assessed with the GATB. . . .The GATB will portray these job seekers as of very low cognitive abilities because of language difficulties, lack of formal education, and lack of experience with paper-and-pencil tests. Yet many of them. . . .are very bright and can demonstrate job-relevant skills in hands-on work simulations."[59]

The study concludes that "It is not reasonable to use the GATB to estimate the abilities of foreign-born applicants who have a marginal command of the English language."[60] Nevertheless, the GATB continues to be used for referrals in many States[61] and is regularly administered to persons with limited English proficiency.

A participant at the Commission's Houston Roundtable Conference was concerned about the Texas Employment Commission's policy of not allowing the GATB exam to be taken more than once.[62] Many recent arrivals want to take the GATB test as soon as possible so that they can be referred to jobs for which they are quali-

---

58   See John A. Hartigan and Alexandra K. Wigdor, *Fairness in Employment Testing* (Washington, DC: National Academy Press, 1989), pp. 75-82, for a more detailed description of the GATB test.

59   Ibid., pp. 219-20.

60   Ibid., pp. 232. A Spanish version of the test is available, especially for testing skills for jobs that require Spanish, rather than English.

61   Since the Commission received the complaint about the use of the GATB exam in the Houston area, the Department of Labor has issued proposed regulations that would suspend the use of the GATB for 2 years so that additional validation of the GATB could be undertaken to respond to the major concerns raised in the National Academy of Sciences report. (These issues do not include the issue of the validity of the GATB for persons with limited English proficiency.) The *Federal Register* notice of the proposed regulations suspending the use of the GATB provided for a period of comment. As of November 1991, the Department of Labor had not yet made its final decision about whether or not to suspend the use of the GATB. In the interim, some States are continuing to use the GATB as before, others are modifying their use of the GATB, and still others are phasing out its use. John Hawk, U.S. Employment Service, U.S. Department of Labor, telephone interview, July 16, 1991.

62   According to the testing supervisor for the Texas Employment Commission (TEC), TEC policy is to allow persons to take the GATB test again if they have had intervening education or experience that would change their aptitudes. Decisions about whether to allow the test to be retaken are made on a case-by-case basis. He did not think that informal exposure to the English language with time in the country would generally be sufficient to allow a person to retake the test, however. (Charles Larpenter, Testing Supervisor, Texas Employment Commission, telephone interview, Jan. 23, 1990.)

One reason proffered for polices against allowing the GATB to be retaken is that GATB scores are significantly improved by practice. The General, Verbal and Numerical Aptitude scores are among those least affected by practice, however, although the clerical perception score is one of those most affected by practice. Furthermore, practice improves scores only about half as much when an

fied. Yet, knowing that if they take the GATB soon after arriving in the country their scores on the portions of the exam requiring greater English proficiency will be low, many recent arrivals are also afraid that if they take the GATB exam now their low scores on those portions of the test will prevent them from obtaining better jobs later on when their English has improved.[63]

The following example of how the use of the GATB exam in referring job applicants to a Houston-area employer adversely affected Asian American applicants in the Houston area may be typical of a much more pervasive situation across the country.[64]

A subsidiary of a Japanese firm opened a plant in Houston in 1988. Because the jobs it was filling required an aptitude for mechanical assembly—skills not required by other employers in the Houston area—the firm turned to the Texas Employment Commission (TEC) to help it screen its job applicants. The firm explained its needs to TEC, which recommended that job applicants be given the GATB exam. TEC undertook to administer the exam to all of the firm's job applicants and refer to the firm only those applicants who "passed" the GATB. The firm was not told the scores of those referred to it for employment.

Shortly after the testing and referral process began, the firm noticed that several of its workers of Vietnamese and Cambodian origin, who had been hired as temporary employees pending the test results and who were performing very well on the job, were not subsequently recommended by TEC, presumably because their limited English proficiency prevented them from doing well on the GATB. The firm did not hire these employees as permanent employees in the mechanical assembly jobs even though they appeared to be performing well, because the firm felt that this would not be "fair."[65] The firm did, however, go back to TEC, which agreed to lower the weights of the GATB test components requiring English in calculating the final score of applicants for jobs at the firm.

Honesty Tests—In 1988 Congress passed the Employee Polygraph Protection Act,[66] which prohibits most private employers from using any

---

alternate form of the GATB is used at retake. Unfortunately, until 1983, Employment Services offices only had one version of the GATB to administer. Since 1983 two additional forms have been available. The National Academy of Sciences' recent study of the GATB has recommended the development of additional alternate forms, and indeed two are underway. (Hartigan and Wigdor, *Fairness in Employment Testing*.)

The Department of Labor currently issues no policy on retesting or interpreting the GATB score of non-native English speakers. Instructions issued before 1980 did specify that retesting was appropriate when there was some reason to believe that a job seeker's skills had changed (e.g., had received education, experience, or training). These instructions were abolished in the early 1980s, but many State and local offices continue to follow them. One Department of Labor official stated that if the Department were to resume issuing policies to State and local test administrators, it would permit much more retesting than in the past. Instead of issuing instructions, however, the Department currently counsels test administrators to follow sound testing practices. For non-native English speakers, such practices include not taking test scores at face value and providing other testing accommodations and individual counseling to those for whom test scores may be invalid. The Department's research program has demonstrated that use of a translator for giving instructions or giving oral versions of the test are not promising alternatives for Southeast Asians. Without Federal guidance, State are free to set their own policies or allow local Employment Service Offices to make them.

63   David Mathias, YMCA International Services, telephone interview, Jan. 23, 1990.

64   The following is based on information obtained in a telephone interview with Sharon Gerchow, Personnel Office, MHI Forklift America, Jan. 18, 1990.

65   One of the affected employees, a Vietnamese man, was reassigned as a permanent employee with the job of "painter," a job classification that the firm did not require to take the GATB exam. This man has not tried to retake the test, because he is happy with his current job assignment, according to a personnel officer in the firm.

66   29 U.S.C. §§ 20001, *et seq*. Also see 29 C.F.R., Part 801.

lie detector tests for preemployment screening or during the course of employment. Since then, many employers have turned to using paper-and-pencil honesty tests.[67] Paper-and-pencil honesty tests have not been as carefully scrutinized, validated, and researched as employment tests measuring skills and abilities. Indeed, a recent report by the U.S. Congress' Office of Technology Assessment cautioned that "[t]he research on integrity tests has not yet produced data that clearly supports or dismisses the assertion that these tests can predict dishonest behavior."[68] Although research suggests that honesty tests generally do not have an adverse impact, that research looks primarily at blacks. Asian Americans are almost never included in such studies, although Hispanics sometimes are. Furthermore, paper-and-pencil tests of honesty require the test taker to have considerable English proficiency as well as a grasp of American social customs and values. If the level of English required by the job is less than that necessary to take the test, a paper-and-pencil honesty test may adversely affect non-native English speakers.

Concerns about the adverse effect of honesty tests on Asian American job applicants were raised at the Commission's Houston Roundtable Conference.[69] According to a job counselor who places Asian refugees in jobs in the Houston area, when one area employer used polygraph exams (with interpreters when necessary) to screen job applicants, most of the Asian Americans he referred to the employer were hired; but after the employer switched to an honesty test, for which interpreters/translators were not allowed, no more Asian Americans were hired.[70]

English-Only Rules in the Workplace

Employers often seek to impose rules requiring their employees to speak only English while they are on the job. Sometimes these English-only rules are blanket rules banning the use of any language other than English at any time while the employee is at work. Other times the rules are more specific, banning the use of non-English languages when the employee is performing certain duties. English-only rules are a common source of frustration and resentment for many Asian Americans and others whose primary language is not English. They feel that the rules single them out for adverse treatment based on their national origin, that they are often adopted for the purpose of discrimination, and that they repress their ability to express themselves freely.

In some instances English-only policies may be illegal discrimination based on national origin, but in other instances they may be lawful. English-only policies are unlawful when the rules are adopted for the purpose of discrimination based on national origin. Thus, the Equal Employment Opportunity Commission explicitly

---

67   However, two States—Massachusetts and Rhode Island—also ban written examinations that purport to detect deception, verify truthfulness or measure honesty.

68   The Office of Technology Assessment report was presented at a hearing before the Subcommittee on Employment Opportunities of the Committee on Education and Labor, U.S. House of Representatives, on Sept. 26, 1990.

69   Quan Statement. In following up on his concerns, staff discovered that the allegation involved two honesty tests—the Phase II Profile Integrity Status Inventory (developed by Lousig-Nont & Associates) and the Stanton (the complaint did not specify whether the reference was to the Stanton Survey or the Stanton Survey Phase II)—in particular. (David Mathias, YMCA International Services, telephone interview, Dec. 21, 1989.) Although neither of these tests has been shown to have an adverse impact, neither has been adequately validated for Asian Americans or for members of language minorities. Furthermore, independent reviewers concluded that the Lousig-Nont test is inadequate for making hiring decisions at all without further validation and gave the Stanton mixed reviews.

70   David Mathias, YMCA International Services, telephone interview, Dec. 21, 1989.

states that these policies are invalid when they are applied differentially to members of different national origin groups.[71]

Even when they are not adopted for the purpose of discrimination, English-only policies may violate Title VII under an adverse impact theory if they are not justified by business necessity.[72] The EEOC has held that blanket rules banning the use of non-English languages at all times are almost always illegal, because they will never be justified by business necessity.

A rule requiring employees to speak only English at all times in the work place is a burdensome term and condition of employment. The primary language of an individual is often an essential national origin characteristic. Prohibiting employees at all times, in the work place, from speaking their primary language or the language they speak most comfortably, disadvantages an individual's employment opportunities on the basis of national origin. It may also create an atmosphere of inferiority, isolation and intimidation based on national origin which could result in a discrimina-tory working environment. Therefore the Commission will presume that such a rule violates Title VII and will closely scrutinize it.[73]

However, EEOC regulations state that more specific English-only rules may be lawful if they can be justified by business necessity.[74] The EEOC elaborates on what is necessary for an English-only rule to be justified by business necessity in its Compliance Manual:

Typically, narrowly drawn rules justified by business necessity are applicable only to certain employees and only apply to those employees while they are actually performing a specific job duty or under specific circumstances. To prove an overriding business purpose sufficient to override the adverse effects of the rule, the respondent must establish that the rule is necessary to safe and efficient job performance or the safe and efficient operation of the business. In appropriate circumstances, either safety or efficiency considerations alone may justify a speak-English-only rule.[75]

---

71   EEOC Compliance Manual, vol. II, §623.3. Differential application of employment rules is generally held to be proof of intentional discrimination.

72   The EEOC regards it as self-evident that an English-only policy must have an adverse impact based on national origin: "In recognition of the fact that the primary language of an individual is often an essential national origin characteristic, the Commission will presume that rules requiring employees to speak only English in the work place adversely affect an individual's employment opportunities on the basis of national origin where that employee's primary language is not English." EEOC Compliance Manual, vol. II, §623.6(a).

73   29 C.F.R. Ch. XIV §1606.7(a).

74   29 C.F.R. Ch. XIV §1606.7(b).

75   EEOC Compliance Manual, vol. II, §623.6(c)(1)(ii).
An example of an English-only rule that the EEOC held to be justified by business necessity is the following: "Reasonable cause does not exist to believe that petroleum company violated Title VII when it adopted rule requiring only English to be spoken by refinery employees who work in laboratory and processing areas—where potential of fires and explosions exists—and by all employees during emergencies, where rule is narrowly drawn to accomplish specific purpose of assuring effective communication among employees during specified times and in specific areas." (EEOC Decision 83-7, 31 FEP Cases 1861.)
An example of an English-only rule that may not be justified by business necessity is: "CPs [Complaining Parties], Polish Americans, allege that the speak-English-only rule of R [Respondent], a nursery, discriminates against them on the basis of national origin, since their primary language is Polish. R's speak-English-only policy applies only to employees working inside the store itself who serve and assist customers. The rule is inapplicable to outside employees who care for the shrubs, flowers, and other plants grown on the premises. Although the rules does apply to casual discussions among employees working inside the store, it does not apply to conversation in the employee lounge during work breaks or lunch. Although R's policy is not an absolute prohibition and is applied only at certain times, depending on R's justification, it still may not be narrowly drawn enough to be justified by business necessity." (EEOC Compliance Manual, vol. II, §623.6(a)(2).)

The courts have differed in their treatment of English-only rules. In a case that predated the EEOC policy on English-only rules, the Fifth Circuit held that an employer's policy requiring all employees to speak English while on duty at all times did not violate Title VII's prohibition of national origin discrimination,[76] because the employees were all bilingual and therefore could choose to obey the rule. The court cautioned, however, that its decision applied only to English-only policies affecting *bilingual* employees:

Our opinion does not impress a judicial imprimatur on all employment rules that require an employee to use or forbid him from using a language spoken by him at home or by his forebears. We hold only that an employer's rule forbidding a bilingual employee to speak anything but English in public areas while on the job is not discrimination based on national origin as applied to a person who is fully capable of speaking English and chooses not to do so in deliberate disregard of his employer's rule.[77]

Despite this caveat, however, the Fifth Circuit decision is at odds with EEOC policy, which does not distinguish between English-only rules applied to bilingual persons and those applied to persons with limited English proficiency.

In a decision that was later rendered moot by the Supreme Court,[78] the Ninth Circuit agreed with the EEOC's approach to English-only rules:

The EEOC guidelines, by requiring that a business necessity be shown before a limited English-only rule may be enforced, properly balance the individual's interest in speaking his primary language and any possible need of the employer to ensure that in particular circumstances only English shall be spoken. The business necessity requirement prevents an employer from imposing a rule that has a disparate impact on groups protected by the national origin provision of Title VII unless there is a sufficient justification under the Civil Rights Act of 1964 for doing so. Accordingly we adopt the EEOC's business necessity test as the proper standard for determining the validity of limited English-only rules.[79]

Because the *Gutierrez* decision was rendered moot, it cannot be used as a precedent in deciding future cases dealing with English-only rules in the workplace. Furthermore, because the EEOC regulations were adopted after the *Garcia* decision, the *Gutierrez* court itself did not view the EEOC guidelines as decisive.[80] Thus, at

---

76   The rule did not apply to breaks or other employee free time. Garcia v. Gloor, 618 Fed. 2d 264, 270 (1981).

77   *Id.* at 272.

78   Municipal Court v. Gutierrez, 873 F.2d 1342 (9th Cir. 1989). The Ninth Circuit decision may have been rendered moot because the case was settled after the decision was rendered or because the Gutierrez no longer worked for the court. Linda M. Mealey, "English-Only Rules and 'Innocent' Employers: Clarifying National Origin Discrimination and Disparate Impact Theory Under Title VII," *Minnesota Law Review*, vol. 74, no. 2 (December 1989), p. 418, n. 183]

79   838 F. 2d 1031, 1040 (9th Cir., 1988), *dismissed on remand* 873 F.2d 1342,1343. In an accompanying footnote, the court explained that if the English-only policy was shown to be the product of discriminatory intent, the stricter bona fide occupational qualifications standard applies instead of the business necessity standard: "We note that the part of the EEOC guidelines that refers to business necessity is, under general principles of equal employment opportunity law, applicable only to cases in which the employer has acted without invidious intent. Where a rule is shown to have been adopted for the *purpose of* discriminating against a protected group, the employer's conduct is permissible only if the discriminatory rule constitutes a bona fide occupational qualification (BFOQ) for the job. Thus even a limited English-only rule must meet the strict BFOQ test if it is the product of discriminatory intent." *Id.* at 1040 n. 9.

80   The *Gutierrez* decision states: "We need not decide in this case, whether, in the absence of decisional law, EEOC guidelines and decisions can constitute clearly established law. Here, judicial precedent existed and it appears to have been inconsistent, at least in part, with the guidelines. If contrary judicial precedent had been issued subsequent to the guidelines, there is no question that we would hold that the guidelines do not 'clearly establish' the law. Although the answer is not as certain when the guidelines are issued

this time, the law regarding English-only rules in the workplace is not clearly established.

A case currently before the Ninth Circuit may help to resolve some of the law's ambiguities with respect to English-only rules, however. In this case, a Filipino nurse is charging that a California hospital discriminated against her on the basis of national origin by instituting an English-only rule that applied to all staff conversations "at any time or any place,"[81] and retaliated against her for filing a discrimination complaint by demoting her and transferring her from the hospital's maternity unit to the hospital's emergency room even though her skills and training are in maternal care.[82] The EEOC has intervened in the case on behalf of the nurse.[83] The case went to trial on April 18, 1991, and closing arguments were heard on May 3, 1991.[84] The case has received considerable attention in Asian American communities throughout the United States because it involves an Asian American nurse who sought to speak Tagalog during work hours and because such English-only rules are common in hospitals employing large numbers of Filipino nurses across the country.

The Certification of Foreign-Educated Professionals

Many Asian Americans and others who received their professional training outside of the United States have difficulty obtaining jobs commensurate with their education and experience in this country.[85] Sometimes they are unable to provide documentation of their professional training and experience in their countries of origin and are forced to retrain in this country or to switch careers. Other times they find that, although they can provide diplomas and transcripts as proof of their professional education abroad, State professional certification boards often have different requirements for foreign-educated professionals than for U.S.-educated professionals. Although differential treatment of professionals educated in foreign countries has not been found to be *per se* illegal discrimination under Title VII, it can erect barriers to obtaining professional jobs that are a source of enormous frustration for Asian and other professional immigrants to this country.[86] Furthermore, many

after a judicial decision, where that decision has been rendered by a federal circuit court and the subsequently issued guidelines remain largely untested, we think it appropriate to reach the same conclusion. Thus, we hold that in the case before us the EEOC guidelines did not serve to clearly establish the law regarding the validity of English-only rules." *Gutierrez* at 447.

81   Gigi Santos, "Nurse in 'English-Only' Case Gets Support," *Philippine News*, vol. 20, no. 21 (Jan. 31- Feb. 6, 1990).

82   Ibid.

83   Jean Guccione, "EEOC Will Intervene in Lawsuit Challenging English-Only Policy," *Los Angeles Daily Journal*, Apr. 3, 1990, and Kathryn Imahara, attorney for plaintiff, telephone interview, Apr. 12, 1990.

84   Kathryn Imahara, attorney for plaintiff, telephone interview, Jan. 28, 1991, and Kathryn Imahara, letter to Nadja Zalokar, Office of Programs, Policy, and Research, U.S. Commission on Civil Rights, Sept. 4, 1991.

85   See California Advisory Committee to the U.S. Commission on Civil Rights, *A Dream Unfulfilled: Korean and Pilipino Health Professionals* (1975), for an earlier report touching on this topic.

86   Although discrimination based on country of education is not illegal under Title VII, it may be illegal under some local ordinances. For instance, the city of Chicago recently banned discrimination based on "origin of education or professional training, from an accredited institution." Municipal Code of Chicago, §21-10.

Asian immigrant professionals suspect that the differential treatment they receive as foreign-educated professionals may in fact be a pretext for discrimination on the basis of national origin.

A case in point is the situation of graduates of foreign medical schools (FMGs), who make up roughly one-fifth of all physicians practicing in the United States. Approximately 30 percent of FMGs are U.S citizens, and 70 percent are foreign nationals.[87] A large proportion of foreign national FMGs come from Asian countries, especially India and the Philippines. Many FMGs came to this country in the mid-1960s when they were given preferential visa status because of a shortage of physicians in the United States. By the 1970s, however, the physician shortage had apparently become a physician surplus, generating some resentment of FMGs by graduates of U.S. medical schools (USMGs). Nevertheless, there remain many places in which America's basic health care needs are not yet being met, especially in rural and depressed areas. According to one expert, data appear to show that FMGs service these basic health care needs disproportionally:

FMGs serve in disproportionate numbers in rural areas, often in solo and partnership practices, in pub-lic hospitals, in smaller not-for-profit hospitals, and in regions of the country that have experienced emigration of population because of declining industry and high unemployment. Poor populations and Medicaid recipients also are often reliant on FMGs.[88]

Furthermore, foreign-born FMGs also play a critical role in providing for the health care needs of Asian immigrant communities, since recent immigrants are often prevented by language, cultural, or informational barriers from seeking treatment from American-born physicians.[89]

To practice medicine in the United States, FMGs, like USMGs, need to be licensed by a State medical licensing board. Many FMGs have not completed residencies before coming to the United States and thus also need to obtain positions as residents in U.S. hospitals. Some FMGs charge that they are the victims of unfair discrimination by State licensing boards, hospitals with residency positions, and others in the medical community.[90]

In fact, State medical licensure boards throughout the country have imposed stiffer certification requirements for FMGs than for USMGs.[91] USMGs are required to pass a single examination, usually the National Board of

---

87   U.S. General Accounting Office, *Medical Licensing By Endorsement: Requirements Differ for Graduates of Foreign and U.S. Medical Schools* (May 1990), p. 3, n. 3.

88   Stephen S. Mick, "Contradictory Policies for Foreign Medical Graduates," *Health Affairs*, Fall 1987, pp. 5-18.

89   See chap. 7 for a discussion of the health care needs of Asian Americans.

90   Several lawsuits have been filed by Asian Americans against State licensing boards. In 1986 Dr. Kar, who had received his medical education at the University of Medical Sciences in New Delhi, and was licensed to practice medicine in two other States, filed a suit against the State of Vermont for denying his application for a license. In denying his application, the State licensing board said that his medical school had not been approved by the American Council for Graduate Medical Education of the American Medical Association (ACGME). Dr. Kar pointed out that there was no published requirement to that effect in Vermont and that the decision to adopt the requirement was made after his application was complete. (Lynn Hudson, "Doctor to Sue Vermont on License," *India Abroad*, Mar. 7, 1986.)

         In 1987 two Vietnamese American doctors who had received their medical degrees from the University of Saigon filed a suit against the State of California's medical licensing boards seeking damages because they were denied medical licenses after fulfilling all the requirements. The State licensing board had decided, in a closed meeting, not to issue licenses to persons who had graduated from the University of Saigon after 1975, because it felt that it could no longer verify the quality of the education received there. (Harriet Chiang, "Foreign-Trained MDs Charge License Bias," *San Francisco Chronicle*, June 8, 1987.)

91   The following description of the differences between State requirements for FMGs and USMGs is derived from U.S. General Ac-

Medical Examiners exam (NBME), which is taken in parts throughout the student's medical education. FMGs, on the other hand, are required first to be certified by the Educational Commission for Foreign Medical Graduates (ECFMG)—which requires that they pass a basic medical exam, the Foreign Medical Graduate Examination in Medical Sciences (FMGEMS), and an English-language-proficiency examination—and then to pass a second examination, the Federal Licensing Examination (FLEX), which is equivalent to the NBME but must be taken in one 3-day sitting. Most States also require that FMGs serve longer periods in postgraduate training, or residencies, than USMGs. Furthermore, FMGs are often required to provide information showing that their medical school provided an education that meets the standards of the Liaison Committee on Medical Education (LCME), which accredits U.S. and Canadian medical schools. Typically, States also have stiffer endorsement requirements (requirements for physicians already licensed to practice in one State seeking to become licensed in another State) for FMGs than for USMGs, even for FMGs who have practiced in the United States successfully for many years.

Defenders of stiffer licensing requirements for FMGs cite the wide range in quality of foreign medical schools. For a variety of reasons, it is not thought practical for the LCME or other American agencies to accredit foreign medical schools.[92] Thus, the stiffer requirements for FMGs are said to be necessary to ensure that they meet U.S. professional standards.

FMGs, on the other hand, point to research showing that the performance of FMGs and USMGs as physicians is indistinguishable.[93] They stress the hardships imposed on many FMGs by requirements that they document in detail the course content, faculty resumes, facilities, etc. of their medical schools. These time-consuming requirements allegedly amount to harassment. They also argue that it is particularly unfair to base endorsement requirements for FMGs on the quality of their medical education rather than on their individual records as practicing physicians because in many instances these FMGs have been practicing medicine in the United States for many years.

Representatives of all sides of the debate have reached agreement to develop a national clearinghouse "to maintain and verify information on licensure applicants' educational backgrounds and credentials," and the American Medical Association has taken some steps in that direction.[94] The clearinghouse would ease hardships for FMGs in obtaining original documents over and over again as they apply for licensure and then endorsement. Federal funding for such a clearinghouse is proposed in a bill sponsored by Congressman Mervyn Dymally (D-CA) currently before Congress.[95] The medical profession is also moving to a "single examination pathway to licensure" for USMGs and FMGs.[96] FMGs are now allowed to take parts I and II of the NBME, but it is still less widely available abroad than the FMGEMS.[97]

counting Office, *Medical Licensing by Endorsement: Requirements Differ for Graduates of Foreign and U.S. Medical Schools* (May 1986).

92   Prof. Stephen Mick, Department of Health Policy, University of Michigan, telephone interview, Mar. 7, 1991, and U.S. General Accounting Office, *Medical Licensing by Endorsement*, p. 7, n. 10.

93   U.S. General Accounting Office, *Medical Licensing by Endorsement*, p. 7.

94   U.S. General Accounting Office, *Medical Licensing by Endorsement*, pp. 6-7.

95   H.R. 319 is sponsored by Representative Dymally. Senator Simon has introduced a similar bill (S. 802) in the Senate.

96   U.S. General Accounting Office, *Medical Licensing by Endorsement*, p. 10.

97   Prof. Stephen Mick, Department of Health Policy, University of Michigan, telephone interview, Mar. 7, 1991.

FMGs have also charged that they are discriminated against in the allocation of residency positions and hospital privileges.[98] A bill currently before Congress, H.R. 319, may provide some relief for FMGs. Under this bill, it would be illegal to have differential treatment of FMGs in licensing, endorsement, hiring for staff positions, or granting of clinical privileges. For now, however, FMGs may be in some instances protected under Title VII, which prohibits discrimination on the basis of national origin. A recent court case is pertinent here:

A physician, educated in Iran, was offered employment with an Alabama medical corporation on the condition that he was given admitting privileges at a nearby hospital. When he was initially denied hospital privileges at the hospital and later given privileges with a longer probationary period than customary, he sued the hospital, charging national origin discrimination under Title VII.[99]

In deciding the case, the Eleventh Circuit Court ruled that a hospital that denies a doctor's application for admitting privileges can be sued for discrimination under Title VII even though it is not in any sense the doctor's employer if that denial interferes with the doctor's employment opportunities elsewhere.[100]

Discrimination Caused by the Immigration Reform and Control Act

In 1986 Congress passed the Immigration Reform and Control Act (IRCA),[101] which authorized legal status for 3 million undocumented aliens who had entered the United States before 1982 while imposing civil and criminal penalties, "employer sanctions," on employers who hire unauthorized workers. To allay concern that employer sanctions would lead employers to discriminate against foreign-looking and foreign-sounding workers, IRCA also contained provisions aimed at preventing such discrimination. Under IRCA, employers are required to verify the work authorization of *all* workers, not just those workers employers suspect might not be authorized to work. Furthermore, IRCA makes it illegal for employers with four or more employees to discriminate in hiring, firing, or referrals against any authorized worker based on the individual's national origin or citizenship status. To enforce its antidiscrimination provisions, IRCA set up the Office of the Special Counsel for Immigration-Related Unfair Employment Practices (OSC) within the Department of Justice.[102]

Fears that the IRCA's antidiscrimination provisions would prove to be insufficient to prevent discrimination led Congress to require the General Accounting Office (GAO) to conduct a series of three studies to determine whether IRCA's employer sanctions provision had caused discrimination. In March 1990 the third and final GAO report (hereafter, "GAO report") concluded that "a widespread pattern of discrimination has resulted against eligible workers. . .[and] it is more reasonable to conclude that a substantial amount of these discriminatory

---

98   Materials provided by Dr. Kishore Thampy, International Medical Council of Illinois.

99   The ultimate resolution of the case was still pending as of November 1991.

100   Pardazi v. Cullman Medical Center, 838 F.2d 1155 (11th Cir. 1988).

101   8 U.S.C. §§1101 *et seq.* (1988).

102   Before IRCA, the Equal Employment Opportunity Commission (EEOC) had authorization under Title VII of the Civil Rights Act of 1964 to investigate employment discrimination complaints involving charges of national origin discrimination against employers with 15 or more employees, but discrimination on the basis of citizenship status was not illegal. Under IRCA, complaints charging employers with 15 or more employees with national origin discrimination can be brought either to the EEOC or to the OSC. Citizenship discrimination complaints and complaints involving employers with 4 to 15 employees can only be brought to the OSC.

practices resulted from IRCA rather than not."[103] The GAO report confirmed the findings of numerous other reports that IRCA has resulted in widespread discrimination against foreign-looking and foreign-sounding workers.[104]

IRCA-related discrimination is likely to fall most heavily on groups that have large numbers of immigrant workers, such as Asian Americans. If employers assume that more individuals in ethnic groups with high proportions of immigrants are likely to be unauthorized workers, then they may be more suspicious of the work authorization of *all* members of the group, and they might be reluctant to hire *any* members of

that group at all. For Asian Americans, this tendency is likely to be compounded by the common misperception that all Asians are foreigners. Furthermore, employers who are not thoroughly informed about all the documents that can establish an individual's work authorization may prefer familiar documents, such as social security cards, U.S. passports, or green cards, to the less familiar work authorization documents that are frequently held by new immigrants and refugees, many of whom are Asian. Other employers may mistakenly require green cards from all foreign-seeming workers, even U.S. citizens, who do not have them.

---

103   U.S. General Accounting Office, *Immigration Reform: Employer Sanctions and the Question of Discrimination* (Mar. 29, 1990), p. 71.

104   GAO's conclusions are based in part on the results of a survey of employers that led GAO to project that 891,000 employers, about 19 percent of all employers, began illegal discriminatory practices as a result of IRCA. Further analysis of the GAO employer survey data reveals that roughly 499,000 employers began to discriminate on the basis of national origin, and 687,000 employers began to discriminate on the basis of citizenship. Of those starting illegal discriminatory practices, 757,000 employers began a policy of not hiring a certain category of workers, and 381,000 employers began a practice of selectively asking for work authorization papers. Other government reports that concluded that IRCA had caused discrimination include:

● U.S. Commission on Civil Rights, *The Immigration Reform and Control Act: Assessing the Evaluation Process*, September 1989.

● Arizona Advisory Committee to the U.S. Commission on Civil Rights, *Implementation in Arizona of the Immigration Reform and Control Act* (December 1990).

● Colorado Advisory Committee to the U.S. Commission on Civil Rights, *Implementation in Colorado of the Immigration Reform and Control Act: A Preliminary Review*, January 1989.

● Rhode Island Advisory Committee to the U.S. Commission on Civil Rights, *Implementation in Rhode Island of the Immigration Reform and Control Act: A Preliminary Review*, May 1989.

● New Mexico Advisory Committee to the U.S. Commission on Civil Rights, *Implementation in New Mexico of the Immigration Reform and Control Act: A Preliminary Review*, May 1989.

● Texas Advisory Committee to the U.S. Commission on Civil Rights, *Implementation in Texas of the Immigration Reform and Control Act: A Preliminary Review* (September 1989).

● State of Illinois, Human Rights Commission, *Summarizing Data and Information Gathered on Employment Discrimination Caused by Enactment and Implementation of the Immigration Reform and Control Act of 1986*, Report to the U.S. General Accounting Office, Sept. 23, 1988.

● New York State Inter-Agency Task Force on Immigration Affairs, *Workplace Discrimination under the Immigration Reform and Control Act of 1986: A Study of Impacts on New Yorkers*, Nov. 4, 1988.

● John E. Brandon, City of New York Commission on Civil Rights, *Tarnishing the Golden Door: A Report on the Widespread Discrimination Against Immigrants and Persons Perceived as Immigrants Which Has Resulted from the Immigration Reform and Control Act of 1986*, August 1989.

● State of California, Fair Employment and Housing Commission, *Report and Recommendations of the California Fair Employment and Housing Commission: Public Hearings on the Impact and Effectiveness in California of the Employer Sanctions and Anti-Discrimination Provision of the Immigration Reform and Control Act of 1986*, Jan. 11, 1990.

● New York State Inter-Agency Task Force on Immigration Affairs, *Immigration in New York State: Impact and Issues*, Third Report, Feb. 23, 1990.

The GAO report provides confirmation that Asian Americans experience IRCA-related discrimination disproportionately. The report found that the proportion of employers adopting discriminatory practices was higher in the Western States, New York City, Chicago, and Miami, and especially high in Texas and Los Angeles.[105] Reviewing these data, the Task Force on IRCA-Related Discrimination (Task Force)[106] observed:

Considering all of the GAO data, it appears that the problems of IRCA-related discrimination are most prevalent in areas which are heavily populated by Hispanics and Asians. This highlights that Hispanics and Asians—whether they are citizens or work-authorized non-citizens—are bearing the brunt of IRCA-related discrimination.[107]

The Task Force Report continued: "Further analysis of the GAO survey data made available to the task force suggests that IRCA-related discrimination is more prevalent among employers with high percentages of Hispanic or Asian employees."[108]

Additional evidence that Asian Americans are experiencing illegal employment discrimination as a result of IRCA is provided by a study by San Francisco State University's Public Research Institute (PRI) jointly with the Coalition for Immigrant and Refugee Rights and Services (CIRRS), which analyzed data collected from a telephone survey of 416 San Francisco employers. The PRI/CIRRS report found that a large majority of San Francisco employers engage in illegal discriminatory practices:

An overwhelming majority (97%) of sample business firms regularly engage in at least or mployment practice that may be discriminatory undei .::'A or other anti-discrimination laws, and 53% regularly engage in three or more.[109]

Furthermore, the report finds that San Francisco employers are particularly wary of hiring Asian Americans:

Fifty percent of employers in the sample feel that the INS's documentation requirements make it riskier to hire people who speak limited English. A large proportion feel it is riskier to hire Latinos (40%) and Asians (39%).[110]

---

105   GAO report, pp. 40-44.

106   GAO's finding that IRCA had caused a widespread pattern of discrimination triggered a provision in IRCA requiring the convening of a Task Force on IRCA-Related Discrimination to review GAO's findings and make recommendations to Congress. This Task Force was chaired by John R. Dunne, Assistant Attorney General, Civil Rights Division, U.S. Department of Justice. The other members of the Task Force were R. Gaull Silberman, Vice Chairman, U.S. Equal Employment Opportunity Commission, and Arthur A. Fletcher, Chairman, U.S. Commission on Civil Rights. The Task Force issued its report to Congress in September 1990.

107   Task Force on IRCA-Related Discrimination, *Report and Recommendations of the Task Force on IRCA-Related Discrimination*, Report to Congress Pursuant to 8 U.S.C. 1324a(k) (September 1990), p. 21.

108   Task Force Report, p. 23. The Task Force based this contention on an analysis of the GAO data undertaken by the U.S. Commission on Civil Rights. The Commission analysis revealed that 2.0 percent of the work force of employers who did not discriminate because of IRCA was Asian, as compared to 2.7 percent of the work force of employers who did adopt discriminatory practices as a result of IRCA. Asian Americans appear to be particularly subject to selective screening of their work authorization documents. The percentage Asian among the work forces of employers who did not screen selectively was 1.9 percent, whereas the percentage Asian for employers who did screen selectively was 4.0 percent.

109   Lina M. Avidan, *Employment and Hiring Practices Under the Immigration Reform and Control Act of 1986: A Survey of San Francisco Businesses* (Preliminary Report, Public Research Institute, San Francisco State University, and Coalition for Immigrant and Refugee Rights and Services, January 1990), p. iii.

110   Ibid., p. iv.

There are no other studies of the effects of IRCA document discrimination specifically against Asian Americans, but many studies have found that employer confusion about IRCA has caused discrimination against foreign-looking or foreign-sounding individuals, noncitizens, or immigrants. For instance, the New York City Commission on Human Rights (NYCCHR) conducted a hiring audit in which carefully matched individuals, one with a heavy accent and the other without an accent, responded to help-wanted advertisements in major New York papers. NYCCHR found that the accented job applicants were often treated less favorably than the job applicants without accents.[111]

Thus, there is little doubt that many Asian Americans have been discriminated against because of IRCA's employer sanctions provisions. Aggravating this situation, many Asian Americans are not aware of their rights under IRCA and do not know where or how to file IRCA-related complaints. As one observer puts it:

Even if an applicant is aware that he is not hired due to his not being a citizen, many would not be aware that this is an illegal form of discrimination. For Asian Americans, cultural barriers to filing a complaint also exist. Most Asian cultures have limited traditions of asserting individual legal rights. Even those born in America have substantially lower tendencies to take legal action in the face of discrimination. This is changing, but will be especially pronounced among immigrant groups.

Finally, information on how to file a complaint under the Immigration Reform and Control Act is not well known. Outreach, to the extent that it has been done, has been limited. . . .In the Asian American community, such outreach must consider the myriad languages spoken by many of those affected. . . .[112]

OSC has made some efforts to inform Asian Americans of their rights under IRCA. These efforts include speaking to Asian American community organizations; printing and distributing informative posters in Chinese, Japanese, and Korean; and grants to promote the outreach efforts of community organizations, including a $100,000 grant to the Chinese American Planning Council in New York and grants to two other organizations with Asian American clientele. OSC's 800 number is staffed only by English- and Spanish-speaking operators, however, and OSC's informational pamphlets for the public are only available in English and Spanish.[113]

After the GAO released its finding that IRCA has caused a "widespread pattern of discrimination," the U.S. Commission on Civil Rights issued a statement calling for the repeal of IRCA's employer sanctions provisions. That statement said:

The United States Commission on Civil Rights. . .calls on Congress to repeal the employer sanctions provisions of the Immigration Reform and Control Act (IRCA). . . .With the U.S. General Accounting Office's announcement. . .that employer sanctions create a "widespread pattern of discrimination" against legal workers, there is no longer doubt that America's efforts to stem illegal immigration through sanctions have seriously harmed large numbers of Hispanic, Asian, and other "foreign-looking" and "foreign-sounding" American workers. This discrimination is unacceptable, and its root cause—employer sanctions—should be eliminated.[114]

---

111   NYCCHR observed that "[t]he audit's findings indicate substantial discrimination by employers in New York City. Of the 86 employers tested, 41% were found to demonstrate differential treatment towards job applicants with accents." John E. Brandon, *Tarnishing the Golden Door: A Report on the Widespread Discrimination Against Immigrants and Persons Perceived as Immigrants Which Has Resulted from the Immigration Reform and Control Act of 1986* (City of New York Commission on Human Rights, August 1989), p. 29.

112   Paul Igasaki, Statement to the U.S. Senate Committee on the Judiciary, Apr. 20, 1990, pp. 10-11.

113   Juan Maldonado, Office of Special Counsel, U.S. Department of Justice, telephone interview, Feb. 15, 1991.

The Commission's position was reiterated several months later at a House Judiciary Subcommittee on Immigration, Refugees, and International Law hearing:

There are those who implicitly seem to believe that added discrimination against American workers is a small price to pay to stem the flow of illegal immigration. The Commission on Civil Rights takes strong exception to this point of view. Discrimination, irrespective of its source and form, is intolerable, but discrimination caused by a policy of the Federal government is especially offensive and can never be justified. . . .I urge Congress to. . .take a hard look at how employer sanctions have actually worked. They are not cost effective in stopping illegal immigration. More importantly, they have created new discrimination against American workers, which is simply unacceptable. Employer sanctions are bad policy and should be repealed.[115]

In 1990, however, Congress chose not to repeal employer sanctions. Instead, Congress chose to attempt to reduce the discriminatory effects of IRCA's employer sanctions provisions by implementing some, but not all, of the recommendations made by the Task Force on IRCA-Related Discrimination.[116] Congress did not adopt several critical Task Force recommendations. In particular, Congress did not:

- establish regional offices for the Office of Special Counsel,
- appropriate funds for a new outreach effort to educate employers and employees about IRCA's antidiscrimination provisions,
- simplify employers' work authorization verification process,
- broaden the authority of the Department of Labor to enforce document check requirements, or
- request a future GAO study to determine the extent of remaining discrimination,

all of which were recommended by the Task Force.

In September 1991 bills entitled the Employer Sanctions Repeal Act of 1991 that would repeal employer sanctions were introduced in the Senate by Senator Kennedy (D-MA) and Senator Hatch (R-UT)[117] and in the House of Representatives by Representative Roybal (D-CA) and Representative Richardson (D-NM).[118] As November 1991, no action had been taken on these bills.

Discrimination in Construction Unions

Participants at the Commission's New York Roundtable Conference alleged that Asian Americans are virtually shut out of construction unions in New York City and as a result are forced to take lower paying jobs restoring or repairing buildings.[119] These allegations resurfaced several months later at a series of New York City hearings on discrimination in the construction industry,[120] and similar allegations were made at the Commission's San Francisco

---

114   U.S. Commission on Civil Rights, "Civil Rights Commission Calls for Repeal of Employer Sanctions," News Release, Mar. 29, 1990.

115   Arthur A. Fletcher, Chairman, U.S. Commission on Civil Rights, statement to the House Judiciary Subcommittee on Immigration, Refugees, and International Law, June 27, 1990.

116   Changes to IRCA were part of the Immigration Act of 1990, Pub. L. No. 101-649.

117   S.1734, 102nd Cong., 2nd Sess. (1991).

118   H.R. 3366, 102nd Cong., 2nd Sess. (1991).

119   Stanley Mark, Mini Liu, and Jackson Chin, Statement at the U.S. Commission on Civil Rights Roundtable Conference on Civil Rights, New York, NY, June 23, 1989.

120   Wing Lam, Testimony at New York City Human Rights Commission and New York City Office of Labor Services Hearing on Discrimination in the Construction Trades, Mar. 12, 1990; Stanley Mark, Testimony at New York City Human Rights Commission and

Roundtable Conference.[121] Among the discriminatory practices allegedly engaged in by construction unions to keep Asian Americans out are selective use of English-proficiency requirements and unfair hiring hall practices.

Although resource constraints prevented the Commission from undertaking a complete investigation of these allegations, available statistics confirm that Asian Americans are underrepresented in construction unions. Nationwide, Asian Americans constituted 0.8 percent of the membership of construction unions in 1990, although they made up 2.9 percent of the U.S. population.[122] Asian American representation is even lower in New York State,[123] where Asian Americans constituted 3.9 percent of the population in 1990 but made up only 0.3 percent of the membership of construction unions.[124] Furthermore, among persons in New York State with skill levels comparable to those of construction workers (i.e., the pool of potential construction workers), Asian Americans are considerably less likely to be employed in construction jobs than are whites: in 1980 only 2.6 percent of the Asian Americans who reported their occupations as craftsmen, operators, or laborers were in construction jobs, as compared to 14.5 percent of whites with these occupations. Based on these statistics, further investigation of the allegations of construction union discrimination against Asian Americans in New York City and of anti-Asian discrimination by unions in general is warranted.

Employment Discrimination Against Asian American Women

Although Asian Americans of both genders encounter employment discrimination based on their race, the barriers to equal employment opportunity may be greater for Asian American women because of their gender. As women, they may be the victims of gender discrimination and sexual harassment on the job. And as Asian American women, especially if they are immigrants, they may be less equipped to handle such discrimination than women of other races for two reasons. First, Asian American women, especially those who are immigrants, may find that the small number of Asian American women in the workplace is an impediment to their joining informal networks of co-workers on the job; and this in turn may mean that when Asian American women encounter discrimination they do not have easy access to the support and advice of their co-workers. Second, immigrant Asian American women may be less well-informed about their rights in the workplace and culturally conditioned not to complain about mistreatment. Their isolation from their co-workers, their ignorance of their rights, and their reluctance to complain all make Asian American immigrant women vulnerable to sexual harassment in the workplace and other forms of employment discrimination.

New York City Office of Labor Services Hearing on Discrimination in the Construction Trades, Apr. 25, 1990.

121   Harold Yee, Statement at the U.S. Commission on Civil Rights Roundtable Conference on Civil Rights, San Francisco, CA, July 29, 1989.

122   "Membership in Referral Unions, By Type, By International, and by Race/Ethnic Groups/Sex, 1990," table provided by the U.S. Equal Employment Opportunity Commission.

123   Unfortunately, comparable data were not readily available for New York City.

124   "Membership in Referral Unions, By State, By Type, By International, and by Race/Ethnic Groups/Sex, 1990," table provided by the U.S. Equal Employment Opportunity Commission.

Briefly presented below are three illustrative cases:

Case 1—In May 1989 a Filipino American woman working as a secretary in a medical laboratory at one of the University of California campuses fainted on the job. The rescue squad called to the scene happened to include a Tagalog-speaking man, who learned that the fainting was related to job stress and ultimately discovered that the stress had been caused by sexual abuse by the woman's supervisor.[125] The rescue team member reported his finding to the school authorities and advised the woman to seek legal and psychological counsel. The university found the supervisor guilty as alleged, and the case is in progress.

The victim came to the United States as a student in 1983 and found a part-time job the same year. Three months after she started her job, her supervisor, a medical doctor, took her to his home on the pretext of giving her a ride home and raped her. Her supervisor's sexual abuse continued for years, up to the time of the fainting incident. During this time, she was ashamed and dumbfounded, felt lost, and did not know what to do. She was totally ignorant of what rights she might have and what means of recourse she could pursue. In early 1989 she accidentally discovered that the same supervisor had sexually harassed other women at the same laboratory. Upon hearing what had happened to the victim, some of these women advised her to file a complaint. Being uninformed of the complaint procedure and its ramifications (she was then an undocumented alien), the victim sought counsel from another supervisor, a non-Asian American medical doctor in the same laboratory. She was discouraged from pursuing the case, and she became hesitant and afraid of filing a complaint. It was at about this time that she fainted.

In this case, the victim was too ashamed to talk about her ordeal, which deprived her of the advice and support of close workplace friends. Not knowing what rights and means of recourse she had as an employee, she had to endure the abuse for 5 long years. When she finally ventured out seeking assistance, she was discouraged from seeking justice.

Case 2—The second case concerns a Korean American woman working at a United States Air Force base in California:[126]

A technical support division at the base was placed under the management of a new supervisor a few years ago. This new supervisor was perceived by many to be anti-Asian in subtle ways, and except for a Korean American female computer programmer, the staff members of Asian ancestry all moved to other divisions one by one.

When the Korean American programmer asked her new supervisor informational questions regarding new office policies or practices being instituted, she was rarely given straight explanations or answers. She was made to feel as if she was asking something she was not supposed to. While the supervisor treated questions from her co-workers with courtesy and professionalism, she felt that her questions were handled in an unfriendly way, sometimes with hostility. At one of the office meetings, the division chief pointedly said her behavior of questioning office policies was out of line. She soon began to feel that she was being singled out and that she was a target of harassment and disparate treatment.

The new division chief's harassment and mistreatment intensified when she signed a document that chronicled a long series of simultaneous absences by the division chief and his female secretary during regular business hours. The suspicious absences had continued for quite some time, and they were a matter of

---

125   This account is based on information provided by Madge Kho, Equal Rights Advocates, interview, Feb. 22, 1990, Oakland, CA.

126   This account is based on information supplied to Commission staff. This case is undergoing adjudication, and the complainant requested anonymity.

common knowledge. Although the document was submitted to a higher commanding officer, there was no official investigation or response to the revelations contained in the document.

From the time that she submitted the signed document to a higher authority, the Korean American employee began to experience adverse turns in her work life. Her promotion was denied twice without what she considered an adequate explanation. Her request for a transfer to another division was turned down by the division chief on the grounds that the chief of the division to which she was requesting the transfer had shown favoritism to her in the past. While her transfer request was being denied on this frivolous ground, her immediate supervisor was advising her, "If I were you, I would move out of this division." The supervisor repeated this unsolicited advice three more times after she made it clear that she did not want to move under coercion or intimidation.

According to her, the harassment continued. For instance, one time she received an official reprimand for abusing government resources for personal use (i.e., using an office typewriter to fill out her son's college applications). She filed a grievance, and an official investigation concluded that the accusation was unfounded. She soon found out that the amount of time she took for lunch was being closely monitored, while there was no such monitoring of others. The people she had been going to lunch with gradually dropped out; she found out that they were getting comments from their immediate supervisors which apparently discouraged them from going to lunch with her. Finally, she was left with only one person who was willing to eat lunch with her. Whenever they went to lunch at the cafeteria, these two people felt certain that

someone was watching them, trying to overhear their conversation. This Asian American woman finally filed a discrimination complaint. An internal EEO investigation and reconciliation efforts were not successful, and the case is now under investigation by an outside source.

This case illustrates the influence a manager can exert in the workplace in setting a particular tone regarding race and gender. Through exemplary behavior, a manager can help set a racially supportive atmosphere in the workplace, but through subtle maneuvering, the manager can turn an entire workplace against an employee or employees of a particular race or ethnicity. It underscores the need for top management to be alert to signs of potential civil rights problems in subordinate units, such as high turnover rates among minorities or different racial patterns of promotion and assignment to desirable jobs.

Case 3—The third case concerns a Filipino American woman working at a United States Army base in the San Francisco Bay area.[127]

The woman reported sexual harassment by her immediate supervisor to the base commander. The base commander talked to the department head about the complaint. Instead of investigating the alleged harassing official, the department head started a series of what appeared to be retaliatory actions against the complainant, including work-related harassment, disparate work assignments, demeaning treatment, and general hostility. The complainant heard her co-workers make comments which seemed to imply that the base leadership was taken aback not so much by the substance of the complaint as by the fact that it came from an Asian American woman. According to her, it was as if an Asian American woman was not supposed to complain. Because of the stereotypic

---

127   This case is based on the information provided at a meeting of Filipino community representatives held at the Filipinos for Affirmative Action, Oakland, CA, Feb. 22, 1990.

expectation of compliance and docility, a formal complaint from an Asian American woman might have been considered as a personal affront or challenge. Her notification of the alleged retaliation to the base authorities was to no avail: it aggravated an already bad situation. The complainant finally suffered a nervous breakdown and had to quit her job. A lawsuit is now in progress.

Several aspects of this case are noteworthy. First, the base leadership did not follow up on the original complaint to make certain that appropriate actions had been taken. The charge of ensuing retaliation filed with the authorities went unheeded. Second, the number of Asian Americans was too small to serve as a basis for collective mobilization. In addition, probably for fear of blacklisting and retaliation (as alleged by Filipino community representatives),[128] the few Asian American employees at the base were unable to register a collective concern with the base authority. Deprived of collegial support, the complainant became a vulnerable target for harassment by management.

---

128   Ibid.

Chapter 7

Other Civil Rights Issues Confronting Asian Americans

Topics discussed in the preceding chapters by no means exhaust the civil rights issues of vital concern to Asian Americans. This chapter discusses six other fundamental civil rights issues: political representation, access to health care, access to the judicial system, public services for battered women, coverage and representation in the media, and religious accommodation. Although limited resources precluded indepth examination of these issues, the chapter discusses each issue in sufficient detail to define the nature of the problem and to heighten public officials', legislators', and the general public's awareness of and sensitivity towards the issue.

Political Representation

Even though the numbers of Asian Americans have been increasing steadily for several decades, Asian Americans are only just now beginning to become a political force. Many of the participants at the Commission's Roundtable Conferences expressed concern about Asian Americans' lack of political representation and political empowerment and decried the dearth of Asian American elected officials and political candidates.[1]

Indeed, outside of the State of Hawaii, there are very few Asian American elected officials across the country. The State of California has two Asian American Congressmen,[2] but the only elected State position held by an Asian American is that of California Secretary of State.[3] Although Asian Americans now make up close to 10 percent of the State's population, there have been no Asian Americans in the California State Legislature for over a decade.[4] A similar pattern prevails in local districts. For instance, in Daly City, California, where Asian Americans are over 42 percent of the population, there has never been an Asian American elected to the city council.[5] New York City, which has an Asian American population of more than 400,000, has never had an Asian American elected to its city council.[6] According to a participant at the New York Roundtable Conference, "Right now we don't have one single elected official at any level, be that state assembly, city council, or any other type of office."[7] Asian Americans who have been elected usually are not identified with

1   Michael Yuan, Statement at the U.S. Commission on Civil Rights Roundtable Conference on Civil Rights, Houston, TX, May 27, 1989; Stanley Mark, Charles Wang, Rockwell Chin, and Jackson Chin, Statements at the U.S. Commission on Civil Rights Roundtable Conference, New York, NY, June 23, 1989; Vu Duc Vuong, Kevin Acebo, and Harold Yee, Statements at the U.S. Commission on Civil Rights Roundtable Conference, San Francisco, CA, July 29, 1989.

2   Rep. Robert T. Matsui (D-CA-3) and Rep. Norman Y. Mineta (D-CA-13).

3   Tim W. Ferguson, "California Ethnic Politics, Chinese Style," *Wall Street Journal*, May 23, 1991. March Fong Eu is California's Secretary of State. Asian/Pacific American Municipal Officials, *Directory of Asian/Pacific American Elected and Appointed Officials* (1990).

4   Ibid.

5   William Tamayo, Robin Toma, and Stewart Kwoh, "The Voting Rights of Asian Pacific Americans," Asian American Studies Center, University of California, Los Angeles, July 1991, p. 3.

6   Asian American Legal Defense and Education Fund, "Asian American on City Council in 1991? AALDEF Works with Commission to Create Asian American Seat," *Outlook* (Winter 1991), p. 1 (hereafter cited as "Asian American on City Council?").

an ethnic constituency. For instance, Los Angeles City Councilman Michael Woo was elected from a district that is only 5 percent Asian American.[8]

Asian Americans' political underrepresentation and consequent lack of political power result both from demographic factors, such as low percentages eligible to vote, and barriers to political participation, some of which are discriminatory.

Two demographic factors operate to reduce the voting participation and hence the political power of Asian Americans. First, because many Asian Americans are recent immigrants, a large proportion of the Asian American population has not yet attained citizenship and hence is not eligible to vote. In 1980 almost 70 percent of Asian Americans aged 15 and over were foreign born, and only 55 percent of the total Asian American population were U.S. citizens.[9] With the continuing large-scale immigration of Asians to this country after 1980, it is likely that an even larger percentage of Asian Americans today is foreign born. Second, some Asian American groups, especially Southeast Asians and Pacific Islanders, are much younger than the U.S. population as a whole.[10] Thus many Asian Americans are either under the voting age of 18 or in their young adulthood, which is the age at which those eligible to vote have the lowest participation rate. Asian Americans' noncitizenship and age combined substantially reduce their eligibility to vote. In New York City, for instance, out of a total Asian American population of 245,220 in 1980, only 76,400, or 31 percent, were citizens of voting age.[11]

Even among Asian Americans who are eligible to vote, however, the voter participation rate is lower than for many other population groups. For example, a survey of California voters found that only 48 percent of Asian Americans overall and 69 percent of Asian Americans who were citizens voted in 1984, compared with 80 percent of non-Hispanic white and black citizens.[12] A number of factors has been suggested as contributing to the low voter participation of eligible Asian American voters, including the recent immigration status of many, which means that they have not yet become accustomed to the American political system,[13] and cultures and historical experiences that discourage participation in the political process.[14]

---

7   Charles Wang, Chinese American Planning Council, Statement at the U.S. Commission on Civil Rights Roundtable Conference on Asian American Civil Rights Issues for the 1990s, New York, NY, June 23, 1989. Since that statement, three Asian American judges have been elected.

8   Seth Mydans, "Vote in a 'Melting Pot' of Los Angeles May Be Mirror of California's Future," *New York Times*, June 2, 1991.

9   U.S. Bureau of the Census, 1980 Census of Population, vol. 2, Subject Reports, *Asian and Pacific Islander Population in the United States: 1980* (January 1988), table 16. Almost two-thirds of foreign-born Asian Americans were not citizens, and two-thirds of non-citizen Asian Americans had immigrated to the United States between 1975 and 1980. Ibid.

10   Whereas the median age for the U.S. population as a whole is around 30, the median age for Southeast Asians is 21.5 for Vietnamese, 16.9 for Laotians, 22.4 for Cambodians, and 16.3 for Hmongs; and the median age of Pacific Islanders is 23.1. Ibid., tables 48, 54, 66, 84, and 90.

11   Stanley Mark, Asian American Legal Defense and Education Fund, "Voting Rights, A Summary of the Issues," September 1989.

12   Bruce E. Cain, "The Political Impact of Demographic Changes," pp. 304-19 in U.S. Commission on Civil Rights, *Changing Perspectives on Civil Rights*, Report on a Forum Held in Los Angeles, CA, Sept. 8-9, 1988.

13   Vuong Statement.

14   Bruce E. Cain, "The Political Impact of Demographic Changes," p. 309. As explained by a *New York Times* article, "Participation in government is often looked on with suspicion by Asian immigrants who fled repressive governments. For them government at its best has meant taxation and military service, and at its worst, oppression, persecution or death." "Randolph Journal: Asian Refugee Sends Voters a Signal," *New York Times*, Aug. 21, 1990. Congressman Matsui, a Japanese American, attributes the reluctance to enter politics of Asian Americans who have lived in this country for generations to the history of anti-Asian legislation and the

Several factors limiting Asian Americans' political representation and political power are serious civil rights concerns, however. Participants at the Commission's Roundtable Conferences named several specific barriers to the political participation and hence the political representation of Asian Americans: 1) apportionment policies that dilute the voting strength of Asian American voting blocks;[15] 2) the unavailability of Asian-language ballots and other election materials;[16] 3) problems with the implementation of the Census of Population; and 4) anti-Asian sentiments among non-Asian voters and the media[17] and the consequent dearth of Asian American political candidates (which may also be partly caused by political parties that ignore the Asian American population and do not actively seek or promote Asian candidates).[18] Each of these causes is discussed in turn.

1) Apportionment policies—Asian American political power may have been diluted by apportionment schemes that split the Asian American population in an area into several districts and by at-large election systems within districts.[19] One study, for example, notes that San Francisco's State senate district boundaries have split the Asian American population in that city; that Koreatown, Chinatown, and Filipinotown in Los Angeles are each split into several city council districts; and that Daly City and other cities in the south Bay and San Gabriel Valley have at-large elections.[20]

Drawing districts that give Asian Americans significant political power is not always easy, however. Despite heavy increases in recent years, the Asian American population remains small in comparison to the population as a whole, and even though geographically concentrated in certain States, Asian Americans generally are not so concentrated at a local level that they can even potentially become a majority population in more than a handful of electoral districts.[21] Furthermore, Asian Americans are less likely to vote as a block than other minority groups.[22] For instance, in the State of California, Asian Americans are roughly equally divided among Democratic and Republican registrants.[23] These facts make it very difficult to draw electoral districts in which Asian Americans can be assured of being the majority of voters or a block of voters of sufficient size to have a major electoral influence.

With the release of the 1990 census data showing large increases in the numbers of Asian

---

    forced internment of Japanese Americans during World War II. (Ibid.)

15   Acebo Statement; Yee Statement; Mark Statement; Wang Statement; Jackson Chin Statement.

16   Mark Statement; Rockwell Chin Statement.

17   Vuong Statement; Mark Statement.

18   Vuong Statement; Mark Statement.

19   This argument has been made by Tamayo, Toma, and Kwoh, "The Voting Rights of Asian Pacific Americans."

20   Ibid., pp. 3-4.

21   For instance, with a 57.5 percent Asian population, Monterey Park, CA, is the only city on the U.S. mainland with a majority Asian American population. Ferguson, "California Ethnic Politics."

22   Bruce E. Cain, "The Political Impact of Demographic Changes," pp. 311-12.

23   Bruce E. Cain, Statement at the U.S. Commission on Civil Rights Forum on Changing Perspectives on Civil Rights, Los Angeles, CA, Sept. 8-9, 1988, p. 104. A case in point is the city of Monterey Park, where Asian Americans are roughly 58 percent of the population. A 1988 exit poll of Asian American voters in Monterey Park found that 45 percent of Chinese American voters identified themselves as Republican and 30 percent as independent, with only one-quarter identifying themselves as Democratic; whereas 60 percent of Japanese Americans identified themselves as Democratic, 30 percent as Republican, and 10 percent as independent. (Southwest Voter Research Institute Exit Poll, Apr. 12, 1988, as reported in Leland T. Saito, "'Asian American' Politics: Emerging Tendencies in the City of Monterey Park" (paper presented at the 86th Annual Meeting of the American Sociological Association, Cincinnati, OH, Aug. 23-27, 1991), p. 14.)

Americans, however, Asian Americans have begun to get involved in the politics of the redistricting process. Buoyed by a recent court decision suggesting that a minority group does not necessarily have to constitute over 50 percent of a district's population to be protected by the Voting Rights Act,[24] Asian American groups in California have formed the Coalition of Asian Pacific Americans for Fair Reapportionment to "ensure that the voice of Asian Pacific Americans on the redistricting process is heard in order to facilitate fairly drawn districts that do not fragment the Asian Pacific vote."[25] As part of this effort, the Asian American Studies Center at the University of California at Los Angeles is helping to analyze voting districts and to conduct studies on Asian American voter patterns.[26] Some are working for the creation of a San Gabriel Valley district that would include many Asian American voters and would give Monterey Park City Councilwoman Judy Chu a chance of being elected to the State legislature.[27]

In New York City, Asian Americans have been actively trying to influence the decisions of a 15-member districting commission that was charged with drawing a new districting plan required by a decision to increase the number of seats on the city council from 35 to 51.[28] Previous plans had split Chinatown into two different districts. The Asian American Legal Defense Fund and other Asian groups worked to promote two "Asian districts," one in Chinatown and one in Queens.[29] Others sought to join Asian Americans living in Chinatown with other minorities living in the lower East Side or with whites living in SoHo, TriBeCa, and Battery Park City.[30] On June 4, 1991, the districting commission adopted a plan that placed virtually all of Chinatown in a district that included SoHo, TriBeCa, and Battery Park City and had a voting-age population of 114,207, of whom 37.9 percent were Asian American, 40.7 percent were white, 15.3 percent were Hispanic, and 5.8 percent were black.[31] Since all of Manhattan is estimated to have only about 8,000 Asian Americans registered to vote,[32] however, it is not clear that Asian Americans will be able to win representation even in this district with a large plurality of Asians. Nonetheless, because the plan keeps Chinatown mainly intact, the plan does give Asian Americans some potential electoral influence, and it may also signal that Asian Americans are beginning to gain political influence.

---

24   Garza v. County of Los Angeles, 918 F.2d 763 (9th Cir. 1990), *cert. denied*, 112 L. Ed.2d 673 (1991). The case dealt specifically with Hispanic voters in Los Angeles County.

25   Tamayo, Toma, and Kwoh, "The Voting Rights of Asian Pacific Americans," p. 11.

26   Kathryn Imahara, Asian Pacific Legal Center of Southern California, letter to Nadja Zalokar, U.S. Commission on Civil Rights, Sept. 4, 1991, p. 4.

27   Ferguson, "California Ethnic Politics."

28   Felicia Lee, "Blocs Battle to Draw Chinatown's New Council Map," *New York Times*, Apr. 30, 1991, p. B1, and "Minority Districts for Council Added in New York Plan: Political Map Redrawn; Proposal is Quickly Criticized by Some Groups Seeking More Representation," *New York Times*, May 2, 1991.

29   "Asian American on City Council," p. 5.

30   Lee, "Blocs Battle to Draw Chinatown's New Council Map."

31   Felicia Lee, "Plan Adopted to Increase Minorities on City Council," *New York Times*, June 4, 1991. The plan also included two other districts with large Asian American populations (one with 29.6 percent and the other with 28.3 percent Asians), both in Queens. (Ibid.) The U.S. Department of Justice gave its approval to a slightly modified version of this plan on July 26, 1991. (Robert Pear, "New York Plan Wins U.S. Backing: Justice Department Approves City Council District Map," *New York Times*, July 27, 1991.)

32   Stanley Mark, Asian American Legal Defense and Education Fund, "Voting Rights: A Summary of the Issues," September 1989.

A similar situation prevails in District 20 in Flushing, which was drawn to include a sizable number of Asian Americans: 31 percent of the district's 140,000 residents are Asian American. Yet Asian Americans are only 6.7 percent of the registered voters.[33] Nonetheless, there are two Asian American candidates for District 20's city council seat: Pauline Chu, a Chinese American who is running in the Democratic primary against incumbent Julia Harrison, and Chun Soo Pyun, a Korean American, the only Republican in the race.[34]

2) Limited English proficiency—Limited English proficiency is potentially an important barrier to political participation for many Asian Americans. In a provision that is slated to expire on August 6, 1992, the Voting Rights Act of 1982 requires States and political subdivisions for which the "Director of the Census determines (i) that more than 5 percent of the citizens of voting age of such State or political subdivision are members of a single language minority and (ii) that the illiteracy rate of such persons as a group is higher than the national illiteracy rate"[35] to distribute all election materials, including ballots, in the language of the applicable minority group. Because the Asian American population is generally small, speaks a variety of languages, and is not very residentially concentrated, Asian Americans from a single language almost never constitute 5 percent of a district's voting-age population. Thus, the 5 percent requirement means that Asian Americans almost never receive federally mandated bilingual election materials.[36] Because the benefits of the Voting Rights Act do not extend to Asian Americans, limited English proficiency is a serious barrier to the political participation of many Asian Americans.

A particularly egregious example is New York City, where there were almost 100,000 Chinese Americans of voting age in 1980.[37] Because New York City's population is very large, this number fell just short of the 5 percent cutoff.[38] Voter surveys undertaken by the Asian American Legal Defense and Education Fund found that:

in Chinatown, four out of five voters have language difficulties. These voters stated. . .that they would vote more often if bilingual assistance were provided. Similarly in Queens, four out of every five limited-English-proficient Asian American voters indicated that they would vote more if bilingual assistance were provided.[39]

Thus, many Asian Americans are deterred from voting because of limited English proficiency.

3) 1990 Census—Because it is very closely related both to the drawing of political maps and to the issue of the provision of bilingual voting materials, it is critical whether the 1990 census was able to obtain an accurate count of Asian Americans. A number of participants at the Commission's Roundtable Conferences underscored the importance of getting an accurate count.[40] For instance, whether or not Chinese Americans in New York City meet the 5 percent

---

33   Donatella Lorch, "In Flushing Council Contest, A Slice of Asian Politics," *New York Times*, Aug. 28, 1991.

34   Ibid.

35   42 U.S.C. §1973aa-1a(b) (1988).

36   In fact, as of 1988, apart from Japanese Americans in three counties in Hawaii, no Asian Americans received federally mandated bilingual election materials. 28 C.F.R. Ch. 1 (7-9-89 Ed.), app.

37   U.S. Bureau of the Census, 1980 Census of Population, vol. 2, Subject Reports, *Asian and Pacific Islander Population in the United States: 1980* (January 1988), table 18.

38   Margaret Fung, Executive Director, Asian American Legal Defense and Education Fund, telephone interview, Jan. 29, 1991.

39   Margaret Fung, Executive Director, Asian American Legal Defense and Education, Statement before the New York City Districting Commission, Nov. 1, 1990.

40   Stephen Wong and Martha Wong, Statement at the U.S. Commission on Civil Rights Roundtable Conference on Asian American

threshold specified in the Voting Rights Act for mandatory bilingual voting materials may turn on how accurately Chinese Americans in New York City were counted. Whether or not "Asian American" districts are drawn in the redistricting process is also likely to hinge on an accurate count of Asian Americans. Many participants were concerned that the Census Bureau's form is not provided in Asian languages, that there were not enough bilingual/bicultural census takers, and that the Census Bureau's postenumeration survey might be too small to detect and pinpoint an inaccurate count of Asian Americans.[41]

As important as the accuracy of the data is their timely release. Asian Americans expressed frustration and exasperation at the delayed release of detailed data on Asian Americans from the 1980 census.[42] They pointed out that the 1980 census data were not released until 1988 and that by the time the data were released, they were no longer useful in documenting the numbers and characteristics of the Asian American population, since Asian Americans had undergone a dramatic transformation during the intervening 8 years. According to one participant, the

Census Bureau has agreed to release the data much earlier this time, probably in 1991 or 1992.[43]

4) Bias against Asian Americans—Asian American candidates for public office across the country often say that they had difficulty in getting their candidacies taken seriously by the major political parties.[44] Furthermore, they contend that the parties are not always responsive to the concerns of Asian Americans. A 1989 *Washington Post* article, which argued that the Democratic Party has been slow to adjust its political agenda to attract Asian American voters and in many issues has been guilty of anti-Asian sounding rhetoric, supports their view. It said:

The new [Asian and Hispanic] Americans often feel a personal stake in shifting U.S. priorities towards a more Asian and Latin American orientation. Yet to date, the Democrats have been remarkably resistant. . .to the idea of a less Eurocentric foreign policy. Perhaps the most ominous is the increasingly anti-Asian tone of Democratic rhetoric, all too clearly demonstrated in the "Japan-bashing" and "Korean-bashing" campaign ads used last year by both Michael Dukakis and Rep. Richard Gephardt (D-Mo.)[45]

Civil Rights Issues for the 1990s, Houston, TX, May 27, 1989; Acebo Statement; Mark Statement; Wang Statement; Rockwell Chin Statement.

41 See, e.g., Acebo Statement, Mark Statement, Martha Wong Statement. In November 1990 the Census Bureau agreed to do more postcensus sampling in areas with large Asian American populations. ("Census Bureau to Study U.S. Asian Populace," *Wall Street Journal*, Nov. 19, 1990.) Although this sampling will provide better data on Asian Americans, it will have no effect on the apportionment process, because the Federal Government decided not to adjust the 1990 census figures based on the postcensus enumeration survey.

42 Wang Statement. Both the general booklet, *We, the Asian and Pacific Islander Americans*, and the detailed census statistics, *Asian and Pacific Islander Population in the United States: 1980*, were published in 1988.

43 Wang Statement.

44 For instance, Congressman Matsui described the incredulity with which his colleagues greeted his decision to run for office in a speech given at "Asian and Pacific Americans: Challenges in the New Decade," a conference sponsored by Senators Simon and Daschle, Washington, DC, Oct. 5, 1990. Judy Chu, who is planning to run for the California State legislature, complained "that 'Blacks and progressive whites' set [the Democratic Party's] agenda, and Asians are given short shrift." (Ferguson, "California Ethnic Politics.") However, she feels that "Republicans promote Asian candidacies and issues such as college admission quotas. . . ." (Ibid.) Tom Hsieh, a San Francisco City Supervisor currently running for mayor, voiced similar feelings. (Jay Mathews, "San Francisco Campaign May Accent Asian Clout," *Washington Post*, June 11, 1991.)

45 Joel Kotkin and Bill Bradley, "Democrats and Demographics; Asians, Hispanics and Small Business are the Party's Future," *Washington Post*, Feb. 26, 1989.

In recent years, however, there has been an aggressive outreach effort made by both political parties to the Asian American community.[46]

Roundtable Conference participants gave several examples that they felt demonstrated that anti-Asian sentiments are one of the underlying factors limiting or discouraging Asian Americans' political participation. One participant pointed out that many San Franciscans considered one Asian on the San Francisco Board of Supervisors to be enough:

The population of the City of San Francisco is 35 percent Asian. There are 11 members of the City Council, but there's only one Asian. And already the talk is that Asians are already represented adequately, so you don't need any more.[47]

He also charged that an influential California paper had recently written an editorial asking people not to vote for a Korean American candidate for local election because he had an accent.[48]

Access to Health Care

Many Asian Americans, especially recent immigrants, have serious health care needs that are not being met. Refugees from Southeast Asia arrive in this country with serious physical and mental health problems stemming from their experiences in their home countries.[49] Other Asian Americans, especially those in lower socioeconomic strata, also do not receive the care they need. Two factors appear to limit Asian Americans' access to health care in the United States: language and cultural barriers and a lack of data on Asian American health status. Although limited resources prevent a discussion of Asian Americans' access to other public services in this report, it should be noted that similar problems hamper Asian Americans' access to most other public services as well.

Language and Cultural Barriers

Although there are no nationwide statistics documenting the numbers of health care interpreters who speak Asian languages, it is clear that the national health care system is not adequately meeting the interpretation needs of the limited-English-proficient Asian American population. The bilingual family members and other untrained interpreters frequently used by health care providers are a poor substitute for trained health care interpreters. As noted by a health

---

46 Melinda Yee, letter to James S. Cunningham, Assistant Staff Director for Programs, Policy, and Research, U.S. Commission on Civil Rights, Sept. 6, 1991. For example, in May 1991 the Democratic Party hosted an Asian Pacific American Democratic Summit in Washington, DC. (Democratic News, "Democratic Party Chairman Ron Brown Forms Asian Pacific American Democratic Advisory Council," May 8, 1991.) The summit brought together party officials, including Democratic Party Chairman Ron Brown, and Asian American party activists "to discuss public policy issues, increased political participation, and the 1992 presidential campaign." (Ibid.) At the summit meeting, the party set up the Asian Pacific American Advisory Council to "coordinate activities between registration and education, outreach to naturalized citizens, candidate development, campaign training, fundraising, and increased participation within [the Democratic National Party.]" (Ibid.)

47 Vuong Statement.

48 Ibid.

49 According to a Connecticut State official: "the chief disease [among Southeast Asian refugees] has been tuberculosis, followed by intestinal parasites, hepatitis Type B, and syphilis. The chief personal health disorders are abnormalities in dental conditions, vision, and hearing." (George Raiselis, Refugee Health Program Director, State of Connecticut Department of Health Services, as cited in Connecticut State Advisory Committee to the U.S. Commission on Civil Rights, *Southeast Asian Refugees and Their Access to Health and Mental Health Services* (December 1989), p. 16 (hereafter cited as Connecticut SAC Report).) Another Connecticut State official said that his estimates suggested that between 45 and 72 percent of Southeast Asian refugees have mental health problems. (John Cavenaugh, Administrator, State of Connecticut Department of Mental Health, as cited in Connecticut SAC Report, p. 18.)

care official for the State of Connecticut, interpreting medical information to Southeast Asians requires considerable expertise:

Not all medical/health terminologies are translatable into the various Southeast Asian languages and dialects nor can the Southeast Asian expressions of their physical and mental states be directly translated for western health care providers. The interview of a Southeast Asian refugee must be interpreted by one who is aware of the nuances of the various cultures. Many Southeast Asian medical terms or health conditions when translated literally to English tend to mislead or confuse western health care providers.[50]

The shortage of interpretive services seriously limits the access of many Asian Americans to health care. Furthermore, when a physician's ability to communicate with a patient is hampered by the lack of an interpreter, he or she may be violating the American Medical Association's (AMA) Principles of Medical Ethics. The AMA's Council on Ethical and Judicial Affairs has offered the opinion that the patient's right of informed consent "can be effectively exercised only if the patient possesses enough information to enable an intelligent choice."[51] The council has not addressed directly physicians' obligations to use medical interpreters when communicating with limited-English-proficient patients, however.

In addition to language barriers, cultural barriers compound the problems faced by many Asian Americans in gaining access to proper health care. To render effective health care to Asian Americans, health care providers need considerable knowledge of and sensitivity towards Asian American cultures. Participants at

the Asian American Health Forum (AAHF) noted that:

A health provider's appreciation and understanding of Asian/Pacific values and practices remains a critical factor in access. Imposing Western medical models without considering Asian/Pacific responses will lead to confusion and conflict, rather than cooperation and health promotion.[52]

A health care provider's insensitivity might result in misdiagnosis. For example:

Asian cultures with hierarchical social structures revere authority figures. . . .As a result, a patient of Korean descent may not question a physician's diagnosis and treatment. He or she may indicate understanding, agreement and compliance when none are intended.[53]

Researchers caution that effective health care provision requires health care providers to "recognize culturally-appropriate responses to illness."[54]

Health care providers sometimes need to take steps to reach out to some Asian American groups who may be reluctant to seek their services. A participant at the San Francisco Roundtable Conference said:

[F]or many Asian families it is a stigma to be identified as having [mental health problems]. We need to begin to explore different ways of presenting mental health services. . . .We have an excellent program here in San Francisco, the China Health Child Development Center, that uses a sort of non-stigmatized way of getting some Asian families—Chinese families in particular–to come into their center so that they can be evaluated for mental health problems. . .[This way]

---

50   George Raiselis, Director, Refugee Health Program, State of Connecticut Department of Health Services, as cited in Connecticut SAC Report, p. 17.

51   Council on Ethical and Judicial Affairs of the American Medical Association, "Current Opinions," no. 8.08, "Informed Consent."

52   Malaya Forman, Michael Chunchi Lu, Mingyew Leung, and Ninez Ponce, "Ethnocultural Barriers to Care," Asian American Health Forum Policy Paper, November 1990, p. 4.

53   Ibid.

54   Ibid.

we have been able to increase the number of families receiving mental health services.[55]

Here is an example of a successful outreach effort. Soon after three Hmong children died from measles in the Twin Cities area in the spring of 1990, the public television station in Minneapolis-Saint Paul quickly put together a half-hour Hmong-language broadcast to provide the Hmong community with information about measles symptoms, treatment, and prevention and to encourage parents to vaccinate their children. The unique outreach program featured a discussion in question and answer format between Hmong medical professionals and Hmong community leaders and was widely publicized in the Hmong community before it was broadcast. Copies of the program have since been made available to social services agencies serving Hmong communities across the country.[56]

Several examples illustrate how the lack of interpretation and/or culturally sensitive staff can obstruct or complicate Asian Americans' access to proper health care are given below.

[Speaking of inadequate mental health care for northern California youth of Asian ancestry]. . .it is unconscionable when often times we find that family members are asked to go into therapy sessions to serve as translators for the therapy itself. It is unethical, it is unprofessional, and it is totally inappropriate. But these things happen all the time.[57]

A [Cambodian] woman suffering from convulsions was termed uncooperative for not permitting medical personnel to perform brain tests. It turned out that she had been tortured by the Khmer Rouge who tied plastic bags on her head until she would pass out. As a result, she could not bear having her head touched or covered.[58]

A man who had suffered a serious stroke in a refugee camp and who still had markedly high blood pressure was denied supplemental security income because he had no physical handicaps from the first stroke. None of the four physicians who had examined him noticed that he was confused and did not know where he lived or what day it was. He could not work, and his family could not leave him alone because he would wander off and become lost.[59]

One woman, who had lost her first husband and seven children during the Pol Pot regime and who was tortured and raped, was hospitalized after threatening to kill herself; she was kept only a short time because she could not communicate and was told that long-term therapy was unavailable because the therapist refused to work through a translator.[60]

A father was excluded from the treatment plan of his psychotic daughter because he believed that the spirits must be consulted before his daughter received medicine; the translator was ashamed of this belief and refused to communicate the father's concern. . . .[61]

It is unlawful to discriminate in health services based on national origin. According to the U.S. Department of Health and Human Services (HHS) regulations implementing Title VI of the Civil Rights Act, health-service-providing organizations receiving Federal funds are prohibited, on grounds of national origin, from:

---

55   Leland Yee, Statement at the U.S. Commission on Civil Rights Roundtable Conference on Asian American Civil Rights Issues for the 1990s, San Francisco, CA, July 29, 1989 (hereafter cited as Yee Statement).

56   Materials provided by Gail Feichtinger, KTCA-Channel 2, St. Paul, MN.

57   Yee Statement.

58   Theanvy Kuoch, Khmer Health Advocates, as reported in Connecticut SAC Report, p. 5.

59   Ibid.

60   Ibid., p. 4.

61   Ibid., pp. 4-5.

providing any service to an individual, which is different or is offered in a different manner from that provided to others;[62]

treating an individual differently from others in determining eligibility for receiving services;[63] and

utilizing criteria or methods of administration that have the effect of subjecting an individual to discrimination.[64]

For these reasons, a Federal fund recipient that is unable to communicate with a substantial limited-English-proficient (LEP) population in its service area effectively subjects that population to discrimination based on national origin.[65] In recent years, lawsuits and complaints alleging discrimination against LEP Asian Americans in health services resulted in consent decrees or voluntary compliance agreements. Several examples are provided below:

[M]any working [Asian Americans, particularly recent immigrants] have private health plans, particularly the Kaiser prepaid health plan. Because of language and cultural barriers, these people were coming back to private physicians in Chinatown [instead of using Kaiser services] in order to get adequate health care, and in many instances were *double paying*. . . .Chinese for Affirmative Action. . .filed a Title VI complaint against Kaiser Hospital. . .[After much foot-dragging] Kaiser agreed to sit down to talk about a consent decree. . . .Unfortunately, Kaiser was very slow in responding to the agreement but minor improvements

were made. They tried to tag medical folders so when appointments were made it was identified that a translator was needed. They also tried to revamp their Patient Assistance Office so that people were there if they needed translation.[66]

On October 10, 1985, the Vietnamese Society of Rhode Island filed a complaint of discrimination based on national origin against Health Services Incorporated (HSI), RI, with the HHS Office for Civil Rights (OCR). The complaint alleged that HSI discriminated against a class of LEP persons whose primary language is Vietnamese and specifically that HSI required LEP persons to bring their own interpreters with them to obtain services. When the OCR investigation found a failure on the part of HSI to comply with the Title VI regulations, HSI indicated a willingness to comply voluntarily, resulting in the execution of a voluntary compliance agreement between HHS and HSI on October 1, 1986.[67]

On May 8, 1989, OCR received a complaint against the Maine Medical Center (Hospital) alleging that the hospital had failed to provide interpreters for persons with limited English proficiency whose primary languages were Khmer and Vietnamese. When notified that OCR found a probable cause of allegation, the Hospital indicated its desire to be in voluntary compliance. In September 1991, OCR and the

---

62   45 C.F.R. §80.3(b)(1)(ii).

63   45 C.F.R. §80.3(b)(1)(v).

64   45 C.F.R. §80.3(b)(2).

65   Caroline J. Chang, Regional Manager, Region 1, U.S. Department of Health and Human Services, Office for Civil Rights, "Letter of Findings Re: Complaint No. 01-86-3004," to Rhode E. Perry, Executive Director, Health Services Incorporated, Woonsocket, RI, Sept. 26, 1986, p. 1.

66   Henry Der, Chinese for Affirmative Action, as reported in Asian American Health Forum, *Asian American Health Forum National Agenda for Asian and Pacific Islander Health* (1988).

67   Chang, "Letter of Findings Re: Complaint No. 01-86-3004," and accompanying compliance agreement. The agreement includes the following specific provisions:

"When scheduling appointment for patients of limited English proficiency, HSI appointment personnel will identify the language spoken by the patient and explain that HSI will arrange for an interpreter.

"[Institute] cultural awareness programs for staff who may be unfamiliar with the customs, attitudes and traditions of LEP populations in HSI's service areas." Ibid., p. 1-2.

hospital entered a compliance agreement detailing a series of steps that would ensure nondiscriminatory services to LEP persons.[68]

Although there are many Asian American doctors and other health professionals in this country, it is said that there are "persistent problems such as cultural and linguistic gaps between service providers and patients, which hinder the provision of health services to [Asian Americans], specifically Southeast Asian immigrants and refugees."[69] The ethnic backgrounds and languages spoken by most Asian American physicians are not those of the immigrant populations needing services.[70] Furthermore, Asian American physicians are underrepresented in the Western United States, where the bulk of the Asian immigrant population is concentrated.[71] Despite the need for culturally and linguistically capable health professionals to serve many Asian American populations,[72] the Federal Government generally does not include Asian Americans in its minority recruitment programs for health care professionals, because it deems Asian Americans to be "overrepresented."[73] By not taking account of the heterogeneity of the Asian American population, this policy fails to address the health care needs of many Asian Americans.[74]

Data Needs

An understanding of the health status of the Asian American population is dependent on detailed data on the health and health care participation of Asian Americans as well as general background data on their demographic and socioeconomic characteristics. Such data are indispensable in assessing the health care needs of

68   Caroline J. Chang, "Letter of Findings Re: Complaint No. 01-89-3040," to Donald L. McDowell, President, Maine Medical Center, Portland, ME, Sept. 9, 1991, and accompanying compliance agreement. The agreement includes the following specific provisions: "The Hospital will immediately name a Title VI Coordinator who will act as the overall coordinator of the Hospital's Title VI policies and practices including. . .the up-dating of the interpreter lists, obtaining interpreters. . .and as liaison with community groups and agencies in matters relating to. . .equal service to LEP persons.

"The Hospital will identify and record the primary language of its patients at the earliest opportunity. In order to alert its staff to a patient's primary language and the need for assigning a bilingual worker or the need to use an interpreter, a distinctive mark or notation shall be made on the patient's history or other record that accompanies him or her during treatment.

"The Hospital will post and maintain a sign (or signs) in English, Khmer and Vietnamese reading as follows: 'Maine Medical Center will provide interpreting services to non-English speaking patients and families. Patients do not have to provide their own interpreters. Interpreter services are also available for the deaf. Please ask for assistance.'" Ibid., pp. 5-7.

69   Malay Forman, Michael Chunchi Lu, Mingyew Leung, and Ninez Ponce, "The Development of Asian/Pacific Islander Health Professionals: The Myth of 'Overrepresentation,'" Asian American Health Forum Policy Paper, November 1990, pp. 1-2.

70   Ibid, p. 4.

71   Ibid.

72   The Federal Government does recognize this need. The Department of Health and Human Services recently listed the following as one of its goals for improving the health of Asian and Pacific Islander Americans: "Increase to at least 50 percent the proportion of counties that have established culturally and linguistically appropriate community health promotion programs for racial and ethnic minority populations." U.S. Department of Health and Human Services, Healthy People 2000: National Health Promotion and Disease Prevention Objectives (Washington, DC: Government Printing Office, 1991), p. 601 (hereafter cited as Healthy People 2000).

73   For instance, in August 1989 the guidance for staff of the National Heart, Lung, and Blood Institute's minority biomedical research, training, and career development programs defined eligible minorities as those who are underrepresented in biomedical research relative to their proportion in the population and explicitly finds that Asian/Pacific Islanders are not underrepresented. National Heart, Lung, and Blood Institute Guidance for Minority Activities, Aug. 22, 1989.

74   As noted in chap. 6, policies that make it difficult for foreign-trained physicians to become certified to practice medicine in the United States may also have the effect of restricting the supply of physicians with the language skills and cultural background to treat Asian American immigrants effectively.

Asian Americans and developing policies to meet these needs. They need to be collected separately for each major Asian American ethnic group and broken down by immigration status, region of residence, and socioeconomic status. Without such data, critical needs of Asian Americans will go officially undocumented and politically unrecognized, and hence unmet.

Yet most States and Federal health agencies make only minimal efforts to collect health-related data on Asian Americans. Vital statistics records collect critical information for assessing the health status of our population but generally do not collect separate information on different Asian groups. The State of California's vital statistics has check-off boxes for 11 Asian groups and encodes information on 14 groups, but the National Center for Health Statistics (NCHS), which provides model birth and death certificates for the Nation, has put out a form with no check-off boxes. The race question asks for the individual's race to be written in and in parentheses specifies "American Indian, Black, White, etc." It is clear that such a form will not elicit accurate information about individual Asian American groups. Yet the NCHS model form is used by several States with large concentrations of Asian Americans, namely, New York, Texas, and Illinois. Many other national level health data sets collect information only on Asian Americans in aggregate. Furthermore, because such data sets are usually designed to be representative of the population, their Asian American samples are almost always too small to provide meaningful data, even when Asian Americans can be disaggregated into individual groups.[75]

The Federal Government has begun to recognize the data needs of Asian Americans. A 1991 Department of Health and Human Services report, *Healthy People 2000*, lists the following goal among its objectives for improving the health status of Asians and Pacific Islanders: "Develop and implement a national process to identify significant gaps in the nation's disease prevention and health promotion data, including data for racial and ethnic minorities, people with low incomes and people with disabilities, and establish mechanisms to meet these needs."[76]

Access to the Judicial System

Many Asian Americans, especially those who are immigrants or limited in English proficiency, do not have equal access to the American judicial system. This section first highlights the shortage of trained interpreters as a critical barrier to access to our courts for limited-English-proficient Asian Americans and examines Federal and State laws and regulations pertaining to the provision of courtroom interpreters. It then notes that cultural barriers and discriminatory court treatment may also impede Asian Americans' access to the court. Finally, the section considers the underrepresentation of Asian Americans in the legal profession, which may also affect Asian Americans' access to legal representation and fair treatment in the courts.

Court Interpreters

One major obstacle to justice faced by Asian Americans is the unavailability of quality court interpreters to facilitate understanding for those Asian Americans who are not fluent in English.[77] Incidents where litigants' rights have been denied due to an insufficient understanding of English have been reported in the media

---

75 Nina Ponce, "Public Health Statistics for Asian and Pacific Islander Americans" (San Francisco, CA: Asian American Health Forum, April 1989).

76 *Healthy People 2000*, p. 602.

77 The need for professional, qualified court interpreters has been documented and well demonstrated. It has been reported that there are 43,000 annual requests in Federal court for interpreters in 60 languages. During 1988 the Cook County, IL, State court system

168

and by several State task forces established to study minorities and their experiences in the court systems.[78]

The following is an example of a situation where a Vietnamese immigrant who spoke very little English was forced to stand trial for a crime he had not been charged with and was unable to communicate with either his lawyer or the court because he did not have access to an interpreter:

In Florida in 1985, Nguyen Hen Van, a Vietnamese defendant, who had been charged with theft, was placed on trial for 2 days as the defendant in a murder trial because the jail staff simply brought the wrong man from the cell, and no one else in the court process noticed the error. Two testifying witnesses in the murder trial even identified Mr. Nguyen as the murderer. The actual murder defendant was Nguyen Ngoc Tieu, also Vietnamese, who was sitting in the county jail three blocks away. Even Mr. Tieu Nguyen's lawyer, who had interviewed him for an hour only 2 weeks before the trial did not realize that the wrong man was on trial, even when Mr. Hen Van Nguyen tried to protest saying, "Not me, not me."[79]

When interpreters are unavailable, linguistic minorities are often deterred from using the courts. Even when these people do use the courts, they are often misinformed, intimidated, demeaned, and sometimes denied important rights. Often when interpreters are not available, defendants rely on family members, court personnel, and even law enforcement officers to translate for them.[80] Such persons, although possibly fluent in the defendant's primary language, lack the necessary familiarity with legal terminology and guidelines for interpreting court proceedings.[81] Also, conflicts of interest may arise when a family member interprets for a defendant or other witness.[82]

Federal Regulation

Federal regulation of the availability and quality of court interpreters has been scarce. In 1970 the U.S. Court of Appeals for the Second Circuit upheld the decision of a district court to reverse a murder conviction because the lack of an interpreter for the defendant did not meet constitutional requirements of fairness.[83] The case was of critical importance in setting precedent because it held that since most of the trial

---

processed 40,000 requests for interpreters, and in the New York State courts, parties sought interpreters 250 times per day. ("Libertad and Justicia For All," *Time*, May 29, 1989.)

78   See, e.g., "Libertad and Justicia for All"; "Disorganized Interpreter System Hurts Asian-Americans, Panel Says," *Philadelphia Inquirer*, Nov. 1, 1989, p. 9-B; "Race and Blind Justice Mixup in Court," *New York Times*, Nov. 3, 1985; see also New York Judicial Commission on Minorities, *Report of the New York Judicial Commission on Minorities*, vol. 4 (1991) (hereafter cited as New York Report); New Jersey Supreme Court Task Force on Minority Concerns, *Interim Report* (1990); Washington State Minority and Justice Task Force, *Interim Report* (March 1989); Michigan Supreme Court Task Force on Racial/Ethnic Issues in the Courts, *Final Report* (December 1989).

79   "Mixup in Court"; "Wrong Vietnamese Defendant Undergoes 2 Days of Murder Trial," *Seattle Times*, Oct. 26, 1985. Near the end of the trial, someone in the courtroom did recognize Mr. Nguyen as the wrong defendant and a mistrial was declared.

80   Washington State Minority and Justice Task Force, *Interim Report*, 1989, p. 3 (hereafter cited as Washington State Report).

81   New Jersey Supreme Court Task Force on Interpreter and Translation Services, *Equal Access to the Courts for Linguistic Minorities* (May 22, 1985), pp. 102-03, and Washington State Report, pp. 2-3, as cited in New York Report, p. 217.

82   The American Bar Association's Model Rules of Professional Conduct require attorneys "to explain a matter to the extent reasonably necessary to permit the client to make informed decisions regarding the representation." (American Bar Association, "Model Rules of Professional Conduct," 1989, Rule 1.4, "Communication.") The accompanying comment is silent on whether this rule obliges attorneys to use interpreters when their clients are limited English proficient.

83   United States *ex rel* Negron v. State of New York, 434 F.2d 386 (1970). The court of appeals granted a writ of habeas corpus, the effect of which is to release the defendant from imprisonment without a determination of guilt or innocence.

must have been incomprehensible to the defendant, Mr. Negron,[84] his trial "lacked the basic and fundamental fairness required by the due process clause of the Fourteenth Amendment."[85] The court relied on two basic tenets of law to reach its decision. First, the sixth amendment of the United States Constitution[86] guarantees the right to be confronted with adverse witnesses[87] and includes the right to cross-examine those witnesses. These requirements are "essential and fundamental" to the achievement of a fair trial.[88] The defendant's confrontation rights were clearly violated when he could not understand the witnesses nor partake in his defense.[89] Second, "[c]onsiderations of fairness, the integrity of the fact-finding process, and the potency of our adversary system of justice forbid that the state should prosecute a defendant who is not present at his own trial, unless by his conduct he waives his right."[90] To give meaning to this requirement, the court reasoned that the defendant must possess "sufficient present ability to consult with his lawyer with a reasonable degree of rational understanding."[91] The court also rejected the argument that the defendant had waived his right to an interpreter, for it was clear that the defendant was not so aware of his rights that he should be made to assert them on his own, particularly when his language disability was plainly obvious.[92]

In 1978, just 8 years after the *Negron* case, Congress enacted the Court Interpreters Act.[93] The statute sets forth that the Director of the Administrative Office of United States Courts shall prescribe qualifications for court interpreters and shall institute a program that will certify qualified interpreters.[94] The Director is also required to maintain a list of all certified court interpreters and other qualified interpreters and to establish a reasonable schedule of fees. Under the statute, each district court is also directed to maintain a list of certified interpreters, which shall be made available upon request.[95] The presiding judge[96] has discretion to use an

---

84   *Id.* at 387. The court stated that the defendant, at the time of trial a 23-year-old indigent, with a sixth grade education in Puerto Rico, neither spoke nor understood any English. His court-appointed lawyer spoke no Spanish. Negron, the defendant, was unable to participate in his defense, except for "spotty instances when the proceedings were conducted in Spanish, or Negron's words were translated into English, or the English of the lawyer, the trial judge, and the witnesses against him were translated into Spanish." *Id.* at 388.

85   *Id.* at 389. The Bill of Rights was originally intended as a limitation of the power of the Federal Government. Subsequently, most of those guarantees have been incorporated into the 14th amendment, so that they now also serve as limitations on State governmental authority.

86   "In all criminal prosecutions, the accused shall enjoy the right to a speedy and public trial, by an impartial jury of the State and district wherein the crime shall have been committed, which district shall have been previously ascertained by law, and to be informed of the nature and cause of the accusation; to be confronted with the witnesses against him; to have compulsory process for obtaining witnesses in his favor, and to have the Assistance of Counsel for his defence." U.S. Const., amend. VI.

87   434 F.2d at 389. This also applies to the States through the 14th amendment. Pointer v. Texas, 380 U.S. 400 (1965).

88   434 F.2d at 389 (citing Pointer v. Texas, 380 U.S. 400, 405 (1965)).

89   *Id.*

90   *Id.* (citations omitted).

91   *Id.* (citing Dusky v. United States, 362 U.S. 402 (1962) (*per curiam*)).

92   *Id.* at 390.

93   28 U.S.C. §1827 (1988).

94   *Id.* at §1827(a)-(b).

95   *Id.* at §1827(c).

96   The statute uses the term "judicial officer" rather than judge to indicate applicability to "any judge of a United States district court including a bankruptcy judge, a United States magistrate, and in the case of grand jury proceedings conducted under the auspices of

interpreter's services in judicial proceedings initiated by the United States whether or not they are requested by any of the parties.[97] The judge is to make the decision based on whether the party or testifying witness in question speaks only or primarily a language other than English, "so as to inhibit the party's comprehension of the proceedings or communication with counsel or [the judge], or so as to inhibit the witness' comprehension of questions and the presentation of such testimony."[98]

There are two problems with the Federal statute, one regarding its implementation and the other resulting from one of its provisions. In terms of implementation, as of 1989 only 308 people had passed the rigorous certification standards,[99] and the certification program tests only in Spanish,[100] leaving the identification of Asian-language interpreters totally untouched. As a result, individual district courts turn to local commercial vendors to provide freelance interpreters for Asian languages. Since these freelance interpreters are necessarily uncertified due to the absence of a certification program for Asian languages, the statutory requirement of quality control remains unenforced.

The second failing of the statute may be its provision delegating responsibility to the trial judge. Recent challenges under the Court Interpreters Act illustrate that placing discretion with the judge has given appellate courts the freedom to strike the challenges of defendants who claim that they did not receive a fair trial, either because they were not given an interpreter or because the interpreter who was present was not of sufficient quality.[101] The two cases discussed below do not involve Asian Americans, but they clearly affect the prospect of legal protection under the Court Interpreters Act.

In *Hrubec v. United States*,[102] the U.S. District Court for the Eastern District of New York emphasized that the fact that the defendant's primary language is other than English does not create upon the judge a duty to inquire about the need for an interpreter.[103] The court held that for such a duty to arise, the defendant's language difficulties must, as stated in the statute, inhibit the party's comprehension of the proceedings or communication with counsel or the judge.[104]

In *Valladares v. United States*,[105] the U.S. Court of Appeals for the Eleventh Circuit also found that the trial court had not abused its discretion when it did not question the adequacy of the defendant's interpreter. The court reiterated that the use of an interpreter is committed "to the sound discretion of the trial judge,"[106] stressing that the decision hinges on a number of factors to be balanced by the judge, including "the defendant's knowledge of English and the complexity of the proceedings and testimony. . .and the economical administration of criminal

---

the United States attorney, a United States attorney." *Id.* at §1827(i).

97   28 U.S.C. §1827(d) (1988).

98   *Id.* at §1827(d)(1).

99   "Libertad and Justicia for All."

100   Ibid.

101   *See* Valladares v. U.S., 871 F.2d 1564 (11th Cir. 1989); Hrubec v. U.S., 734 F. Supp. 60 (E.D.N.Y. 1990).

102   *Id.*

103   *Id.* at 67.

104   *Id.* In the *Hrubec* case, the court relied on the magistrate's finding that the defendant had a sufficient command of the English language to understand proceedings and consult with counsel. The court stated that there was no indication that he needed an interpreter and for this reason, found no constitutional or statutory violation. *Id.*

105   871 F.2d 1564.

106   *Id.* at 1566.

law."[107] This reasoning seems to contradict the *Negron* mandate, which was codified by the Court Interpreters Act.[108] *Negron* would seem to imply that the right to confrontation and the fundamental fairness of a trial are constitutional matters that cannot be diluted merely because of the simplicity of the proceedings. If a party does not have the fluency to understand his trial fully, no matter how simple the trial, the judge should use the services of an interpreter, pursuant to the Court Interpreters Act. Similarly, economic administration should not be balanced against a fundamental right such as the right to be meaningfully present at one's own trial.[109]

State Regulation

Because the Court Interpreters Act applies only in Federal court, it is up to the individual States to implement requirements regarding the use of interpreters in the State courts. A number of States have recognized the need for court interpreters and, through specially assigned task forces, have recommended comprehensive plans to rectify the problem. However, these plans are just being initiated and will probably take years to enact and implement. For example, in New York, interpreters are provided for by statute, but like the Federal statute, discretion is left to the local court administrators.[110] Each city is permitted to appoint one interpreter, to be selected jointly by the city judge and the district attorney. The statute also permits the temporary appointment of interpreters. Nevertheless, few interpreters are available. Many witnesses who testified before the New York State Judicial Commission on Minorities (hereafter referred to as the New York Commission) described a number of inadequacies of the existing system, including the specific need for Asian-language interpreters.[111] In particular, a witness in Albany "attested to the need for certain Asian language interpreters in the state's capital."[112] Spanish is the only language for which there are full-time interpreters.[113] Here again, the interpretation needs of Asian Americans are totally unserved.

A New Jersey task force concluded that linguistic minorities feel that they are foreclosed from the court system due to a "lack of interpreter skills, including familiarity with legal terminology; the absence of translated forms and documents; the lack of defined qualification for interpreters; and the absence of guidelines for interpreting court proceedings."[114] A Washington State study came to the same conclusions and recommended that interpreter qualifications should be prescribed by the highest court and that the legislature should establish a State

---

107   *Id.* (citing United States v. Coronel-Quitane, 752 F.2d 1284, 1291 (8th Cir. 1985)).

108   28 U.S.C. §1827 (1988).

109   *See* United States *ex rel* Negron v. New York, 434 F.2d 386, 389 (2d Cir. 1970) ("[I]t is equally imperative that every criminal defendant—if the right to be present is to have meaning—possess 'sufficient present ability to consult with his lawyer with a reasonable degree of rational understanding.'").

110   New York Report, pp. 204-05, citing N.Y. Jud. Law §§386-87 (McKinney 1988).

111   *Id.* at 205.

112   *Id.* (citing *Albany Hearings*, at 35-51 (testimony of Walter Kiang)).

113   *Id.* at 205.

114   New Jersey Supreme Court Task Force on Interpreter and Translation Services, *Equal Access to the Courts for Linguistic Minorities* (May 22, 1985), pp. 102-03, as cited in New York Report, p. 217, nn. 49-50.

Board of Court Interpreting and Legal Translating to ensure a uniform certification process.[115]

Other Barriers

Asian Americans' equal access to justice is further impeded by cultural barriers and negative experiences in the courts.[116] For example, certain cultural barriers, in addition to language barriers, may discourage minorities from using the courts. The New York Commission states that "largely due to the influence of Buddhist, Taoist, or Confucian doctrines, 'in Asian society the use of law as a method for settling disputes is regarded as something to be avoided.' Thus, there is a preference among some first-generation Chinese-Americans, for example, to settle legal disputes through informal mediation and community groups."[117]

The experiences of minorities in courts today are generally regarded as quite negative. Minorities are often uninformed about courtroom procedures, such as where one should go to appear for a hearing. Additionally, because most court personnel, including judges, court officers, stenographers, law assistants, district attorneys and their staffs, as well as private counsel, are white,[118] minority litigants have the perception that the environment is unfriendly, and sometimes hostile, to them.[119] Asian Americans are no exception, and a generally negative encounter or an expectation thereof would discourage Asian Americans from assertive use of the judicial system. Asian Americans, along with other minorities, are sometimes the victims of racial stereotyping, as testified by one Asian American witness to the New York Commission:

[T]here is. . .a real insensitivity to all minorities. . .be it Asian or other, because when you have an Asian defendant. . .[judges] assume that they're part of a gang; and that kind of guilty-until-proven-innocent applies to Asian defendants who are charged with robbery or whatever because the media or everyone else assumes they're part of a gang.[120]

One litigator told the New York Commission that he had heard judges say to Asian litigants that they "do not have a Chinaman's chance."[121]

Representation of Asian Americans in the Legal Profession

Overall minority representation in the legal profession has remained small and, according to the report of the New York State Judicial Commission on Minorities, "lags far behind the representation of minorities in the general population."[122] According to the 1980 U.S. Census, minorities were 20.3 percent of the population, but only 5.5 percent of the 501,834 lawyers in the United States. Representation of Asian

---

115   State of Washington, Office of the Administrator for the Courts, *Initial Report and Recommendations of the Court Interpreter Task Force* (1986), pp. 15-18, as cited in New York Report, pp. 217-18.

116   Asian Americans have encountered discriminatory treatment in American courts since the 1850s. *See, e.g.,* People v. Hall, 4 Cal. 309 (1854); Terrace v. Thompson, 263 U.S. 197 (1923). As noted in chap. 1, courts restricted and often completely denied Asians' rights of land ownership, earning a living in the trade of one's choice, and alienation and inheritability of land. Many decisions revealing the courts' suspicion of and animosity toward Asian Americans were passed down, even from the Supreme Court through the 1940s, when the Court upheld the decision to detain Japanese Americans in internment camps during World War II. *See* Korematsu v. United States, 323 U.S. 214 (1944). The wartime internment of Japanese Americans is discussed in chap. 1.

117   Kahng, "Asian Americans and Litigation," *Equal Opportunity Forum*, vol. 2 (March 1977), as cited in New York Report, p. 96.

118   New York Report, p. 45.

119   Ibid., p. 45.

120   Ibid, p. 55, n. 167.

121   Ibid., p. 58.

122   Ibid., p. 23.

Americans is even more sparse: Asian Americans were only 0.7 percent of the lawyers nationwide, although they constituted 2.9 percent of the U.S. population.[123] Figures in New York State yield the same percentage; while the statewide total number of lawyers is 62,032, only 433 are Asian American (0.7 percent).[124]

In New York, representation of Asian American lawyers in law firms has increased to the point where it now exceeds the representation of Asian Americans in the total attorney population;[125] however, a 1989 survey of 49 New York law firms reflects that Asian Americans still represent only 2.1 percent of firm lawyers.[126] Of these lawyers, only 0.8 percent or 31 Asian Americans were partners.[127]

With regard to attorneys' experiences in law firms and other legal organizations, the New York Commission's report reflects that Asian Americans, like most minorities, have felt some degree of difficulty or animosity within the profession. In New York City, 17.4 percent of Asian American litigators agreed with the statement that "minority lawyers have fewer opportunities to participate in continuing education or training opportunities," while no white litigators agreed with the statement.[128] Large percentages of Asian Americans also agreed that minority lawyers have fewer opportunities for advancement or choice assignments, and are less likely than white lawyers to make partner.[129]

The Plight of Battered Asian American Women

This section examines the plight of Asian American women who are battered by their husbands and discusses barriers to their access to social services, police protection, and the judicial system. Finally, it addresses the ill effects of the Immigration Marriage Fraud Amendments on battered Asian American immigrant women.

Access to Social Services

According to shelter providers for battered women and advocates for Asian American women's rights,[130] the problem of battered women is neither properly recognized nor well understood by law enforcement agencies, funding agencies, and the general public. Shelters and agencies serving Asian American battered women are few to begin with, and the ones serv-

---

123   U.S. Bureau of the Census, *1980 Census of the Population, Detailed Occupation and Years of School Completed by Age, for Civilian Labor Force by Sex, Race and Spanish Origin: 1980* (Supplementary Report PC89-S1-8), p. 6, as cited in New York Report, p. 23.

124   New York Report, p. 25 (citing 1980 Census of Population, Equal Employment Opportunity Profile, prepared by the New York State Data Center) (on file with the New York Commission). Other minorities are also underrepresented in New York's legal profession: minorities represented 25 percent of the New York State's population, yet 96 percent of the state's lawyers were white. Ibid., p. 23. In New York County, where the minority population is 51 percent, the minority lawyer population is only 6 percent, with Asian Americans at only 1.1 percent (195 attorneys). Ibid.

125   New York Report, p. 27.

126   Ibid, citing Jensen, "Minorities Didn't Share in Firm Growth," *National Law Journal*, Feb. 19, 1990, p. 1.

127   Ibid.

128   Ibid., p. 44. Thirty-one percent of black litigators and 25 percent of Hispanic litigators agreed with the statement.

129   58.2 and 59.45 percent, respectively. Ibid. Agreement of Asian American lawyers responding to the survey was generally lower than agreement among black and Hispanic lawyers; however, Asian American agreement is still significantly higher than that of white attorneys responding to the survey.

130   Madge Kho, Equal Rights Advocates, interview, Feb. 22, 1990, Oakland, CA (hereafter cited as Kho interview); Patricia Eng, New York Asian Women's Center, "Problems Faced by Battered Asian Women," Statement at the U.S. Commission on Civil Rights, Roundtable Conference on Asian American Civil Rights Issues, New York, NY, June 23, 1989 (hereafter cited as Eng Statement); Nolda Rimonte, Los Angeles Center for Pacific Asian Family, telephone interview, Dec. 14, 1989 (hereafter cited as Rimonte interview); Debbie Lee, Family Violence Project of San Francisco, telephone interview, June 15, 1990 (hereafter cited as Lee interview).

ing Asian American women with limited English proficiency (LEP) are fewer. Some battered women's shelters do not accept women who do not speak English.[131] Advocates contend that in some cases shelters require LEP women to pay exorbitant per diem rates.[132] Furthermore, the shelters serving Asian American women are disproportionately underfunded. As a result, many battered Asian American women are discouraged from using existing shelters, and those who do do not always receive adequate services.

Several factors appear to contribute to the underserving of battered Asian American women. The first factor is that incidents of spouse battering are not routinely recorded and tabulated by race/ethnicity, which makes it nearly impossible either to assess the relative frequency of incidents by race/ethnicity or to monitor trends over time. Lack of supporting statistics in turn makes it difficult to justify establishing new shelters or requesting additional funds.[133] Established shelters on the West Coast and in New York serve a large number of clients, however: the New York Asian Women's Shelter, which operates a multilingual hotline, received more than 2,000 calls and helped about 250 battered women in 1990.[134]

A second contributing factor is the widely acknowledged problem of underreporting. The sources contacted for this report all agreed that incidents of wife battering are underreported and that the phenomenon is far more prevalent than is publicly known.[135] These sources cited several reasons for underreporting by battered Asian American women. Many Asian Americans consider marital problems highly private matters that ought to remain within families. Therefore, for an Asian American woman, particularly an LEP immigrant, to confront the issue of domestic violence and bring it into the public arena is "often synonymous with condemning herself to isolation and ostracization."[136] The dominant cultural norm for many Asian American women is to accept their fate.[137] Additional reasons cited for why Asian American women are particularly unlikely to report spouse abuse are: 1) the behavioral norm for most Asian American women does not include divorce as a viable option, although divorce is becoming more common and gaining legitimacy; and 2) LEP Asian American women are not adequately informed about the means of recourse they have against spouse battering, services they may expect from shelters and public service agencies, and the possible benefits of reporting incidents to proper authorities.

The third factor has to do with fund allocation formulas that do not take into account the higher cost of servicing LEP Asian American clients. According to providers catering to Asian American clients, the per-client service cost is considerably higher for LEP clients than for English-speaking clients because it is frequently necessary to provide interpreters and to spend

131   Eng Statement, p. 5.

132   Ibid., p. 6.

133   Rimonte interview.

134   Marvine Howe, "Battered Alien Spouses Find a Way To Escape an Immigration Trap," *New York Times*, Aug. 25, 1991.

135   Eng Statement, Rimonte interview, Lee interview. Pertinent statistics are hard to come by, but there is one study that shows the prevalence of wife battering among Asian Americans. The statistics compiled by the Center for Asian American Family in Los Angeles, CA, reveal that of the 1,429 cases reported to the center in 1982, one-third involved Southeast Asian families. L. Smith, "Viet Women In a New World," *Los Angeles Times*, May 30, 1983 (cited in J. Chu, "Southeast Asian Women: In Transition," in *In America and In Need: Immigrant, Refugee, and Entrant Women*, ed. Abby Spero (Washington, DC: American Association of Community and Junior Colleges, 1985), p. 44).

136   Eng Statement, p. 3.

137   Chu, "Southeast Asian Women," p. 44; Rimonte interview.

time explaining procedures and other basics. Yet, the formulas most commonly used in fund allocation are dividing available funds equally among service providers or distributing funds based on the number of clients served.[138] Until funding agencies take into consideration different per-client costs, there will be an economic disincentive to serving LEP Asian American women. Service providers will be forced either to sacrifice the quality of service to LEP Asian American clients or to refuse to serve them.

Access to Police Protection and the Judicial System

Many battered Asian American women, according to shelter operators who work with them,[139] believe that it is futile and even harmful to involve law enforcement officials in domestic violence cases. One reason for this feeling is that police departments oftentimes fail to carry out a thorough investigation of the situation by talking to both the husband and the wife. As noted in chapter 3, it is rare for the police to bring bilingual police officers or interpreters to the scene. Thus, when visiting the site of reported domestic violence, the police often talk only to the person who speaks English. This English-speaking person is usually the husband, who often succeeds in minimizing the seriousness of the situation.

A second reason is that battered women are vulnerable and feel totally unprotected by the police against retaliation from their abusers. Many battered women are convinced that reporting abuse to the police will only serve to further anger the abuser and encourage him to inflict even more abuse when the police leave. Furthermore, even if the abuser is arrested, they feel certain of having to face the consequences when he is released.[140]

Battered Asian American women consider the judicial system equally ineffective and frustrating. Court orders for the abuser to stay away from the victim are rarely enforced. They are viewed as hardly "worth the paper they are written on. . . .There are numerous stories of women clutching these orders as they are beaten or even murdered."[141]

Furthermore, obtaining orders of protection is often a long and complicated process. In New York City, for instance, an entire day must be spent in court, and even then the order is not always granted.[142] For those battered women who are limited in their English proficiency, unfamiliar with court procedures, and compelled to work every day out of financial necessity, it is almost unthinkable to go to the courthouse and spend an entire day trying to obtain an order of protection.

Vacate or exclusionary orders, which require the batterer to vacate the place of residence, could allow battered women to remain in their homes and prevent displacement or homelessness for those battered women who have no place to go. However, vacate orders are rarely issued. Judges are said to be "reluctant to order a man out of his castle and they certainly are even more reluctant to do so for Asian males."[143] It is considered virtually impossible for battered Asian American women to obtain orders of exclusion.[144]

The 1989 sentencing in New York of an immigrant Chinese man to 5 years on probation for the slaying of his wife[145] sent a disheartening signal to battered Asian American women.

---

138 Rimonte interview.

139 Eng Statement; Rimonte interview; Lee interview.

140 Eng Statement, p. 6.

141 Eng Statement, p. 7.

142 Ibid.

143 Ibid.

144 Ibid., p. 8.

This case[146] involved a Chinese man, Dong Lu Chen, 50, who immigrated from China to New York in 1986 with his wife, 30, and three children. He worked as a dishwasher in Maryland until he moved to New York 2 months prior to the incident to join his wife, who was working part time in a garment factory in New York. On September 7, 1987, he bludgeoned his 99-pound wife to death by striking her eight times with a hammer after she confessed to having an affair. At the bench trial, the defense expert witness argued that Mr. Chen was under extreme emotional stress aggravated by his isolation from family and community: in China, marriages are sacred, and husbands are expected to become extremely angry on hearing of their wives' infidelity. Ordinarily, however, friends and family exert a moderating influence on husbands, and violence is avoided. Isolated from friends and community in the new setting, the defense argued, Mr. Chen had no one to keep him from translating his anger into violence. Noting that "[The] court cannot ignore the very cogent powerful testimony [of the expert witness]" and that "Chen took all his Chinese culture with him to the United States except the community which would moderate his behavior,"[147] the judge acquitted Chen of second-degree murder charges and instead convicted him of second-degree manslaughter.

A spokesperson of a battered women shelter on the East Coast testified that "the message. . .inherent in this sentencing is that the criminal justice system will not protect Asian American women [against spousal abuse], and this message is received loudly and clearly in the Asian American community."[148] After the sentencing, many clients at the shelter showed their outrage and said they would not consider going through the court system because it would not protect them at all. This spokesperson noted that even under the guise of respecting cultural background, justice should not be administered under a double standard.[149]

Efforts are being made in some areas of the country to increase battered Asian American women's information about and decrease their distrust of the judicial process. For instance, the city of Los Angeles, along with nonprofit agencies and other groups serving the Asian American community in Los Angeles, began raising money in the spring of 1990 to produce a videotape in Korean showing a woman going through the entire process of seeking protection from her abusive husband. The goals of the project are to "educate victims about why prosecution of domestic violence is often necessary; help prepare victims who are called to testify; [and] explain the potential benefits of counseling programs for batterers, victims and children."[150]

Immigration Marriage Fraud Amendments

In 1986 Congress enacted the Immigration Marriage Fraud Amendments (IMFA),[151] amending the Immigration and Nationality Act

145 Shaun Assael, "Judge Defends Sentencing Wife-Killer to Probation: Pincus Accepts Immigrant's Novel Defense," *Manhattan Lawyer*, Apr. 4, 1989, pp. 4, 17.

146 Accounts of this case are drawn from Shaun Assael, "Wife-Killer May Get Probation," *Manhattan Lawyer*, Mar. 14, 1989, pp. 1, 11, and Assael, "Judge Defends Sentencing."

147 Assael, "Probation," p. 11.

148 Eng Statement, p. 8.

149 Ibid, p. 9.

150 Domestic Violence Video Project brochure obtained at a reception to publicize and raise money for the video held at the KSCI-TV Studios in West Los Angeles, CA, Feb. 28, 1990.

151 Immigration Marriage Fraud Amendments of 1986, Pub. L. No. 99-639, 100 Stat. 3537 (1986) (codified at 8 U.S.C. §1186a). Implementing regulations for these amendments were published as Marriage Fraud Amendments Regulations, 53 Fed. Reg. 3011

of 1982[152] to cope with the allegedly large and growing number of immigrants who were using marriage to U.S. citizens as a ploy to obtain permanent residency.[153]

Under the 1986 amendments, foreign spouses of U.S. citizens who enter the United States are granted 2-year "conditional" residency,[154] instead of permanent residency as they would have been previously. To remove the conditional status and obtain permanent residency, the couple must file a written petition, Form I-751, with the Immigration and Naturalization Service (INS) and appear for a personal interview with an INS official within 90 days of the expiration of the 2-year period.[155] The written petition must be accompanied by evidence that

---

(1988) (codified at 8 C.F.R. §§1,204.205, 211-12, 214, 216, 223, 233a, 235, 242, 245).

152   8 U.S.C. §1101-1557 (1982).

153   In supporting this legislation, the U.S. Department of Justice, the parent agency of the Immigration and Naturalization Service (INS), noted that: "present protections against marriage fraud are totally inadequate. Once permanent status has been granted, it is almost impossible to revoke, rescind, deport, or even locate the alien or the original spouse. By postponing the privilege of permanent resident status until two years after the alien's obtaining the status of lawful admission for permanent residence, the bill provides a balanced approach. . . .[I]t strikes at the fraudulent marriage by the simple passage of time: it is difficult to sustain the appearance of a *bona fide* marriage over a long period. . . .it still. . .provides for family unification." John H. Bolton, Assistant Attorney General, U.S. Department of Justice, letter to Rep. Peter W. Rodino, Jr., Chairman, Committee on the Judiciary, House of Representatives, July 31, 1986, reprinted in *U.S. Code Congressional and Administrative News* (1986) no. 6, p. 5980.

Similar reasoning is also found in the legislative history of the amendments: "[A]liens who either cannot otherwise qualify for immigration to the United States or who, though qualified, are not willing to wait until an immigrant visa becomes available, frequently find it expedient to engage in a faudulent marriage in order to side-step the immigration law. . . .[A]pproximately 30% of all petitions for immigrants visas involve suspect marital relationships. . .the bill perpetually bars from immigrating to the United States any alien who has conspired to engage in a fraudulent marriage or who has attempted to obtain an immigration benefit on the basis of such marriage." H.R. Report No. 906, 99th Cong., 2nd Sess. 6, reprinted in 1986 *U.S. Code Congressional and Administrative News* (1986), no. 6, p. 5978.

Alan C. Nelson, then-Commissioner of the Immigration and Naturalization Service, testified before Congress in July 1985 that up to 30 percent of marriages between aliens and U.S. citizens were suspected of fraud. More recently, however, David Nachtsheim, Special Assistant to Clarence Coster, INS Associate Commissioner for Enforcement, stated that the 1984 survey that served as the basis for fraud claims by then-INS Commissioner Nelson was flawed and that it was not appropriate to use the survey for recommending legislative reform concerning marriage fraud. He also noted that he and others at the INS knew the survey was flawed before Nelson's congressional testimony and that the then-INS Deputy Assistant Commissioner for Investigations had received a recommendation that "The estimation of fraudulent cases. . .should be avoided." *Interpreter Releases*, vol. 66 (Sept. 11, 1989), pp. 1011-12.

One advocacy group claims that "prior to the passage of the law, the INS launched a xenophobic media campaign focusing on the plight of U.S. citizen women who were duped into marriage by foreign men only looking for a quick way to a green card and later were abused and deserted by them. No media attention was given to the plight of battered immigrant women." Coalition for Immigrant and Refugee Rights and Services, Immigrant Women's Task Force, memorandum to National Lawyers' Guild, National Lawyers Project, June 12, 1989, p. 2 (hereafter cited as "Immigrant Women's Task Force Memorandum").

One researcher points out that the estimate of the number of fraudulent cases was questioned during the congressional hearing, alerting Congress to the possible unreliability of the estimated figure. However, Congress was also made aware of the problem of fraudulent marriages by the INS's discovery of marriage fraud rings around the country and national media attention (e.g., ABC's "Nightline: Marriage Fraud," Aug. 26, 1985, and CBS's "60 Minutes: Do You Take This Alien?" Sept. 22, 1985). Vonnell C. Tingle, "Immigration Marriage Fraud Amendments of 1986: Locking In by Locking Out?" *Journal of Family Law*, vol. 733, no. 3 (1988-1989), p. 735.

154   8 U.S.C. § 1186a(a)(1).

155   8 C.F.R. § 216.4.

the marriage was entered into in good faith and "not for the purpose of evading the immigration laws of the United States"[156] and that the marriage has not been terminated other than through the citizen spouse's death. Failure to file the petition[157] or appear for the interview would result in the revocation of the alien spouse's conditional status and the initiation of deportation proceedings.[158]

Critics contend that this requirement subjects immigrant spouses, a significant number of whom are women from Asian countries, to exploitation and abuse, since it effectively forces abused, battered foreign-born spouses to become helpless hostages for 2 years, even when their marriages are not working out right. It is said that batterers, usually the U.S. citizen husbands, have often refused to petition for the wife or have threatened to withdraw the petition once it has been filed or to call the INS and report that the marriage was a sham. Being dependent upon her citizen spouse to petition, a battered woman or a victim of a destructive marriage is forced to stay in an abusive or life-threatening situation, since to do otherwise is to risk the danger of deportation and separation from her children.[159]

Furthermore, critics point out that although the IMFA provides for "extreme hardship" and "good faith/good cause" waivers[160] of the joint petition requirement, many battered condi-tional-resident spouses are limited in their English proficiency and are unaware of this waiver option. Not infrequently abusers and their relatives withhold information on waivers from the battered spouses. Being new to the United States, most of the abused, battered spouses are not well informed of resources and means of recourse, such as shelters, social service agencies, and legal services, available to them.[161] In addition, the statutory language on the standards of extreme hardship and good cause termination of a marriage is not specific. Indeed, a congressional inquiry[162] was prompted because of this ambiguity.

According to an article appearing in the *Wall Street Journal*, "The problem seems to affect Asian women more than other immigrants."[163] This article gave two examples of Chinese women who had been forced to stay with their abusive husbands for fear of being deported:

A 30-year old Chinese woman in San Francisco says she finally left her husband after months of abuse. Repeated beatings and her husband's disregard for her infant son's health finally drove her to leave their home. "He bring the spray for ants," she says, recalling an incident when she hadn't cleaned the bathroom. "He spray my face."[164]

[A] Chinese woman's husband had abused her for almost two years and repeatedly threatened not to sign

---

156   8 C.F.R. § 216.4(a)(5).

157   8 C.F.R. § 216.4(a)(6).

158   The act provides for two types of waivers of the petition requirement, commonly referred to as "extreme hardship" and "good faith/good cause" waivers. The Attorney General may remove the conditional basis of the permanent resident status if an alien spouse demonstrates that: "i) extreme hardship would result if the alien is deported; or ii) the qualifying marriage was entered into in good faith, but was terminated by the alien spouse for good cause." 8 U.S.C. §1186a(c)(4) and 8 C.F.R. §216.5(a).

159   Kho interview; Immigrant Women's Task Force Memorandum; Eng Statement; Rimonte interview; Lee interview.

160   See n. 158.

161   Eng Statement, pp. 2-4; Kho interview; Rimonte interview.

162   A letter of inquiry signed by Sen. Mark O. Hatfield (R-OR) and Rep. Louise M. Slaughter (D-NY) was sent to the INS on Sept. 14, 1989, to which Bonnie Derwinski, Acting Director for Congressional and Public Affairs, INS, responded on Sept. 19, 1989.

163   Cecile Sorra, "Americans' Immigrant Spouses Seeking U.S. Status Can Be Trapped in Marriage," *Wall Street Journal*, Aug. 28, 1989.

164   Ibid.

sign the petition. Pregnant with her second child, she delayed filing for divorce for fear of losing custody of the children.[165]

On June 7, 1989, Congresswoman Louise M. Slaughter (D-NY) introduced a bill, H.R. 2580, granting permanent residency to foreign spouses victimized by their spouses. H.R. 2580 was later incorporated into a larger bill, H.R. 4300, "Family Unity and Employment Opportunity Immigration Act of 1990," which was finally approved by Congress as part of the Immigration Act of 1990.[166] The story of one woman who was helped by this law may be typical.

Raco M. came to the United States 3 years ago from a small village in south China to marry her Chinese American husband. Three months after she arrived, her husband began to hit her in the face. When she refused to have a child right away, the beatings increased. Her husband threatened not to sponsor her for permanent residency if she did not carry her baby to term, but continued to batter her even after she agreed to have the baby. Finally, afraid for her baby, she ran away, was directed by the police to the New York Asian Women's Center, where she was provided with a safe house. Because of the changes in the law, she has received her green card, and she is now commencing divorce proceedings.[167]

Asian Americans and the Media

The mainstream media are the primary source of information for most Americans, and they consequently have a powerful influence on the American public's perceptions, attitudes, and opinions. Television alone reaches 98 percent of all American homes. The average family watches television for 6 hours and 55 minutes each day, according to Nielsen Media Research statistics.[168] Not only are television and other forms of media the American public's prime source of information, but they also are a major vehicle for transmitting the norms, beliefs, and values of our culture. As such, the media play a dominant role in shaping the general public's perceptions and attitudes about members of different races and ethnic groups.

Since the Asian American population is relatively small and concentrated in a few geographic areas, many Americans may not frequently come into contact with Asian Americans in their daily lives. The media, therefore, may exert a particularly important influence on the development of the general public's views of Asian Americans. Insensitive or unidimensional portrayals of Asian Americans by the media might foster prejudice and promote anti-Asian bias, whereas balanced coverage might dispel long-standing myths and prejudices and build understanding for Asian Americans.

The employment of Asian Americans in the media, especially in influential positions, is likely to have a significant impact on how Asian Americans are covered and on how the general public comes to view them. Asian Americans working in the media may be essential for eliminating superficial and sporadic coverage and arriving at portrayals that promote understanding of Asian Americans. Furthermore, underrepresentation of Asian Americans in the media work force, and in decision-making positions in particular, may have resulted from dis-

---

165 Ibid.

166 Pub. L. No. 101-649. §701(a)(4) of the final bill provides that permanent residency will be granted when: "the qualifying marriage was entered into in good faith by the alien spouse and during the marriage the alien spouse or child was battered by or was the subject of extreme cruelty perpetrated by his or her spouse or citizen or permanent resident parent...."

167 Howe, "Battered Alien Spouses Find a Way to Escape."

168 "A Short Course in Broadcasting," *The Broadcasting Yearbook 1991* (Washington, D.C.: Broadcasting Publications, Inc., 1991), p. A-3.

criminatory barriers restricting the employment and advancement of Asian Americans in the media. For these reasons, this section discusses first the portrayal and then the representation of Asian Americans in the mainstream media.

The Portrayal of Asian Americans by the Media—Stereotypes and Invisibility

Over the years, the portrayal of Asians in the American news and entertainment media has been largely dominated by foreign affairs. Until the early 1970s, the mainstream media in the United States depicted Asians largely as citizens of Asian nations, and often in connection with wars (e.g., World War II, Korean War, Vietnam War). As the economies of Japan, Korea, and other Asian countries have become increasingly competitive with the United States economy, the media have begun to cover Asians as citizens of our economic competitors. For the most part, therefore, the Asians portrayed in film, on television, and in the news media are foreign Asians, and they often have been portrayed in a negative light.[169]

The distinctions between citizens of Asian nations and citizens or intending citizens of the United States who happen to be of Asian ancestry has remained largely unarticulated by the media. Therefore, many in the public do not differentiate between Asians who are citizens and residents of countries in Asia and Asian Americans who are citizens or intending citizens of the United States, and media stereotypes of foreign Asians have come to affect the general public's views of Asian Americans as well. These blurred distinctions are in part attributable to the media's inadequate coverage of Asian Americans: in contrast to the extensive media coverage of foreign Asians, Asian Americans have been largely invisible in the media.[170] For example, a recent study found that only three Asian Americans appeared regularly on the spring 1989 prime time television lineup.[171] Similarly, Asian Americans are seldom the focus of news media coverage. When the news media do portray Asian Americans, they often treat them in a superficial, stereotypical fashion. For instance, a common focus of the stories about Asian Americans is the success of some immigrants and refugees who arrived in the United States with nothing, overcame all barriers, and achieved high levels of education and income. At the same time, the news media almost never cover other aspects of Asian American communities,

169 The film character, Dr. Fu Manchu, a cruel, violent, diabolical villain, and early films based on the Chinese warlord period (e.g., *Bitter Tea of General Yen* (1933), *Oil for the Lamps of China* (1935), and *The General Died at Dawn* (1936)), are historical examples of negative portrayals of Asians. More recent examples are the portrayal of the Vietnamese in *The Deer Hunter* (1978) and *Apocalypse Now* (1979).

170 Textbooks also may pay too little attention to the history and culture of Asian Americans and other minorities. (California State Board of Education, *History-Social Science Framework For California Public Schools: Kindergarten Through Grade Twelve* (July 1989), pp. 20-21.) A 1990 survey of graduating seniors in San Francisco public schools showed that many of the students felt that their textbooks failed to "give them accurate depictions of any ethnic groups but whites." As a result, minority students, including Asian American students, leave school with meager knowledge of not only other cultures but of their own as well. (Raul Ramirez, "Ethnic Students Often Treated as Foreigners," *San Francisco Examiner*, May 7, 1990, p. A-9, and K. Connie Kang and Dexter Waugh, "Minority Students Feel Like Outsiders Who Were Robbed of Their Past," *San Francisco Examiner*, May 6, 1990, p. A-1.)

171 Sally Steenland, *Unequal Picture: Black, Hispanic, Asian, and Native American Characters on Television* (Washington, DC: National Commission on Working Women of Wider Opportunities for Women, August 1989), pp. 21, 31-33. Ioki, an Asian American officer in a racially diverse undercover unit on "21 Jump Street"; Chao-Li, a butler on "Falcon Crest"; and Billy, a radio producer on "Midnight Caller," were all supporting roles. Asian characters appearing in two Vietnam war series, "Tour of Duty" and "China Beach," were usually found in the background of the scenes or did not have continuing roles. "Murphy's Law" featured an Asian American female lead, but was canceled in the spring and relied heavily on ethnic stereotyping. Ibid.

such as poverty or the problems of limited-English-proficient youngsters. Thus, the news media have played a role in disseminating the "model minority" stereotype of Asian Americans.

Asian American Representation in the Media Work Force

In 1968 the Kerner Commission, appointed by President Johnson in response to growing racial unrest in the late 1960s, concluded that a mass medium controlled by whites could not portray minorities accurately and that a white-dominated mass medium would ultimately fail to serve minority audiences.[172] Almost 25 years later, Asian Americans and other minorities continue to be underrepresented in the media work force (i.e., television, film, and print media), particularly at the management level.

With respect to minority representation in television, a 1977 study by the U.S. Commission on Civil Rights found that:

(1) white males held most of the decision-making positions in the television industry, while women and minorities held subsidiary positions;

(2) television executives often assumed that a realistic portrayal of women and minorities on television would diminish the medium's ability to attract the largest possible audience.[173]

More recent data suggest that minorities are still not in a position to influence program content. Of the 162 producers working on 1989 spring season prime time programs, only 12 producers (7 percent) were minorities. Of those 12 minority producers, only 2 were Asian American.[174] One observer wrote:

On television today, the portrayals of people of color, and whites too, are created almost solely by white producers and writers. In such a scheme, all viewers lose. White viewers lose because they rarely see their reflection from someone else's eyes. In addition, they are absorbing images of others which lack dimension and authenticity. Black, Hispanic, Asian and Native American viewers suffer because the complexity and reality of their lives are distorted into something that is unrecognizable.[175]

As for film, although several talented Asian American actors began to make a visible impact on the Hollywood screen in the 1980s,[176] over the years only a handful of Asian American performers[177] have been recognized as having Hollywood "star" status, most Asian American actors have been cast in minor roles. The absence of Asian American film stars was not only due to a dearth of Asian roles: even Asian roles were often not given to Asian American actors.[178] Historically, an overwhelming majority of leading Asian roles in films were played by white actors.[179]

---

172 U.S. Commission on Civil Rights, *Window Dressing on the Set: Women and Minorities in Television* (Washington, D.C.: U.S. Government Printing Office, 1977), p. 2.

173 Ibid., p. 148.

174 Steenland, *Unequal Picture*, p. 37.

175 Ibid., p. 43.

176 They are: Pat Morita playing "Miyagi" in *Karate Kid*; John Lone appearing in *Iceman*, *Year of the Dragon*, and *The Last Emperor*; and Joan Chen starring in *Taipan*, *The Last Emperor*, and *The Salute of the Jugger*.

177 E.g., Anna May Wong, Sessue Hayakawa, and James Shigeta.

178 Furthermore, Asian actors have not customarily been given the opportunity to play non-Asian roles.

179 Three of the most well-known Asian characters were portrayed in "yellowface," by white actors: after Charlie Chan became a major box-office draw, the part was always played by white stars, while Chan's bumbling sons were usually played by Asian American actors; and Dr. Fu Manchu and Mr. Moto, a Japanese version of Charlie Chan, were also played by white actors. (Patti Iiyama and Harry H.L. Kitano, "Asian Americans and the Media," in Gordon L. Berry and Claudia Mitchell-Kernan, eds., *Television and*

A similar pattern prevails on Broadway, as demonstrated by the recent controversy concerning the casting of a white actor, Jonathan Pryce, as the Eurasian engineer in the New York version of the London hit musical, *Miss Saigon*.[180] Advocacy groups such as Association of Asian American Artists (AAPAA) and Asian Pacific Alliance for Creative Equality (APACE) have argued that it exacerbated the problem of limited opportunities for Asian American actors and prevented the engineer character from being portrayed more sensitively.[181]

As for the news media, although they have acknowledged that minority readership is vital to the growth of their businesses and have made a concerted effort to diversify their newsrooms,[182] a study by the American Newspaper Publishers Association released in 1990 indicated that news/editorial departments had the lowest minority representation (10 percent) in the news media, and that there had been no improvement in minority representation in these departments over the previous 2 years.[183] Inside the newspaper business, Asian Americans accounted for 1 percent of the executives and managers in advertising, circulation, general management, news/editorial and production; 2 percent in in-

formation systems; and 3 percent in accounting/finance.[184] The Asian American Journalists Association (AAJA) reports that Asian/Pacific Americans are only 1.3 percent of newsroom employees, primarily reporters, although they are 2.9 percent of the population at large and Asian Americans have high average education levels, meaning that many Asian Americans have the basic qualifications necessary to become journalists. In fact, 54 percent of the Nation's 1,500 dailies employ no minorities at all.[185]

A similar pattern of underrepresentation prevails in broadcast news, where minorities make up 17 percent of the work force at commercial television stations and 9 percent at commercial radio stations.[186] The U.S. civilian work force, in comparison, is about 22 percent minority. Asian American men constitute an estimated 1.7 percent of the television news work force and a mere 0.7 percent of the radio news work force.[187] Among television correspondents, there are still only a few Asian American faces. Only 4 Asian American journalists were ranked among the 100 most visible men and women network television reporters in a 1990 Network Correspondent Visibility report.[188]

the Socialization of the Minority Child (New York, NY: Academic Press, 1982), p. 154.)

180   "Miss Saigon: Deja Vu 100 Years Later," *Inside Movies*, Fall 1990, p. 1.

181   Ibid., p. 2.

182   *Cornerstone for Growth: How Minorities are Vital to the Future of Newspapers* (Task Force on Minorities in the Newspaper Business, date unknown), p. 39.

183   News Release from American Newspaper Publishers Association (ANPA), June 1, 1990 (Regarding ANPA survey of Employment of Minorities and Women in U.S. Daily Newspapers).

184   Ibid.

185   David A. Louie, President, and Diane Yen-Mei Wong, Executive Director, Asian American Journalists Association, letter to Ki-Taek Chun, Deputy Director, Eastern Regional Division, U.S. Commission on Civil Rights, Mar. 13, 1991 (hereafter cited as Louie and Wong letter).

186   "Study Finds Little Change in Status of Minorities in News Media," *Newsletter of the Asian American Journalists Association*, Fall 1990, p. 19.

187   Louie and Wong letter.

188   "Few Asian Americans among Most Visible TV Correspondents," *AAJA Newsletter*, Summer 1991, p. 11. Among the male correspondents, Ken Kashiwahara of ABC and CBS's James Hattori were ranked 45th and 74th, respectively; of the female correspondents, Linda Taira of CBS and Ann Curry of NBC were ranked 15th and 27th. (Connie Chung was not ranked, because news anchors were not included in the survey.)

Journalists are information gatekeepers. By deciding what to cover, they help define what constitutes major social issues; by presenting information in a certain way or at a certain time, they can affect how society views and decides issues.[189] Minority journalists may be able to uncover otherwise inaccessible information. They may also provide an understanding and insight necessary to balanced and accurate coverage.[190] Yet, these statistics suggest that Asian Americans are underrepresented as a whole and are not yet in a position to determine or implement broad policy as to "what is news" in news organizations.

There are indications that the underrepresentation of Asian American journalists at critical junctures may adversely affect the media's ability to cover incidents involving the Asian American community with due balance and sensitivity. When specific incidents require coverage of Asian American communities, the media may be ill-prepared to provide balanced coverage of the issues; instead they may oversimplify situations and fail to provide the public with crucial insights. For instance, some critics have alleged that the local news media in Los Angeles exacerbated racial tensions in that city following the murder of a black customer by a Korean American storeowner by turning an isolated incident into a racial issue[191] and by turning to an unqualified person (a Japanese American professor) as spokesmen for Los Angeles' Korean American community and printing his statement implying that Korean American businessmen are wealthy and higher class than their inner-city customers.[192] Similarly, it has been alleged that a series of Associated Press articles about a prostitution ring staffed by Korean American wives of American soldiers gave the inaccurate and unsupported impression that "Korean women—mostly married to U.S. servicemen—are involved in a growing network of sex for sale and the Korean American communities are engaged in a conspiracy of silence,"[193] while at the same time failing to take the opportunity to examine the related issue of the "enormous needs of tens of thousands of Asian women (including Koreans) who have been victimized or abandoned by their former GI husbands."[194]

The stereotype shared by some newsroom managers that Asians are not sufficiently aggressive in their reporting may create a "glass ceiling" that impedes the advancement of Asian Americans in the industry. A 1989 survey of 50 news managers across the Nation revealed that some news directors still believe that Asian American journalists are not assertive, do not like risk, and avoid confrontation.[195] Approximately one in four Asian American journalists

---

189 Louie and Wong letter.

190 For example, the Asian American Journalists Association notes: "Members of a community of color often feel more comfortable talking with journalists of color, especially journalists whom they can identify as being of their community, whether because of color, ethnicity, culture or interest. Without adequate representation of journalists of color, communities can sometimes be effectively cut off from access to the media in that geographic area. A community's alienation from its own local, and the national, media means important issues are not covered, key community resource people are not consulted, and the community is left voiceless about how their community is covered, if at all." Ibid.

191 K.W. Lee, editor, *Korea Times*, as quoted in Marlene Adler Marks, *Jewish Journal*, Apr. 12-18, 1991.

192 K. Connie Kang, letter to James S. Cunningham, Assistant Staff Director for Programs, Policy, and Research, U.S. Commission on Civil Rights, Sept. 19, 1991 (hereafter cited as Kang letter).

193 K.W. Lee, President, Korean American Journalists Association, letter to Louis D. Bocardi, President, Associated Press, Dec. 11, 1986, as quoted in Kang letter.

194 Ibid.

195 Mark Hokoda, "Are Asian Americans 'Too Nice'?—Managers Share Views on AA Journalists," *AAJA Newsletter* Spring-Summer 1989, pp. 2, 21.

responded to a 1987 survey by saying that they perceived "a specific career barrier based in either ethnic or sexual discrimination, particularly as impediments to the move into management."[196] Asian American journalists are likely to quit their jobs because they found limited opportunities for advancement in their organization or field.[197]

Representation of Asian Americans in the media needs to be improved, particularly at the management level, because:

These managers are the ones who help decide who is hired, retained and fired; they help set policy and tone both in the newsroom and in the news reports. Without adequate representation of Asian Pacific Americans and other journalists of color, these decisions are all to often made without a full understanding of the impact on minority communities and minority journalists.[198]

For these reasons, the Asian American Journalists Association offers the reminder that:

In these times of increased diversity in society, we need more journalists who can reflect accurately and sensitively this diversity in their reporting, producing, editing and photography. . . .And, it is only through this type of enlightened journalism that we can expect this country to learn to live with, and embrace, differences in color, ethnicity, culture, religion, sex, . . .and physical abilities.[199]

Religious Accommodation

Many Asian Americans belong to non-Western religions that are minority religions in the United States, such as Buddhism, Hinduism, Islam, Shinto, Sikhism, Taoism, and tribal religions. Not only do the religious differences between Asian Americans and the majority of the U.S. population contribute to anti-Asian bigotry and violence, but they can at times cause other conflicts when the practices and requirements of Asian American religions are incompatible with majority traditions, established business practices, and laws. This section discusses protections available to members of minority religions under the law and gives examples of when society at large has failed to accommodate Asian Americans' religious convictions.

First Amendment Rights to Religious Accommodation by Federal, State, and Local Government

The rights of individuals to be free of government interference with their religion are protected by the first amendment, which forbids the Federal Government (and through the 14th amendment, State and local governments) from interfering with the free exercise of religion. The first amendment has been interpreted to provide an absolute guarantee against government inter-

---

196   Edgar P. Trotter, *The Asian American Journalist* (Los Angeles, CA: Institute for Media-Society Studies, Department of Communications, California State University, Sept. 24, 1987), p. 19.

197   Alexis S. Tan, *Why Asian American Journalists Leave Journalism and Why They Stay* (Pullman, WA: The Edward R. Murrow School of Communication, Washington State University, 1990), p. 3.

198   Louie and Wong letter, p. 2.

199   Ibid.

ference with religious *beliefs*,[200] but government interference with religious *conduct* is allowed under certain circumstances. For instance, government laws ban polygamy, sacrifice of human beings, and funereal immolation of widows, and that is permissible.[201] In the past, the first amendment was generally interpreted to exempt individuals from general laws and regulations that required conduct prohibited by their religion (or prohibited conduct required by their religion) except when the government could show a compelling state interest for why they should not be exempted. In *Sherbert v. Verner*, the U.S. Supreme Court argued that there needs to be a "compelling state interest"[202] for government interference with religious conduct. It held that:

It is basic that no showing merely of a rational relationship to some colorable state interest would suffice; in this highly sensitive constitutional area, "[o]nly the gravest abuses, endangering paramount interests, give occasion for permissible limitation."[203]

In April 1990, however, the U.S. Supreme Court decision in *Employment Division v. Smith*[204] considerably narrowed the first amendment rights of individuals by allowing the government to deny exemption from laws that interfere with religious conduct as long as such laws are generally applicable and not adopted for the purpose of discrimination:

[T]he "exercise of religion" often involves not only belief and profession but the performance of (or abstention from) physical acts; . . .It would be true, we think. . .that a state would be "prohibiting the free exercise [of religion]" if it sought to ban such acts or abstentions only when they are engaged in for religious reasons, or only because of the religious belief that they display. . . .The government's ability to enforce generally applicable prohibitions of socially harmful conduct, like its ability to carry out other aspects of public policy, "cannot depend on measuring the effects of a governmental action on a religious objector's spiritual development." To make an individual's obligation to obey such a law contingent upon the law's coincidence with his religious beliefs, except where the State's interest is "compelling"—permitting him, by virtue of his beliefs, "to become a law unto himself," contradicts both constitutional tradition and common sense.[205]

The *Smith* decision has already had an effect on the religious rights of some Asian Americans. For example, the decision prompted the reversal of a 15-year-old Occupational Safety and Health Administration (OSHA) exemption of Sikhs and Amish from regulations requiring the wearing of hard hats by construction workers.[206] The *Smith* decision has also had consequences for Hmongs and others whose religions prohibit autopsies. In a case that was brought before the *Smith* decision, a Hmong couple in Rhode Island sought damages from the chief medical examiner of the State because his office had performed an autopsy on their 23-year-old son, who had died suddenly, without their knowledge and against their will. The Hmong religion holds that bodies are sacred and does not allow any form of muti-

---

200 "The door of the Free Exercise Clause stands tightly closed against any governmental regulation of religious *beliefs* as such. Government may neither compel affirmation of a repugnant belief; nor penalize or discriminate against individuals or groups because they hold religious views abhorrent to the authorities; nor employ the taxing power to inhibit the dissemination of particular religious views." Sherbert v. Verner, 374 U.S. 398, 402 (1963).

201 U.S. Commission on Civil Rights, *Religion in the Constitution: A Delicate Balance*, (Clearinghouse Publication no. 80, September 1983), p. 36, quoting Reynolds v. United States, 98 U.S. 145, 165-66 (1878).

202 374 U.S. 398 at 406.

203 374 U.S. at 406, quoting Thomas v. Collins, 323 U.S. 516, 530 (1945).

204 110 S. Ct. 1595 (1990).

205 *Id.* at 1599, 1603 (citations omitted).

206 OSHA Notice CPL 2, signed by Patricia K. Clark, Director Designate, Directorate of Compliance Programs, Nov. 5, 1990.

lation of bodies, including autopsies. The chief medical examiner defended the autopsy as necessary to "ensure that the cause of death was not attributable to some act or agent that posed a threat to the health, safety and welfare of the citizens. . .of Rhode Island."[207] Citing the *Sherbert* "compelling interest" standard, and finding that the interests cited by the defense "fall far short of being compelling," the U.S. District Court of Rhode Island initially held that the chief medical examiner had impermissibly interfered with the Hmong couple's free exercise of their religion.[208] Following the *Smith* decision, however, the district court reversed its ruling.[209]

As the religions adhered to by many Asian Americans come into conflict with mainstream America, the *Smith* decision could have a wide-ranging effect on Asian Americans and others who subscribe to minority religions. The Religious Freedom Restoration Act of 1991, introduced in the House of Representatives by Congressmen Stephen Solarz (D-NY) on June 26, 1991, and co-sponsored by 41 members of the House, would mandate a compelling interest test for determining when government can interfere with religious conduct.[210]

Religious Accommodation by Civilian Employers

In addition to their first amendment rights, individuals have also received protections against religious discrimination from the Civil Rights Act of 1964. As amended in 1972, Title VII of the Civil Rights Act requires employers not only to refrain from differential treatment on the basis of religion (e.g., not hiring a prospective employee because he or she is of the Hindu religion) but also to take affirmative steps to accommodate the religious convictions of their employees "unless an employer demonstrates that he is unable to reasonably accommodate to an employee's or prospective employee's religious observance or practice without undue hardship on the conduct of the employer's business."[211] For example, employers are required to take steps to accommodate employees whose religious convictions are in conflict with the employer's work schedule and employees who seek to wear religious garb or follow religious grooming practices that conflict with the employer's regulations. There are, however, limits to employers' obligations to accommodate

---

207   You Vang Yang v. Sturner, 728 F. Supp. 845 (D.R.I. 1990) citing Defendant's Memorandum in Support of a Motion for Summary Judgment at 8.

208   *Id.*

209   Ruth Marcus, "Reins on Religious Freedom? Broad Coalition Protests Impact of High Court Ruling," *Washington Post*, Mar. 9, 1991.

210   *Congressional Record*, vol. 137, no. 101, June 27, 1991. Specifically, the bill states: "(a) Government shall not burden a person's exercise of religion even if the burden results from a rule of general applicability, except as provided in subsection (b).

"(b) Exception—Government may burden a person's exercise of religion only if it demonstrates that application of the burden to the person—

"(1) is essential to further a compelling governmental interest; and

"(2) is the least restrictive means of furthering that compelling government interest."

H.R. 2797, 102nd Cong., 1st Sess. §3.

211   42 U.S.C. §2000e(j). The issue of what is reasonable has not been definitively resolved. In a landmark case, Trans World Airlines v. Hardison, 432 U.S. 63 (1977), the Supreme Court held that Title VII does not require employers to accommodate religious convictions when the accommodation necessitates more than a *de minimus* cost. The Equal Employment Opportunity Commission guideline "states that undue hardship will be identified when an employer, labor organization, or other entity can demonstrate that accommodation would require more than a *de minimus* cost or would require a variance from a bona fide seniority system when doing so would deny another employee his or her job or shift preference as guaranteed by the system." EEOC Compliance Manual 628.7(a).

their employees' religious convictions. A 1987 decision by the Equal Employment Opportunity Commission (EEOC) is illustrative. Despite the then-existing OSHA exemption for Sikhs from its requirement that hard hats be worn in construction areas, the EEOC held that the employer's need to guarantee the safety of its electrician employees was sufficient that it would cause the employer undue hardship to exempt a Sikh employee from wearing a hard hat and a gas mask.[212] (Sikh men are required by their religion to wear a turban that prevents the wearing of a hard hat, and to leave their facial hair unshaved, which would prevent the mask from achieving a proper seal.)

Religious Accommodation by the Military

The military is not under the same obligation to accommodate religious differences among its members as civilian employers are, and even after the *Smith* decision, it probably faces a lesser standard than other government entities in determining when it must accommodate religious needs. In a decision made before *Smith* (i.e., at a time when many thought that a compelling interest standard applied to government entities), the U.S. Supreme Court held that the military must be given more leeway than other governmental bodies:

Our review of military regulations challenged on First Amendment grounds is far more deferential than constitutional review of similar laws or regulations designed for civilian society.[213]

The Court stated that the judiciary owes considerable deference to the military's own judgment about military needs:

[W]hen evaluating whether military needs justify a particular restriction on religiously motivated conduct, courts must give great deference to the professional judgment of military authorities concerning the relative importance of a particular interest. Not only are courts "'ill-equipped to determine the impact upon discipline that any particular intrusion upon military authority might have,'" but the military authorities have been charged by the Executive and the Legislative Branches with carrying out our Nation's military policy. "[J]udicial deference is at its apogee when legislative action under the congressional authority to raise and support armies and make rules and regulations for their governance is challenged."[214]

In separate dissents, Justices William Brennan and Sandra O'Connor each pointed out that the majority had not only accepted the military's judgment that military discipline is an important military interest, but also had accepted the military's unsupported word that allowing a Jewish officer to wear a yarmulke would have serious adverse consequences for military discipline. Thus, the *Goldman* decision apparently gave the Armed Forces considerably greater protections from first amendment challenges than other governmental bodies.

Concerned about the implications of the *Goldman* decision for religious minorities, such as Jews who seek to wear yarmulkes and Sikhs who seek to wear turbans, the 100th Congress enacted a provision explicitly allowing members

---

212   Commission Decision no. 82-1, CCH EEOC decisions (1983) ¶6817, 28 FEP Cases 1840.

213   Goldman v. Weinberger, 475 U.S. 503, 507 (1986).

214   *Id.* at 507, 508 (citations omitted).

of the armed forces to "wear an item of religious apparel while wearing the uniform of the member's armed force" except when "the wearing of the item interferes with the performance of the member's military duties" or if the apparel is "not neat and conservative."[215] The law gives the Secretary of Defense discretion in deciding which items of religious apparel are allowable. Although the law itself does not mention yarmulkes or turbans, the Conference Report makes clear that Congress expected these to be allowed:

The conferees are concerned about reports that the implementing regulations may be written so narrowly as to exclude virtually all religious apparel. The law does not list eligible items of apparel, but the conferees note that the Army in the past has permitted the wearing of Sikh turbans and that the Senate and the House floor debates cited various examples of the wearing of Jewish yarmulkes by members of the armed forces.[216]

Despite the legislative history and the intent of Congress, the Department of Defense (DoD) has issued regulations banning the wearing of Sikh turbans with the uniform. Responding to a letter of concern about the DoD regulations from Rep. Les Aspin, Chairman of the House Committee on Armed Services, then-Secretary of Defense Frank Carlucci defended the DoD regulations as in compliance with the law:

The DoD implementing directive defines neat and conservative to preclude items that replace or interfere with the regular uniform. We do not believe either of these requires the Army to permit the wearing of visible religious apparel in place of required items of the uniform, such as Service caps, hats, or other headgear.[217]

---

215   National Defense Authorization Act for Fiscal Years 1988 and 1989, 10 U.S.C. §774 (Supp. 1991).

216   House Conference Report no. 100-46 p. 638. The Conference Report also gives the following guidance: "The provision also permits the Secretary concerned to prohibit the wearing of an item of religious apparel when 'it would interfere with the performance of the members' military duties.' The conferees note that the 'nonuniform' aspect of religious apparel should not be used as the sole basis for involving the interference with duties provision, except in unique circumstances, such as those involving ceremonial units, and, even then, only when actually performing ceremonial functions." Ibid.

217   Frank C. Carlucci, Secretary of Defense, letter to Rep. Les Aspin, Chairman, Committee on Armed Services, Dec. 8, 1988.

Chapter 8

Conclusions and Recommendations

This report presents the results of an investigation into the civil rights issues facing Asian Americans that was undertaken as a followup to the Commission's 1989 Asian Roundtable Conferences. Contrary to the popular perception that Asian Americans have overcome discriminatory barriers, Asian Americans still face widespread prejudice, discrimination, and denials of equal opportunity. In addition, many Asian Americans, particularly those who are immigrants, are deprived of equal access to public services, including police protection, education, health care, and the judicial system.

Several factors contribute to the civil rights problems facing today's Asian Americans. First, Asian Americans are the victims of stereotypes that are widely held among the general public. These stereotypes deprive Asian Americans of their individuality and humanity in the public's perception and often foster prejudice against Asian Americans. The "model minority" stereotype, the often-repeated contention that Asian Americans have overcome all barriers facing them and that they are a singularly successful minority group, is perhaps the most damaging of these stereotypes. This stereotype leads Federal, State, and local agencies to overlook the problems facing Asian Americans, and it often causes resentment of Asian Americans within the general public.

Second, many Asian Americans, particularly immigrants, face significant cultural and linguistic barriers that prevent them from receiving equal access to public services and from participating fully in the American political process. Many Asian American immigrants arrive in the United States with minimal facility in the English language and with little familiarity with

American culture and the workings of American society. There has been a widespread failure of government at all levels and of the Nation's public schools to provide for the needs of immigrant Asian Americans. Such basic needs as interpretive services to help limited-English-proficient Asian Americans in their dealings with government agencies, culturally appropriate medical care, bilingual/English as a Second Language education, and information about available public services are largely unmet.

A third, but equally important, problem confronting Asian Americans today is a lack of political representation and an inability to use the political process effectively. Asian Americans face many barriers to participation in the political process, in addition to the simple fact that many Asian Americans are not yet citizens and hence ineligible to vote. Although some Asian Americans are politically active, the large majority have very little access to political power. This lack of political empowerment leads the political leadership of the United States to overlook and sometimes ignore the needs and concerns of Asian Americans. It also leads to a failure of the political leadership to make addressing Asian American issues a national priority.

This chapter lays out specific conclusions and recommendations. Many of the civil rights issues facing Asian Americans also confront other minority groups. For example, issues related to the rights of language minorities are equally important for other language-minority groups. Thus, many of our conclusions with respect to violations of Asian Americans' civil rights and our recommendations for enhancing the protection of their civil rights are applicable to other minority groups as well.

Bigotry and Violence Against Asian Americans

In 1986 the Commission drew attention to the problem of bigotry and violence against Asian Americans.[1] Our investigation shows that bigotry and violence against Asian Americans remains a serious national problem today. This report has recounted numerous incidents of bigotry and violence directed against Asian Americans. These incidents include the vicious bias-related murders of Vincent Chin, Jim Loo, Navroze Mody, and Hung Truong, and the recent massacre of Southeast Asian schoolchildren in Sacramento, California; attacks on Asian American homes and places of worship; racially motivated boycotts against Asian-owned businesses; racial harassment of Asian Americans on college campuses; and racial slurs made by public figures, one of whom was a candidate for governor. The incidents reported here are by no means exhaustive: for every incident reported here, there are many more that have not been reported.

The root causes of bigotry and violence against Asian Americans are complex. Racial prejudice; misplaced anger caused by wars or economic competition with Asian countries; resentment of the real or perceived success of Asian Americans; and a lack of understanding of the histories, customs, and religions of Asian Americans all play a role in triggering incidents of bigotry and violence. The media have contributed to prejudice by promoting stereotypes of Asian Americans, especially the model minority stereotype; by sometimes highlighting the criminal activities of Asian gangs; and by failing to provide the indepth and balanced coverage that would help the public to understand the diverse Asian American population. Furthermore, the media give little attention to hate crimes against Asian Americans, thereby hindering the formation of a national sense of outrage about bigotry and violence against Asian Americans, a critical ingredient for social change. Schools contribute to the problem by not teaching students about the histories, cultures, experiences, and contributions of Asian Americans. Political leaders contribute to the problem when they unthinkingly lash out at Japan as the cause of United States economic difficulties. More important, political and government leaders have yet to make it a national priority to prevent and denounce anti-Asian prejudice and violence.

Recommendation 1:

Local and State governments should review whether their laws adequately protect the rights of Asian Americans and others to be free from bias-related intimidation and violence; all jurisdictions should enact and implement effective anti-bias laws.

Recommendation 2:

The media should make concerted efforts to increase public awareness of incidents of anti-Asian discrimination and hate crimes against Asian Americans and to build a national consensus about the urgency of combating all acts of bigotry and violence.

Recommendation 3:

Political leaders should refrain from activities and remarks that promote or play upon racial and ethnic bias, such as "Japan bashing." Accordingly, the political leadership of both national political parties should agree to refrain from "race-baiting" tactics in upcoming election campaigns.[2]

---

1   U.S. Commission on Civil Rights, *Recent Activities Against Citizens and Residents of Asian Descent* (Clearinghouse Publication 88, 1986).

2   This recommendation was originally made by the Commissioners in July 1991. In letters to President Bush and to the leaders of the U.S. House and Senate, Commission Chairman Arthur Fletcher urged the President and congressional leaders "to convene a sum-

Recommendation 4:

The Federal Government should mount a coordinated national effort to promote understanding for Asian Americans, particularly immigrants, and to prevent hate activities against them. This effort should include as active participants the schools, police, and local and State governments, as well as the Federal Government. The U.S. Department of Justice's Community Relations Service is a logical agency to be involved in coordinating the national effort.

The Hate Crimes Statistics Act,[3] enacted in 1990, provides an opportunity to learn more about and document the extent of hate-motivated violence against Asian Americans and others at a national level. The experiences of local jurisdictions across the country that have made efforts to collect data on hate crimes make it clear that proper implementation of the Hate Crimes Statistics Act will require more than developing a national reporting system. Additional ingredients necessary for a successful implementation of the act include:

1) improved outreach to victim communities to encourage hate crime victims to recognize and report hate crimes;
2) improved police training so that officers on the beat can readily identify hate crimes;
3) the formation of new police units that specialize in identifying, investigating, and reporting hate crimes as well as guiding community outreach and police training efforts.

Recommendation 5:

To implement the Hate Crimes Statistics Act properly, police departments should provide enhanced police officer training and community outreach efforts to ensure that hate crimes are correctly recognized, reported, and recorded, and large police departments should create special units to investigate and collect data on hate crimes.

Police-Community Relations

There are serious fissures in the relationship between the Asian American community and the police that leave many Asian Americans without effective access to police protection and some with the fear that they themselves may become the victims of police misconduct.

For many Asian Americans, recent immigrants in particular, access to police protection is severely limited by their lack of English proficiency. Persons with limited English proficiency need interpretive services to communicate effectively with the police. Yet, interpretive services are rarely provided by police departments across the country, and when provided, they are generally inadequate. As a result, limited-English-proficient Asian Americans are often reluctant to call the police, and when they do, they often have difficulty in making their side of the story known to the police. This miscommunication frequently results in incomplete police reports, and sometimes in police harassment or false arrests of limited-English-proficient Asian American witnesses.

Sometimes, immigrant Asians bring with them a legacy of distrust of authority, including the police, that results from unfortunate encounters with governmental or law enforcement agencies in their countries of origin. The residue of such experiences makes them reluctant to talk to or seek help from the police. This distrust is aggravated by difficulties in bridging the cultural and

---

mit conference, comprised of major public officials from Federal, State and local government, the media, and private citizens, to address [the issue of inflammatory racial rhetoric in political campaigns] and to prepare guidelines for proper conduct." U.S. Commission on Civil Rights, letter to President Bush and Leaders of the U.S. House of Representatives and Senate, July 18, 1991.

3   28 U.S.C. 534.

language gap that exists between many Asian Americans and the police. Few police officers across the country have been given sufficient training about Asian cultures, and as a result, Asian Americans often receive culturally insensitive treatment from police officers. Police misconduct towards Asian Americans exacerbates the distrust. Our investigation revealed that there have been incidents of police misconduct in all parts of the country, ranging from harassment of Asian American youth to cases of serious brutality against Asian Americans.

A third barrier to Asian Americans' access to police protection is the underrepresentation of Asian Americans among police officers in most law enforcement jurisdictions across the country. This lack of representation severely restricts police access to information about crime in Asian American communities, which in turn hampers police efforts to protect these communities from growing criminal activity.

Some police departments across the country are experimenting with alternative ways of reaching out to the Asian American communities in their cities. These alternative approaches, commonly known as "community policing," have been reported to help bridge the gap between Asian Americans and the police. Community policing entails 1) hiring Asian American community service officers to serve as liaisons between regular police officers and Asian Americans; 2) setting up Asian American police advisory boards consisting of representatives of the Asian American community who meet regularly with the police to voice community concerns and who help gain community support for police investigations of criminal activity in Asian American communities; and 3) providing cultural sensitivity training for police officers.

Recommendation 6:
Police departments should take aggressive action to increase the representation of Asian Americans among police officers.

Recommendation 7:
Police departments should provide interpreters to limited-English-proficient Asian Americans both on an emergency and on a nonemergency basis.

Recommendation 8:
Police departments and civilian review boards should make a commitment to monitor actively alleged incidents of police harassment and brutality, to undertake thorough followup investigations, and to take appropriate action based on the results of these investigations.

Recommendation 9:
Police departments should adopt community policing methods to build a trusting relationship with Asian American communities. In particular, they should consider:

- creating Asian American police advisory boards;
- hiring Asian American community liaison officers;
- providing cultural sensitivity training to all police officers; and
- disseminating information about the police department to immigrant Asian Americans.

Access to Primary and Secondary Education— Immigrant Asian American Children

Many Asian American immigrant children, particularly those who are limited English proficient (LEP), are deprived of equal access to educational opportunity. These children have to overcome both language and cultural barriers before they can participate meaningfully in the educational programs offered in public schools.

Providing equal educational opportunity to Asian American LEP students requires sound student assessment procedures and programs that can orient them and their parents to American society and American schools. Asian American LEP students need bilingual education and

English as a Second Language (ESL) programs staffed by trained teachers to enable them to learn English and at the same time to keep up in school. They need professional bilingual/bicultural counseling services to help them in their social adjustment and academic development. Our investigation has revealed that these needs of Asian American LEP students are being drastically underserved. In particular, there is a dire national shortage of trained bilingual/ESL teachers and counselors.

Title VI of the 1964 Civil Rights Act requires school systems to take "affirmative steps to rectify the language deficiency in order to open programs to LEP children."[4] In recent years, the U.S. Department of Education's Office for Civil Rights (OCR), the designated agency for monitoring and enforcing the provisions of Title VI, has been criticized for not adequately enforcing these Title VI requirements for LEP students. Recently, OCR has made protecting the rights of LEP students a top priority and has pledged to carry out more compliance reviews in this area.

There is little information on how Asian American immigrant children are faring in public schools. Many national data sets on educational achievement, such as the National Assessment of Educational Progress, do not collect information on the achievement of students with extremely limited English proficiency, and most do not have adequate samples of Asian American students or do not differentiate between immigrant and nonimmigrant students. Available information suggests that many Asian American immigrant students, although performing well by some measures, are leaving our public schools with serious deficiencies, particularly in the areas of reading and writing, and that some subgroups have high dropout rates.

Recommendation 10:
Federal, State, and local governments should collect systematic data on how the needs of limited-English-proficient (LEP) students are being met and on the educational achievement of LEP students.

Recommendation 11:
Colleges and universities, in conjunction with the U.S. Department of Education, State education agencies, and local school districts, should establish programs that recruit and train bilingual/English as a Second Language teachers specifically for underserved languages, such as the Southeast Asian languages.

Recommendation 12:
Every school system with immigrant students should have in place a comprehensive program to ease the transition of newly arrived immigrant students and their families into the American school system and into American society at large. Such a program should include intensive English as a Second Language classes offered to adults, as well as classes for children in school.

Recommendation 13:
The Office for Civil Rights (OCR) in the U.S. Department of Education should step up its enforcement of Title VI's *Lau* requirements for instruction for LEP students. In particular, OCR should carry out more compliance reviews for compliance with *Lau* guidelines.

Asian American immigrant students frequently encounter fellow students, teachers, and administrators who know little or nothing about their cultures and histories. Oftentimes, school officials do not understand their new students and are unprepared to help them cope with their transition into American schools; their fellow students have no background to help them appreciate why their new classmates are different

---

4   Lau v. Nichols, 414 U.S. 563 (1974).

and are likely to react to them with unease or hostility. For Asian American students to realize their full potential at school, they need school environments that are understanding and supportive, not insensitive and hostile. Aggressive programs to educate school personnel and students about Asian (and other) cultures and histories and to combat racism in our schools are urgently needed.

Even more serious, our investigation found that a high degree of racial tensions is prevalent in public schools across the country. Asian American students are frequently the targets of racial remarks by fellow students, and are often provoked into physical fights because of their race or national origin. Furthermore, school officials often fail to take appropriate preventive steps to deal with the racially charged environment. Allegedly, teachers and administrators frequently minimize or overlook the seriousness of anti-Asian sentiments in public schools. Many Asian Americans are convinced that when Asian American students get involved in disputes or fights with other students, teachers and administrators come down harder and impose harsher disciplinary actions on Asian American students.

Recommendation 14:

Federal, State, and local government and school officials, in partnership with parents and students, should make a concerted effort to defuse racial and ethnic tensions in public schools and to promote mutual tolerance and understanding among racial and ethnic groups. As part of this effort,

• public school officials should become aware of racial tensions in the schools; take steps to defuse them; and respond to racial incidents rapidly and aggressively; and

• school curricula should be revised to provide a truly multicultural education.

Admissions Discrimination Against Asian Americans in Higher Education

In the early 1980s, the admit rates of Asian American students to elite colleges and universities fell at a time when the number of Asian American applicants to these colleges and universities was increasing rapidly. Charges that colleges and universities were placing ceilings on the numbers of Asian American students admitted, and that Asian American applicants were discriminated against in the admissions process relative to white applicants, began to be made with increasing frequency. Because researchers and other interested parties could not gain access to the necessary admissions data, the issue could not be resolved. Starting in 1988, the controversy became embroiled in the national debate on affirmative action, with opponents of affirmative action maintaining that admissions discrimination against Asian Americans is the inevitable outcome of affirmative action programs. The ensuing politicization of the controversy obscured the central issue, whether or not elite colleges and universities had instituted discriminatory admissions practices against Asian American students.

This report reviewed the admissions discrimination controversy at three universities: Brown University, the University of California at Berkeley, and Harvard University. At Brown, the issue led to the university's admission that "Asian American students have been treated unfairly in the admissions process,"[5] and recommendations for "immediate remedial measures,"[6] which were implemented shortly thereafter. At Berkeley, an investigation of the

5   Brown University Corporation Committee on Minority Affairs, "Report to the Corporation Committee on Minority Affairs From Its Subcommittee on Asian American Admissions," Feb. 10, 1984, p. 2.

6   Ibid.

issue by a Special Committee of Berkeley's Academic Senate pinpointed several factors that may have been responsible for a precipitous decline in Asian American admissions in the fall of 1984, including a decision to cease guaranteeing admission to economically disadvantaged applicants who did not qualify for affirmative action[7] and a decision to raise the minimum grade point average that would guarantee admission to Berkeley without at the same time raising the minimum test score threshold.[8] The Special Committee also revealed one episode at Berkeley that, although it ultimately had no effect on Asian American admissions, was particularly disturbing. In December 1983, the director of the Office of Admissions and Records imposed a minimum SAT-verbal requirement on immigrant students (and not on other students).[9] Although the policy was revoked less than 2 weeks later, it was implemented with the full knowledge of its discriminatory effect on Asian American applicants and without any apparent purpose other than to limit the number of immigrant students on campus. Furthermore, while the controversy on admissions discrimination was in high gear, the Berkeley administration repeatedly denied that the policy had ever existed, until copies of the directive putting the policy in effect were released by the California State Legislature in early 1988.

At Harvard, the issue prompted a Title VI compliance review initiated in 1988 by the U.S. Department of Education's Office for Civil Rights (OCR). In late 1990, OCR issued its report finding that Harvard had not discriminated against Asian American applicants. The report concluded that the lower admit rate for Asian American applicants in comparison to white applicants could be entirely explained by admissions preferences given by Harvard to athletes and children of alumni ("legacies"). OCR concluded that Harvard's policy of giving preferential consideration to children of alumni does not violate Title VI.[10] This conclusion rests on three considerations. First, OCR argued that existing case law does not suggest that legacy preferences are *per se* illegal. Second, OCR noted that there was "no evidence to suggest that these preferences were instituted to intentionally or deliberately limit the number of Asian Americans at Harvard,"[11] since these preferences had been in place long before the number of Asian American applicants increased significantly. Finally, OCR applied a disparate impact analysis to Harvard's legacy preference policy and determined that it was designed to serve the legitimate institutional goal of obtaining financial and volunteer support for the university from alumni, and that there were no viable alternative policies that would accomplish the same goal.

Despite the determination that legacy preferences are not *per se* illegal, the issue of the legality under Title VI of legacy preferences that have a disparate impact by race remains unresolved. To date, although OCR determined that the information supplied by Harvard was sufficient to justify its legacy preference policy under Title VI, there is no established Federal policy

---

7 The vast majority of these students were Asian Americans.

8 Berkeley guaranteed admission to candidates who met either a minimum grade point average (GPA) threshold or a minimum test score threshold. Asian American applicants were more likely to be admitted on the strength of their GPAs, whereas white applicants were more likely to be admitted on the strength of their test scores. Thus, raising only the GPA threshold had the effect of disadvantaging Asian American applicants relative to white applicants.

9 Because Hispanics, the other large immigrant group among Berkeley's applicants, were eligible for affirmative action, the vast majority of students who would have been affected by this policy were Asian American.

10 U.S. Department of Education, Office for Civil Rights, "Statement of Findings" (for Compliance Review No. 01-88-6009 on Harvard University), Oct. 4, 1990, p. 43.

11 Ibid., p. 40.

guidance on when a university admissions policy with a disparate impact by race, color, sex, religion or national origin can be justified under Title VI.

Recommendation 15:

Colleges and universities should examine thoroughly their admissions policies for adverse effects or unintentional bias against Asian Americans and put in place safeguards to prevent them. Such safeguards should include:

- providing training to admissions staff;
- routinely reviewing new policies for adverse impact;
- including Asian Americans in the admissions process; and
- making data on the racial and ethnic breakdown of applicants and admitted students available to the public when requested.

Recommendation 16:

OCR should require colleges and universities covered under Title VI of the Civil Rights Act of 1964 to provide OCR regularly with data on the racial and ethnic breakdown and qualifications of applicants and admitted students, and OCR should use these data in deciding whether or not to institute Title VI compliance reviews of these institutions. Furthermore, OCR should make such data available to the public when requested.

Recommendation 17:

OCR should issue policy guidance clarifying specifically what a university needs to show under Title VI to justify a legacy preference policy or other admissions policies that have a disparate impact by race, color, sex, religion, or national origin. At a minimum, OCR should require universities to be prepared to prove that such policies are truly necessary, i.e, that they have a necessary purpose; that they in fact accomplish that purpose; and that there are no alternative ways to accomplish the purpose with less discriminatory impact.

Employment Discrimination

Asian Americans face a number of barriers to equal participation in the labor market. Many of these barriers are encountered to a greater degree by the foreign born, who often confront linguistic and cultural barriers to finding employment commensurate with their education and experience, but even third- or fourth-generation Asian Americans find their employment prospects diminished because employers have stereotypical views of Asians and prejudice against citizens of Asian ancestry. Employment discrimination, to varying degrees, is a problem facing all Asian Americans.

The perception that there is a "glass ceiling" barring most Asian Americans from attaining management positions (especially upper level management positions) for which they are qualified is perhaps the concern most frequently voiced by Asian American individuals and advocacy groups across the country. Because the choice of whom to put in a management position is usually a highly subjective decision, Asian Americans are vulnerable to managers who are biased against Asian Americans or who subscribe to stereotypical views of Asian Americans as not having the qualities that make strong corporate leaders, executives, and high-level decision makers. In addition, the subjective nature of promotion decisions usually makes it difficult to prove that the adverse employment decision was a discriminatory one. The evidence accumulated in this study convinces the Commission that the problem is a serious one and that it pervades both private corporations and government agencies. The issue merits serious research and increased enforcement efforts on the part of Federal, State, and local antidiscrimination agencies. Such enforcement efforts should build upon the pilot studies of Fortune 500 corporations carried out by the Department of Labor's Office of Federal Contract Compliance Programs as part of the Department's Glass Ceiling Initiative.

Recommendation 18:

Federal and State monitoring agencies should periodically collect, disseminate, and analyze data on the number of Asian Americans as well as other minorities and women in upper level management positions.

Recommendation 19:

Federal and State enforcement agencies should take aggressive steps to enforce anti-discrimination provisions with respect to the glass ceiling, including initiating compliance reviews of firms' employment practices that follow the lead of the Office of Federal Contract Compliance Programs' pilot studies of Fortune 500 companies.

Recommendation 20:

All glass ceiling monitoring and enforcement efforts should include Asian Americans as well as women and other minorities.

Our investigation revealed that many Asian Americans, particularly immigrants, face unlawful discrimination in the workplace because of limited English proficiency, accent, or the desire to speak their native language on the job. Asian Americans with limited English proficiency or who speak accented English are unnecessarily barred from jobs and promotions because of artificially high English-proficiency requirements imposed by employers. For example, employers at times use the results of employment tests that require more English proficiency than necessary to do the job for which they are hiring. Few employment tests are professionally validated for the limited English proficient in general and for Asian Americans in particular. Similarly, employers may sometimes exclude persons who speak with accents from promotion even when these accents are easily understandable. Finally, many Asian Americans have found the use of their native languages on the job arbitrarily banned by employers when there is no compelling business justification for doing so.

Recommendation 21:

Employers should review their employment practices with a view to ferreting out and eliminating (unless justified) those practices that discriminate on the basis of language, such as English-only workplace rules, artificially high minimum-English-proficiency requirements, and the use of nonvalidated employment tests for limited-English-proficient job applicants.

Recommendation 22:

Federal, State, and local civil rights enforcement agencies should make an increased effort to protect the rights of language-minority workers. As part of this effort, they should, for example:

- increase outreach efforts to educate employers and the public about the rights of language-minority workers;
- monitor the development and use of employment tests given language-minority workers to ensure that they are professionally validated for those with limited English proficiency.

Many Asian Americans and others who received their professional training outside of the United States have difficulty obtaining jobs commensurate with their education and experience in this country. Sometimes they are unable to provide documentation of their professional training and experience in their countries of origin and are forced to retrain in the United States or to switch careers. In many fields, State professional certification boards have different requirements for foreign-educated professionals than for U.S.-educated professionals. In medicine, for instance, foreign medical school graduates face stiffer licensing and endorsement requirements than graduates of United States medical schools. Such disparate certification requirements are a major employment barrier for foreign-educated professionals. Although differential treatment of professionals educated in foreign countries has not been found to be illegal discrimination under Title VII, many

Asian American immigrant professionals suspect that the differential treatment they receive as foreign-educated professionals may in fact be a pretext for discrimination on the basis of national origin. State certification boards, on the other hand, contend that differential certification requirements are necessary because persons trained abroad often are not trained up to U.S. standards or because it is difficult to ascertain the quality of their training.

Recommendation 23:

Professional licensing boards that have differential requirements for U.S.-educated and foreign-educated professionals should examine their policies in light of the disparate impact on immigrants of diverse national origins to ensure fair treatment of foreign-educated professionals while maintaining U.S. professional standards.

The Immigration Reform and Control Act (IRCA),[12] enacted in 1986, imposes civil and criminal penalties (i.e., "employer sanctions,") on employers who hire unauthorized workers. To allay concern that employer sanctions would lead employers to discriminate against foreign-looking and foreign-sounding workers, IRCA also contained provisions aimed at preventing such discrimination. There is considerable evidence, however, that many Asian Americans, along with other minorities, have been discriminated against because of IRCA's employer sanctions provisions. In addition, many Asian Americans are not aware of their rights under IRCA and do not know where or how to file IRCA-related complaints. The Office of the Special Counsel of the U.S. Department of Justice, which has as one of its duties the dissemination of information about the IRCA's

antidiscrimination provisions, targets the bulk of its dissemination efforts towards Spanish-language speakers. Last year, Congress declined to repeal employer sanctions and implemented only some of the recommendations made by a Task Force on IRCA-Related Discrimination with a view to reducing the discriminatory effects of IRCA's employer sanctions provisions. In September 1991 bills entitled the Employer Sanctions Repeal Act of 1991 that would repeal employer sanctions were introduced in the Senate by Senator Kennedy (D-MA) and Senator Hatch (R-UT)[13] and in the House of Representatives by Representative Roybal (D-CA) and Representative Richardson (D-NM).[14]

Recommendation 24:

Congress should repeal employer sanctions provisions of the Immigration Reform and Control Act (IRCA) by passing the Employer Sanctions Repeal Act of 1991.[15]

Recommendation 25:

In the event that Congress chooses not to repeal IRCA's employer sanctions provisions,

a) Congress should, at the least, adopt all remaining recommendations made by the Task Force on IRCA-Related Discrimination for reducing IRCA-caused discrimination, namely:

- establish regional offices for the Office of Special Counsel;
- appropriate funds for a new outreach effort to educate employers and employees about IRCA's antidiscrimination provisions;
- simplify employers' work authorization

---

12   Immigration Reform and Control Act of 1986, 8 U.S.C. §§1101 *et seq.*, Pub. L. No. 99-603, 100 Stat. 3359.

13   S.1734, 102nd Cong., 2nd Sess. (1991).

14   H.R. 3366, 102nd Cong., 2nd Sess. (1991).

15   The U.S. Commission on Civil Rights has previously called for the repeal of IRCA's employer sanctions provisions. U.S. Commission on Civil Rights Statement, "Civil Rights Commission Calls for Repeal of Employer Sanctions," Mar. 29, 1990.

verification process;
- broaden the authority of the Department of Labor to enforce document check requirements; and
- request a future GAO study to determine the extent of remaining discrimination.

b) The Office of the Special Counsel of the Department of Justice should make increased efforts to inform Asian Americans and those who employ them of their rights under IRCA's antidiscrimination provisions.

The Commission has received allegations that Asian Americans are virtually shut out of construction unions in New York City and as a result are forced to take lower paying jobs restoring or repairing buildings. Although resource limitations prevented the Commission from undertaking a full investigation of this issue, available statistics confirm that Asian Americans are underrepresented in construction unions in New York City.

Recommendation 26:

The New York City Commission on Human Relations and the U.S. Equal Employment Opportunity Commission should undertake indepth studies of New York City's construction unions to determine whether they are discriminating against Asian Americans; should these investigations uncover evidence that construction unions are discriminating, they should take vigorous steps to enforce Federal, State, and local antidiscrimination laws.

Although Asian Americans of both genders encounter employment discrimination based on their race, the barriers to equal employment opportunity may be greater for Asian American women because of their gender. As women, they may become the victims of gender discrimination

and sexual harassment on the job. And as Asian American women, especially if they are immigrants, they are often less equipped to handle such discrimination than women of other races for two reasons. First, Asian American women may find that the small number of Asian American women in the workplace is an impediment to their joining informal networks of co-workers on the job, and this in turn may mean that when Asian American women encounter discrimination, they do not have easy access to the support and advice of their co-workers. Second, immigrant Asian American women are often not well-informed about their rights in the workplace and culturally conditioned not to complain about mistreatment. Their isolation from their co-workers, their ignorance of their rights, and their reluctance to complain all make Asian American women, especially immigrants, particularly vulnerable to sexual harassment in the workplace and other forms of employment discrimination.

Recommendation 27:

Employers and civil rights enforcement agencies should take steps to reduce the special employment barriers facing Asian American immigrant women; such steps should include special outreach efforts to inform Asian American women and other vulnerable groups of their rights and how to vindicate them.

Employment discrimination on the basis of race or national origin is prohibited under Federal laws. However, several recent Supreme Court decisions had a negative effect on Asian Americans' and other minorities' ability to obtain legal redress for discrimination against them. *Patterson v. Mclean Credit Union*[16] limited the types of employer behavior that are illegal under section 1981, meaning that Asian Americans could no longer sue for damages when their employers racially harassed them on the job. *Martin v. Wilks*[17] allowed consent decrees to be

---

16   491 U.S. 164 (1989).

challenged in court after they were entered, making made it more difficult for Asian Americans to seek to be included in consent decrees requiring affirmative action in municipal and State government employment. *Wards Cove Packing Co. v. Atonio*[18] increased plaintiffs' burden in disparate impact suits, making it more difficult for Asian Americans and others who face artificial barriers to employment to prove their case in court. In 1990 the Commission recommended the enactment of the Civil Rights Act of 1990 that would undo the effects of these three decisions.[19] Although the Civil Rights Act of 1990 was not enacted, in 1991, after exhaustive debate, Congress passed and President Bush signed into law a compromise bill, the Civil Rights Act of 1991,[20] containing most of the provisions of the Civil Rights Act of 1990.

Recommendation 28:

The Equal Employment Opportunity Commission and the Federal courts should make every possible effort to enforce vigorously the Civil Rights Act of 1991.

Political Participation

Asian Americans as a group lack political representation and empowerment. There are very few elected Asian American officials across the country, and Asian Americans as a group have low participation in the political process. This report has identified several barriers to Asian Americans' participation in the political process.

In a provision that is slated to expire on August 6, 1992, section 203(c) of the Voting Rights Act of 1982[21] requires States and political subdivisions to provide bilingual election materials in non-English languages when persons of that language group constitute more than 5 percent of the citizens of voting age in a district and have a higher than average illiteracy rate. Because the Asian American population is generally small and speaks a variety of languages, Asian Americans with a single language almost never constitute 5 percent of a district's voting-age population. Even in New York City, where 100,000 Chinese Americans were enumerated in 1980, Chinese Americans are less than 5 percent of the population. Thus, the 5 percent requirement means that Asian Americans almost never receive federally mandated bilingual election materials. Because the benefits of the language requirements of the Voting Rights Act do not extend to Asian Americans, limited English proficiency is a serious barrier to the political participation of many Asian Americans.

In the past, Asian American political power may have been diluted by apportionment schemes that split the Asian American population in an area into several districts and by at-large election systems within districts. As the fastest growing minority group in the Nation over the past decade, however, Asian Americans are increasingly becoming involved in the redistricting process, and several redrawn districts across the country have large Asian American populations.

Because of its effect on reapportionment and on the provision of bilingual voting materials, it is critical whether the 1990 census can provide an accurate count of Asian Americans. As important as the accuracy of the data, however, is their timely release, since the data are critical for gaining support for programs to help Asian Americans. The detailed data on Asian Ameri-

---

17   490 U.S. 755 (1989).

18   490 U.S. 642 (1989).

19   In June 1990 the Commissioners voted to endorse the Civil Rights Act of 1990 and released a report on the proposed legislation. U.S. Commission on Civil Rights, *Report on the Civil Rights Act of 1990* (July 1990).

20   Pub. L. No. 102-166.

21   42 U.S.C. §1973aa-1a(b) (1988).

cans from the 1980 census were not released until 1988. By the time the data were released, they were no longer useful in documenting the numbers and characteristics of the Asian American population, since Asian Americans had undergone a dramatic transformation during the intervening 8 years. The Census Bureau has agreed to release the 1990 data without undue delay, probably in 1991 or 1992.

Other factors limiting Asian Americans' political influence are anti-Asian bias among the public and difficulty in getting Asian American candidacies and issues taken seriously by the major political parties.

Recommendation 29:

Congress should reauthorize section 203(c) of the Voting Rights Act of 1982 with the following change:

- The section should be modified to apply to language-minority groups with more than a specified minimum number rather than a percentage of citizens of voting age.

Recommendation 30:

The Bureau of the Census should release detailed data on Asian Americans promptly, as promised.

Recommendation 31:

The major political parties and civic organizations (e.g., the League of Women Voters) should launch a major effort to promote voter registration and political participation among Asian Americans.

Access to Health Care

Many Asian Americans, especially recent immigrants and those in lower socioeconomic strata, have serious health care needs that are not being met. Refugees from Southeast Asia arrive in this country with serious physical and mental health problems stemming from their war-related experiences in their home countries.

Many Asian Americans face both language and cultural barriers to access to health care. Our national health care system is not adequately meeting the interpretation needs of the limited-English-proficient Asian American population. The bilingual family members and other untrained interpreters frequently used by health care providers are a poor substitute for trained health care interpreters. Cultural barriers compound the problems faced by many Asian Americans in gaining access to proper health care. To render effective care to Asian Americans, health care providers need considerable knowledge of and sensitivity towards Asian American cultures. Federal policies that exclude Asian Americans from Federal programs that recruit and train minority health care professionals have contributed to the dearth of trained health care professionals to serve Asian American communities.

Detailed data on the health and health care participation of Asian Americans as well as pertinent background data on their demographic and socioeconomic characteristics are indispensable in assessing the health care needs of Asian Americans and in developing appropriate policies to meet these needs. Such data need to be collected separately for each major Asian American ethnic group and broken down by immigration status, region of residence, and socioeconomic status. Without such data, critical needs of Asian Americans will go officially undocumented and politically unrecognized, and hence unmet. Yet most States and Federal health agencies make only minimal efforts to collect health-related data on Asian Americans.

Recommendation 32:

Public health and other social service programs should strive to meet the specific needs (e.g., interpretation, cultural sensitivity) of low-income and immigrant Asian American communities. Federal funding for such programs should be increased.

Recommendation 33:

The Department of Health and Human Services should raise the priority given to increasing the number of trained health care professionals who have the linguistic and cultural skills to serve immigrant Asian American communities. Asian Americans who meet these qualifications should be included in programs targeted at increasing the numbers of minority health care professionals.

Recommendation 34:

The Council on Ethical and Judicial Affairs of the American Medical Association should offer an opinion clarifying physicians' obligations to use medical interpreters when dealing with limited-English-proficient patients.

Recommendation 35:

Public health data should be collected and reported separately for Asian American subgroups.

Access to the Judicial System

Many Asian Americans, especially those limited in English proficiency, do not have equal access to the American judicial system. The severe shortage of trained interpreters is a critical barrier to access to our courts for limited-English-proficient Asian Americans. When interpreters are unavailable, linguistic minorities are often deterred from using the courts. When they do use the courts, they are often misinformed, intimidated, demeaned, and sometimes denied important rights. In the absence of court-appointed, qualified interpreters, defendants have no choice but to rely on family members, untrained court personnel, and even law enforcement officers to translate for them, creating the potential for inaccurate interpretation due to lack of familiarity with legal terminology or conflict of interest. It is for these reasons that the Court Interpreters Act[22] provides that the Federal courts set standards for and certify qualified interpreters. However, very few interpreters have been certified, and the certification program set up under the act only tests in Spanish. Furthermore, the use of an interpreter is left to the discretion of the presiding judge.

Recommendation 36:

Federal and State authorities should launch a national effort to train and certify court interpreters and to ensure that all limited-English-proficient persons have access to certified interpreters in their dealings with the judicial system. In particular, the Court Interpreters Act should be implemented more vigorously and should be modified to give judges precise instruction about when the provision of certified interpreters is warranted.

Recommendation 37:

The American Bar Association should amend Rule 1.4 of its "Model Rules of Professional Conduct"[23] to clarify attorneys' obligations to use interpreters when dealing with limited-English-proficient clients.

Battered Asian American Women

Foreign-born Asian American women who are battered by their spouses do not have adequate access to police protection and social services. These women have significant linguistic and cultural barriers that prevent them from seeking help. When they seek police protection,

---

22   28 U.S.C. § 1827.

23   American Bar Association, "Model Rules of Professional Conduct," Rule 1.4, "Communication."

they find that police arriving at their door are likely to listen only to their husbands, particularly if they speak better English than they do. Furthermore, few social service agencies have linguistically and culturally trained staff who can help them. In fact, social service agencies who seek to serve the needs of battered Asian American women often are unable to obtain the necessary funding, sometimes because of rigid funding formulas that provide a fixed amount of money per client served and do not make allowances for the extra costs of serving Asian American women.

Recommendation 38:
Federal, State, and local funding agencies should fund social services programs that meet the specific needs (e.g., interpretation, cultural sensitivity) of battered Asian American wives. In particular, such agencies should adopt flexible funding formulas to allow social service agencies to serve higher cost clients, such as Asian American battered wives.

Media Portrayal of Asian Americans

The public's perceptions and attitudes towards Asian Americans are heavily influenced by the way Asian Americans are portrayed by the media. Many of the civil rights problems confronting Asian Americans are fashioned by stereotypes, especially the model minority stereotype, that are promoted by the media. Others are the result of a general ignorance about Asian Americans that arises from a lack of coverage of Asian Americans and their concerns by the mainstream media. The underrepresentation of Asian Americans in decision-making positions in the media contributes to determining the slant and depth of the media's coverage of Asian Americans. The media have a major role to play in modulating racial tensions and shaping the future of relations between the Asian American community and the public at large. As such, they have the responsibility to provide accurate and indepth coverage of Asian American communities to the American public.

Recommendation 39:
The media should make every effort to provide balanced, indepth, and sensitive coverage of Asian Americans and to improve the representation of Asian Americans in their decision-making ranks.

Religious Accommodation

For Asian Americans who belong to non-Western religions, the practices and requirements of their religions are sometimes incompatible with majority traditions, established business practices, and laws. Asian Americans practicing non-Western religions are vulnerable to discrimination based on their religion in the employment arena, where employers set requirements that fail to accommodate the religious needs of Asian Americans. A recent Supreme Court decision, *Employment Division v. Smith*,[24] has considerably narrowed the rights of religious minorities by allowing the government to deny exemption from laws that interfere with religious conduct as long as such laws are generally applicable and not adopted for the purpose of discrimination. The Religious Freedom Restoration Act[25] currently before Congress would require the government to show a compelling State interest before religious minorities could be forced to comply with laws that significantly interfere with their religion.

Recommendation 40:
Congress should move quickly to hold hearings on the effects of the *Employment Division v.*

---

24   110 S. Ct. 1595 (1990).

25   H.R. 2797.

Smith decision on the religious practices of Asian Americans.

General Recommendations

Accurate, reliable, and complete data on Asian Americans are vital for government, private sector, and other efforts to develop plans to meet the needs of Asian Americans. Yet data on Asian Americans are sorely lacking in many critical areas, including demographics, socioeconomic status, educational achievement, and public health. Often, available sample sizes of Asian Americans are too small to provide information about them. In many large-scale data collection efforts, Asian Americans are grouped together with Native Americans and sometimes with blacks and Hispanics in "other" or "nonwhite" categories. Asian Americans are sometimes identified as a separate group, but data on individual Asian American subgroups are almost never collected. The diversity of the Asian American community, which is comprised of persons with many national origins, immigration dates and statuses, and socioeconomic levels means that until data collection efforts differentiate among these diverse subgroups, our understanding of Asian Americans will continue to be inadequate to develop plans to meet their needs.

Recommendation 41:

Federal, State, and local governments should provide for enhanced data collection on Asian Americans in all areas—including socioeconomic statistics, education, vital statistics, health, etc. The data need to be disaggregated by Asian/Pacific group and include such information as immigration date and status. In most cases, Asian Americans need to be oversampled, and in some cases special surveys may be needed.

Racial tensions appear to be escalating across the country, yet the political parties have done little to defuse them, and some political candidates have even exacerbated racial tensions by using racial rhetoric in their campaigns. Political leaders in the United States need to provide effective moral leadership in the area of civil rights, thereby once again making civil rights an urgent national issue given sustained public attention. The general absence of moral leadership carries over to the civil rights concerns of Asian Americans: this report has found that the political leadership, the media, and the public have in most instances failed to respond to the needs and concerns of Asian Americans. Violations of Asian Americans' civil rights are not given the high priority on the national agenda that they deserve. This observation leads the Commission to recommend:

Recommendation 42:

This country's political leadership should endeavor to create a national climate that discourages anti-Asian discrimination and ensures equal opportunity for Asian Americans. In particular, political leaders at all levels need to make a top priority:

- combating prejudice and violence against as well as stereotyping of Asian Americans;
- increasing public awareness and sensitivity towards the needs of Asian American immigrants;
- ensuring that all necessary measures are taken to guarantee equal opportunity to Asian Americans.

Recommendation 43:

Federal, State, and local government should mount a coordinated national effort to reach out to new Asian American immigrants, to educate them about our system of government, to inform them of their civil rights, and to encourage their participation in the political process. As part of this effort, the Department of Justice should coordinate the development of a civil rights handbook to provide Asian American immigrants with basic information about our system of government and their rights as American residents/citizens.

Recommendation 44:

The President should appoint a national council on refugees to review Federal activities and programs designed to help refugees and the communities in which refugees reside, to work with State and local governments and private organizations on refugee-related efforts, to collect and disseminate information on refugees and refugee policy, and to make recommendations to the President and Congress for improving aid to refugees and the communities in which they live. Also the Office of Refugee Resettlement in the Department of Health and Human Services should undertake a comprehensive review of its programs and policies to determine their effectiveness in meeting the needs of refugees and of the communities in which refugees live.

Appendix

THE CITY OF NEW YORK
OFFICE OF THE MAYOR

VIRGO Y. LEE
DIRECTOR

OFFICE FOR ASIAN AFFAIRS
52 CHAMBERS STREET
NEW YORK, N.Y. 10007
(212) 566-4010

October 11, 1991

Dr. James Cunningham
Assistant Staff Director
U.S Civil Rights Commission
1121 Vermont Avenue, N.W., Room 700
Washington D.C., 20425

Dear Dr. Cunningham,

Mayor Dinkins has asked my office to comment on the portion of the draft of the report entitled "Civil Rights Issues Facing Asian Americans in 1990's." The report refers to the boycott of two Korean grocery stores in the Flatbush Section of Brooklyn that started on January 18, 1990.

Your draft primarily takes quotes from newspaper articles and published reports such as: the Mayor's Committee, the New York City Council and NYC Police Department. As such, there is little to be said about previously published opinions regarding the boycott issue.

I would only offer the opinion that when the boycott issue is referred to as a "black" boycott of Korean stores, a more accurate description would be "Caribbean" since the surrounding community was primarily a Haitian Community and the initial boycotters were of Caribbean descent.

Beyond this opinion and the attached comments, the report adequately attributes the comments to the appropriate sources.

Sincerely yours,

Virgo Y. Lee

207

CITY OF HERCULES

111 CIVIC DRIVE, HERCULES, CA 94547

PHONE: 415 • 799 • 8200

October 4, 1991

Mr. James S. Cunningham
Assistant Staff Director
 for Programs, Policy and Research
1121 Vermont Avenue, N.W., Room 700
Washington, D.C. 20425

Re: Comment on Draft Report: Civil Rights Issues Facing Asian Americans in the
        1990's

Dear Mr. Cunningham:

This letter responds to correspondence which the City received from Staff Director
Wilfredo Gonzales, dated September 27, 1991. In that correspondence, Mr. Gonzales
requested the Hercules Police Chief to review a portion of the above-entitled draft
report regarding an arrest of a number of juveniles in the City of Hercules on
August 28, 1989, and to comment on the accuracy of the report.

The City appreciates the opportunity to comment on the draft report. The Chief of
Police, the City's Attorney and I have reviewed the draft report, and have
concluded that it does not accurately describe the August 28, 1989, juvenile arrests
in several respects. In particular, the draft fails to describe the diligent efforts the
City's Police Department made to work with its minority community to resolve these
important issues of police/community relations.

For your convenience, I have redrafted the report so that it is consistent with both
the facts that were revealed through the Department's investigation of the matter,
and the City's willingness to eliminate even the appearance of police harassment of
juveniles. For your convenience, I have also enclosed a copy of the City's
investigative response to the matter.

Draft Report Revision

Between 1900 and 1970, Hercules was a small, predominantly white town of 1,000
residents. Since then, Hercules, has grown rapidly to 17,000 residents, 25 percent
of whom are Filipino (see 1990 Census material). The community has evolved as
multi-racial with fully integrated neighborhoods during the past 15 years of growth.
The City Council has been composed of a "majority of minorities" since the early
1980's, including Filipino representation since 1979. The community is highly
educated and is at a high middle income level of $60,000 average per household.

208

Regular social interaction among the different races and ethnic groups is routinely enjoyed as seen in our annual Cultural Fair, at special community events throughout the year, in our parks, on the trail system, tennis courts, etc.

On November 17, 1989, the American Civil Liberties Union and the Asian Law Caucus filed a complaint with the Hercules Police Department. The complaint was made on behalf of 11 Hercules juveniles and their parents regarding the Department's response to a citizen report on August 28, 1989, that several juveniles were fighting at a private residence.

When the police arrived on the scene, approximately 20 to 25 juveniles were fighting and running through the front and back yard of a vacant home on a residential street. Further investigation revealed that the back door of the vacant home had been pried open. The police arrested 18 juveniles in the vicinity and charged them with trespassing and fighting. Police also confiscated two baseball bats and a knife from the juveniles. Police identified two juveniles at the scene who had previously been released to the custody of their parents three days before the fighting in a shopping center parking lot. The August 28, 1989, fight appeared to be an expansion of the prior fight.

The complaint charged that the arrested juveniles, some of whom were allegedly handcuffed, were driven to the police station and detained for "two to five hours." The Police Department responded that it processed the group of 18 juveniles as quickly as possible, releasing each to the custody of his or her parents as soon as the juvenile was photographed and fingerprinted. Although many were released much sooner, the last of the several juveniles has completed processing after only three hours and 45 minutes had elapsed. Several juveniles had to wait the extended time due to their parent's request to pick up their child after work.

The juveniles also alleged in the complaint that they were refused permission to make telephone calls. The Department responded that the Department itself contacted each parent or guardian in order to facilitate the efficient processing of the juveniles and to assure that a responsible adult was notified. Several juveniles had expressed objections to their parents being notified. In response to the allegation that one girl was refused permission to use the bathroom for over an hour and a half, the Department's investigation revealed that there was no female officer available to accompany the girl during that time. The complaint further charged that the arresting officers used excessive force and had sought to intimidate the juveniles, including threatening them. The Department responded that it had acted only to the extent necessary to maintain control over the boisterous group.

Following the August 28, 1989, incident, Filipino juveniles also came forward with the allegation that the police had frequently stopped them for no apparent reason, searched the trunks of their cars, and asked them if they were members of gangs. Until that time, not even the parents of the Filipino juveniles were not aware of such allegations nor were any complaints lodged with the Department or the City.

The City and the parents of the juveniles worked together to resolve these issues. City representatives met with the parents and their representatives on several occasions to devise strategies to improve police and community relations. Juveniles, parents, and City representatives also attended a Contra Costa Human Rights Commission Hearing on the treatment of minority juveniles in order to gain a better understanding of the issues.

The Police Department chose to modify several of its operating procedures in an effort to address all concerns raised. The Department revised its procedures to specify both the criteria to be used to identify gang members and the juvenile arrest rights regarding the use of telephones and bathroom facilities. There have been no reports of police harassment in Hercules since that complaint was filed.

On behalf of the Hercules Mayor and City Council, we hereby formally request that this revision be substituted, in its entirety, for the draft language which was originally provided. We believe it to be a forthright and accurate portrayal of the community, the City and of the incident. Please contact me if you have further questions or concerns.

Very truly yours,

Marilyn E. Leuck
City Manager
City of Hercules

MEL:kc

cc: The Honorable Mayor and City Councilmembers of Hercules
       California Delegation of the House Judiciary Committee
       Ms. Eve Maldonado, California League of Cities - Washington, D.C.
       Mr. Richard Whitmore, Attorney at Law
       Mr. Russell Quinn, Hercules Chief of Police

UNITED STATES DEPARTMENT OF EDUCATION

OFFICE FOR CIVIL RIGHTS

THE ASSISTANT SECRETARY

NOV 7 1991

Mr. Wilfredo J. Gonzalez
Staff Director
U.S.Commission on Civil Rights
1121 Vermont Avenue, N.W.
Room 700
Washington, D.C.   20425

Dear Mr. Gonzalez:

Thank you for the opportunity to comment again on your proposed
report. As you recall, on September 27, 1991, you asked the
Office for Civil Rights (OCR) to review and comment upon two
sections of your draft report, "Civil Rights Issues Facing Asian
Americans in the 1990s." One section provided a summary of the
Office for Civil Rights' enforcement of Title VI of the Civil
Rights Act of 1964 regarding the provision of services to
limited-English-proficient children, and the other section was a
lengthy discussion of OCR's 1990 compliance review of Harvard
University. I sent comments to you on October 16, 1991, pointing
out OCR's concerns with the report. Some revisions were
subsequently made, and on October 23, 1991, you again forwarded
the two sections and asked for additional comments. I have
reviewed the draft and submit the following comments. These
comments, supersede my previous comments and I have no objection
to your not including my previous letter with your report.

<u>OCR's Enforcement of the Rights of Language Minority Students</u>

I am disappointed that this section of the report presents such a
one-sided view of OCR's activities in this critical area. The
provision of services to limited-English-proficient students was
first identified as a priority issue for OCR in 1990. As such,
the resources of this agency that are not consumed by the
investigation of complaints are focused on this, and a limited
number of other, high priority issues. The effort OCR is
devoting to this issue is greatly disproportionate to the
extremely small percentage of complaints we receive alleging that
school districts are not providing services to limited-English-
proficient children; however, its priority status reflects my own
sense of this issue's importance. Access to educational programs
is a civil right, and it is essential to the successful
accomplishment of the President's national education goals.

Page 2 - Mr. Wilfredo J. Gonzalez

Your summary criticizes this agency's performance in the 1980s, citing a decline in the number of compliance reviews, inadequate monitoring of the corrective action plans obtained as a result of those reviews, and selected quotes from various Congressional reports. The draft report leaves the reader with the strong impression that OCR was willfully ignoring this issue and the criticism leveled by various representatives of the Congress. This is simply incorrect.

In the 1980s, OCR followed a consistent and responsible path of enforcement, policy development and compliance review activity. Due to OCR's inappropriate reliance on the <u>Lau</u> Remedies from 1975 to 1981 as a <u>de facto</u> compliance standard and the failed effort to require bilingual education through regulation, OCR began the 1980s with no viable Title VI policy or procedures on the provision of services to limited-English-proficient students. Essentially, OCR started from scratch to develop workable guidance to begin to address the policy vacuum that existed in 1981.

Following the Secretary's withdrawal of the "Language Minority NPRM" in February 1981, OCR developed interim procedures for conducting Title VI investigations. Under these procedures, more than 170 compliance reviews and complaint investigations were carried out during the 1981-1985 time period. Following an update of these interim procedures in the December 3, 1985, document, OCR continued to review the practices of school systems on this issue. For example, in June 1986, OCR reviewed survey data from school districts nationwide to determine which districts reported significant numbers of unserved limited-English-proficient students. OCR's regional offices followed up with each of these districts.

At several points in the draft report, reference is made to various studies or Congressional reports on OCR's performance. <u>What concerns me is not the reference to such documents, but that the Commission's draft report uncritically accepts the conclusions of these reports and their interpretation of the data OCR provided without examining whether they interpreted the data correctly.</u> I can only imagine that the Commission would, itself, be quite concerned if committee studies and reports or a congressman's comments regarding your performance were taken as gospel without being subjected to critical analysis.

For example, on pages 35-37, the draft report discusses the conclusions of a 1988 report generated by the House Committee on Education and Labor. A brief summary of OCR's response to the report's charges follows. OCR provided the Congressional committee with a detailed response to every allegation their report made. OCR also noted, in the cover letter to the Chairman of the Committee, that

> [I]t is also clear that many of the report's criticisms
> are inaccurate or misleading. The report does not
> accurately take into account the effects on OCR of
> certain major legal changes. . . nor does it display a
> sound understanding of OCR's enforcement procedures.

Also, on pages 34 and 35, the draft report states a journalist's
conclusion that the 1981 to 1985 OCR Title VI compliance activity
data on limited-English-proficient students show that "school
districts were nine times less likely to be scheduled for a
compliance review [from 1981 to 1985] than during the previous
five-year period. During this same period, OCR conducted only 95
compliance reviews covering 65 districts compared with 573
districts reviewed between 1976 and 1980. . . ." Using a
newspaper article as evidence to reach conclusions about a
Federal agency's civil rights enforcement practices in an area
where there are complex policy and legal issues is, in my view, a
dubious practice. Aside from that, the statement is very
misleading. It leaves the impression that OCR, from 1976 to 1980
conducted on-site compliance reviews of 573 school systems. It
did not. In the mid-1970s, based on statistical data, OCR
developed a list of about 330 school systems nation-wide that
might not be serving limited-English-proficient students. Many
of these districts were required to submit corrective action
plans without any on-site investigation ever being conducted.
Another group of about 175 systems was required to submit plans
to qualify for the Emergency School Aid Act funding.

OCR has made numerous ongoing efforts since 1988 to improve its
performance as an enforcement agency. We are still improving.
The agency has not accomplished all that I would like to achieve,
particularly in the number of compliance reviews we have been
able to conduct, but given the enormous increase in complaints we
have received since 1989 (up 37 percent) and the budgetary
constraints under which we have been asked to operate, I am
extremely proud of OCR's performance during my tenure.

As noted in your report, my National Enforcement Strategy
establishes the enforcement of the rights of limited-English-
proficient children as a priority issue for OCR for compliance
reviews and technical assistance activities in FY 1991. It is
also a priority issue in FY 1992. In FY 1991, OCR initiated 12
Title VI compliance reviews on the provision of services to
limited-English-proficient students, or 30 percent of the 40
reviews initiated, although complaints on this issue account for
an extremely small percentage of the complaints received by this
agency. By comparison, in 1990 OCR initiated no reviews on this
issue. In 1992, we will significantly increase the number of
compliance reviews OCR initiates, including additional reviews on
the provision of services to limited-English-proficient students.

In FY 1991, several regional offices conducted monitoring and technical assistance outreach activities with school districts that had corrective action plans as a result of previous OCR investigations. For example, our regional office in Chicago conducted a comprehensive on-site monitoring review of a major mid-western school system, found specific violations of previous plan agreements, and obtained detailed corrective actions. Another regional office assisted a major school district in its efforts to develop a plan to address problems with its procedures for assigning students to bilingual education. Additionally, we have participated in over 35 technical assistance workshops on limited-English proficiency during 1991 in cities across the country from Boston to Springfield to Portland.

To further assist our regional offices in conducting investigations on this issue, on September 27, 1991, I issued a memorandum entitled, "Policy Update on Schools' Obligations Toward National Origin Minority Students with Limited-English Proficiency (LEP) Students." This is an update of the 1985 policy statement. OCR's regional offices were also provided with detailed investigative guidance and training on how to conduct investigations of this issue.

In order to ensure that our enforcement policy guidance reaches all aspects of the education and limited-English community, I have initiated a dissemination plan for the policy update that includes mailings to over 1,900 interested groups, briefings for all interested Department personnel, as well as for House and Senate staffers and a briefing for interest groups scheduled for November 14, 1991, to which you have been invited. Additionally, we have put together a fact sheet that contains frequently asked questions and provides answers in terms that are less legalistic and easier to understand. I am enclosing a copy of the fact sheet for your information.

Your report aims to summarize OCR's enforcement of the rights of limited-English-proficient students. I ask that you describe OCR's efforts in this area in the context of OCR's total workload and the efforts we have made to improve our effectiveness as a civil rights enforcement agency. It is my hope that you will give additional focus to these efforts in your report. By not doing so, your report does a disservice to this agency and to its staff.

Harvard Compliance Review

I am pleased to see that in response to my earlier comments much of the discussion in the report on the Harvard Compliance Review has been revised and made more accurate. However, there continue to be statements in this section of the report that misinterpret, or misconstrue, OCR's investigation and findings.

In the discussion of the methodology of OCR's logistic regression analysis, which appears on page 39, footnote 112 states that "a more appropriate specification [of the independent variables] would have been to enter [them] as categorical variables [rather than as continuous variables.]" Variables such as the academic rating were treated as continuous and not categorical variables because of the large number of possible comparisons involved in the latter approach. When this analysis was conducted, OCR had no preconceived notion that particular categorical comparisons required closer review than others. Consequently, we examined the general impact of all available variables.

With regard to the decision to use the stepwise procedure, we disagree with the draft report's implication that this was somehow incorrect or inappropriate. Although this procedure did "[discard] some variables," as noted in footnote 113, we "employed logistic regression to try to identify which of the ten admissions variables could account for the admit rate disparity." (Statement, p.34.) Thus, the procedure was _supposed_ to discard those variables that clearly did not account for the disparity. While it is true that the coefficients would have been slightly different with the inclusion of all of the variables, these differences would have been extremely small, given the statistical power involved and the p<.05 inclusion criteria. The differences would have had no effect on either the conclusions OCR drew from the statistical analyses conducted or the direction of OCR's investigation as a whole.

The statistical analyses were only one part of our investigation, and they were based on _available_ information only. As explained in the cautionary note that preceded the statistical section in OCR's Statement of Findings: "More importantly, perhaps, is the understanding that, while there is a great deal of information relevant to the admit/reject decision contained in the quantitative variables we analyzed, there may be other unmeasured variables which affect the decision." (Statement, p.32.)

In addition, on page 41, the report concludes that OCR "gives too little prominence to its discussion of the logistic regressions and as a result may leave the casual reader with little understanding of the basis for OCR's statistical findings." It is doubtful that the "casual reader's" understanding of OCR's statistical findings would be enhanced by further discussions of logistic regression analyses.

One of my major concerns with the draft report focuses on the discussion of the use of legacies, which appears on pages 48-49. First, on page 48, the report implies that OCR should have, and did not, ask for supporting evidence that alumni support would drop off without the legacy preference, and that there were no reasonable alternatives to the use of the preference. OCR did, indeed, ask Harvard for any data, studies or other information that demonstrated the effect of the legacy preference on alumni giving. In response, Harvard provided no quantifiable data, but asserted that "based on hundreds, perhaps thousands, of conversations with alumni whose sons and daughters have applied [to Harvard]," they believed that the legacy preference stimulated financial contributions and that "alumni whose children have been rejected may sever all connections with the University." (Letter to OCR, July 2, 1990).

Also on page 48, the report concludes that "[t]he issue of the legality of alumni preference under Title VI remains unresolved." This is not true with repect to its use at Harvard. Harvard's use of the legacy (alumni) preference as one factor in the admit/reject decision is not inconsistent with the requirements of Title VI. While the Commission may have more general concerns about the legality of alumni preferences under Title VI, it should not obscure the distinction between those concerns and OCR's specific findings with respect to Harvard.

On page 49, the report suggests that OCR, by relying upon the Rosenstock decision, erroneously employed a "rational relation" test, developed under the due process and equal protection clauses of the U.S. Constitution, when it should have looked to the more demanding "strict scrutiny" standard in conducting its review of Harvard's use of legacy tips. Neither proposition is correct.

OCR did not use a "rational relation" test. Instead, OCR, in making a determination under Title VI, utilized a legal standard and analytical framework derived from Title VII "disparate impact" cases. Griggs v. Duke Power Company, 401 U.S. 424 (1971); McDonnell Douglas v. Green, 411 U.S. 792 (1973), Wards Cove Packing Co. v. Antonio, 490 U.S. 642 (1989). Following the approach developed in these cases, OCR's investigation: (1) identified whether there was a significant disparity in the rate of acceptance for Asian-American applicants; (2) identified criteria that caused the disparity; (3) ascertained whether the recipient was able to offer a legitimate justification for the criteria; (4) identified whether there were any alternative criteria that are less divisive that would have accomplished the recipient's legitimate ends; and (5) if there were such alternatives, determined whether the recipient had legitimate reasons for not adopting them.

OCR should not have applied the constitutional standard of "strict scrutiny" to its review of the Harvard legacy policy, because the policy does not employ, implicitly or explicitly, a racial or ethnic classification. OCR found that the application of the legacy tips resulted in a disparate impact on the basis of national origin. Therefore, analysis under the Title VII disparate impact standard was most appropriate.

Page 7 - Mr. Wilfredo J. Gonzalez

Finally, on page 49 the report criticizes OCR for basing its approval of legacy tips "on 'one Federal district court's willingness to recognize a link' between an institution's economic interest and alumni contribution." OCR's determination on the legitimacy of the use of the legacy tip at Harvard was based on a standard Title VI analysis following Title VII precedents, not on the decision of "one Federal district court."

Thank you for affording me this additional opportunity to comment on the Commission's draft report. If I can be of further assistance to you, please contact me at FTS 732-1213.

Sincerely,

Michael L. Williams
Assistant Secretary
for Civil Rights

Enclosure

FACT SHEET -- OCR POLICY UPDATE ON SCHOOLS' OBLIGATIONS TOWARD NATIONAL ORIGIN MINORITY STUDENTS WITH LIMITED-ENGLISH PROFICIENCY

Purpose of the Policy Update

Q: Why is this issue important?

A: Without special language assistance, an estimated two million limited-English proficient students from a wide variety of ethnic and racial backgrounds may not have meaningful access to their schools' programs. In his AMERICA 2000 strategy, the President calls for meeting the educational needs of all students.

Q: Why is OCR involved in this area?

A: OCR is responsible for enforcing Title VI of the Civil Rights Act of 1964, which prohibits discrimination on the basis of race, color, or national origin in programs or activities that receive Federal financial assistance. OCR has interpreted Title VI to require that school districts "take affirmative steps to rectify [English] language deficiencies which have the effect of excluding national origin minority children from participation in the educational program offered." In Lau v. Nichols, 414 U.S. 563 (1974), the Supreme Court upheld this interpretation of Title VI.

Q: What is the purpose of the policy update?

A: The policy update is designed to provide additional guidance to our regional offices about what schools must do to comply with Title VI. OCR has distributed this policy widely to make schools, parents, and students aware of schools' obligations under Title VI and to ensure better compliance with Title VI. This policy update does not change OCR's policy under Title VI.

Acceptable Alternative Language Programs

Q. Must school districts use a particular type of alternative language program, such as transitional bilingual education or English as a Second Language, to comply with Title VI?

A.   No. Districts may use any program that is recognized as sound by some experts in the field or is considered a legitimate experimental strategy. Examples of such programs include transitional bilingual education, bilingual/bicultural education, structured immersion, developmental bilingual education, and English as a Second Language.

Q.   Has a school district satisfied its responsibilities under Title VI once it chooses an appropriate alternative language program?

A.   No. The district must also carry out the program properly and provide the teachers and resources necessary for the program to succeed. In addition, the school district must modify its program if, after a legitimate trial, it does not succeed in enabling LEP students to overcome their language barriers. As a practical matter, school districts will be unable to comply with this requirement without periodically evaluating their programs.

Staffing Requirements

Q.   What sort of qualifications must teachers in a bilingual education program have?

A.   Teachers of bilingual classes must be able to speak, read, and write both languages, and they should have received adequate instruction in the methods of bilingual education. They must also be fully qualified to teach the subject matter of the bilingual courses. In addition, the school district must be able to show that it has determined that its bilingual education teachers have the required skills.

Q.   If a school district uses a program other than bilingual education, what sort of qualifications must the program's teachers have?

A.   The program's teachers must have received adequate training in the specific teaching methods required by that program. This training can take the form of in-service training, formal college coursework, or a combination of the two. The district should ensure, through testing and classroom observation, that teachers have actually mastered the skills necessary to teach in the program successfully.

Q. How can a school district comply with Title VI if qualified teachers for its program are unavailable?

A. First, a district should be prepared to describe the efforts it has made to hire qualified teachers. If qualified teachers are temporarily unavailable, the district must require its teachers to work toward obtaining formal qualifications. In addition, the district must ensure that those teachers receive sufficient interim training to enable them to function adequately in the classroom, as well as any assistance they may need from bilingual aides that may be necessary to carry out the district's interim program.

Q. Can LEP students be taught solely by bilingual aides?

A. No. Bilingual aides must work under the direct supervision of qualified classroom teachers. LEP students should not be receiving instruction from aides rather than teachers.

Q. What qualifications must bilingual aides meet?

A. To the extent that the district's chosen educational program requires native language support, and if the district relies on bilingual aides to provide such support, the district should be able to demonstrate that it has determined that its aides have the appropriate level of skill in speaking, reading, and writing both languages. Aides at the kindergarten and first grade level, however, need not demonstrate reading and writing proficiency.

Exit Criteria for Language Minority LEP Students

Q. When can a school district exit a student from an alternative language program?

A. Students may not be exited from an alternative language program unless they can read, write, and comprehend English well enough to participate meaningfully in the district's regular program. Exit criteria that simply measure a student's oral language skills are inadequate. The district's exit criteria should be based on objective standards, such as test scores, and the district should be able to explain why students meeting those criteria will be able to participate meaningfully in the regular classroom.

Q.   If a school district elects to emphasize English over other subjects when LEP students first enroll, does the district have any obligation to provide special instruction to the students once they learn English well enough to function in the regular classroom?

A.   Yes. While schools with such programs may discontinue special instruction in English once LEP students become English-proficient, schools must provide the assistance necessary to remedy academic deficiencies that may have occurred in other subjects while the student was focusing on learning English.

Gifted/Talented Programs

Q.   Can school districts refuse to consider admitting LEP students to gifted/talented programs?

A.   No. If a district has a process for locating and identifying gifted/talented students, it must also locate and identify gifted/talented LEP students who could benefit from the program. Exclusion of LEP students from gifted/talented programs must be justified by the needs of the particular student or by the nature of the program.

OCR Compliance Activities

Q: How does OCR ensure that school districts fulfill their obligations under Title VI?

A: OCR investigates complaints filed by individuals or groups who believe that they, or others, have been subjected to discrimination. Even if no formal complaint has been filed, OCR can conduct compliance reviews of school districts to determine whether they are fulfilling their obligations under Title VI. In addition to conducting investigations, OCR provides technical assistance to state and local education agencies and program beneficiaries to inform them of their obligations and rights under Title VI. Technical assistance is provided using a variety of methods including on-site consultations, training, workshops, and meetings.

Q: What happens if OCR finds that a school district's treatment of LEP students violates Title VI?

A: If OCR finds a Title VI violation, we try to negotiate a
     corrective action plan under which the district specifies
     the actions it will take to remedy the violation. If
     negotiations are successful, OCR issues a letter of findings
     detailing the Title VI violation and stating that the
     district has agreed to remedy the violation. We then
     monitor the district's actions to ensure that it has carried
     out the corrective action plan.

     If OCR is unable to get the district to agree to a
     corrective action plan, we initiate formal enforcement
     activities which, after an administrative hearing, can lead
     to the termination of all Federal financial assistance to
     the district unless the district agrees to remedy the Title
     VI violation.

Q: Who can we contact for information on how to file a
     complaint or obtain technical assistance?

A: You can call OCR at (202) 732-1213 to obtain the address and
     telephone number of the OCR regional office responsible for
     your area. The regional office will be able to give you
     specific information about filing a complaint or obtaining
     technical assistance.

UNIVERSITY OF CALIFORNIA, BERKELEY

BERKELEY · DAVIS · IRVINE · LOS ANGELES · RIVERSIDE · SAN DIEGO · SAN FRANCISCO   SANTA BARBARA · SANTA CRUZ

OFFICE OF THE CHANCELLOR   BERKELEY, CALIFORNIA   94720

October 16, 1991

Mr. James S. Cunningham
Assistant Staff Director for Programs, Policy, and Research
United States Commission on Civil Rights
1121 Vermont Avenue, N.W.
Washington, D.C. 20425

Dear Mr. Cunningham:

Thank you for the opportunity to review sections of the draft report *Civil Rights Issues Facing Asian Americans in the 1990s*. As an active member of the Berkeley faculty during most of the 1980s, I was very interested to revisit many of the issues with which we struggled. I am also impressed by the thoroughness of the research reflected in the draft and in the extensive use of primary sources.

At the same time, however, I must say that I am somewhat troubled by the tone of the sections dealing with Berkeley. I believe the current draft places too much emphasis on the allegations against the University and too little on the findings of the investigative bodies. Overall, much less attention is devoted to the University's side in the current draft, and much more is given to speculation about motivations. I believe the draft should cite the facts of the controversy more concisely and in a more balanced manner.

I hope these comments will be helpful.

Sincerely,

Chang-Lin Tien
Chancellor

HARVARD UNIVERSITY

DANIEL STEINER
Vice President and General Counsel

MASSACHUSETTS HALL
CAMBRIDGE, MASSACHUSETTS 02138
(617) 495-4778

November 7, 1991

Mr. James S. Cunningham
Assistant Staff Director for Programs,
 Policy and Research
U. S. Commission on Civil Rights
1121 Vermont Avenue, N.W.
Washington, D. C. 20425

Dear Mr. Cunningham:

Thank you for your letter of October 28, 1991 and for the revised version of the Harvard University portion of the draft report of the Commission on Civil Rights. The changes from the earlier version are, as you wrote, significant, and we accept your suggestion that we substitute this letter and the enclosure for our earlier letter as the Harvard comments that will be included with the final report as an appendix.

As set forth in the enclosed memorandum, some of the earlier expressed serious concerns still remain. The criticism of the methodology employed by the Office of Civil Rights, Department of Education (OCR) in its investigation of Asian American undergraduate admissions at Harvard and Radcliffe Colleges seems unwarranted and based largely on speculation that different approaches might have produced different results. The draft report fails to provide any solid argument for faulting the OCR methodology. The draft report also tries to make an issue of the extent to which Harvard in fact uses an ethnic reader to review applications for admission. Title VI does not require Harvard to involve an ethnic reader in its admission process, and the extent to which one is used is irrelevant to the question of discrimination. In respect to the two factors that accounted for the small difference in the admission rate of Asian American applicants, the Commission's discussion of the legal issues shows an inadequate understanding of the analysis performed by OCR, which is the Department charged by law with the interpretation of Title VI, and of the applicable legal concepts under established case law.

Both OCR and Harvard invested enormous amounts of time, thought, and energy in the two-year investigation into the questions of alleged quotas on Asian American admissions and other forms of discrimination. OCR definitively concluded that Harvard did not discriminate in any way. The range of the analysis and the amount of data -- from regression analysis involving thousands of numbers to folder-by-folder review of hundreds of applications -- demonstrates the breadth and quality of the review. Over the years, Harvard has devoted a great deal of attention not only to compliance with Title VI but also to affirmative action in Asian American admissions. Our affirmative action program, particularly our extensive recruiting efforts, has been effective: Asian Americans in 1990 and 1991 constituted over 19% of the entering freshman class as opposed to under 5% in the late 1970s. The conclusions reached by OCR fairly reflect Harvard's actions in an area that has great meaning to us as we seek an able and diverse student body, and we would hope that the Commission on Civil Rights, before criticizing an extensive OCR investigation, would provide a better reasoned, sounder basis for its criticism.

We appreciate your courtesy in sending us the revised draft report for comment. If we can be helpful in any way in the process of further consideration of the draft report, we are prepared to review any later drafts or to meet with you and your staff.

Sincerely,

Enc.

MEMORANDUM OF HARVARD UNIVERSITY ON DRAFT REPORT

This memorandum presents Harvard University's comments on that section of the U.S. Civil Rights Commission's draft report that concerns the Title VI review of Asian American admissions conducted by the Department of Education's Office for Civil Rights (OCR). Harvard's comments concern three parts of the draft report: the statistical analysis, the examination of the admission process, and the preference given to children of alumni.

Before turning to these matters, we have one preliminary comment. The Commission characterizes OCR's report as providing for the first time "well-guarded institutional proprietary information about Harvard's admissions procedures." (p.35) In fact, however, previous public statements by Harvard and reported research about its admissions process had disclosed the essential elements of the process; OCR's report corroborated those prior accounts. Our admissions process has been studied by innumerable faculty committees, by many graduate students (including the researcher referred to in the Commission's footnote), and by various publications. Indeed, a recent book by the former Dean of the Faculty included an entire chapter on Harvard admissions. Far from being secret, Harvard's admissions process has been extensively discussed in the public domain.

Statistical Analysis

Some of the Commission's comments on OCR's statistical methods seem to speculate without basis that alternate methodological approaches would have had different results. The Commission criticizes OCR's aggregation of data without addressing OCR's justification (mentioned in footnote 114) that the sample size was too small to be completely reliable. Note that OCR's statistical analysis aggregated data from 10 years, looked at data from individual classes, and analyzed particularly the more recent classes (the classes of 1991 and 1992). While we are confident that no discrimination occurred in any of the years reviewed, we agree with OCR's approach that ensuring current compliance is the proper goal of a Title VI review. There are, after all, sound policy reasons for statutes of limitation; not only is proof less "stale" and more likely to be available, but also governmental resources are focussed on what a recipient of federal funds is doing now and not in the distant past.

More significantly, we find troubling the discussion that ends the section on statistical analysis (p. 41). The Commission speculates at length that admissions officers might have held biases that might have affected personal ratings that might have affected admissions decisions. The report does not mention at this point that OCR itself considered this hypothesis, addressed it by reviewing files, and concluded that there was no evidence of such bias. While the

Commission discusses this aspect of OCR's analysis later in its draft report, its raising this issue in this way -- based purely on speculation and without immediately acknowledging that OCR's review disproved it -- unfairly implies discrimination. If a reader looked only at this section of the report without turning to the later discussion (which is not cross-referenced), that reader could easily conclude that subjective bias might have affected the process.

Examination of Harvard's Admission Process

We believe that the Commission' report exaggerates the "problems" that it highlights in this section, and shows a misunderstanding of the careful process used by Harvard's admissions committee. The statement in the introductory paragraph that OCR found "several potential sources of discrimination" in the admissions process overstates the case: indeed, the Commission's report mentions only two (the ethnic read and the "stereotyping comments"), neither of which is or was found to be discriminatory in practice, and the former of which could not be a "potential source of discrimination".

On the issue of the Asian American ethnic reader, we believe that the Commission misconstrues OCR's findings. First, it should be recognized that Harvard has chosen to use an ethnic reader as an additional method of ensuring that applicants from varying ethnic backgrounds are treated sensitively. The members of the admissions staff who serve as ethnic readers are particularly knowledgeable about certain ethnic groups and serve as additional advocates for such candidates. The ethnic readers may be the admissions officers routinely assigned as the first, second, or third readers of a folder; sometimes, they give a folder an extra read, a "fourth read", in their capacity as the ethnic readers. They also serve as informal advisors to other readers in the office, and often give oral comments as asked by other admissions officers. The ethnic reader is generally assigned to the dockets (geographical groupings of applications) from which most of the applicants in that particular ethnic group come. The ethnic readers are thus involved in some capacity with most ethnic applicants to Harvard.

OCR found that approximately 19% of the folders of Asian American applicants that it reviewed contained written comments by the ethnic reader. Harvard explained that this percentage did not accurately reflect the ethnic reader's involvement, since much of that involvement was oral and was thus never noted in writing in the folder. For the two classes that OCR reviewed, we continue to believe that the ethnic reader's involvement in the applications of credible Asian American applicants -- including reading files as an assigned "reader", reading without making written comments, giving oral advice, sitting in docket meetings, and participating in committee meetings -- was much closer to 80% than to 19%.

The Commission's draft report shows a lack of understanding of this process, in that it distinguishes between a read done by the ethnic reader in her capacity as first reader and a read done in her capacity as ethnic reader. The ethnic reader brings her particular sensibility to the process whenever she reads the folder, and the Commission's (and indeed OCR's) distinction is therefore meaningless. Moreover, the Commission's report responds to Harvard's explanation

2

that the ethnic reader's involvement was oral, not written, simply by repeating that the written documentation did not support this assertion -- which by definition it could not.

We also find the Commission's footnote 125 confused. OCR stated, quite rightly, that Harvard is not required under Title VI to take affirmative action by providing an ethnic reader. The Commission then argues that if OCR found that the lack of an ethnic read resulted in discriminatory treatment, this lack could violate Title VI. We are puzzled as to how the lack of something that is not required could ever be discriminatory; in other words, does the Commission suggest that this sort of affirmative action may be legally mandated?

Stereotyping Comments

The word "stereotype" implies a negative categorization without foundation. Some of the comments that the Commission and OCR label "stereotyping" comments are not in themselves negative; there is, for example, no negative rating associated with being "shy". Nor is there anything negative in the term "classic": a student from a "classic" blue collar, inner city background is one of the kinds of applicants whom Harvard tries to recruit. Moreover, these characterizations were frequently based on information given to Harvard by others, including, in some cases, the students themselves; those "stereotyping" characterizations can hardly be attributed to Harvard admissions officers when they are founded in the documents submitted by others. We also note that the Commission's report fails to quote that part of OCR's report stating that some readers showed unusual sensitivity to possible bias in teachers' or others' reports. And finally, even if the so-called stereotyping comments were "negative" in themselves and were without foundation, OCR's review showed that they had no effect on the ratings, and no effect on admissions decisions.

Legacy Tips

It is important to put the "tips" for children of alumni in context. First, the great majority of alumni children who apply to Harvard are extremely well qualified. While test scores are only one indication of ability, it is worth noting that, in the most recent classes, the scores of the admitted alumni children are almost the same as the average of the admitted class (an insignificant 10 points less) and above the overall average of applicants. There is a natural self-selection by the children of alumni, and many of the less strong potential candidates simply do not apply. Second, the majority of alumni children who apply are not admitted. And third, the number of alumni children at Harvard is not large: over the past two years, approximately 13% of the incoming class has been comprised of the children of alumni while over 19% has been Asian American.

The Commission's report misconstrues OCR's analysis of this issue and misstates applicable law. OCR addressed the legality of preferences in admissions by analogy to the considerable body of employment law that has grown up under Title VII of the Civil Rights Act of 1964. Specifically, OCR applied to the college admissions process the disparate impact analysis used in such Title VII cases as Griggs v. Duke Power Co., 401 U.S. 424 (1971) and

<u>Albermarle Paper Co. v. Moody</u>, 422 U.S. 405 (1975). Its statistical analyses showed that the somewhat lower acceptance rate for Asian American applicants could be explained by the preferences accorded to legacies and athletes -- categories in which Asian American applicants to Harvard are currently somewhat underrepresented. (This "underrepresentation" exists in comparison to the pools of applicants, not necessarily to the general population. In recent years, more Asian American students have participated in intercollegiate athletics, and the pool of athletes increasingly includes Asian American students; and as the more recent alumni have children applying to college, the pool of Asian American legacy applicants will increase.)

Using the Title VII model, OCR effectively shifted the burden of persuasion to Harvard, which in turn explained and defended its policies. In respect to alumni children, Harvard pointed out the extraordinary importance of alumni financial and other contributions to Harvard's achievement of its educational objectives. Alumni gifts of over $36 million in 1989 were essential to our need-blind admissions program; over 4,000 alumni serve on committees throughout the United States that recruit and interview applicants to Harvard; more than 37,000 dues-paying members of Harvard and Radcliffe Clubs contribute to scholarship funds; and alumni assist Harvard in many other significant ways.

The OCR report examined Harvard's explanations, found them supported by empirical evidence, and concluded that Harvard had shown that the legacy, as well as the athlete, policies served "legitimate institutional goals." OCR then weighed, and accepted, Harvard's assertion that there are no acceptable alternatives that might serve these legitimate goals. OCR also recognized the latitude that courts have given universities in selecting their students and achieving diversity.

The Commission's report seems to be confused on the case law and to put an impossible burden of proof on Harvard, a burden that is not called for under the analogous Title VII law. The <u>Rosenstock</u> case, which OCR mentioned, is simply one case in which alumni preferences were addressed. It does not control in Harvard's situation because, as OCR noted and as the Commission notes, it involves constitutional law, not Title VI. The Commission's discussion about "suspect classes" is thus irrelevant; that is a concept used in constitutional cases but not in Title VI cases.

Moreover, the Commission states that OCR "might have asked for supporting evidence" that alumni support would drop if the preferences were not given, and that there are no reasonable alternatives for such support. Harvard in fact provided ample supporting evidence for the policy by explaining the rationale and giving facts concerning alumni involvement. But the Commission seems to be asking for something more: that Harvard prove what would happen if it chose not to give a preference for alumni children. Harvard would then be faced with the impossible task of proving the consequences of a hypothetical condition.

As to reasonable alternatives for support, OCR presumably knew from its close involvement with higher education in the United States today that many educational institutions are facing significant shortages of funds. Federal government support has been declining

4

steadily; state support is even more depleted; and many grant making entities have reduced their awards. Tuition and fees are already high and cannot be significantly increased. Budget cutbacks and general retrenchment prevail. The generosity of alumni and other donors to Harvard remains the one potential source of revenue that can help to make up for the decline in other sources of support.

We would also point out that there are many tips commonly granted by colleges in addition to the tip for alumni children, such as the tip for recruited athletes or for in-state residents. The legal and policy issues on tips should thus be considered in this larger framework. For example, if a private college in a state that has a small Asian American community grants a preference to residents of the state, is that tip illegal? If not, under what standards must it be evaluated, and what burden of proof must the college bear? Similarly, how could a college prove the legitimacy of a tip for athletes? And how do the legal issues mesh with the academic freedom traditionally granted to colleges in the province of admissions?

The admission of ethnic minorities to Harvard has greatly increased the diversity -- in its broadest sense -- and vitality of the college. We are committed to continuing our policies that have resulted in Asian American students constituting nearly 20 percent of the freshman class. We consider OCR's report to be impartial and thorough, and view it as objective corroboration that Harvard's policy is not only nondiscriminatory but also fundamentally fair.

November 7, 1991
MCP7:CIVRTCOM.2

THE OFFICE OF THE ASSISTANT SECRETARY OF DEFENSE

WASHINGTON, D.C. 20301-4000

**FORCE MANAGEMENT
AND PERSONNEL**

1 8 OCT 1991

Dr. James S. Cunningham
Assistant Staff Director
  for Programs, Policy and Research
1121 Vermont Ave., N.W., Rm 700
Washington, D.C. 20425

Dear Dr. Cunningham:

Thank you for your letter of September 27 to the Secretary of Defense concerning a section of the draft report, Civil Rights Issues Facing Asian Americans in the 1990s. I have been asked to reply.

The section of the report we received is entitled Religious Accommodation by the Military. You asked for our comments on the accuracy of this section. Attached are our comments for your consideration.

I hope that these comments are of some benefit to you. If you have any questions, please call me or my Deputy, Lieutenant Colonel Jim Schwenk, at (703) 697-3387/5947.

T. D. Keating
Captain, JAGC, USN
Director, Legal Policy
(Requirements & Resources)

DoD Comments
"Religious Accommodation by the Military"
from
Civil Rights Issues Facing Asian Americans in the 1990s

We believe that your comments on page 59 of the report fairly
summarize the standard of review of military decisions that was
discussed in <u>Goldman</u>. However, we do not agree with your analysis of
the legislative intent in passing 10 USC 774. Three sentences in
your report state opinions that we do not believe are accurate.

The first sentence of the first full paragraph on page 60 of the
report contains the phrase "such as Jews who seek to wear yarmulkes
and Sikhs who seek to wear turbans." The phrase is used to explain
why Congress enacted 10 USC 774. While we agree that Congress
enacted that statute because of concern for religious accommodation
in the wearing of uniforms, we do not believe that Congress, as a
whole, focused explicitly on Jews and Sikhs.

In our view, the statute clearly demonstrates that, as a whole,
Congress focused on the broader issue of religious apparel for all
groups. Although certain members may well have considered the
statute to be a relief measure for one particular religious group or
another, the statute does not address any particular group. Moreover, the statute authorizes the Secretary concerned to prohibit the
wear of <u>any</u> item of religious apparel, if the Secretary determines
either that the item is not neat and conservative or that its wear
would interfere with military duties. We do not believe that Congress would have passed a bill with such broad language, and given
the Secretary concerned such broad authority, if Congress had
intended to authorize the wear of yarmulkes and turbans. Instead, we
believe that Congress would have simply authorized their wear,
clearly and explicitly, in the statute. This Congress did not do, so
we recommend that you delete this phrase from the report.

Six lines below the line discussed above, the report states,
"Although the law does not mention yarmulkes or turbans, the Conference Report makes clear that Congress expected these to be allowed."
The cited conference language states, in pertinent part, "The law
does not list eligible items of apparel, but the conferees note that
the Army in the past has permitted the wearing of Sikh turbans and

that the Senate and the House floor debates cited various examples of the wearing of Jewish yarmulkes by members of the Armed Forces."

The cited language does not "make clear" that Congress intended yarmulkes and turbans to be allowed in all circumstances. The conferees merely noted that, in the past, one service had permitted turbans to be worn, and that the wear of yarmulkes was common in certain circumstances. The conferees' intent was that the Secretary consider that practice when deciding how to implement the law. Had the conferees intended to mandate the wear of turbans and yarmulkes, they would not merely have "noted" our past practice, but would have clearly expressed their intent that DoD allow the wear of those specific items of apparel. This the conferees did not do, so we recommend that you delete the sentence that begins with "Although" including the cited conference report language.

Finally, the first sentence of the first full paragraph on page 61 states, "Despite the legislative history and the intent of Congress, the Department of Defense (DoD) has issued regulations banning the wear of Sikh turbans with the uniform." We believe, as the Secretary of Defense said in the letter cited in the report, that our regulation fully complies with the law, the legislative history and the intent of Congress. We recommend that you rewrite the quoted sentence to read, "In implementing this law, the Department of Defense has issued regulations that prohibit the wear of religious apparel, such as turbans, that replace the wearing of required items of the uniform or interfere with the wearing of protective equipment such as helmets and gas masks."